D0742077

DON
REVIE

DON REVIE

THE BIOGRAPHY

CHRISTOPHER EVANS

BLOOMSBURY SPORT
LONDON • OXFORD • NEW YORK • NEW DELHI • SYDNEY

For Jasmine

BLOOMSBURY SPORT
Bloomsbury Publishing Plc
50 Bedford Square, London, WC1B 3DP, UK
29 Earlsfort Terrace, Dublin 2, Ireland

BLOOMSBURY, BLOOMSBURY SPORT and the Diana logo are trademarks of
Bloomsbury Publishing Plc

First published in Great Britain 2021

A catalogue record for this book is available from the British Library

Library of Congress Cataloguing-in-Publication data has been applied for

ISBN: HB: 978-1-4729-7336-8; ePub: 978-1-4729-7337-5; ePDF: 978-1-4729-7338-2

2 4 6 8 10 9 7 5 3 1

Typeset in Adobe Garamond Pro by Deanta Global Publishing Services, Chennai, India
Printed and bound in Great Britain by CPI Group (UK) Ltd, Croydon CR0 4YY

To find out more about our authors and books visit www.bloomsbury.com
and sign up for our newsletters

CONTENTS

FOREWORD

I always judge how good a football manager is by the difference between (a) the state of a football club when he takes over and (b) the position that he leaves the club in at the end of his tenure. All the great managers of recent history – Jock Stein, Bill Shankly, Sir Alex Ferguson and Sir Matt Busby – left their mark on their respective clubs, changing them significantly, and Don Revie most definitely falls into the same category.

When Don took over as Leeds United manager in 1961, Leeds United were a struggling second division team with no real footballing history in a city dominated by rugby league. Don had the foresight to give youth a chance and made some shrewd signings in the transfer market, which led to the creation of a footballing dynasty between 1963 to 1974 and arguably one of the best football teams in the history of English football.

Although we were never that close personally, I always got on well with Don professionally and he had a big influence on my career. He bought me as a right-winger from Manchester United in 1963, but I was always a central midfield player. After an injury to the great Bobby Collins in 1965, Don gave me my chance in my favoured central midfield position. My career flourished from then on and I owe a debt of gratitude to him. In my opinion, Don Revie was certainly one of the great football managers in English football history and it was a privilege to be part of the fabulous team he moulded.

Looking back on the end of his time as England manager, I'm sure that if Don had his time again with the national side, he would have left the job differently. In fact, he admitted this to me shortly before his death in 1989.

This excellent book by Chris Evans gives an honest and balanced assessment of Don Revie's career, and I hope that everyone enjoys reading it.

John Giles, legendary Leeds United midfielder
August 2021

PROLOGUE

4 p.m., 7 July, 1974, Olympic Stadium, Munich

After the events of the past week, he had almost forgotten it was his 47th birthday in a few days' time. Things had moved so quickly. Instead of enjoying his annual golfing holiday with his wife in Scotland, he had travelled from his Yorkshire home to take his seat in an executive box in one of the most impressive arenas in the world.

The stadium, with its steel and glass canopies, had been designed just six years earlier to resemble the German Alps and offered no shelter from the biting wind. Even though it was the middle of summer, the burly man who had arrived an hour-and-a-half ago to be greeted by various dignitaries was wrapped in a dark blue overcoat more suited to winter.

All day it had been threatening to rain, but the light drizzle could not dampen the carnival atmosphere that had enveloped the Bavarian city. Everywhere he looked, supporters in the streets, dressed either in bright orange or red and yellow, had mingled happily, singing and chanting. Their mood contrasted with the grey skies overhead.

Looking out across the pitch, the green advertising hoarding nestled behind the goal line implored fans to drink Heineken lager. For those who did overindulge, the billboard directly opposite reminded everyone there was always Alka-Seltzer for the morning after.

He had spent the last hour sitting increasingly impatiently with a fixed smile through the closing ceremony. Now there was a further delay of 26 minutes as the officials hunted around for corner flags.

Like the rest of the 70,000 people in the ground, he wanted the game to kick off. The longer the delay the more he fidgeted, gently rocking back and forth in his seat. Things were not helped by the man next to him sucking on a large cigar, wafting plumes of smoke over them both, creating an unpleasant atmosphere.

More than once he made an exaggerated action with his hand as if to wave the smoke away, but it had no effect. Eventually, he chose to ignore it as very soon the two most famous footballers in the world, Holland's Johan Cruyff and West Germany's Franz Beckenbauer, would be shaking hands in the centre circle, one of them destined to lift the trophy as the winner of the 1974 World Cup.

For the next 90 minutes, he watched and made notes. For this man was not merely an interested spectator. This was Don Revie and just 72 hours earlier he had been appointed England manager. The hopes and dreams of an expectant nation rested on his broad shoulders.

4 p.m., 4 July, 1974, Elland Road, Leeds

The heavy cables and wires which were attached to the various cameras and microphones made it difficult to find a place to sit. When a suitable place was found it was quickly lost as a technician barged in trying to find the best possible angle for the early evening news.

The press conference was supposed to begin at 2.30 p.m., now with no word from either party it was just coming up to 4 p.m. As the assembled journalists waited, they talked and smoked and very soon the rumours began. There had been an argument over money? Perhaps he didn't want the job after all and it had all been a wasted journey?

As four men finally entered the room after a 90-minute wait, a heavy fug of tobacco smoke hung in the wood-panelled boardroom, adorned with pendants from celebrated games of the past. They took their places in chairs so close together they struggled for elbow room.

Holding a piece of paper, the new Football Association Secretary, Ted Croker, with his longish dark-brown hair swept over into a side parting, and pristine white shirt, flared dark suit and modern tie fashioned in a huge knot, read out a joint statement which had been prepared by the FA and Leeds United.

'We have accepted the resignation of Don Revie to free him to accept the appointment as England team manager. Revie has agreed terms with the FA.'

Looking tanned, fit, and happy with fashionable long, trimmed sideburns, his wavy hair swept into an unruly quiff, Revie looked directly into the cameras. Wearing a cobalt blue double-breasted blazer with gleaming silver buttons, matching kipper tie and light grey flannel trousers he looked every inch the England manager.

In contrast, the two other men from the FA – chairman Dr Andrew Stephen and his counterpart on the international committee Dick Wragg, with their bald heads framed by wispy white hair – looked like they belonged to another era.

As Revie spoke, they both slumped in their chairs wearing sombre expressions, their regulation FA jackets open to reveal high-waisted trousers which touched their chests and did nothing to conceal their large bellies.

'I am delighted to be given the chance to manage England. This must be any manager's dream. I also have a feeling of sadness after 13 years as manager of Leeds. I have tried to build the club into a family and there must be sadness when anybody leaves a family.

'The first result I will be looking for on a Saturday night will always be Leeds United's. Leeds gave me the chance to start my managerial career and we have had our ups and downs, but everybody in the club, the directors, coaching staff and, in particular, the players, have stood by me through thick and thin.

'I was in contact with the players about leaving them. They all understood and said the England job was a little bit special in their minds. They would have been upset if I had been going to another club.'

Then he got serious. With a look of determination he set out his aims: 'I would like to build up for the World Cup in 1978. Four years seems a long way off, but it isn't.

'I would like to build England on club lines. I am going to be interested in the youth policy and I would like the under-23s to play their matches at a different time.

'They go on tour at the same time as the seniors. I would like to go with the under 23s and then with the senior side and build up the same way as you build a club side and try to develop the same family spirit we have at Leeds.'

Finally breaking into a smile, Ted Croker told the press, 'We have signed England's most successful manager. We are happy to get him.'

With Revie committed to leaving and having applied for the England job two months earlier, for Leeds United the only real issue had been one of compensation and, despite interest in this from the gathered press, Croker said combatively, 'We are saying nothing about compensation at all. We are not discussing figures. It is a personal thing. The salary is commensurate with managers' salaries these days. We are talking in terms of a five-year contract.'

This comment led Revie to quip, 'I was offered a 10-year contract, but I took only five. If I can't make it in that time then perhaps I am not the man for the job!'

Revie seemed to many to be the logical choice. Writing in the *Sports Argus* the day before the announcement, Randall Northam said, 'Don Revie, the man who has just guided Leeds United to the League Championship, should succeed Sir Alf Ramsey as England team manager.

'I believe the Football Association want him and I think Revie could be tempted away from his dream of bringing the Champions Cup to Leeds, but the FA would have to pay him more than Sir Alf... Revie has the most obvious qualifications.'

...

Back in the Olympic Stadium, Revie had hardly got his notepad out before the Dutch scored from the penalty spot. He could take heart from Holland's experience – this was their first appearance in the final stages for 36 years and now thanks to their coach, Rinus Michels, they were making their first appearance in a World Cup Final.

Just like Revie, Michels had been a successful club coach responsible for Ajax's recent European dominance. Now he was replicating that success on the world stage. If Holland and Michels could do it then so could Revie and England.

Another penalty, this time converted by the West Germans, and the capacity crowd was in for an exciting final. The watching Revie was a happy man; the reaction to his appointment in the press back home could not have been better. Hardened sports writers confirmed their support of Revie's appointment and Frank Taylor wrote in the *Daily Mirror*, 'Of the one thing I am sure, this is the start of a revolution in England's approach to international soccer. I must confess to some degree I was surprised as I did not expect the FA to go to such expense. We can expect the cobwebs to be swept away and a renaissance of our national game.'

Even the *Liverpool Echo,* home of Leeds' closest rivals, was fulsome in praise of Revie, 'The appointment of Revie has been hailed as a tremendous triumph… at this time Revie is the hero of the hour. The knight in shining armour riding up on a white charger to rescue England from the depths of despair.'

When *Shoot!* magazine posed the question, 'Is Don Revie the right manager for England?' the answer was 'Definitely…they have the best man to ensure England football recovers from being in the doldrums.'

Even his two immediate predecessors, Sir Alf Ramsey and Joe Mercer, were quick to back the appointment. At a reception at the Royal Lancaster Hotel to mark the eighth anniversary of England's 1966 World Cup win, Ramsey told the gathered press, 'England could not be in safer hands.' While Mercer, who had been linked to the job but at the age of 61 ruled himself out of the permanent position, said, 'When you look at the candidates, you come up with him all the time. He has had so much success and is brave in defeat.'

In a sit-down interview with the *Daily Mirror's* Frank Taylor, Revie demonstrated no fears about other international sides: 'The only teams worth watching in this World Cup have been Holland and West Germany. In the past we have produced players like Cruyff and Beckenbauer and I believe they are still there.'

Revie said he wanted his England players to express themselves as his old team Leeds had done in the last few years. In their early days in the top division they had a reputation for hard tackling and gamesmanship. By the time Revie had masterminded the league win in 1974, Leeds had spent six years winning every domestic trophy with the type of free-flowing, attractive football that won plaudits from all quarters. But his achievements with Leeds were in the past; the new challenge was fashioning an England side capable of going to the top of world football.

Writing in his column for the *Sports Argus* just six weeks before he was appointed, Revie set out the importance of reaching the World Cup finals: 'As far as international football is concerned the World Cup and, to a lesser extent, the European Nations Championship, are the tournaments to win.

'Whoever replaces Sir Alf as England manager has my full sympathy!'

Now it was Revie with the biggest job in football. There was no hint of any doubts when he told the press, 'All the players need is confidence. I am sure we can be number one in world football again. The players can do it if they are prepared to work hard at their shooting and passing and are ready to improve their skills. We must get the players to think alike, as if they are one man.'

As if Revie needed telling about the enormity of the task in hand, Frank McGhee of the *Daily Mirror*, offered this piece of advice: 'When Don Revie, England's new manager, watches West Germany play Holland for the 1974 World Cup here tomorrow, he will be exposed to the frightening truth about the enormity of the challenge he has accepted, getting England to the 1978 final.

'Both West Germany and Holland started this tournament with teams that were already of a very high quality and both have now matured into sides of genuine greatness. Both are certainly very much better, stronger and much more skillful than any side England could put into the field right now—but no better than England under Revie must become.'

At the final whistle, Revie rose from his seat to applaud the new world champions. There was nothing to fear, West Germany were worthy 2–1 winners but, from what he had seen, the standard in the tournament was not particularly high. As he watched Franz Beckenbauer lift the brand new FIFA World Cup trophy, Revie glanced at the scoreboard and it could have been a personal message to him: 'Ciao and thanks West Germany, see you in Argentina in 1978.' There was no reason in the world to believe he would not be there.

'I'm not worth that much, I've still got a lot to learn.'

Don Revie, on being told a record price tag of
£28,000 was on his head, 5 November, 1949.

'Only a master footballer like Revie can make the plan succeed.'

Preston North End and England's Tom Finney
on Manchester City's 'Revie Plan'

'No doubt about it – Don Revie, hub of the machine that has taken Manchester City to the Cup Final was the best possible choice as Footballer of the Year… although he never pretended to be a centre-forward. Now he is one of the most dangerous in the country.'

England legend Stanley Matthews

PART ONE

1

BEGINNINGS

'I want to be a footballer, and I want to join your club.'

Don Revie

It was just after dawn on 19 August, 1944, when the train finally pulled into Leicester station after its 130-mile journey from the north of England. After five years of war, the country would soon be waking up to some welcome news – the battle of Normandy, launched on D-Day two months earlier, had been won. The *Daily Mirror*, proudly declared, 'The Hun cannot make another stand and the pursuit is on.'

A gawky young man, underweight for his age, emerged from the station. The 17-year-old was centre-forward for the Middlesbrough Swifts, a well-known Teesside team, and he was in the east Midlands for his first professional trial with Leicester City.

All week he had been thinking about the journey, now he was here. Too shy to ask for time off from his work as an apprentice bricklayer, he had caught the last train from his Middlesbrough home the night before.

He had only been given one instruction: 'Report to Filbert Street, at 14.00.' Knowing no one, with nowhere to go and hours to kill, the young man began wandering the streets of this strange new city.

For a boy who had never been south of Redcar in his life, Leicester, which eight years earlier had been deemed the second richest city in Europe by the League of Nations, was a revelation.

The terraced houses and cobbled streets were much the same as the town he had just left behind, as were the large chimneys from the hosiery factories that had been requisitioned for the war effort. However, with its Art Deco buildings and large covered market, which gave it a busy, bustling feel, Leicester was nothing like anything the young man, who wandered around this strange city with his football boots wrapped in brown paper under his arm, had seen before.

It stood in stark contrast to the Middlesbrough he had just left behind. In 1862, just 12 years after the iron ore discovery that transformed it from a hamlet of just a few farms to one of the most populous towns in the country, the Prime Minister, William Gladstone, visited. Among the thriving blast furnaces and steel mills he declared, 'This remarkable place, the youngest child of England's enterprise, is an infant, but if an infant, an infant Hercules.'

By the end of the 19th century, Gladstone's prediction had come true as the town underwent remarkable growth in both the local economy and population. This once quiet place on the banks of the Tees River became responsible for one third of the country's iron and steel production.

By 1914 Middlesbrough-based Dorman Long had become the largest company in the country, employing 20,000 people. It constructed many of the most famous bridges built in the first half of the 20th century, including the Sydney Harbour Bridge, the Tyne Bridge, the Tees Newport Bridge and the Omdurman Bridge in Sudan. This new-found wealth was reflected in the smart Georgian houses, theatres and an opera house found in the town centre. Not for nothing was Middlesbrough called Ironopolis.

When Don Revie was born on a sweltering day on 10 July, 1927, at 20 Bell Street, the novelist Sheila Kaye-Smith was writing *Iron and Smoke*. Published in 1928, she described Middlesbrough as 'a land of everlasting fog' and a 'frontier-stretch of hell'. Decline of this once thriving town had set in.

Worse was to come when writer Kingsley Amis called the town 'a hole'. A 'hideous mushroom' declared travel writer Douglas Goldring. Novelist Aldous Huxley compared Middlesbrough to 'a fungus in a test tube'. 'Dismal, even with beer and football' was the verdict of playwright and novelist JB Priestley.

Talking to Gordon Burn of the *Sunday Times* in 1976, Revie was much more upbeat about his hometown: 'For the time, where we lived wasn't considered rough, not compared to the areas around Dorman Long's, the iron and steel works, down by the docks. But we only had two bedrooms, a front room and a kitchen, and then dad built a little wooden place in the back yard for the boiler and washer. There was no bathroom, of course. It was a tin bath in front of the fire every Friday night. That was a ritual.

'They were just ordinary back-to-backs, but they were all nice people in the street, and everyone knew everyone else. For generations most families lived there, and we all seemed to be in the same boat at that time during the Depression.'

The Teesside town had been hit particularly hard by economic woes. The year before Revie was born half the town had found itself out of work. Dependent on heavy industry, which was already struggling because of overcapacity, a downturn in exports and overseas competition, communities built around chemicals, iron and steel were at breaking point. There was not a single family who had not been affected by the Great Depression that now engulfed the country.

Years later Revie would recall those days: 'Yes, I came from a very poor home but a very warm home. I think poor homes are warm places. I think that when your mother and father can't afford a pair of football boots for you, they can't afford a new pair of shoes – possibly only once a year – and all your trousers have to be patched and your pullovers have to be darned, and you've got to go to market on a Saturday night to get cheap things that are left over at the end of the week in order to live for the next seven days, I think it gives you a bit of strength in later life. But I think it also gives you a little bit of insecurity, and you always feel that around the corner there's a pitfall.'

To many of the residents, the workhouse, which only closed its doors in 1930, was still a very real prospect. Punctuated with the harrowing stories that came from there of a child who burned to death in 1880 because there was no fire screen, and another young child who drowned in a plunge bath seven years later after two inmates were put in charge of up to 70 children, the Holgate workhouse was the stuff of nightmares.

Even after it closed, its main building still served as a Public Assistance Institution. It was to this place that unemployed men now came to claim the dole. It was here that local officials would go through every agonising detail of a person's finances to decide whether someone qualified for the benefit or not.

One of those workers who found himself going through the humiliation of the means test was Revie's father, Don Sr, a joiner, who for two long years found himself out of work, during which he received the grand total of 24 pence a week for the upkeep of the family of five. It was a desperate time and there were family accounts of Revie's father looking for sticks to put on the fire, just to keep the house warm.

To make ends meet, the whole family were put to work. Revie said: 'Father was a joiner but he was out of work for a couple of years and my mother had to take in washing, big baskets of washing that Joyce and Jean, my twin sisters and me used to have to collect from Acklam, which was the posh area of Middlesbrough. We had to walk a couple of miles to get them and a couple of miles back, and she used to wash all this stuff with a poss stick in the old iron pot where you had to light a fire underneath to heat the water. Then she had to scrub them on the old scrubber, and then she had to iron it all. Five bob it was, five bob a basket.

'I can't remember very much about the town centre. Our house was only a 10-minute walk away but we didn't go there a lot, only on Saturday nights to carry the groceries back. Middlesbrough always had a good market and, especially when father was out of work and things were a bit hard, I'd get there just before it packed up for the weekend, because you could pick up things cheaper, cheap meat and vegetables. We always used to get the shank end for the soup the following week.'

It was not all doom and gloom for the young Revie. 'I can remember my father going for a pint on a Sunday lunchtime; and the Tees bridge, where we used to go and play at times, on it and under it, on little rafts on water, waiting for the middle to go up to let the big boats through.'

With no television in the North East and radio only a luxury, it was football that consumed Revie's time. Writing in his autobiography he remembered: 'For in those early 1930s there wasn't much else to do but talk football. Unemployment and its attendant miseries stalked through Teesside in those years. There was no money; precious few toys for children. Men might have lost hope altogether but there was always that great British institution – football – to occupy the minds, some of the time at any rate. Soccer was the safety valve which kept men from wallowing in self-pity. And for little Don Revie it was a safety valve too.'

The most famous footballer in the North East during the 1930s was George Camsell, a goal machine who had hit 59 league goals in the 1926–27 season. He was the face of Erimus Hair Cream and every day along with his teammates he would pass through Bell Street on his way to training at Ayresome Park. It was little wonder Revie would pester his father to take him to see his heroes in action.

Even though Camsell was the star, Revie's idol was Wilf Mannion from the moment Mannion pulled on a Middlesbrough shirt in January 1937. As a fair-haired, good-looking young man he was called 'Golden Boy' because of his unrivalled ball control and trickery.

'We never missed a home game at Ayresome Park and my father used to take me to Sunderland and Newcastle for away games when I was a kid. I collected the autographs and photographs of the team, the Micky Fentons and George Camsells and Bobby Baxters and Billy Forests. But my idol was always Wilf Mannion. I had his autograph a dozen times and the big pictures of him you used to get with *Topical Times* I had plastered all over the bedroom walls.'

After every home game, Revie would make the short trip home to the back streets behind his house. In a space measuring only 10 feet wide, using whatever could pass for a football, whether it was rags tied together or an old tennis ball, he would re-enact the game he had just seen.

'In fading light – often until darkness fell – I would flick a ball against the wall, fasten on to the rebound and go dribbling it round the iron gratings. In my mind I could hear the roar of the crowd. I was, as my father said, "Football daft!"'

It wasn't until Christmas 1936, when Revie's father had found work and the family's finances had returned to something like normality, that he received his first pair of football boots. Just weeks earlier he had been picked to represent Archibald Secondary Modern School at outside-right. His best friend at the time was a boy called George Tinsley who lived at number 44 – and more importantly was the proud owner of Bell Street's only leather football.

Revie recalled, 'There was a lad called George Tinsley, his mother and father were better off than other people in Bell Street. Well he had a real football, so he was everybody's pal. A leather football with a bladder and lacing. We used to look after it, dubbin it and blow it up and let it down at the right times. It was like a piece of gold.'

To those who lived on Bell Street, Revie was remembered as one of the boys who got up to the same mischievous pranks as other lads his age but, in the main, he was seen as a nice boy who was forever kicking a ball up and down the alleyway.

As 1936 turned into 1937, Revie felt happy days were here at last: 'All the kids in the North East in those days had street teams that would play each other in little leagues. They were called 'friendlies' but they were really tough matches, played between coats as goals at either end of the street. You played at least two or three hours a day, and this is where you got all your natural skills.'

At the start of the 1939–40 Football League programme, Middlesbrough, with its team of England internationals, was expected to challenge for the title after finishing fourth the year before. Then everything changed. On 3 September, with the league campaign only three games old, World War II was declared.

Inside 20 Bell Street the world of the Revie family was falling apart. Margaret Revie, the woman who had done so much to keep her family fed and clothed while her husband searched for work, was ill. The doctors told them it was cancer and incurable. While it was important to remain strong at home there were occasions when Revie would burst into tears in front of his friends, who would put an arm around him and tell him his mother was going to get better.

The place that had haunted Don Sr for so long was now where all his fears came true. After undergoing many changes in use, the former workhouse had become Middlesbrough Municipal Hospital. It was here Revie's mother passed away at the age of 50, on 27 November, 1939.

Her death was a devastating blow for Revie. 'Although my father was a staunch Middlesbrough supporter my mother encouraged me as much as he did. She wanted me to enjoy my sport; and when she died it was the greatest tragedy of my young life. Only a boy who has lost his mother knows what heartache means.'

Teachers at his school would remember Revie repeatedly kicking the ball against the wall before the day even started with tears rolling down his cheeks.

'My dad used to leave for work at 7 a.m. My sisters, Joyce and Jean, went to their employment at 8 a.m. There was no point in me waiting around moodily at home. So, from eight o'clock until school opened at 8.45 a.m. I stayed in the school yard, kicking my ball against the school wall. In the dull grey mornings of winter, flicking the ball against the wall helped pass the time. I didn't feel so lonely, I didn't miss my mother so much.' By his own admission, all Revie could think about at that time was, 'Football, football, football.'

Appearing on the TV programme *This is Your Life* in 1974, Revie's sister Jean recalled how he was so obsessed with the game he failed to attend her wedding: 'My wedding was arranged on a particular Saturday afternoon and, at that time, Don was 14 years of age and playing for the Swifts [a prominent Teesside junior club]. However, instead of being a guest at my wedding, he slung his football boots over his shoulder, walked past the parlour and said, "Well, I'm off, see you after the match!"'

Unlike a large number of children in Middlesbrough, Revie was not evacuated and football went on for the youngster. A few months before Revie's mother died, the Archibald Secondary Modern team had finished fourth in the Middlesbrough Schools league and went on to win a few cups. It was testament to Revie's ability that he was made captain of the side in 1941, the year he turned 14.

But that was also the year it seemed the young man's dream of becoming a professional footballer was destined to disappear. Finances meant he had to leave school and earn a wage.

As Revie recalled: 'Any ideas I may have had of taking up football as a career were knocked on the head when my father decreed that I must learn a trade. So, at 14, I became an apprentice bricklayer. I can't say that I liked laying bricks as much as I liked laying on passes for my teammates on a football field.'

In the long run, perhaps, Revie would not have made a great bricklayer after all. His daughter Kim later recalled an incident where he attempted to put his apprenticeship to good use: 'Dad's legendary DIY skills! Having served as an apprentice bricklayer, he reminded us with confidence and a wink how he was more than capable of putting up a toilet roll holder in the bathroom, which was in a different room to the toilet.

'I remember mum's face as I ran downstairs to announce that dad had knocked a hole through the wall and you could see from one room into the other, which resulted in the whole wall having to be knocked down!'

One day stands out as significant on Revie's road to football stardom. Revie was sitting at the back of the crowded front room in Keith Road, the Middlesbrough Swifts' unofficial headquarters. The day before he had faced the Swifts with his Newport Boys Club and now he was hoping to catch the eye of Bill Sanderson.

To everyone who knew him, Sanderson ate, slept and drank football. A local train driver, he was Swifts' club secretary and the 14–16 age group team played in the Middlesbrough Junior League. Every Sunday, on a model pitch, Sanderson used brightly coloured corks to represent the players he wanted to analyse after the previous day's game, pointing out various errors he had noticed and then running through moves to correct them.

'This is a private club, what are you doing here?' Sanderson asked the small stranger in his parlour. 'I want to be a footballer, and I want to join your club,' came Revie's reply.

It was not as if Sanderson did not know of the young man in his front room. He had been impressed enough by his performance for Newport the previous day to say he wished he had Don Revie in his side. Now Revie had made Sanderson personally aware of his presence.

Revie recalled, 'I started playing for Newport Boys Club at outside-right when I was 13. I was transferred for five shillings when I was 14 to Middlesbrough Swifts who were possibly the best team in the North East at the time.'

Even though he had learned his skills on the cobbled surface of Bell Street, it was under the tutelage of Bill Sanderson that Revie learned football is not a game for self-glorification, with players making brilliant solo dribbles, but a team game.

In those early tactical talks, the beginnings of a football philosophy was laid down. Writing in 1956 Revie said, 'In these days of defence in depth and a defence complex which threatens to paralyse all attacking ideas, it was absolutely vital to discuss opposition; their strengths and weaknesses; and also for your own team to have their own pet moves thoroughly worked out.

'You cannot lay down a final and foolproof winning plan of campaign around a blackboard because the other side have their own ideas. But no one will ever convince me that pre-match tactical talks do not serve a useful purpose. They help the player – especially the young player – to get a clearer picture of what is expected of him.

'I know from my own experience with the Swifts that these Sunday morning tactical discussions opened up for me new visions of the game.'

A no-nonsense man, with little time for prima donnas, Sanderson never let his charges forget it was an honour to turn out for his team. Unable to get into the first team on his arrival, the promising Revie spent his first six months as 12th man, carrying and sorting the kit for the other boys.

But it was not long before he broke into the side, making it into the line-up for the 1941 Ellis Cup semi-final where the Swifts lost to a Cleveland Works side that went on to lift the cup. In doing so he won praise from local newspapers for his ability at such a young age.

Marked out for his partnership with Freddie Watkin, Revie was complimented on his pace and his knack of being able to float a ball from the corner with pinpoint accuracy for a striker to head.

It wasn't long before the big clubs came calling. As the war neared its end, professional football, which had been suspended for the past five years, was about to begin again.

On 16 May, 1944, Leicester City team manager Tom Bromilow reported to his board on a scouting visit to Middlesbrough and Scotland. In particular, he was keen to come to an agreement to make the Swifts a nursery club. He felt there could be a profitable relationship for both clubs.

Just over a month later *The People* reported: 'Another club looking to the post-war football future is the ever-vigilant Leicester City, who have just adopted Middlesbrough Swifts as their nursery club. Better still, they have appointed George Carr, famous forward with Leicester and Middlesbrough, as their representative on the spot.'

One of four brothers to have played for his hometown side, George Carr was part of the Leicester City team that ended up as runners-up in 1928–29 (their best-ever finish at the time) and briefly captained the side. Now he was charged with finding the best lads in the North East for the City. Almost immediately, he turned his attention to the Swifts' two best players, Revie, and inside-left Freddie Watkin, recommending both for a trial.

However, knowing the boy's father was a fanatical follower of Middlesbrough, Billy Forrest, their former left-half, sidled up to him one Saturday afternoon and asked whether his son wanted a trial with the club.

Revie said: 'I always wanted to play for Middlesbrough, always Middlesbrough, from being six. When the brass band struck up on a Saturday just before the teams came out, it used to send shivers down my back. I used to think, "Oh, it would be great to run out of that tunnel and play on that pitch in front of all these people."'

Everyone knew Revie was desperate to play for Middlesbrough but the club showed no interest in signing him for their boys' team, so Revie looked elsewhere. 'I had a trial with Leicester City but Middlesbrough never gave me one. But this can happen; possibly their scout didn't fancy me on the day.'

The train tickets had been booked. Watkin was to travel with his friend to Leicester as well but he had doubts, Middlesbrough was all he knew. His friends and family were all at home whereas Leicester was a full five hours away. Besides, there were no guarantees he would make it. Despite having all the gifts in the world, Watkin decided to stay home and accept a factory job. He would continue playing but the opportunity to become a professional footballer was gone forever.

Describing Watkin as 'one of the greatest inside men I have ever seen play,' Revie said of his partner, 'The name will not mean anything to followers of league football, but you can take it from me that Freddie had everything to become another Raich Carter or Wilf Mannion. He had wonderful ball control; a sound tactical sense; and he always seemed to be in open space to receive a pass and when he parted with the ball he sent it on its way with slide-rule accuracy.'

Of Watkin's decision Revie would say, 'He was the complete young footballer, yet he was lost to league football simply because Freddie did not fancy leaving home to become a professional footballer . . . I think professional football is poorer because Freddie did not take the plunge.'

Now all alone in a strange city, Revie sat in a café gulping tea. There was a knot in his stomach. As the clock ticked by, he felt more and more anxious. Finally, he gingerly made his way to Filbert Street. Arriving at the players' entrance, the attendant asked who he was and he replied, 'I am Don Revie and I am here to play for Leicester City.'

2

LEICESTER CITY (1944–49)

'I was beginning to feel my feet in professional football. The nervous
early days were behind me and I was beginning to think I might
make a name in the game.'

Don Revie

When he arrived at Filbert Street, Revie noticed the paint peeling from the once-
whitewashed walls, and the flaking blue sign above the glass doorway which read
'Team Before Self'.

Signing on 19 August, 1944, Revie had only been a professional for a week
when he slipped unnoticed into the dressing room where the men seemed much
older and all knew each other. Nervously, Revie unwrapped his boots and pulled
on the royal blue shirt of Leicester City, ready for his debut against Wolverhampton
Wanderers on Saturday 26 August.

With the country still at war, both teams played with 'guests', usually
footballers turned soldiers who were posted in barracks nearby. That day, Wolves
contained players from Aston Villa and Chelsea, while Leicester boasted Arsenal's
pre-war centre-forward, Leslie Jones.

In the company of such seasoned professionals, Revie did not say a word
until a stern looking man with a receding hairline sat next to him. Revie thought
he recognised him from somewhere.

'Are you Revie?'

'Yes, I am Don Revie,' the nervous teenager replied.

'You from the North, son?'

'Yes.'

'Good, stick with me and we might be able to make a player of you then.'

After he left the dressing room, Revie turned to a man on the door and asked who that was. In total astonishment the man replied, 'Why that's Sep Smith of course!'

At the time, Septimus Smith was one of the most recognisable figures in the game. Club captain and an England international, he had spent his entire career with the East Midlands club. Writing in his autobiography, *Soccer's Happy Wanderer*, Revie said of Smith: 'When you speak of great players no list is complete without Sep. We talk in glowing terms of Raich Carter and Peter Doherty as great inside-forwards. So they were. But Sep Smith in his prime ranks with the greatest of them all as a tactician and accurate passer.'

As they ran out, Revie recalled Smith making a beeline for him, telling him, 'Don't forget, son, if I say "GO" you go. And if I give you the ball and shout "GIVE IT BACK" you give it back straight away. Understand? If you play it that way, soccer is easy.

'I picked up this soccer knowledge at the feet of the master player Sep Smith but as we played together for the first time against Wolves, I don't mind admitting I was overawed by Sep. I just did as he told me, so I could not help but have a reasonable game. He did the thinking for us. I merely obeyed his every shout.'

The players ran out to a bomb-ravaged Filbert Street. The main stand had largely been destroyed by the Luftwaffe, but this did not quell the spirits of the 10,000-strong capacity crowd who loved seeing their local side take on a strong Wolves team.

The opportunity for Revie to impress came early. After only three minutes he found himself with the ball at his feet, just outside the opposition penalty box. A quick pass split the Wolves defence, finding striker George Dewis who promptly smashed the ball past the stranded keeper.

Nodding his approval, Sep Smith shouted, 'Keep at it, son.' The game ended 2–2 with Revie laying on another goal for Dewis. A week later, on 3 September, Revie was named in the programme for the return game. It was not a happy experience; Leicester were routed 4–0 by a rampant Wolves team.

...

When Leicester chairman Alf Pallett asked his club captain if Revie would make the grade, Smith told Pallett the youngster had talent but was a work in progress. Years later Smith would say, 'I could see he had potential when he came down for a trial and I used to coach him lots with the ball. I'd say, "Come on with me" and we'd go into a corner and I'd teach him things.'

Seen as ponderous, prone to sometimes overthinking his play, Smith described Revie as 'an eager young player but I used to make him cry when I told him he did things wrong. He told me he would go home after the match and start to cry. I was pushing him because I believed in him.'

Despite his embryonic career, Revie had promised his father he would continue his apprenticeship, which he did at Sherriff's in Leicester. The next few months were not easy for Revie. Smith was a hard taskmaster. 'Certainly, whenever I played with Sep Smith, he was a wonderful help. Off the field he dictated my style of play as well. I'm not ashamed to admit that after a hard spell of coaching from Sep I have gone to bed and cried. Remember I was a bricklayer by day and trained at night or whenever I had any spare time.'

Thanks to Sep Smith's intense coaching the transformation in Revie was remarkable. When he ran on for his full debut on 31 August, 1946, against Manchester City after 33 war-time games, Revie had added three stones in weight, now coming in at 12 stones. And it was not long before he made an impact. Reporting on Leicester's 1–0 win over Coventry City on Saturday 19 October, 1946, the *Coventry Evening Telegraph* noted the 'lively Revie, eager to do two men's work.' Detailing his climb from junior football to the Second Division (Leicester had been relegated from the top flight in 1939) he was described as 'one of Leicester City's biggest assets'. The same newspaper called him Leicester's 'most dangerous forward' in a 2–1 win over Cardiff City the following month.

The man tasked with bringing Leicester back to the top division was Johnny Duncan, who had replaced Tom Mather as team manager. Duncan was a former team captain who had achieved legendary status at the club by lifting their only major trophy, the Second Division title in 1925.

At the same time as managing the club, Duncan was also landlord of the Turk's Head Hotel. Positioned opposite the prison on Welford Road it was a renowned sports bar, which had counted Matt Busby as a past patron.

Just like Sep Smith, Duncan believed he had a rare talent on his hands with Revie. Revie said, 'Although I was young, he cast me in the role of schemer for Leicester. It was, of course, asking a lot from a young player, but Johnny had confidence in me, just the same as he had confidence in all his players. He had the knack of making ordinary chaps play well above their normal standard.'

As Revie headed into 1947–48 season, he felt things were looking up. 'I was beginning to feel my feet in professional football. The nervous early days were behind me and I was beginning to think I might make a name in the game.'

Away from the pitch, even the loneliness he had felt on his first visit to the city had disappeared. Revie revelled in the family atmosphere 'Uncle Tokey' (as the manager was known to his friends) had created at the club. Duncan's son and Revie had also become firm friends.

The summer before the start of the season, Revie travelled to Lochgelly in Scotland, where he promised to use the skills he had learned as a bricklayer to work on the Duncan family grocery shop. It was here he first laid eyes on Elsie, a headstrong, warm young woman who was training to be a teacher. She was the daughter of Tom Duncan, who played alongside his brother, Johnny, at Leicester City in the 1920s and, just like Revie's mother, had died early at just 39. After that sad event, Uncle Tokey became a surrogate father to young Elsie.

Revie was taken by her wavy hair, delicate features and soft Scottish brogue. Fiercely intelligent and as competitive as Revie, it would not be long before they were making regular trips between the East Midlands and Scotland to spend time together.

'Their first date was a game of tennis and, thanks to their competitive spirits, neither was going to let the other one win,' daughter Kim would later recollect. Upon qualifying as a teacher in Edinburgh, Elsie took a job in Leicester to be near Revie. It would not be long before Revie would desperately need her companionship.

There was no warning that Revie's happy new life was under threat when he trotted out to face Tottenham Hotspur at Filbert Street on 8 November, 1947. There was a quarter of an hour left on the clock and it had been a rotten afternoon for Leicester. According to the *Daily Mirror*, 'For 15 minutes, Leicester's quicksilver approach work dazzled the 34,000 spectators. They produced great things. After 18 minutes their poise went and Tottenham were the dictators.'

With only a quarter of an hour left on the clock, the game was already lost. Three goals orchestrated by the brilliant Tottenham left-half, Ronnie Burgess, had put the game out of the reach of the home side.

Never knowing when he was beaten, Revie threw himself wholeheartedly into a challenge with Burgess. It was the type of 50–50 ball Leicester had been chasing all day with little success. The resulting challenge left Revie in a crumpled mess on the floor and he remembered Burgess telling him, 'Take it easy, Don,' as the Welsh international attempted to help the youngster back to his feet.

Having been reassured by Willie McLean (the joint trainer with George Ritchie) that it was a bad sprain, Revie was told to run it off only to collapse again. This time he was stretchered off with the sympathy of the crowd ringing in his ears.

An X-ray two days later at Leicester Royal Infirmary confirmed the worst. Revie's ankle was broken in three places and he had damaged ligaments. In fact, there was enough damage to pass the death sentence on the young footballer's career. All the months of completing his apprenticeship as a bricklayer, the extra training with Sep Smith, and the nights he had cried through sheer exhaustion looked to be for nothing.

'What are the chances of playing again?' Revie asked orthopaedic surgeon Matthew McCleary. 'I would say 1 in 1,000,' McCleary replied.

Looking at his tearful young player, Johnny Duncan whispered, 'Well let's see if you can be that 1-in-1,000 man.' Just over two months later, in January 1948, the *Daily Herald* reported, 'Revie, Leicester City inside-right, who fractured an ankle… has resumed light training and is expected to be fully fit in three weeks.' It was a remarkable recovery.

Later McCleary commented: 'It was a shocking injury that would have ended anybody else's career. He was in plaster for two months but still managed to come back. No one should underestimate his grim determination to be a footballer.'

On 14 February, 1948, he was named in a reserve 11 to take on Coventry City in a Football Combination Cup match. Despite being apprehensive he came through the match unscathed and celebrated with a double whisky at the Turk's Head.

Upon his return to the first team, Revie needed to summon up all that grim determination. The Leicester crowd that had looked on in sympathy as he was stretchered off months before had now turned on him. Not appreciating his defence-splitting passes and critical of his perceived lack of pace, the fans would often voice their displeasure by telling him to 'get rid of it'. And a newfound nervousness while challenging for the ball meant that, for the rest of his career, Revie jumped out of tackles. Derek Temple, who won the league championship in the 1960s with Everton later said, 'Don had a reputation as a hurdler.'

As Leicester City kicked off their 1948–49 season, Revie was determined to win over the crowd. After an impressive fifth place in the Second Division in 1948, there was now a big push for promotion. For his part, Revie could not have got off to a better start. Scoring after only 90 seconds in the opening match against Leeds United, Revie almost claimed the quickest goal of the day.

When Leeds hit back with two goals to take the lead, Revie levelled the score, which finished at 2–2. A week later the *Coventry Evening Telegraph*, reporting on the local derby between Coventry and Leicester, said of Revie's goal in a 2–1 win for the away side at Highfield Road: 'Leicester took the lead after 20 minutes, Revie was the scorer and he got his goal with a brilliant solo effort from halfway. He ran through on his own and crashed a shot, which Wood could only partially clear, and then the left-half fastened on to the ball again at full speed to follow up and sidestep the ball into the net.'

Two things kept Revie going. The first was the faith Johnny Duncan placed in him, telling him that he intended to build the side around him. The second was the encouragement of Sep Smith, who told him if he did not think he was worth it he would not have invested time in him in the first place. Years later, writing about the Busby Babes, Smith said, 'It needs a wise head to reassure young players when the going gets tough, otherwise they will lose confidence and be lost to the game.'

More goals for Revie then followed in September against Sheffield Wednesday and West Bromwich Albion. Performances like this soon made some of the bigger clubs sit up and take notice.

After an indifferent start to the season, Leicester slipped down the Second Division and Duncan was under huge pressure. The lack of faith in the side was reflected by local bookmakers who initially offered odds of 400–1 of Leicester lifting the FA Cup in May 1949. The prospect of dropping into the Third Division after 40 years in the top two tiers was a distinct possibility.

As they struggled, Sep Smith was usually nowhere to be found at Filbert Street on Saturday afternoons. Instead, Duncan had tasked him with visiting the grounds of upcoming opponents in the FA Cup.

In the third round Leicester were paired with First Division Birmingham City and two hours of football failed to settle the tie as Leicester left with a creditable 1–1 draw to bring the tie back to Filbert Street the following Saturday. Over 30,000 were there when, yet again, the 90 minutes failed to produce a winner before Birmingham took the lead early in extra time. Leicester looked to be heading out and a feeling of doom swept over the club when Revie missed a spot kick. Minutes later, Mal Griffiths saved his side and forced a second replay back in Birmingham.

The two clubs sportingly agreed that the third game, two days later, would be at a neutral venue chosen by the winner of a coin toss. When Birmingham won the toss, they chose nearby Villa Park. Unfortunately for Leicester, Villa were also involved in a cup marathon of their own and needed to use their ground, leaving Birmingham with no choice but to take their home advantage.

Illness and injury forced Birmingham to make a host of changes for the third match while an unchanged Leicester coped better with the heavy conditions. Jimmy Harrison deservedly gave Leicester the lead shortly before the interval only for Don Dorman to level the game yet again two minutes into the second half. Any thoughts among the 30,000 fans that this tie might yet again run into extra time were quickly ended when Revie made amends for his penalty miss two days earlier to settle matters.

The fourth round threw up Preston North End as Leicester's opponents. Thanks to dossiers produced by Sep Smith, which urged the Leicester defence to neutralise the Preston wingers, Leicester made it to the fifth round, with goals from Jack Lee and Mal Griffiths.

A scout from Arsenal, Joe Shaw, was in the capacity crowd at Filbert Street on 19 February, 1949 for the fifth round against Luton Town, tasked with watching Revie. He was lucky to get in. Such was the interest in the game that the gates had been closed a full hour early. Leicester and Luton Town were about to replay their FA Cup fifth round having drawn 5–5 at Kenilworth Road. In another thrilling end-to-end contest Leicester booked their place in the quarterfinals with a 5–3 win.

The journalists and other seasoned watchers had no doubt about Revie's ability. Although Shaw would have read the *Daily Herald* the following morning, he would have been told by Johnny Duncan that he had no chance of enticing young Revie away.

It was not only Arsenal who were interested. While Joe Shaw was watching Revie, the *Daily Herald* ran a story that claimed Middlesbrough, his boyhood team, had offered him the opportunity to return to his roots. The press statement from the Leicester board was terse: 'We have spoken to the player in question and he has no intention of returning to that area.'

The sixth-round victory against Brentford proved to be Leicester's most routine win of the entire cup run. Jack Lee opened the scoring in the first half while Mal Griffiths settled affairs in the second, on a day when Leicester forward Ken Chisholm stood out as Brentford's chief tormentor. There was little in the way of sympathy for the home fans who were roundly criticised in the press for their treatment of the Leicester players and Lee in particular.

No team in the 20th century had won the 'double' of the league championship and FA Cup in a single season. As the teams ran out for the semi-final it looked as though Portsmouth, who had already secured the First Division title by eight points, were odds-on favourites to achieve the impossible. The bookmakers, who had never rated Leicester's chances, agreed, offering odds of 8–1 on favourites Pompey to send the City back to the East Midlands with their tails between their legs. Even the Pathé News commentator told viewers Leicester City had no chance.

Demonstrating why they were the best team in the country, Portsmouth swamped Leicester for the first 15 minutes. Then with Pompey heavily committed to attack, the ball was intercepted and slid to Chisholm on the halfway line. Thinking quickly, he found Mal Griffiths steaming up the wing with half of Arsenal's Highbury pitch almost to himself as Jack Lee raced into the box. Griffiths' pass fell behind Lee but he had enough time to tee it up for Revie to lash a first-time shot past stranded goalkeeper Ernest Butler.

A quick Pompey equaliser made the Leicester goal look like a minor blip before the inevitable onslaught from the league champions. Despite some scares the game was still level as the referee blew for half time.

As the sides came in, Sep Smith was waiting in the Leicester dressing room. He had been watching Portsmouth all season and had noticed that every time keeper Butler came out for a cross he had a habit of palming the ball over the head of his opponents. All the Leicester strikers had to do was hang back and wait for the ball to fall to them.

With barely two minutes on the clock in the second half, Jack Lee got to the byline and swung the ball back to Ken Chisholm on the edge of the area. Butler looked to have Chisholm's goal-bound shot covered before it deflected off Harry Ferrier's shin and past the helpless keeper to put The City back in front.

Pompey almost saved the tie with 15 minutes to go. Len Phillips got into the Leicester penalty area, shook off Ted Jelly's challenge and, as keeper McGraw raced out of goal, slipped the ball across the six-yard box to Peter Harris who had the simple task of tapping the ball into a net guarded only by defender Sandy Scott. But Harris overstretched, getting the slightest of touches on the ball before knocking it wide.

Later, Pompey's Butler came for a cross and got nowhere near it to leave Revie to squeeze the ball into the net and make it 3–1.

The remaining minutes ticked by like hours as many of the Leicester players looked up at the big clock in the Highbury North Bank and the realisation set in that, if they could hang on for another few minutes, they were going to Wembley. Portsmouth continued to press but never again created a clear opportunity to get back into the game. Leicester were in the cup final for the first time. Writing in *Soccer's Happy Wanderer* Revie said, 'I was only 21 and could scarcely believe that at this early age I was going to fulfil an ambition denied to many great players in their long careers. I felt on top of the world. The dread days when the Leicester crowd barracked me were over. I had regained my confidence. Instead of the jeers it was cheers and "Have you got any cup final tickets Don?"'

...

Reaching the FA Cup Final was only a distraction from Leicester's league position. By the end of April, they faced the very real prospect of kicking off the following season in the Third Division. A 3–0 home defeat to Fulham on 16 April had *The People* lamenting a lack of goals that was leaving them on the verge of relegation.

Even the *Daily Mirror* weighed in on Leicester City's chances by saying, 'It now appears for the first time, a team will contest the cup final at Wembley shadowed by the threat of relegation to the Third Division.'

In an Easter Monday league clash a ball cleared by the Leicester keeper bounced in West Ham United's half and both Revie and opposing centre-half Richard Walker jumped for the ball. A forehead connected with a nose and at the end of the 1–1 draw Revie left the pitch covered in his own blood. A slight nose bleed, nothing to worry about?

When Johnny Duncan was asked about the game he made no mention of Revie's condition to the *Daily Mirror* saying, 'Well, at least we got one point and made it through with 11 fit players.' More pressing was the win fellow strugglers Nottingham Forest had registered against bottom-placed Bradford Park Avenue, leaving the two Midlands clubs level on points in the race for safety.

Standing third from bottom with two teams relegated, the Blackburn Rovers game on Thursday of the same week was now a must-win for The City. However bad Revie's nose looked there was no way Duncan would countenance dropping his young inside-right.

The manager had made the right call. Replicating the form they had shown in the semi-final against Portsmouth, the cup finalists overcame Rovers with a thumping 3–1 victory. Despite sporting two black eyes and a swollen nose, Revie scored with what the *Daily Herald* described as the 'best shot of the match'. They were now third from bottom with a two-point cushion over Forest, and a game in hand.

The major concern for Johnny Duncan was left-half Johnny King limping off with a suspected broken bone in his leg. While these fears would prove unfounded, the manager could not risk losing any more players so rested Revie for the game against Plymouth Argyle. He watched the game from the stands before joining up with the rest of the team for pre-final training at Skegness.

After a 1–1 draw, Leicester were left needing one win for safety. With attention now on the cup final, only a week away, Revie turned in for an early night. It was Ken Chisholm, Revie's roommate and scorer of Leicester's second goal in the semi-final, who raised the alarm. As a former bomber pilot in World War II there were not many things he hadn't seen, but when he saw Revie bent over a wash bowl for 90 minutes with blood streaming from his nose he knew something was very wrong.

Revie was rushed to Plymouth Hospital where the nose was plugged, and the bleeding brought to a trickle. Then Johnny Duncan decided to get in a taxi with Revie and drive all the way back to Leicester Royal Infirmary. The trip was horrendous – Revie lost more blood and got weaker and weaker. 'Had he arrived more than half an hour later he would have been dead, such was the amount of blood he lost,' Elsie Revie later recalled.

Reflecting in *Soccer's Happy Wanderer,* Revie wrote, 'I was as weak as a kitten as we rolled into Leicester. Two specialists were waiting as I was carried into the hospital. I hardly knew what was happening, but such is the fever of Wembley that I managed to stammer weakly: "Can you stop the bleeding in time for me to play in the final." Then I must have fainted. An emergency transfusion took place and treatment for ruptured blood vessels.'

The team followed all the normal cup final traditions of taking a training base near London and then setting up at a city hotel the night before the final while the players' wives were given head scarves depicting caricatures of the team to be worn at Wembley.

As the teams lined up to be introduced to the Duke of Edinburgh on a bright April day for the 1949 FA Cup Final, Don Revie was not among them. As the 100,000 fans who had come to Wembley sang 'Abide With Me', Revie was lying in a hospital bed and tuning into the game on a bedside radio at Leicester Royal Infirmary, over 100 miles away.

The first half of the final proved to be the one-sided affair many had expected and Wolves cruised into a two-goal lead, but Leicester got the lift they needed at the start of the second half when Mal Griffiths pulled a goal back. That set up a nervy 10-minute spell when Leicester threatened to equalise – and thought they had when Ken Chisholm fired in from close range, only for the goal to be ruled out for offside. The scare seemed to wake up Wolves and they soon restored their two-goal lead, which they never again looked in danger of losing.

And the man whose goals had done so much to get them to the hallowed twin towers was not there. Readers of the *Daily Mirror* would have spotted Revie dressed in Paisley pyjamas with headphones on waiting for the game to start. Just a few days earlier Johnny Duncan had delivered the news Revie was dreading. Not only would he not be playing but he was even too weak to travel to London.

Lying there, Revie knew he was helpless but the team had sent a telegram, 'Don't worry Don, we'll pull out that little extra for you and bring the cup into the ward on Monday night.' When they did come there was no cup – only an apology that they had not been able to win it for him.

Nobody could feel sorrier than Revie. His dreams of playing in an FA Cup Final and winning an England cap were shattered. Instead of touring Scandinavia with the national side, he would be kicking his heels in rural Ireland.

...

As if to underline how important Revie was to the club's plans, Johnny Duncan had appointed the 22-year-old as his new team captain for the coming season. Don's relationship with Elsie was becoming serious, marriage was in the offing. Therefore, fans were led to believe that for as long as Duncan remained manager there was no way Don Revie was going anywhere. Then came the bombshell.

Just two weeks into the new season, George Chisholm of the *Daily Herald* reported that Revie had requested a transfer. According to Revie in *Soccer's Happy Wanderer* things had changed in the dressing room: 'When I reported back to Filbert Street at the start of 1949–50 season I discovered I had been made captain. I should have been the happiest man in the world yet for some strange reason there wasn't the same spirit among the boys. I don't know what it was. Maybe the reaction after our wonderful cup run.'

Things were changing for Revie on the personal front. A month after his transfer request, Revie and Elsie exchanged vows at the Robert Hall Baptist Church, on 17 October, 1949. Elsie was now a fully qualified teacher and was working at a Leicester school. They made their home at Danvers Road where they lived with her mother and sister, but to the couple it was only a temporary arrangement.

If anything, marriage made Revie more determined to leave the club. He worried that now, as a full member of the Duncan family, teammates and fans would think he only owed his place in the side to his connection to 'Uncle Tokey'. He had already been stung by a report in *The People* which called him 'Leicester's blue-eyed little boy'.

Revie later said, 'In October 1949 I married Johnny Duncan's niece, Elsie. That made me one of the Duncan family and it complicated my football future. If I had a bad spell and was retained in the first team, unkind tongues would soon have been suggesting that it was only because of the influence of the manager.'

The request to Johnny Duncan was blunt in its simplicity: 'Boss, I want a transfer.' Duncan agreed to put it to the board who quickly accepted the player's decision. However, they insisted on the caveat that Revie would only leave the club in exchange for other players and they had to be the right fit for the club.

A board meeting around that time saw an extraordinary turn of events that killed off any hope of Revie staying on – the club was under investigation by the FA.

An allocation of tickets given to the club for the cup final had appeared on the black market at inflated prices. The club was unable to provide any evidence as to who had bought the original tickets as all paperwork had been destroyed. This was a serious allegation that could have resulted in not just a charge by the governing body, but also a criminal investigation.

Halfway through the meeting, after discussing potential transfer targets, Duncan was asked to leave the meeting. He must not have thought there was anything untoward happening but was shocked to receive a phone call the next day asking him to resign as manager.

In the press the following day, Duncan insisted he was sacked but Len Shipman, the Leicester chairman, told journalists he had resigned. Speaking to the *Daily Herald* Duncan said: 'I went to the Tuesday board meeting as usual and was asked to leave before it finished. I believe it went on for some time after I left. It was not until the morning when I was going about my normal duties, including team selection, that I was told of my sacking from today.'

In the same article Shipman said, 'He was asked to resign but I cannot state the reason for the decision.' Either way one thing was clear, by accident or design, Johnny Duncan was no longer manager, ending a 27-year association with the club. Despite rumours, the real reason for Duncan's departure was never adequately explained.

At the same meeting board members were informed that there had been two approaches for Revie, one from Fulham and the other from Hull City. But for the press, who were aware of scout Joe Shaw's regular visits to Filbert Street, there was only one place Revie was heading – Arsenal.

Just two weeks after Johnny Duncan had been sacked the Leicester chairman, secretary and Revie headed to London. They told no one where they were going and refused to confirm or deny they were meeting with Tom Whittaker, the Arsenal manager.

Years later Revie claimed the vastness of London and the marble halls of Highbury had filled him with doubt. 'Here was a situation most footballers would be happy to be in. But I was suddenly assailed with doubt. Would I make the grade at the fabulous Arsenal side? What would happen if I lost my form? Perhaps I would be relegated to the reserves and never heard of again?'

The meeting did not go as planned. The Leicester board minutes of 25 October stated, 'Negotiations with Arsenal for the transfer of D Revie based on the exchange of players has not materialized. The transfer of Revie is to be carried out on a cash basis to the highest bidder. To date enquiries had been received from Hull City, Manchester City, Fulham, Wolves, Cardiff City, Southampton and Derby County.'

Time was now dragging on. It was nearly November and Revie had submitted his transfer request on 13 September. Each day the press was full of speculation. One day he was heading back to the North East and Newcastle; on another day Derby County, who in March 1949 had broken the British transfer record to buy Manchester United's Johnny Morris, were willing to go beyond £25,000 to get their man.

But once Arsenal were out of the running there was one clear favourite – Manchester City. City were keen to build on their seventh-place finish in the First Division and Revie was seen as a vital part of their post-war rebuilding, which included the reconstruction of their bombed and burned out main stand.

As long ago as 1 October, Bob Smith, the City chairman, was in the crowd at Gigg Lane when Bury hosted Leicester. He made his intentions to the newsmen clear: 'I went to Bury in general line with our system of keeping well-informed about the form of players we are interested in.'

A month later, the Leicester board, after accepting an offer of £26,000 from Manchester City, which would have broken the British transfer record, granted the club permission to talk to Revie. At the same time, Hull City were told their bid of £20,000, while a club record, was way below what they had been offered by the other interested party. It looked as though Revie would soon be exchanging the royal blue of Leicester for the sky blue of Manchester City. All the player had to do was say 'yes'.

The following day Revie and new bride Elsie travelled to Manchester. Stepping off the train they encountered smoke hanging in the air from factory chimneys and gloomy cobbled streets that reminded Revie of his childhood. Their first impressions of the city were not good and things were not helped by torrential rain.

Matters went from bad to worse when they viewed the house on Maine Road that the club was offering the young couple. They were just not impressed, so by the time City manager, Jock Thomson, sat down to discuss personal terms, he was wasting his time. Don and Elsie had already made their minds up – he would not be signing for Manchester City.

According to the press, the player himself was fed up and frustrated that Leicester had now put a record price tag of £28,000 on his head. 'I'm not worth that much, I've still got a lot to learn about soccer,' Revie told Bill Holden of the *Daily Mirror* in November 1949. Until his transfer was resolved, his and Elsie's lives were on hold. She had resigned from her job as a teacher ahead of a move which had so far failed to materialise but, despite all the speculation in the newspapers, Revie was quite clear about his intentions. To Holden he said, 'I am not going to join Manchester City. My wife and I looked over the place, but we shouldn't like to live there. I've decided not to go. I want to go to Hull City where I believe Raich Carter can teach me a lot more about the game.'

Regarded as the finest English inside-forward of his generation, Carter had led Sunderland to the 1937 FA Cup Final, having won the league championship a year earlier. He won the cup again in 1946 after moving to Derby County. Throughout his career Raich Carter had known only success.

As player/manager of Hull City he quickly led the unfashionable Tigers out of the Third Division (North) at the first attempt. Signing a player of Revie's calibre would be a statement of intent as Carter did not want to hang around in the Second Division for any longer than was necessary. He was sure that under his watch Hull City were going to do great things.

From Revie's point of view, it was a win-win situation. He could continue his footballing education under one of his great heroes, all the while being part of a team that was going places. The only sticking point was the Leicester City board who were yet to grant Hull permission to speak to the player.

The board had run out of options. There was no chance of resurrecting the deal with Arsenal and the player himself had blocked the move to Manchester City. They were faced with a choice of either keeping an unhappy player or letting him go. Reluctantly, on 8 November, the Leicester board accepted Hull City's bid of £20,000. By Saturday that week, Revie was running out in Tigers' colours for his home debut against Coventry City.

3

HULL CITY (1949–51)

'I couldn't wish for anybody better than Don to groom as my successor.
He is young, strong, fast and one of the cleverest ball players in the game.'

Raich Carter, Hull City player/manager

When Revie put pen to paper for Hull City it seemed he was about to enter a golden period in his life. Revie, who told the press he had been given 'carte blanche' from his wife to find a house, was given a home in Hessle on the outskirts of the city. The family atmosphere he flourished in at Leicester City looked sure to continue with the newlyweds asking Elsie's mother, Jenny Duncan, to move in.

Kim Revie recalled: 'Both were busy working, dad with his football and mum with her teaching. Both were no good around the house, so they moved my grandmother in to help with the cooking and cleaning.'

To many observers, turning down glamour clubs like Arsenal and Manchester City in favour of Hull seemed an odd choice. Even though they had won the Third Division (North) championship and had run the mighty Manchester United close in a 1–0 FA Cup quarter-final defeat the previous season, they had no history to speak of except for an FA Cup semi-final in 1930.

But for Revie, the one reason to move to Humberside was Raich Carter. Revie said, 'I had seen him play many, many times and always recognised his genius and felt being attached to the same club would automatically enable me to learn a lot more about the game.'

Known as the 'Great Horatio' while playing for his hometown club, Sunderland, by the age of 23 Carter had won all the game's major trophies in a

29

career interrupted by World War II. After the war, he transferred to Derby County where he became the first man to win the FA Cup with two different clubs, either side of the war.

Generally seen as the finest inside-forward of his generation, winger Stanley Matthews, who partnered him in the England team, said of Carter: 'Bewilderingly clever, constructive, lethal in front of goal, yet unselfish. Time and again he'd play the ball out wide to me and with such service I was in my element.'

Appointed player/manager of Hull City in April 1948, his talent and example on the pitch saw the Tigers win their first nine matches of his first full season and win the Third Division (North) with record-breaking attendances. However, Carter was an abrasive character who told the *Hull Daily Mail* in February, 1949, 'I used to be arrogant but I've matured and grown more tolerant; now I'm just conceited.'

To Revie, with his family settled and an opportunity to learn from a master, Hull seemed the perfect place to begin married life. Carter suggested Revie stay at his house the first night in Hull while he waited to arrange digs. Remembering the long sessions with Sep Smith when he first joined Leicester City, Revie looked forward to a long night talking tactics and the state of football in general. Instead, he was met with silence.

Sitting in a chair in his parlour, Carter folded his arms and did not say a word. All Revie's attempts to strike up a conversation were met with one-word answers. For a long time they sat in awkward silence, only broken by Revie asking Carter if he had anything to read. Fumbling around the house Carter tossed Revie a few football books then headed for bed.

'To say the least, I was mildly surprised. But then I didn't know that Raich was never a manager to talk a lot about the game off the field. As he was still playing, he preferred to set his own example on the field. He did most of his shouting there and for those who played with him his call for the ball made it easy for them to part with it.'

Even though the manager was renowned for the 'Carter Roar', where he would shout sharp instructions to other teammates, off the pitch he had very little to say. Commenting on his managerial style Carter explained: 'My aim is to play high-class football and let the result take care of itself.'

For someone who was used to the attention to detail of Johnny Duncan or Sep Smith, Revie was shocked by Carter's instructions on his debut on 12 November, 1949, against visitors Coventry City. 'OK Don just go out there and play your normal game,' were the only words Carter said to him. Despite announcing his new signing would play in his own favoured inside-right position, Carter took up a deep-lying role, hindering Revie in the process.

Such was Carter's performance, scoring two goals in the 2–1 victory, the shine was taken off Revie's debut. As the *Hull Daily Mail* reported, 'Carter's match-winning brilliance overshadowed Don Revie's debut. But Revie gave occasional samples of stylish work even though he was not in the picture to anything of the same extent as City's player/manager.'

Originally, Carter had seen Revie as a long-term replacement for him in the Hull side, telling the *Daily Herald*, 'I couldn't wish for anybody better than Don to groom as my successor. He is young, strong, fast and one of the cleverest ball players in the game. My chief concern has been to find a forward to fill the gap when I pack up to concentrate on management. I don't think I need worry anymore.'

But now that Revie was at the club, there didn't seem to be a natural role for him. It didn't help when the manager told the press, 'I am determined to play on as long as I can raise a gallop.'

Trouble came when Revie came to understand that Hull City's game was not his normal game. Whereas Revie was brought up with Leicester City's short passing, Hull City relied on long, defence-splitting balls played out of midfield by the deep-lying Carter. Very often, Revie drifted out of games.

It was a full three months before Revie finally found the net, on 12 January, 1950, against Southport in an FA Cup tie. This was a poor return for a player who had scored 16 times in 36 league matches and whose four goals in the FA Cup had fired Leicester to the final a few months earlier.

Come the fourth round of the cup, Revie was dropped for a replay with Stockport County, a particularly low point for Carter and Hull City as they were humbled 2–0 by a side a division below them.

The goal against Southport was to be the only time Revie scored in the 1949–50 season. He later commented, 'Perhaps the reported price tag of

£20,000, which Hull City were said to have paid for my services, affected my play. Perhaps it was because I was young and taking time to settle down which made me such a flop at Boothferry Park at first. Whatever the reason, the fact remains I could just not put a foot right. In my first season I did not score a league goal.'

After the *Daily Herald* announced on 3 March, 1950, 'Yes, Hull City have dropped their £20,000 signing for the game against Preston North End,' there was only one thing to do – turn to family. A call to Johnny Duncan, asking him to come and see him play and tell him where he was going wrong, saw Uncle Tokey head to Humberside to run the rule over his nephew.

In his long career Duncan had learned that good players do not suddenly become bad overnight. Watching from the stands at Boothferry Park, Johnny only needed a few minutes to see what everyone else could not – Raich Carter was playing in Revie's position.

Duncan told Revie, 'You cannot have two schemers playing deep. With Raich doing all the necessary, your best position now is at right-half.' When Revie asked Carter if he could move position, the response surprised him. 'I was waiting for you to ask!' This would prove to be a challenge as at Leicester he had never really impressed in his few appearances in that role.

The first time Revie was tested in his new position was in a reserve game against Worksop. Instantly, matters improved. Instead of trying to turn with the ball, Revie was now able to face it, giving him a better view of the pitch. Soon he was talked about as a potential wing-half for England.

A frustrating first season ended in May 1950 with Hull finishing in seventh place, well off the pace of Tottenham Hotspur and Sheffield Wednesday, who were promoted. Failing to justify his price tag, Revie could not find the net in 35 league games – 13 for Leicester, 22 for Hull.

But come the 1950–51 season, Revie felt his new position would improve his fortunes and he started to enjoy spending time with his new teammates. His first league goal for Hull came against Swansea in the third match of the season.

On the team front, the Hull board demonstrated its willingness to match Raich Carter's ambitions by making an offer for Stoke City's highly rated centre-half, Neil Franklin. However, Revie could not have known he was about to be the subject of controversy when transfer negotiations began in November 1950.

According to reports in the *Hull Daily Mail*, Revie was not happy at Hull and wanted a transfer. The paper went on to say Revie was on his way to Stoke with Franklin coming the other way. The rumour became so serious the player himself was forced into making a statement. 'I am quite happy at Hull City. I never wanted a move, nor do I intend to ask for one. Moreover, I have never heard any suggestion in official quarters that the Franklin negotiations would involve me in any way, shape or form.'

With Neil Franklin now in the side alongside Revie and Welsh international Bill Harris, it looked as though Hull City would be serious contenders for promotion. However, injuries took their toll. Revie, who was an ever-present, took a knock that side-lined him in April 1951, while Franklin was ruled out with a knee injury. The club, without its strongest players, slipped to a disappointing 10th in the Second Division and failed to make a dent in the FA Cup.

But Revie was now firmly established in the side, notching up eight goals. This led *Sport* magazine to claim, 'Many folk sneered when Hull, then in a Raich Carter process of rejuvenation, decreased their financial resources to the extent of £20,000 to increase their player strength by taking Revie to Humberside. And the failure of Don to immediately produce his best and brightest form in the old gold of Hull was proclaimed as further proof of the inflated transfer market.

'Now, Hull fans are enthusing over right-half Revie, ace schemer and penalty king and perhaps not far removed from when he will fulfil his soccer ambition of donning the white shirt of England.'

Improved performances for Hull City led to admiring glances from Leeds United and Manchester City (again), both in the First Division. During a summer tour of Spain, where Revie played in a 4–0 loss to Atletico Madrid and a 2–0 defeat to Athletic Bilbao, there was a personal high point for Revie when he bagged a brace in front of 25,000 at the Les Corts Stadium, Barcelona's home before they moved to the Camp Nou in 1957.

However, Revie was not happy, regretting the deal that had fallen through with Arsenal in 1949. He remembered the words of Tom Whittaker, the Arsenal manager, when he turned them down. 'We would have liked you to come to Arsenal. Never forget, if I can be of any help to you in the game or outside it, you only have to ring me.' In the weeks leading up to the 1951–52 season Revie was tempted to make the call.

Just a few months earlier, in April 1951, the *Daily Mirror* asked, '£20,000 Don Revie, who has not settled to form at Hull. Could he do it at Highbury?' The article speculated whether Arsenal and Hull City might be interested in a swap deal involving Arsenal winger Ian McPherson, plus a cheque for Revie.

Secretly Revie hoped a move to Highbury might be back on. 'I must say I was hoping at the back of my mind that I would get a second chance of joining Arsenal. By now I realised that I would have been wiser to have gone to Highbury where I would have been under Tom Whittaker – with all the benefits that every player gets at Highbury.'

Looking back, Revie also rued the decision to rule out Manchester. Simply put, Revie had reached the conclusion, signing for Hull City had been a mistake from day one.

No longer the shy boy brought to tears by Sep Smith, at 24 Revie was a married man with an extended family. He was about to hit his peak as a player and feared another season in the Second Division would see him remembered as a potential star who burnt brightly for a short time before fading into mediocrity. He was at a fork in the road and he had to decide whether to stay or go.

Hull City's most famous player made up his mind – he wanted out. The board spent a week trying to change his mind but to no avail. An announcement on 12 September started the process – manager Raich Carter had written to them a week before informing them of his resignation.

'At a meeting of the Board last night a letter from Carter was considered. He resigned as player/manager to take effect immediately. No reason was given. The resignation was accepted by the Board with regret.'

A month later Revie decided he had had enough, too. The reasons for both Carter's resignation and Revie's transfer request were the same – both were ambitious and a bad start to the season meant it was clear that rather than challenging for honours, Hull City would be sucked into a relegation dogfight.

It had been two years of frustration for Revie. 'Football is like any walk of life. You must be happy to enjoy it. I suppose I was the odd man out, my style wasn't Hull City's style and the only sensible thing in circumstances like these was to get out.'

Any lingering doubts Revie had about leaving came to an end when Carter left the club. From the outset the main reason Revie had come to Hull was to learn from Carter – with him gone there was little reason to stay. He told the board he believed his playing style suited the top division and therefore wanted a move.

Revie later said, 'This may sound selfish. Yet what professional footballer does not feel he would like to reach the very top? It is hypocritical to think otherwise. The game was no longer an enjoyment to me, the high hopes I had as a youngster seemed to have gone forever. There was nothing for it but to ask for a transfer in the hope I might find something like consistent form with a new club.'

To unsettle him even more Revie was aware that Manchester City, the club that had openly courted him through the press in the months leading up to his move to Hull City, had made another offer for him. After initially turning it down, the board changed its mind, telling City they could have Revie as long as they offered a player in exchange.

Having been stung by the negative press publicity surrounding his protracted transfer from Leicester, Revie was keen not to be put through that experience again. On 18 October, 1951, Revie and Elsie got on a train headed for the North West. This time there would be no delays so by the end of that day, after what felt like a two-year chase, Revie was finally a Manchester City player.

The deal saw Manchester City full-back Ernie Phillips head to Hull City, together with a cheque for £6,000 to make up for the shortfall in the valuation of both players. The two clubs were going in opposite directions – Manchester City were newly promoted at the first time of asking (after being relegated in 1950), while Hull City were only saved from relegation to the third tier by Raich Carter making a comeback as a player. Manchester City and Revie were about to enter one of the most fascinating and successful periods in their history, but there would be a few mountains to climb first before they got there.

4

MANCHESTER CITY (1951–56)

'It's the answer to all our problems. You cannot stop when it gets going, the style is made for you, Don.'

Johnny Williamson, Manchester City striker on the Revie Plan

The club that Revie joined on 18 October, 1951, was a world away from what he left behind at both Leicester City and Hull City. Back in the top flight after only one season in the Second Division, Manchester City were determined to regain the championship they last won in 1937.

Relegated the following year in 1938, they were promoted as champions in 1946 only to find themselves going down again in 1950. At the same time, their fierce city rivals, Manchester United, had finished as Division One runners-up in three consecutive seasons and had won the FA Cup in 1948.

Appointed City manager on 1 June, 1950, Les McDowall was a man on a mission. Having played for the club between 1937 and 1948, making 129 appearances, the Scot knew City intimately and was determined to break the cycle of promotion and relegation that had plagued it.

Wasting no time, he set out his stall early by beating Arsenal to the much sought-after signature of right-half Roy Paul, a Welsh international, paying Swansea Town £19,500 for his services just weeks after taking over.

Headstrong and opinionated, Paul was described by teammate Ken Barnes as a 'born leader who was brilliant in the air'. Paul was a winner who played 160 matches for Swansea, winning the old Third Division (South) championship in 1949.

Available after a move to Colombian side Millonarios fell through, Paul could play in all three half-back positions and was tipped as a future club captain.

Revie's arrival came as something of a relief to Paul. As designated penalty-taker he was more than happy to hand over duties to Revie.

Paul's nephew, Alan Curtis, who went on to play for Swansea and Leeds United in the 1970s and 80s, said of his uncle, 'He was a hero in the Rhondda but he loved a drink. He said he only played one game sober and that was when the pub was closed!' It was this lack of discipline that ended up frustrating McDowall.

To further underline the ambition of the club, and just two weeks before capturing Revie from Hull, City broke the British transfer record by securing the services of inside-forward Ivor Broadis from Sunderland, for £25,000. The signing of Broadis was quite a coup. A highly skilled player, he was already being compared to Raich Carter.

An almost unique figure in British football history, Broadis had been appointed as player/manager of Carlisle United at the ridiculously young age of 23 before single-handedly negotiating his move to Sunderland. Bill Shankly, who replaced Broadis as Carlisle United manager, labelled him 'the strongest and most dangerous inside-forward in the game'.

City now had a side in which Revie could flourish and that looked like it was on the cusp of a new golden era. Revie later wrote: 'I joined Manchester City just two weeks after Ivor Broadis, who in my opinion was one of the fastest and cleverest inside-forwards in the game. This City team should have been a world-beating combination. Trautmann in goal; Roy Paul, one of the greatest wing-halves in football at left-half; Ivor Broadis; Roy Clarke, the Welsh international winger; and a most promising group of club men like Roy Little, Jimmy Meadows, Dennis Westcott, Ron Phoenix and Johnny Williamson. Really the list is too long to include all the boys.'

Despite high hopes, City got off to an awful start with only seven points from their first 10 games. A brilliant 2–1 win against Fulham at Craven Cottage on 3 November, 1951, was the high point of an otherwise dismal run. Reporting on the match, the *Sunday Pictorial* wrote, 'High-priced inside-forwards Don Revie from Hull and Ivor Broadis from Sunderland got the goals at Craven Cottage. Manchester got on with the job in hand with quick incisive passing and deserved their win, if only for their opportunism.'

After being handed a 4–1 beating in the FA Cup third round replay against Wolves on 17 January, 1952, where the only highlight was the *Daily Herald* describing Revie as a 'danger man', City went on a run which saw them draw eight games and lose three. It was not until 14 April that City registered a win – 2–1 against Liverpool.

Despite contributing goals against Spurs, Middlesbrough and West Bromwich Albion, Revie's City ended a disappointing season in 15th place – made even more painful as Manchester United lifted the league championship.

Bad form continued into the next season. A pair of losses to Stoke City and Tottenham Hotspur meant City were not looking likely to challenge for honours. Revie only opened his account with a brace against Middlesbrough in a wild 5–4 loss at Ayresome Park on 13 September, 1952.

Despite scoring against Cardiff City and Bolton Wanderers in early October, when Revie missed a penalty against Aston Villa he was convinced he would never be seen in a City shirt again. Unable to find his best position, he played inside-forward and wing-half as Les McDowall could not settle on his favoured formation. Two days later he was in McDowall's office asking to be put on the transfer list. He said his reason was simple: Manchester City did not play in his style. His request was turned down flat.

'Just as happened at Hull with Raich Carter, I found myself playing alongside a chap who liked to play deep. Ivor is a much more spectacular player than me. He is, I would say, quicker on the ball and that wonderful 20-yard burst of his with the ball is one of the most electrifying sights in soccer.

'It should have been easy for us both to link up, leaving Ivor racing through. Instead, we both lay back and got in each other's way. Then, as at Hull, I went upfield and found I couldn't play the role of goal grabber. Maybe the reason is my brand of football needs time and space to flourish properly. I am no speed merchant. I have never pretended to be anything but a schemer and an accurate passer of the ball.'

Things were not helped by the relationship Revie had with Les McDowall. On Revie's part he found his manager aloof and not willing to listen to his player's concerns. For the manager's part, he never trusted Revie, found the player's interest in tactics interfering and disliked his stubborn nature.

On 20 December, 1952, as Manchester City lined up to play Stoke City the situation was dire. Both teams needed the win as they occupied the bottom two places. The lift the 2–1 win gave City was only temporary. A 6–2 defeat against Preston North End left the Blues at the bottom of the table, having failed to register a win away from home all season.

An upturn in form in the New Year, starting with a 1–1 draw in the Manchester derby, saw City put seven past a hapless Swindon Town in the FA Cup, and claim a precious away win against Liverpool at Anfield on 17 January. A 5–1 win at home to Middlesbrough, with Revie getting on the scoresheet, capped a brilliant January that saw Manchester City climb out of the relegation zone.

Any hopes of an FA Cup run came to an end with a 5–1 thrashing at the hands of Luton Town in a fourth round FA Cup replay early in February. Erratic form followed with only a 5–0 win over FA Cup finalists, Blackpool, on 25 April, 1952, saving City from the drop. By the time they lost 3–1 away at Chelsea they had lost four out of their last five games and limped to the end of the season just one point clear of relegated Stoke City.

As everyone gathered in the Revie household for Hogmanay, there was nothing to suggest 1954 was going to be any different to 1953. Manchester City had lost four out of their first five games. A 2–0 win over bitter rivals United in September, with Revie smashing home a goal, made the fans smile but City were hugely inconsistent again.

Despite spending a colossal £200,000 on players since the end of World War II, City seemed destined to be cast as perennial strugglers. As the revellers gathered to see in the New Year, Revie tried to cast to one side his doubts about the direction Manchester City was going in.

Master of ceremonies that night was Revie himself, striking up a rendition of his favourite song, *Bye, Bye Blackbird*. Future England winger Peter Barnes later remembered Revie encouraging the under-23s to sing it when he was England manager.

If Revie was unsettled at Manchester City, so was his main rival, Ivor Broadis. Things had started to go downhill for City's star man. Having gained a regular place in the England side the previous season, Broadis' form dropped off alarmingly; he was not named in the side that beat Manchester United in a 2–0 victory in September, and lost his international place. An official statement from the manager said, 'Following a heart-to-heart talk between the player and myself, it will be in the best interest of the club and player to part.' In that conversation, McDowall had become concerned by some of the comments Broadis was making in his weekly column in the *Manchester Evening News*. Therefore, it was no surprise when Broadis departed for Newcastle United in October, for £18,000.

The same month, Revie was called up to a Football League XI to face a League of Ireland XI at Maine Road, and scored a hat-trick in a 9–1 victory. A call-up to the England B team came in March 1954, leaving him tantalisingly close to the full international team.

But the chopping and changing that marked Les McDowall's tenure in charge of Manchester City continued, to Revie's frustration. Over the Christmas period he had played in three positions, hardly conducive to a settled team. Like Revie, McDowall knew he had some very good players, but the team was really two units, which McDowall found difficult to link together.

The solution had been demonstrated about a month before, on 23 November, 1953. Hungary, the Olympic Champions, arrived at Wembley to take on England. Wearing fashionably high-cut shorts and low-slung boots, they were not expected by the press to pose much of a threat to the national side. Future England manager Bobby Robson, watching as a 20-year-old in the crowd, said of the Hungarians: 'None of these players meant anything to us. They were men from Mars as far as we were concerned. We thought we would demolish this team. England at Wembley; we were the masters; they were the pupils.'

How wrong everyone turned out to be. The team featuring future England manager Sir Alf Ramsey, Wolves' captain Billy Wright and all-time great Sir Stanley Matthews were given a footballing lesson. 'It was like carthorses playing racehorses,' remarked Tom Finney, who missed the game through injury. Matthews agreed, 'They were wonderful to watch, with tactics we'd never seen before. That wonderful Hungarian team, they were the best.' Wright added, 'It was a magnificent performance. Looking back, we completely underestimated the advances that the Hungarians had made.'

It was the tactics that fascinated Revie, watching at home with friends Ken Barnes (father of Peter) and Johnny Williamson. Ever since the 1930s, when Herbert Chapman, manager of the dominant Arsenal side of the era, devised the W-M formation to combat the new offside rule, the lay-out had become the settled view of how football should be played. Little did the England players know when the Hungarians lined up at Wembley that they were about to rip up the rulebook.

When playing the W-M formation, the defending centre-half would traditionally mark the opposition's centre-forward — usually whoever was wearing the number nine shirt. But in the Hungary game, England centre-half Harry Johnston found himself marking Hidegkuti, who was effectively operating as a midfielder.

This meant that Johnston was constantly drawn out of position, allowing the Hungary players to exploit the space. England were also undone by Hungary using Kocsis and Puskás as strikers. These two wore numbers 8 and 10 – England thought they were inside-forwards. This in turn led to uncertainty about who should mark them and, to further confuse the English players, the Hungary forwards were continually swapping positions against the inflexible English defence, who were marking numbers on shirts instead of players.

The magnificent Magyars ran out 6–3 winners – the result led to a review of the training and tactics used by the England team. The so-called 'Match of the Century' also brought Ferenc Puskás to the world's attention.

While the press and commentators raved about the way Hungary had played, Ken Barnes had seen it all before. Writing in his autobiography, *This Simple Game*, Barnes claimed City were already playing that way in the reserves. He wrote: 'It had fuck all to do with the Hungarians, we were playing a deep-lying centre-forward in the City reserves before they turned England over at Wembley.'

As the bottles and food were cleared away after the New Year's party at the Revie house, City's reserves were in fact in the middle of a 30-game run that saw them unbeaten until the end of the season.

A few days later, over a game of snooker at Wythenshawe Conservative Club, Johnny Williamson, the player who got the closest to Revie during his career, tried to convince a sceptical Revie of the plan: 'It's the answer to all our problems.

41

You cannot stop when it gets going, the style is made for you.' Revie laughed, 'It might work in the reserves, Johnny, but in the First Division we cover too quickly. You're over-enthusiastic because you are having a good run with it.'

As City kicked off the New Year, consistency was again the main problem. A 3–0 away win at Cardiff City on 23 January with Revie scoring then saw City go four games without a win, shipping a total of eight goals. Safety was only achieved on 16 April with a 1–0 victory over Chelsea. A groin strain earlier in the month put paid to Revie's season prematurely as City finished 17th, an improvement on the previous season but disappointing for a side which had hoped to challenge for honours.

After the summer break, as Revie turned up for pre-season training a full two weeks early, he was despondent. The early season start had robbed him of precious time with Elsie and son Duncan. His wife's teaching job meant they hardly ever spent any time together. While Revie was off in the afternoons after training, Elsie was in the classroom. When she was free on Saturday, Revie was on the football pitch. The long summer holidays allowed them to spend time together, but, ever-ambitious, he felt that spending another season with a struggling side would mean that his chance of a full England cap would be gone forever.

The depression hanging around the club was reflected in the press who, for the third season running, made City contenders for the drop in 1955. Things were made worse by the emergence of an exciting young side, the Busby Babes, on the other side of Manchester.

With a reputation as a stern Scot, with little interest in what went on on the training pitch, the Manchester City players were surprised to be greeted with a speech from Les McDowall. It was the most Revie had heard from his manager in his three years at the club.

Standing in the centre circle, McDowall began: 'We are going to play football this season. By football, I mean football. Keep the ball down, no big kicking, no wild clearances from the defence. We want to aim for smooth link up from defence to attack, letting the ball do the work and not leaving chaps to chase long balls when short and more accurate passes would suit the situation better.'

After he finished, he gestured to Revie to follow him for a private chat in his office. Knowing that the manager was suspicious of his inside-forward, Revie was half expecting to be told he was being sold. Instead, he was amazed when the manager asked, 'Ever play centre-forward?' When he informed McDowall that he had played there in junior football, his thoughts were 'here we go again!' Yet another position for Revie to play in. Then the manager explained his plan: 'I want you to play there again this season. Only you won't be playing as an orthodox centre-forward. You're always saying you like the square short pass with the ball pushed straight to your feet. We're going to give you that chance. I want you to play deep and I want the other lads to play you in open spaces. It's going to take a lot of stamina on your part to chase all over the field, but the other lads will have to do just as much running around, too. I want a man as a midfield schemer who is happy to wander all over the field and I think you are the man who can do it.'

There was no doubt about it, this is what Revie had wanted, a team built around him. For the past year, the press had been raving about the Hungarian Hidegkuti, the inside-forward with a number nine on his back, who managed to draw England captain and right-half Billy Wright out of position, leaving him on his backside more than once. The return leg in Hungary had resulted in a 7–1 drubbing even with the great Tom Finney in the side, and underlined how powerful the Hungarian plan was.

The opening day of the season, 19 August, 1954, was met with bright sunshine as Manchester City ran out to face Preston North End at Deepdale. The summer's day reflected the optimism within the team. Even though Ken Barnes and Johnny Williamson had developed an understanding which saw the plan work like clockwork in the reserves, neither were named in the starting 11. Instead, Revie was wearing the number nine shirt and a young Scottish lad, John McTavish, was named a wing-half.

The Preston groundsman had done a fine job despite the dry summer so the pitch at Deepdale resembled a bowling green. The conditions could not have been better for playing the ball on the ground.

Any hopes that this was the year Manchester City were going to make a breakthrough soon disappeared. Hampered by a lack of pace from Revie and John McTavish, it was not long before they were torn apart by Tom Finney and his colleagues in a 5–0 annihilation. As Revie later reminisced during a radio interview in 1984, 'I remember Tommy Docherty, the Preston wing-half and future Chelsea manager, having an absolute field day!' Seasoned watchers claimed that had it not been for the heroics of goalkeeper Bert Trautmann the margin could have been as big as eight or nine.

The heavy loss to Preston had brought misery among the ranks. Even with the likes of Roy Paul, Don Revie and Johnny Hart, Manchester City could not make the new plan work. The players approached Les McDowall and told him they wanted to bring it to a close.

Ken Barnes remembers, 'McDowall was closer to dropping the plan. I remember him talking with assistant trainer, Fred Tilson, and he wasn't convinced it would work. It was tried against Preston and they lost 5–0. It was almost scrapped, but Don Revie apparently stressed to McDowall that it had worked so well in the reserves because of my part in it. He urged him to give me a go.'

Later Revie recalled his conversation with the manager, 'I said to him, for this plan to work we need Ken Barnes.' The manager was scathing, saying that in six years with City, Barnes had failed to hold down a regular place. 'Him? He can't tackle his way out of a paper bag.'

Replying, 'No, but he can play,' Revie somehow convinced McDowall to name Barnes in the side to face Sheffield United in a midweek game. Again, the regular snooker games with Johnny Williamson had come in handy. Williamson regularly partnered Barnes in the reserves and told Revie that the attacking wing-half, Barnes, was able to distribute the ball brilliantly. He was the reason why the reserve team had been hugely successful. A 5–2 win over the Blades proved Barnes was the missing link in a system that was about to take English football by storm.

Barnes recalled, 'I played against Sheffield United and the plan worked like a dream. From then on, I became a regular and we started to get noticed as a team – it was a true team effort. Other sides had no idea how to combat it. They tried to get a wing-half to mark Revie, but it still seemed to leave a man spare somewhere else.'

The plan began from the back with Trautmann playing an early version of the modern-day 'sweeper keeper', being expected to throw accurately to Revie, who then played a short pass to Barnes. Revie would then move forward with

Barnes holding the ball up while Revie moved into position. This would allow brave inside-forward Johnny Hart to pop up and take his fair share of goals. It was incredibly effective.

Leading the table briefly in September, the plan seemed to falter as autumn turned into a harsh winter. The lush green grass of August became a faint memory as City failed to move the ball around as effectively on the mud baths of December and January. Despite this, City never lost touch with the top of the table.

After beating Sheffield United 5–2 at Maine Road and then defeating Arsenal 2–1 before Christmas, the Blues did the triple over Manchester rivals United, trouncing them 5–0 in the league clash at Maine Road and 3–2 at Old Trafford. They also beat United 2–0 in the fourth round of the FA Cup with Revie securing safe passage to the next phase. It was the second consecutive round in which Revie had scored, having scored the third in a 3–1 victory over Derby County in the third round.

This assault on the league and progress in the cup inevitably led to talk of a league and cup double. After beating Luton Town 2–0 in blizzard conditions, City lined up to face Birmingham City in the quarter-finals at St Andrews.

'This Revie Plan is overrated,' wrote Peter Ingalls angrily in the *Birmingham Gazette* after witnessing the Brummies' centre-half man-mark Revie, only to see gaps opening for Manchester City to exploit, which they eventually did with a single goal separating the sides.

Just as he saw his side finally make the breakthrough he wanted, Les McDowall tinkered again. This time he convinced the board to purchase another inside-forward in the shape of the exciting young Scot, Bobby Johnstone.

To watchers it looked an expensive folly on the part of the manager but to Revie it looked like there was something more sinister afoot. It was clear Johnstone had been signed to replace him in the system that bore his name. Other members of the team felt that if Revie's position was under threat, then so might theirs be.

And all of this at a time when Revie had become a full England international, even scoring on his debut in a 2–0 victory over Northern Ireland in Belfast in October 1954.

Writing in the *Lancashire Evening Post* on 18 March, 1955, John Tatlock reported: 'The signing of Johnstone, for whom Manchester City are believed to have paid £20,000 to Hibernian a fortnight ago, was the biggest of the late-season moves, and surprisingly enough evoked much criticism from City's own supporters who, content with the effectiveness of their present trio of Hayes, Revie and Hart deem the Scot unnecessary.'

Then ominously for Revie he wrote, 'These critics were answered when Johnstone played so well on his midweek debut that Revie, the man who had done so much to re-establish Manchester City as a power, was not missed.'

As the clock ticked down towards the cup semi-final against league championship rivals Sunderland, a decision needed to be made about the City starting line-up. Having been at the club for four years, Revie was shrewd enough to know the manager was not going to pay out that type of money just to see Johnstone run out for the reserves.

There was only seven days until the semi-final and, after missing out on the final six years earlier, Revie was more anxious than most to play. As it happened, a diving header from Roy Clarke broke down the stubborn Sunderland defence and City were heading to Wembley.

City were one of six teams with a realistic chance of winning the league title, but it all fell apart in the run-in, with only one point earned from the next three games. A 3–1 win against Wolves was followed by an embarrassing 6–1 defeat at home against Blackpool. The title would not be coming to Maine Road.

When City eventually lined up at Wembley for the cup final, they had finished seventh, six points behind champions Chelsea. It was a disappointing end to a league campaign that had promised so much. Nevertheless, it was still a great improvement on the previous year and City had finally been able to genuinely challenge for the league honours.

A month earlier, on 2 April, 1955, Revie achieved a lifelong ambition, pulling on the pristine white shirt of England to play under the hallowed twin towers of Wembley for the first time. As he lined up with Stanley Matthews and Nat Lofthouse, an 18-year-old Duncan Edwards made his debut against the Auld Enemy, Scotland.

The Scotland match found Stanley Matthews in inspired form. England, who had not beaten Scotland since 1934, were rampant. Thanks to a strike by Revie the England team were soon 4–1 up and ran out 7–2 winners. Reports talked of good interplay between Matthews, Lofthouse and Revie.

Commenting on the game later Revie said, 'Stan Matthews didn't talk an awful lot about football on the field. I always remember that famous match when we beat Scotland 7–2 as we came on to the field walking down the tunnel, he said to me "Just leave it to me and get in the box."

'On that day he turned over one of the greatest exhibitions of football I have ever seen. We played it out to Stan who came down the line and beat two or three people, playing out to myself, Nat Lofthouse and Dennis Wilshaw. He was an amazing character.'

After lending his name to the most talked about tactical plan in football, few were surprised just over two weeks later, on 20 April, when Revie was elected as the Football Writers' 'Footballer of the Year'. He would collect the trophy at a luncheon in his honour just days before the cup final.

With City reaching the FA Cup Final Manchester was stirred up to a frenzy. After weeks of pressure, the players were glad to get away to the more relaxing retreat of Eastbourne.

The sun was shining and the players were in a confident mood. After dispatching Sunderland Revie was moved to say of the Manchester City side, 'The defence which so many had at one time thought suspect, was now a well-geared machine. It seemed nothing could shake it. No, not even the mercurial Bobby Mitchell or the thunderbolt efforts of Jackie Milburn in the Newcastle United side, who were now to meet us in the final.'

During this period, teammates noticed Revie was becoming more superstitious and the injury crisis which plagued City in the run-up to the cup final was interpreted by Revie as a bad omen. Joining Johnny Hart and Roy Clarke on the injury list were Bert Trautmann, with fibrosis in his back; Ken Barnes, who was diagnosed with a violent toothache; and centre-half Dave Ewing, who had twisted his ankle.

Adding to the tension were personal appearances and media commitments the City players had agreed to in the run-up to the final. Further to this, Elsie had to sit down and personally reply to more than 300 requests Revie had received for tickets.

The City team also agreed to appear on TV on the eve of the final. Alan Rowlands, Bert Trautmann's biographer, takes up the story: 'The tension was relieved by an appearance on the McDonald Hobley show. Newcastle had declined the invitation and Millwall took their place. The teams were invited to ask scripted sporting questions which "Memory Man" Leslie Welsh would answer.

'In the rehearsal before the live transmission, Hobley had trouble identifying the players and confused the effervescent Joe Hayes for Revie. "I'm not bloody Revie, I'm 'Ayes from Bolton." Hayes, the youngest player at 20, had nerves of iron and was completely unruffled by the media interest.' But it meant that while Newcastle were relaxing, City were busy playing up to the cameras.

A mixture of nerves and excitement were in the air as Les McDowall led his team out of the famous Wembley tunnel. Wearing a smart new kit, Manchester City looked every inch the modern team. Not everyone was impressed though. City star of the 1930s, Eric Brook, didn't like the blue tracksuits. He told Roy Paul, 'Tha looked nowt like a couple of pansies in pantaloons.'

An early goal from Newcastle's Jackie Milburn after only 45 seconds (a record for the fastest goal at Wembley, which stood until 1997) meant City had to chase the game from the off.

Worse was to come after 20 minutes when City full-back Jimmy Meadows caught his studs on the Wembley pitch and tore cruciate ligaments in his knee. The image of him being stretchered off was the last time anyone would see him on the pitch as the injury ended his career.

With no substitutes during this era, City were reduced to 10 men with 70 minutes still left on the clock. Despite going in at half time on level terms thanks to a Bobby Johnstone goal, City faced an uphill battle. Unwilling to reorganise the side, and rather than push Revie forward as an out-and-out centre-forward, McDowall kept faith with the Revie Plan.

But another two goals from Newcastle saw Manchester City trudging up the famous Wembley steps with their heads bowed to receive their runners-up medals. In the end, injuries to Johnny Hart and Roy Clarke, together with playing with only 10 men for most of the match, put paid to City's hopes.

Later that evening, at the traditional FA Cup Final banquet, Roy Paul made this solemn promise: 'We'll be back next year to win it. Sam Cowan knows how I feel. He captained Manchester City's cup final team in 1933 and returned a year later to collect the cup.'

At the time most people put that down to a captain trying to comfort his desolate players. Exactly a year later, in their maroon-coloured change strip, City would return to Wembley and Revie, who had only featured in half of the matches that season, played a pivotal role.

Unlike the year before, City were now one of the most talked about teams in the country. After the success of the Revie Plan in 1954–55, everyone was expecting City to be challenging for major honours.

Then came news that rocked the football world. The 1955 Footballer of the Year had been suspended without pay for 14 days. His crime? He had absented from training without permission – according to manager Les McDowall.

The player himself was incredulous. Revie and Elsie had been married for six years and had yet to enjoy a holiday together. Elsie's job as a teacher restricted her leave to term times, which did not coincide with pre-season training. A planned holiday had been cancelled the previous year when the players were dragged back a full two weeks early.

This year, Revie was determined to enjoy some family time. After a hugely-successful year on the pitch, Revie was determined to get away. According to Revie's version of events, he had been granted authority to leave by trainer Laurie Barnett on the condition he trained while in Blackpool. As he pounded along the sand trying to regain his fitness ahead of the new season, the last thing he expected was the headlines to which he would return.

To further rub salt into the wounds, he didn't even know he was already halfway through his suspension until he had reported back for training at Maine Road after his return from Blackpool. His reaction was one of anger. He told the press he had demanded to be placed on the transfer list with immediate effect.

On 9 August, the Manchester City board duly received a letter from the aggrieved Revie, requesting he be put on the transfer list. Describing Revie as a box office attraction, the *Daily Mirror* reported Arsenal would be the first in with a bid of £30,000 for the unsettled player. But the transfer request was rejected and manager McDowall was ordered to meet with Revie to tell him of the board's decision. A tense 30-minute conversation ended with Revie telling the press he would consider his position in the next 24 hours.

Even though Revie eventually agreed to stay, the players knew the writing was on the wall. Ken Barnes said in his biography, 'McDowall thought Bobby Johnstone somehow a more competent sort of player. Yet Revie had great control for a big man and was a great player of the long ball. But McDowall thought because of his success, he could go one better. My impression was that he had to keep tinkering. I think we were the first to start playing with a sweeper, for instance. But by 1959 the whole side had disintegrated.'

Later Johnstone, who was to take Revie's place as the linchpin of the City side, had this to say: 'It was the beginning of the end. I think McDowall felt he [Revie] had let him down, though Revie was straightforward and truthful about it. From then on, it was only a matter of time before he went. But he [Revie] never said very much to me, he was very quiet, a proper gentleman. McDowall did have some funny ideas. He tried loads of different plans. For instance, he tried to sign as many inside-forwards as he could. He wanted a whole forward line of inside players. I couldn't understand it.'

Despite Revie scoring in the first two games of the season against Aston Villa and in a crushing 7–2 defeat at Wolves, the *Daily Mirror* was particularly scathing about a 2–2 draw with Arsenal describing it as 'kid's play'. There then followed a frustrating time of being in and out of the side.

After being dropped for a league game against Everton, Revie penned another letter to the board asking to be put on the transfer list. With Bobby Johnstone the star of the team, this time it was accepted.

On 1 December, 1955, Revie told the *Daily Mirror*, 'I'll go anywhere.' Certainly, that seemed the case when it was reported Devon non-league club Barnstaple was so desperate to get one over on near-rivals Poole, who had signed former Middlesbrough star Wilf Mannion for free, that they approached

Revie. After sending the Footballer of the Year a telegram he invited them to call him at home in Manchester where he offered to become their player/manager. Unfortunately, Barnstaple did not have the funds to secure his services.

By the turn of the year, as Revie was recovering from a minor operation on a pulled muscle, Sunderland came in for him. Any hopes of a return to his native North East were quickly dashed when Manchester City insisted on swapping him for the Mackems' leading goalscorer Charlie 'Cannonball' Fleming, a request that went unfulfilled.

The road back to the City first team was blocked. Living up to the image of never being satisfied, McDowall had gone out and bought another inside-forward, Jack Dyson, who replaced Bobby Johnstone. Revie now found himself third choice. Add to that a run of going unbeaten in six matches, which made City title contenders, and Revie was resigned to being merely a spectator.

City progressed to their second consecutive cup final, this time against Birmingham City, but Revie played no part until they were drawn to play Liverpool in the fifth round at Maine Road. Having appeared in the previous two league games, Revie was unable to help City find the net as both sides were resigned to a goalless draw. In the return at Anfield, Revie was out in the cold and did not play in any of the rounds until the final.

As Bert Trautmann collected the Footballer of the Year award, the previous year's recipient, Revie, was in the middle of a media storm. Would the man who had lent his name to the most famous tactical plan in history be in the Manchester City line-up for the final? Opinion was split. Some said Revie must play while others wondered if a man who had played only a small role in the road to Wembley warranted a place.

A Manchester City player winning the Footballer of the Year award was not the only similarity to the previous year. At the same Eastbourne pre-final location, City were again beset by injuries. Bobby Johnstone had a niggling calf injury while right-winger Bill Spurdle went down with a severe case of boils.

Despite having been outstanding in form in a 4–2 win at Portsmouth on the final day of the league season, there was no guarantee Revie would be in the final. The directors and much of the press had him down as a troublemaker and six months after his initial request he remained on the transfer list.

It was at the Oatlands Hotel in Weybridge, where City were staying before making the trip to Wembley, that Revie found out he would be playing. But there was little more than three hours on the clock before kick-off.

In the jacket pocket of the suit he had worn in every round of the cup and now considered lucky, he carried two pieces of wood. When Roy Paul noticed them as they were getting changed and asked him what they were, Revie replied that an old gypsy woman had given them to him, explaining they would bring him luck, that his life would change and he would meet with success in his job, fulfilling a lifetime's ambition. It would not be Revie's last brush with gypsies.

This was the first final televised by both the BBC and ITV and as Manchester City came out wearing dark shirts with stripes and white shorts, Roy Paul turned to his players, held up his fist and shouted, 'If you don't fucking win this you will get one of these!'

From the start Revie grabbed the game by the scruff of the neck, setting up City's first goal after three minutes by passing to Roy Clarke who sent it into the middle where Joe Hayes rushed in and scored. City were off to a flier!

Against the run of play, Birmingham managed to equalise. There then followed a bombardment of the Manchester City goal with only heroics from Trautmann keeping them in the game.

McDowall sent his players out for the second half, urging them to keep the ball on the ground. However, Revie had other ideas. Singling out Ken Barnes he asked him, 'Where were you in the first half?' Barnes explained that the manager had told him to closely mark Birmingham forward Peter Murphy, but Revie told Barnes to ignore McDowall and play their own game.

It was a revelation, as midway through the second half City regained the lead. A four-man build-up started by Revie ended with Jack Dyson smashing home past the advancing Birmingham goalkeeper. With 67 minutes gone, Bobby Johnstone wrapped things up and became the first player to score in consecutive finals.

The game is now largely remembered as the final where Bert Trautmann played with a broken neck for the last 17 minutes. However, at the time there was only one player in the headlines.

'Triumph for Revie,' hailed the *Daily Mail*. 'It was Revie, Revie all the way in the FA Cup Final. Within three minutes of the start there could be no doubt he was the man for the job. On the sunlit green carpet of Wembley, Birmingham toiled in his shadow. They could never match the brilliant ball play of the smooth Don.'

5

SUNDERLAND (1956–58)

'There is one thing which will tell you if you are a good player and that is how much money you've got in the bank.'

Don Revie

After masterminding the cup final win, it would have taken a very brave man to leave Don Revie on the bench. As the 1956–57 season began, Revie was now firmly established as the recognised playmaker.

Looking ahead to the new season the *Liverpool Echo* reported: 'Certainties have a habit of failing to materialise in football but one thing that looks "on" concerns Don Revie of Manchester City. Don spent much of last winter in relative obscurity but after his dramatic recall at Wembley and the magnificent part he played in City's success he looks likely to be a regular in the Maine Road attack this term.'

The past two years, with consecutive cup final appearances, had given the City fans hope that they might finally emerge from the shadow cast by their neighbours, United. But those City supporters who travelled to the Black Country on 18 August, 1956, to watch their side kick off against Wolves would have been dismayed by the display. Despite early pressure from the City forwards they went in at half time three down. By the time the game was just over an hour old City had conceded five. Their only consolation was a late penalty from Revie, who the *Birmingham Daily Gazette* described as having 'an insignificant sort of game'.

After a pair of draws against Spurs and Aston Villa, City then went on a dismal run that saw the club lose eight out of its next 10 games. Despite beating Leeds United 1–0 and Sunderland 3–1, with Revie getting on the score sheet, they went four consecutive games without scoring. A 7–3 away defeat against Arsenal on 6 October and City were once again fighting for their survival in the top flight.

As was his reaction to most events while managing City, McDowall changed the system. This time he hit on the idea of pushing Revie to right-half and moving Bobby Johnstone to centre-forward. The experiment failed and it seemed City and their manager were running out of ideas.

At the same time that City were being hammered at Highbury, Revie was across the Irish Sea in Windsor Park, Belfast, returning to the full England team against Northern Ireland. It began well with a cross from Revie finding Stanley Matthews who scored after only three minutes.

From there Revie faded out of the game with Frank McGhee of the *Daily Mirror* scathing. Urging the selectors to drop Revie for the next game, against Wales, for his perceived lack of effort against the Northern Irish. He wrote, 'Stanley Matthews, England's best forward, had, what was for him, a mediocre game and I blame Revie for failing to link up with him and forcing him to go a-wandering.' The 1–1 draw was the last time Revie would pull on an England shirt, ending his international career after six games and four goals.

It was time for Revie to take stock of his career. At 29, he began to wonder what he was going to do next and after he finished playing. He knew this was his last chance at a big-money move. He did not need to be told his career was winding down as injuries mounted up. To underline how much of his career was behind him, in Belfast Revie had lined up alongside Manchester United's Duncan Edwards, who only five days earlier had turned 20.

In the back of Revie's mind was the example of his boyhood hero, Wilf Mannion, who ended up serving tea to the workers of an ICI chemical plant who had once chanted his name from the terraces of Ayresome Park.

Teammate Ken Barnes said, 'I remember him saying when I asked why he wanted to leave Manchester City, "There is one thing which will tell you if you are a good player and that is how much money you've got in the bank."'

Once again, Revie was in McDowall's office. For the third time since signing him from Hull City McDowall had to try to convince Revie to stay at the club.

McDowall's message was, just say the word and the club would be more than happy to remove you from the transfer list. The player was unmoved.

It was November 1956, and all through the previous month there was speculation in the press that Revie would be heading to Sunderland in exchange for Billy Bingham, an outside right who was on the opposing team in the recent Home International in Belfast. After scoring 10 goals in 42 games in 1955, a poor start to the 1956–57 season had seen the Northern Ireland international put in a transfer request. It seemed a perfect solution as both players wanted to move – but nothing came of it.

So after McDowall had failed to convince Revie to stay, the Manchester City board gave permission to sell their player to the highest bidder. Peter Lorenzo of the *Daily Herald* was unconvinced when he said, 'Forgive us for telling you how this will end... Manchester City, afraid of selling their First Division status by transferring Revie, will fix a fee not even Sunderland will pay. Then Revie will make his peace with City by withdrawing his year-old transfer request.'

In the North East, Sunderland were desperate. They had not won since 15 September, 1956, and now found themselves in the relegation zone just above bottom-placed Charlton Athletic, on goal ratio. In their 66-year history they had never played in the Second Division.

The fans were unhappy and gates were down. After breaking the British transfer record twice in two years, including the signing of much sought-after Welsh international Trevor Ford for £30,000 in 1950, they became known as the 'Bank of England' club. In wanting Revie, they hoped to restore the glory days that had seen them finish fourth in the First Division just two years earlier and reach two consecutive FA Cup semi-finals in 1955 and '56.

After a tense two-hour board meeting on 8 November, Sunderland decided they were going to buy big – and in English football at that time there were few names bigger than Revie's. When they spoke to the player his terms were straightforward: he wanted a house that he could in due course purchase from the club and he wanted to ensure Sunderland would help Elsie secure a teaching job. For her part, Elsie told the *Daily Herald*, 'I don't mind where I go as long as Don is happy.'

So Revie became a Sunderland player and when he arrived at Roker Park he was greeted by the faithful as a conquering hero, the man who would finally bring the good times back to the club. The *Newcastle Telegraph* reported, 'The only thing missing was the red carpet as Revie was treated like a VIP.'

When the chairman showed the new signing and his wife to their seats in the stand (Revie had a thigh strain that kept him out of the side for a week), Chelsea were the visitors. The game was disappointing, Sunderland having fallen two behind, but Len Shackleton gave the home side hope in the 74th minute, only for Chelsea centre-forward Ron Tindall to wrap up the game with his second goal four minutes before the final whistle.

Reporting on the performance the *Daily Mirror* said, 'Chelsea's win showed how much Sunderland need Don Revie. But even Revie is going to have a king-sized job to save Sunderland's proud record of never playing out of the First Division.'

Now fit again, Revie was in the side that faced Cardiff City at Ninian Park. The *Newcastle Journal* claimed that Revie carried with him the hopes of the Wearsiders on his shoulders. A disappointing 1–0 loss, where Revie did not look anything like 100 per cent fit, saw the Rokerites extend their losing streak into a third month.

Things did not improve in his first home match against Birmingham on 24 November. According to the *Newcastle Sunday Sun*, 'Playing in his first home game, Revie had an excellent first half, the fact he faded away in the latter stages seems to indicate he is not fully fit.' The 1–0 defeat, their ninth in 10 games, left the Wearsiders firmly rooted to the bottom of the table.

The injury to his thigh was much more serious than first thought and by early December 1956, rather than travelling to Highbury for a game against Arsenal, Revie was in a hospital bed having an operation. The £24,000 Manchester City received for Revie was looking like a shrewd piece of business for the Maine Road outfit.

By the time Revie was called back into the side to play Sheffield Wednesday on 16 February, 1957, it was only the fourth time in three months he had turned out for the club. He had been out of action for seven weeks, but his return was a revelation as Sunderland put five past the Yorkshire team in a 5–2 win.

According to the *Hartlepool Daily Mail*, 'Revie was making excellent use of the ball and there was a good response to much of his play.' A dominant performance was capped off with a curling right-foot shot that hit the top right-hand corner to make it four for the home side.

After being appointed club captain for the 0–0 draw against Preston North End on 16 March, 1957, Revie and Sunderland went on a seven-match unbeaten run. It included an impressive 1–0 home win at fifth-placed Arsenal. With Revie back to full fitness and being praised for his passing ability, by the time the champions, Manchester United, put four past them at Old Trafford on 20 April, 1957, Sunderland were seven points clear of the relegation zone and out of danger. However, trouble was brewing off the field.

The country was just recovering from Christmas and football fans had feasted on a busy fixture list when a letter arrived in early 1957 at the Football League headquarters on Starkie Street, Preston. It was addressed to the Secretary, Mr Alan Hardaker, a gruff Yorkshireman who had only been in post just over a year. Upon reading its contents Hardaker was incredulous.

The letter was signed by an anonymous Mr Smith. It told Hardaker that Sunderland were making illegal payments to their players to induce them to come to the club. The letter writer said the club were selling houses to players at knockdown prices, offering massive signing-on fees and topping up wages.

The maximum wage in football had been in force since 1901 when players were given £4 a week. By the 1950s this had risen to £15 a week with a maximum signing-on fee of £10. It was alleged Sunderland got around this rule by giving players under-the-counter payments. There had been hints of this scandal when former Sunderland and Welsh international Trevor Ford published his autobiography, claiming he had been given a huge discount on his house.

There was no way any club was going to get away with this under Hardaker's watch. A full and through investigation was to be launched. Culprits would be identified and punished if they were found guilty. On 15 January, 1957, the *Daily Herald* reported, 'Sunderland hand over their books to league.' Speaking to the paper, Sunderland chairman Bill Ditchburn said, 'It is quite right the league have our books. They can, of course, examine the books of any club.' The paper then went on to claim the club had paid out £335,000 in transfer fees since the war, including a reported £24,000 for Revie from Manchester City in November 1956.

Despite strong words and deeds the investigation came to nothing. Without the infamous Mr Smith owning up to his identity there was a lack of any real evidence. Players and managers were reluctant to talk. The whole episode was about to be written off as a poison pen letter from an embittered board member when by chance Sunderland's accounts showed an entry for straw. In the days before underground pitch heating, straw was thrown over the pitch during winter months to protect it from snow and ice. It was common practice especially with clubs based in the North. However, the sum of £3,000 seemed a huge amount of money for a commodity that could be picked up pretty much anywhere.

Simon Inglis, in his book *Soccer in the Dock*, takes up the story: 'Hardaker's suspicions were now aroused so he telephoned his brother Ernest, who was Chairman of Hull Rugby League Club, and as the late secretary's autobiography relates a conversation went as follows: "How much does it cost to cover your ground with straw in a normal sort of winter?" When told that Sunderland claimed £3,000 for straw, Ernest replied, "Blow me, for that we'd manage for 25 years."

'It was now clear what Sunderland had been up to. They had placed orders for both straw and tarmac far in excess of what was required. When the suppliers came to deliver, they gave credit notes to the club for the amounts met. In turn the club cashed the credit notes in with the suppliers and used the money to pay the players over and above the permitted maximum wage.'

Punishment was swift and harsh. On 10 April, 1957, the League and FA imposed a fine of £5,000, the largest ever meted out at the time. Five of Revie's teammates – Ray Daniel, Ken Chisholm, Billy Elliot, Willie Fraser and John Hannigan – were banned for life for accepting illegal payments. Even the manager Billy Murray, who had been key in bringing Revie to the club, was fined £200.

On 11 April, 1957, the *Daily Mirror* was asking, who was next? Bill Ditchburn, the Sunderland chairman who, along with two other directors, had been suspended for life, told the paper, 'You can expect fireworks, I am not going to take this lying down.'

Nearly three weeks later, on 29 April, an eight-man committee of the players' union claimed to have a dossier from over a thousand players that they had received under-the-counter payments. Professional Footballers Association (PFA) chairman Jimmy Hill was quoted in the *Daily Mirror* as saying, 'We believe this dossier can prove to be the answer to all the problems in the game. We believe it will show the game has to be cleaned and after an amnesty it will resolve itself.'

The PFA under Jimmy Hill fought back, demanding a wide-ranging enquiry and started a petition, calling on all players who had received illegal payments to sign it. They calculated that so many men would own up that the FA would be forced to drop their charges against the Sunderland men. It was a gamble, but it paid off. The Sunderland men were simply fined and allowed to play again. Later, even their fines were quashed.

This scandal only made the PFA more determined than ever to smash the restrictions on earnings and contracts that professional players were then subjected to. Under intense pressure, the Football League finally gave in and conceded that players were free to earn whatever their clubs were prepared to pay them. Within months, England captain Johnny Haynes was the first £100-a-week player.

But manager Bill Murray was shattered. He had guided Sunderland away from the relegation zone, preserving the club's cherished top-flight status. Revie had played 16 times, scoring just twice. By the season's end the guilt caught up with Murray and he resigned, ending his 18-year association with the club. He never managed again.

The board was quick to appoint a replacement – the no-nonsense Alan Brown, who had worked wonders in keeping his former club Burnley in the top half of the First Division.

Sunderland historian Rob Mason says, 'Brown, a former soldier, was a disciplinarian with a capital D. His nickname was Bomber Brown, pointing to his wartime service and as a nod and a wink to his hero Bomber Harris. He was also a member of the Moral Rearmament Movement which called on the country to start promoting morals and values once again.'

However, to many, Brown was a mentor. Lawrie McMenemy, who shared the same background as the new Sunderland boss, would later credit him with being a role model. Brown gave McMenemy a start when he managed Sheffield Wednesday in the 1960s. Equally, Revie's future nemesis, Brian Clough, would learn much about the importance of disciplining players under the tutelage of Brown when he played for Sunderland in the late '50s and early '60s.

When Brown took over at the start of the 1957–58 season he assured Revie he would build the team around him, but Revie was suspicious.

Rob Mason believes the writing was on the wall for some of the expensive older players and staff when Sunderland legend Len Shackleton, one of the most talented inside-forwards in the country, decided to retire after having played only one game under the new regime. Sunderland had paid a British transfer record when Shackleton left Newcastle United.

Despite never warming to the man himself, Revie did learn about self-discipline from Brown. 'After a particularly fraught game against Everton, the crowd turned on their manager. It was terrible. As we trouped off the pitch I happened to look up into the stand and saw Alan Brown sitting there while the crowd were chanting for his blood and he never moved a muscle or displayed the slightest emotion. I remember being most impressed by his magnificent self-control and I am certain I learned a great deal from him in that unhappy moment.'

There was no doubt that Brown's first season in charge was a disaster. Revie played 39 league matches that season and finished as Sunderland's second-top scorer with 12 goals, which included crucial strikes in single-goal victories against Birmingham City, Manchester City, Leeds United and Spurs.

The player also scored against Birmingham City on Easter Sunday but the away side notched six. Sunderland then lost the next two and fell to bottom spot. Despite victories in the final two matches of the campaign, Sunderland were relegated for the first time.

Life in the Second Division was tough going. Players like Len Shackleton were not replaced. No longer able to pay big money, Brown was forced into trusting youth. Faced with a season in the Second Division, battling injuries and a manager whom Revie felt would ship him out sooner or later, he reverted to type and asked Brown to put him on the transfer list.

Now 31, Don knew time was running out for his football career. It was fine to be in the Second Division when he was a youngster, but he knew he had narrowly escaped a life as a journeyman player at Hull City.

Whereas before he told the press he wanted to move to further his career, this time he was clear about the reasons for wanting to get out – he was simply unhappy. He was also relieved of the Sunderland captaincy.

As Brown put his trust in youth, Revie would be the sixth international player to leave following Shackleton's retirement, with players like Ray Daniel, Joe McDonald, Billy Bingham and Charlie Fleming all exiting the club at the same time.

When Daniel had made the same transfer request as Revie some months earlier, the board simply replied, 'We have no room for disgruntled players.' So, it was no surprise that when the board met on 20 August to discuss Revie's request they simply said, 'Granted.'

After a visit to Fulham on 1 September, 1958, the *Daily Mirror* reported that Alan Brown had offered Revie a job on the coaching staff when his playing days were at an end, only if he stayed with Sunderland. Brown said, 'Don is the last man I wish to lose in the present state of re-organisation here. I regard him as one of the finest people in the game and the type of player any manager would grab for his staff when his playing days are done.

'I will do anything to keep this man. We hit it off well, but he has got this idea into his head that he would do better away.'

Just like the other transfer requests in the past, there was no shortage of interested parties. It was rumoured that Sunderland had agreed a deal with Cardiff City for Revie to move to Ninian Park. Middlesbrough also registered an interest while the press reported Revie's recent happy inclusion in the summer tour of Canada and North America with Manchester City, as a guest, left him hankering for a move back to his old home at Maine Road.

However, Revie was now faced with old rumours that another transfer request added up to one thing – he was a troublemaker. The rumour was so strong this time that Revie felt he had to address it directly.

After claiming Revie was about to sign for Cardiff City, the Welsh newspaper, *Western Mail*, cited a column the player wrote with the headline 'I am not a troublemaker'. Revie was quoted as saying, 'The rumour-mongers are at it again and I don't know what they are saying in their cheap and nasty way. Ever since I made a request for a transfer, stories have been circulating and the latest one is that I am a troublemaker. Some folk, of course, like reading stories about people who are in the public eye.

'I suppose it is inevitable but I am sure that fair-minded members of the public take idle gossip with a pinch of salt.' Going on to cite his invitation to the summer tour with Manchester City and the gift of a brand-new set of golf clubs presented to him by the players after the FA Cup win in 1956, Revie said that this was evidence that he was no troublemaker.

On the pitch, there was finally something to cheer about. Rooted to the bottom of the Second Division, the 4–0 win over Rotherham United near the end of November 1958 gave Sunderland fans hope they could turn the season around and be in the fight for promotion at the end of the season.

In his first game in five weeks, Revie had nabbed the first goal before South African Don Kitchenbrand's hat-trick, the first for a Sunderland player in two years. This broke a string of heavy defeats that saw them concede 17 goals in three games, scoring only two in reply. But once in the dressing room the euphoria quickly disappeared as the players witnessed the extraordinary scene of the former Footballer of the Year engaging in fisticuffs with manager Brown.

There was no report of any fight in the *Newcastle Evening Telegraph* on Monday 24 November, 1958, which carried the headline 'Revi(e)talised', stating, 'For the first time this season, Revie showed his true form and how the Roker attack benefitted from his skill and leadership.'

Sunderland historian Rob Mason says, 'Revie had asked Brown for permission to travel home with his family instead of with the team. He did not want to travel on the team bus. Voices were raised, then both player and manager started shoving each other. Eventually punches were thrown.

'The other players separated them but there was no forgiveness for Revie. For Brown, it was a case of my way or the highway. Revie would never turn out for Sunderland ever again.'

The incident between Revie and his manager was the culmination of two years of frustration for both the player and the club. There was no way Revie could shake the feeling he had made a huge mistake in returning to his native North East from Manchester.

As Revie and Brown traded blows in the Rotherham dressing room, another man was monitoring the situation at Sunderland. Making the journey from West Yorkshire to the south of the county, Leeds United director Sam Bolton had come to watch the man his manager Bill Lambton wanted to replace Welsh superstar and Juventus-bound, John Charles. Very soon he would attempt to make Don Revie a Leeds United player.

There was talk in the press he was about to re-sign for his first club Leicester City, despite making positive noises about moves to his hometown club Middlesbrough or Cardiff City.

The initial interest from Cardiff City and Middlesbrough cooled simply because of his injuries. Further to this, age had also slowed Revie down. Never the fastest of players, he was now more reliant on his footballing brain than ever. The problem was, as well, that Revie's style of play never fitted with what Alan Brown was trying to achieve with the Roker Park outfit. Inside-right Charlie Fleming commented on Brown's style: 'Instead of running five yards and passing the ball, he got them to run 20 and pass the ball five.'

By common consent the game against Rotherham was one of Revie's best displays in a Sunderland shirt. But there was no way back. After the punch-up in the dressing room there would no more coaxing, cajoling or complimentary statements. Alan Brown told the board he was adamant: he wanted Revie out of the club, he did not care where he went.

Officially Revie was on the side-lines due to a sore shin and did not even play for the reserves at the weekend. The future looked bleak and niggling groin injuries meant that clubs were now unwilling to take a risk on an ageing inside-forward.

'As manager of Leeds, I am the man who knows the score better than anyone – I am responsible for the club's past, present and future. Managers stand or fall by the results their teams achieve… or fail to achieve. Managers get the glory – or the sack. Football is funny that way.'

Don Revie

'Don Revie was on trial at Leeds United. And the job was made tough by the fact that he had to switch from being "one of the boys" to "the boss".'

Jack Charlton, Leeds United centre-half, 1967

'The boss was a disciplinarian and wanted to keep everyone in line. If you crossed him, you would be fined.'

Gary Sprake, Leeds United goalkeeper, 1962–73

PART TWO

6

LEEDS UNITED (1958–61)

'I had a lot of respect for what he achieved as a player so listened and
acted on a lot of what he said. We always did have an early night.'

Billy Bremner, Leeds United and Revie's roommate

With any hope of a coaching job with Sunderland gone, proposed moves to
Cardiff City and his home town of Middlesbrough rejected and even the hope of
an emotional return to Maine Road being out of the question, Revie sat down to
watch television on a chilly Thursday night in November 1958 when the
telephone rang.

At the end of the line was Bill Lambton, manager of Leeds United. From the
off, the Yorkshire club was an attractive option for Revie. For a start it was in the
top flight, having finished eighth in the First Division in 1957 after being
promoted as runners-up in the Second Division in 1956.

The Leeds manager had rung Revie to tell him that Leeds and Sunderland
had agreed terms for his services, so would he be interested in travelling to Elland
Road with a view to signing a contract for the Yorkshire club? Lambton was only
the temporary manager but could sign players. He did not hold out much hope
that the former Footballer of the Year and ex-England international would sign
for the club.

Arriving at Elland Road with Elsie, Revie could have been forgiven for
thinking he was visiting one of the bomb sites of his youth. Stix Lockwood,
player liaison officer and someone who has been associated with Leeds United
for 60 years, recalls, 'In 1956, thanks to an electrical fault, the entire west stand
burned to a cinder. This included the club office, the press office and even the
club archives. Everything was lost. The damage from the blaze was to cost

something in the region of £100,000, a huge amount in those days. The club, which just three years earlier had shelled out £7,000 for what was then the most expensive floodlights in the country, was now plunged into deepest, darkest financial crisis. Things had not been helped when it was discovered the insurance the club had taken out would in no way cover the total cost of the damage.'

A public appeal had raised £60,000 and another £180,000 had come from a loan from Leeds City Council. This resulted in the construction of a 4,000-seater stand. But the year Revie arrived the stand nearly burnt down again. Only the swift actions of the club directors, who were on-site at the time, minimised the damage.

These financial problems off the field had affected the team's performances. The club was now in dire straits, which called for desperate measures. Their star player was club captain John Charles, the Welsh superstar generally recognised as one of the best players in the world. In 1956–57 he scored an outstanding 38 goals in 40 games. When Turin outfit Juventus came calling in August 1957, offering a British record transfer fee of £65,000, it was too hard for the club to turn down. Overseeing Charles' development had been Revie's hero and former manager, Raich Carter.

Appointed in May 1953 to his first job after leaving Hull City, Carter had led the Elland Road outfit into the First Division as runners-up. The great form of John Charles saw the club confound their new-found status by finishing eighth. The fire and the departure of John Charles saw a downturn in fortunes with a disappointing 17th-place finish resulting in Carter being shown the door by chairman Sam Bolton.

So it was against this backdrop that Revie encountered a club that was demoralised on the field and almost bankrupt in the boardroom – and with a fire hazard of a stadium. To cap it all, Leeds United were not a club with a storied history. The Second Division title in the 1930s was the only piece of silverware the club could boast about in their near 40-year history. Despite all that, there was something Revie found welcoming in the place.

As always, Elsie's happiness was firmly in the front of Revie's mind as they looked around the Yorkshire town. Having done his homework on his potential signing, Leeds director Harry Reynolds, a self-made steel magnate and millionaire, knew Revie was family orientated.

Upon meeting Revie, Reynolds promised a house in the city plus all the help he could offer in securing Elsie a job with the Leeds Education Authority. Reynolds would go on to become a huge figure in the life of Revie and Leeds United. It was a meeting between Revie and Reynolds that secured the deal. Don Revie would sign for Leeds.

Revie's first act was to tell Bill Lambton there was nothing wrong with his shin and that he was fit to play that weekend against Newcastle United. So, at the age of 31, Revie would run out again in the First Division.

In doing so he became Britain's costliest player, with his various transfers adding up to around £83,000. Not bothering to give him a fitness test, Revie was sent back to Sunderland to pick up his boots, immediately ahead of his debut. Bill Lambton told the press, 'I'm delighted with the deal. Revie is exactly the type of inside-forward we have been wanting. He has agreed to live in a hotel here in Leeds for the present and train at our ground instead of training by himself at Sunderland.'

In Leeds, rugby league and cricket were the favourite sports. This was reflected in attendances for football matches. Only 10,000 people watched as Revie showed his class, creating a winning goal in a 3–2 win over Newcastle United in a game where he was closely marked by centre-half Bob Stokoe. Looking on, the directors thought they had found someone to replace the departed John Charles. The days of living in a city-centre hotel quickly came to an end as Reynolds was as good as his word, securing Revie a club house, while Elsie found a teaching job at Leeds High School, where she would remain for the next 16 years.

There was more good news in the nine weeks after signing. The players elected Revie team captain in place of Wilbur Cush, who had resigned blaming the responsibility of leading the side for the downturn in his personal form.

But the signing of Revie only provided a temporary bounce. The team that had drifted around mid-table was still officially without a full-time manager, though beating Newcastle United, one of four victories, made sure that Lambton had a strong claim on the job.

On 6 December, the *Daily Mirror* gushed about Revie's contribution to a 3–2 victory against West Ham at Upton Park: 'Revie knows when and where to move, he made his colleague Chris Crowe look like a match winner.'

Even though names such as Bill Shankly were bandied around in the press as the new manager of Leeds United, the board was unable to attract a big name and Bill Lambton was named as full-time manager a month after Revie signed, on 9 December, 1958. Having never convinced anyone of his ability in the job and with players disgruntled about his training methods, it seemed as though Lambton's days were numbered. After a 6–2 drubbing at the hands of Wolves, the same players who had elected Revie as the new leader met again, this time with chairman Sam Bolton.

Centre-half Jack Charlton was 23 and had been at the club six years, with a short interruption for national service. By the time Revie arrived he had a reputation for enjoying late nights and was something of a disruptive influence in the dressing room.

Recalling Lambton's dismissal in his autobiography, Charlton said, 'The chairman called a meeting after some of the lads had their say and asked if they wanted the manager to leave and every one of the players said yes. Bill said pathetically, "If you let me stay, we'll have a new start," but nobody said a dicky bird.' It would not be the last time Leeds players would gather to put pressure on the chairman to dismiss their manager. The only hint of discontent was in Lambton's statement to the press, following his enforced resignation, alleging interference by the directors in training sessions as the reason why he was leaving the club.

Previously, when managers were sacked, Revie usually looked for a way to get out of the club. But this time Revie stuck around when Lambton left. He was enjoying life in Leeds and was flourishing as an older professional, mentoring young players.

One player who did not impress Revie was Jack Charlton, who by the arrival of Revie to the club had developed a reputation for being awkward.

After one practice match in front of the Elland Road crowd, where Charlton ran all over the place, with scant regard for passing to the rest of the team or maintaining control of the ball, Revie as captain singled out the big Geordie, telling him if he were manager, he would be the first one shown the door.

Charlton looked at the former Footballer of the Year, shrugged his shoulders and said 'well you are not the manager so why should I care?' The slapdash attitude seemed to permeate the whole club.

No one in football, it seemed, wanted to manage Leeds United. Attempts to find an experienced candidate ended in frustration. Both Arthur Turner of Hebden United and former Leeds captain Tommy Burden turned down the chance to take over the reins of a club which, by common consent, was in freefall.

With no manager available, the board took control for the last three months of the season. Cobbling together three wins and a draw at the close of the season, Leeds managed somehow to finish 15th – well above the relegation places.

There was almost a disaster for the club on the health front in early 1959 when Revie agreed to manage a junior five-a-side team in a televised competition.

During the tournament they had met Birmingham City's right-back Jeff Hall, who had contracted polio. Leeds were concerned that England international Hall could pass the infection on to other players. Luckily Revie was given the all-clear and was back in the Leeds side. Hall died from the disease just a few months later, in April 1959.

Having approached two other candidates for the job, Leeds United finally settled on Jack Taylor. Barnsley born, as a player he enjoyed success with Wolves in the 1930s before passing through Norwich and Watford after the war. He brought his career to a close under Raich Carter at Hull City.

When Taylor got the job as Leeds manager, he had spent seven years at Third Division Queens Park Rangers. They had won nothing, but were known as a solid mid-table side. Being third choice for a vacant post hardly filled anyone with confidence, but the signing of a diminutive Scottish midfielder was a ray of sunshine in a dismal campaign.

Upon his first meeting with Revie, Billy Bremner was in awe of the man who would ultimately do so much to create the legend of Leeds United. And in Bremner, Revie saw a mirror image of himself. The tiny youngster was homesick and missed his native Stirling and his girlfriend Vicky. He would have given anything to return home.

Revie was eternally grateful to Sep Smith and how he had taken the new boy under his wing at Leicester City. Now Revie was happy to do the same for Bremner. Like Revie when he first joined Leicester, Bremner was lonely and unsure of himself. Revie was now the senior professional, club captain and a former England international. And whereas Rangers, Celtic, Arsenal and Chelsea all turned Bremner down because they thought he was too small, Revie, on the other hand, knew talent when he saw it and became Bremner's mentor.

For his part, Bremner, who regularly roomed with Revie, found him as a player to be professional, sincere and honest. Always eager to pass on his vast footballing knowledge to the younger man. Revie was fanatical about players being well rested, believing they were at their most effective after a good night's sleep. To that end, particularly before big matches, Bremner always ensured he was the first to turn in for an early night.

Making his debut on the right wing against Chelsea in a 3–1 win at Stamford Bridge on 20 January, 1960, with Revie at inside-right, Bremner's performance was so impressive that regular Chris Crowe was sold to Blackburn Rovers in March 1960 to make way for the young Scot. In his first season, Bremner made 11 appearances with his first goal coming in a 3–3 draw against Birmingham City on 9 March, in a game where Revie notched up two goals.

However, it was not enough and relegation, which seemed inevitable, finally came at the end of Taylor's first full season in charge, 1959–60, with only Luton Town stopping them from propping up the First Division table. It looked as though Revie was destined to eke out the rest of his career in the Second Division.

The Leeds chairman was getting desperate. The banks were breathing down board members' necks and attendances were on the wane. The football was drab and boring, the average home gate was only 14,000 and performances on the pitch were hardly going to bring the home fans flooding back. Some days spectator numbers fell below 10,000.

Things were so bad that in December 1960 there was a vote of no confidence in the board. With Sam Bolton refusing to hear any requests from Jack Taylor for new players, a sense of frustration hung over the club. On the pitch, Revie was feeling the same way. An offer from Tranmere Rovers in February 1961 to revive his fortunes was turned down as his confidence as a player was now on the floor. He had given up the Leeds captaincy to Freddie Goodwin, one of the few club signings (from Manchester United), citing the armband as bringing bad luck to the team.

With an extended family to care for, Revie's thoughts began to drift to what the future held. Temperamentally he was unsuited to running a pub like Johnny Duncan and countless other footballers. Instead, he was fascinated by football formations and tactics, something that had been with him from an early age thanks to the tutelage of Bill Sanderson. He knew his future lay in securing a coaching job.

When Revie turned down the Tranmere transfer, a very annoyed manager Walter Gilbraith told the *Liverpool Echo* on 21 February, 1961, 'Revie has told me he wanted to wait till Sunday before giving me his decision. I also learn now he stated publicly he wishes to take a player/manager job in the south and my interest in him has ended.'

The club in the south was Bournemouth, sitting in the Third Division (South). A move to the coast would suit Don and Elsie, together with their 'old folk', as they called Elsie's mother Jenny Duncan, her aunts Jean and Jenny Duncan, and her uncle Willie Duncan. Just as Revie was on the point of signing, there was a snag. Before he could arrange terms to become player/manager, the cash-strapped Leeds United board wanted a fee of £6,000 for the ageing inside-forward.

On 3 March, 1961, the *Daily Mirror* reported, 'Bournemouth want Happy Wanderer Revie as successor to Don Walsh, sacked two weeks ago, but they can't afford the fee that would boost Revie into a £90,000 footballer. Fees totaling £84,000 have changed hands when Revie moved from Leicester City to Hull to Manchester City, Sunderland and Leeds United. Now the smallest fee of the lot could wreck his hopes of starting a new career.

'Bournemouth chairman W Brick said last night: "£6,000 is far in excess of what we can afford. There is no question of waiting until the end of the season when Revie could possibly join us as manager without a fee. We want a new man right away."' Had they waited until the summer, likely the man they had identified as their new player/manager would have been unavailable anyway.

Even though Sam Bolton was getting sick and tired of holding things together with the Leeds board, the man who had been instrumental in bringing Revie to the club in the first place had big plans for Elland Road.

And in Revie, Harry Reynolds, a retired, self-made millionaire, who was taking an increasing interest in Leeds United as board member, had found someone who shared his vision. Their friendship was sealed on a scouting trip to Bolton Wanderers with Jack Taylor. The car journey saw the director and club captain talking non-stop about football and how the game should be played.

It was no surprise when Reynolds, who was now the guiding light on the board thanks to his investment, and who was becoming increasingly frustrated with Bolton's handling of the club, turned to Revie when patience with Jack Taylor ran out. Unwilling to sack the manager because of the £2,500 it would cost to pay off his contract, after a quiet word from Reynolds who agreed to pay him off out of his own pocket, with the club stumbling to the lower reaches of the second division, Taylor resigned on 11 March, 1961.

On 17 March, a struggling club with no heritage employed a player with no managerial experience. The new man set his stall out in a statement to the press: 'I've been looking for a manager's job and I'm delighted to accept this appointment. I realise of course that it is a difficult job but I like a challenge and I can meet it. My aim is to be first but I think we shall be successful if we all pull together.'

To the outsider, Leeds United looked like a club in deep trouble. Mired in the lower half of the Second Division with another relegation fight on their hands, Revie was the board's fourth managerial appointment in as many years. However, armed with a tactical brain and keen to try out new ideas and a youth system which was beginning to bear fruit, Revie felt quietly confident in his first managerial appointment.

7

LEEDS UNITED (1961–63)

'He will have all the backing the new board and I can give him. Without
going into details, I can now say Don Revie has more of the sinews
of war – what we Yorkshiremen call "brass" – at his disposal than
his predecessors had.'

Harry Reynolds, Leeds United chairman

As the players readied themselves in the dressing room before a routine training
session on 16 March, 1961, they were met by an unfamiliar sight. Sitting waiting
for them was director Harry Reynolds.

Telling the players he had something important to say he went on, 'I would
like to introduce you to Jack Taylor's replacement.' Then, almost on cue in
walked new manager Don Revie to rapturous applause from the assembled
players.

A photoshoot was quickly arranged with Revie surrounded by players like
Derek Mayers, Peter McConnell, Gerry Francis, Colin Grainger and Jimmy
Ashall. The confident-looking new manager, resplendent in an expensive-looking
grey suit, was pictured shaking hands with Jack Charlton.

The most pressing problem the club faced was revenue. The attendance for
Revie's first home game in charge, on 25 March, 1961, against Sheffield United,
was 13,688 – some way short of the 30,000 the directors knew they needed to
break even.

The board, which now found itself £250,000 in debt, had made it clear the
two best players at the club – centre-half Jack Charlton and midfielder Billy
Bremner – were available at the right price.

Things had got so bad on the financial front that chairman Bolton was forced to admit that four of the directors had to contribute £3,500 of their own money to keep the club afloat. Time was running out, even though Bolton had managed to attract investment in the shape of Albert Morris of Morris Wallpapers and Manny Cussins of John Peters Furnishing Group, who were both happy to part with £10,000 of their own money to join the board.

Even though Harry Reynolds agreed to provide a further £50,000 of financial support to secure Leeds United's immediate future, the worry of trying to keep the club afloat finally got to Bolton. At the Annual General Meeting on 8 December, 1961, citing anxiety, disappointment, hard work, financial problems, staffing issues and a succession of unexpected difficulties, Bolton resigned from his position, imploring the fans to get behind the board.

New chairman Harry Reynolds, who had done so much to bring Revie to the club, was now the man entrusted with seeing Leeds into a new era. His daughter Margaret Veitch recalls: 'When he came on to the board in the 1950s he didn't devote all that much time to the club. But when he retired in 1959, then Leeds United became more or less his hobby... and he wanted to make them a success. Even though money was short initially, he said, "We're going to go first class, we're going to stay at good hotels." His attitude was that if we were going to be a top club, we would do the things expected of a top club.'

Reynold's first speech as chairman underlined his support for the young new manager: 'He will have all the backing the new board and I can give him. Without going into details, I can now say Don Revie has more of the sinews of war – what we Yorkshiremen call "brass" – at his disposal than his predecessors had. How much more must remain our secret. The soccer market is as much a field of business to operate in as you will find. I have all possible confidence in Don Revie who has shown splendid balance and unsurpassable zeal in our recent weeks of adversity.'

With the addition of Albert Morris and Manny Cussins to the board, Leeds were on a firmer financial footing. The signing of centre-forward Billy McAdams for £15,000 from Bolton Wanderers on 13 December, 1961, was a statement of intent. The *Birmingham Daily Post* reported, 'The capture of McAdams is the first signing by Leeds since the policy of buying was started by new chairman, Mr Harry Reynolds.'

On 17 December, the *Daily Mirror* reported on Leeds United's new buying policy: 'New Leeds United chairman Harry Reynolds has given manager Don Revie the transfer go-ahead because the club finds itself with better assets than many supposed.'

It's been commonly believed that Revie changed the Leeds United kit at the start of the 1961–62 season from the blue-and-gold strip they had been playing in since 1934 in order to imitate Real Madrid, a club he had always admired.

According to Jack Charlton, writing in his autobiography, this was a myth: 'This [white] was the gear Real Madrid played in and the initial reaction from the local press was that Revie was aping the Spaniards. Not so, explained Don. In his opinion white is the easiest colour to identify on a pitch. When you have only a split second to make a pass before the tackle comes in you're more likely to pick up the right man if he's wearing, not red or blue or green, but white.'

By the time Revie was appointed manager Leeds had been playing in an all-white kit since first running out against Middlesbrough under Jack Taylor at Elland Road on 17 September, 1960. This became their first-choice strip for the rest of the season.

Even though it looked as though the finances of the club were now on a firmer footing, the playing squad was still in need of reinvigoration. Things were not helped when rumours reached the Hibernian manager Walter McMurray Galbraith that Billy Bremner was homesick and hankered after a move back home to Scotland. Seeing a chance to sign a player both Arsenal and Chelsea coveted, the Edinburgh outfit, then seen as one of the crack sides in Scotland, made a bid of £25,000.

When the potential move to Hibernian was put to Bremner, Revie was disturbed when Bremner told him he was homesick and hankered after a move back to Scotland. To Bremner, who was getting serious with his girlfriend, Vicky, the move made sense on a personal and professional front.

Not realising the talent that they had on their hands in Bremner and desperate for cash, the board were determined to force the transfer through. The final decision, however, remained with the manager. A conversation with the legendary Manchester United manager Matt Busby had convinced Revie the future was with youth. As he told the AGM his vision was firmly based around attracting the best young players in the country and Billy Bremner was counted among that number.

As Revie later recalled when it came to Billy's proposed transfer, 'Unfortunately, the board of directors were keen to accept the bid. It was a good fee and the money would help the club. I was dead set against it; it filled my thoughts every day. I wanted the directors to realise how important he was to my team-building plans. Hibernian gave a deadline for a response and the directors said they would await my decision before responding.

'I waited until the last possible moment then told them not to accept a penny less than £30,000. It was a gamble but my sources in Scotland told me they were stretching their finances to the very limit at £25,000 so an extra £5,000 would hopefully be a bridge too far and end their interest.'

Fortunately for Revie his hunch proved right. He sat down with Bremner and told the disappointed midfielder that Hibs had pulled out of the transfer. By his own admission Bremner was fuming and on the verge of telling Revie to shove Leeds United. It was then that Revie demonstrated the management skills that were to become legendary.

Looking the fiery youngster in the eye, Revie told him of his ambition for Leeds, how he wanted to win league, cup and European honours. For Bremner, who had heard it all before, this was just another false dawn. Why should he care about what Revie was saying? Yet, by Bremner's own admission, this was something different. He believed what his manager had to say. When Revie told him that he wanted to build the side around him, Bremner resolved to buckle down. With it a legendary partnership was born.

Despite the green shoots of recovery, Leeds fortunes' did not improve on the field. Despite recording a 1–0 win over Charlton Athletic on the opening day of the 1961–62 season and a resounding 3–1 win away at Brighton, a 5–0 thrashing at the hands of Bill Shankly's Liverpool at Anfield on 26 August saw the team lose three out of the next four games.

Injuries forced Revie to name himself at right-half against Norwich on 6 September but to no avail, with the team going down 2–0 at Carrow Road.

Coming through uninjured was an achievement itself, with names such as Jack Charlton and Freddie Goodwin among five players who found themselves on the sick list after the game.

Naming himself against his old club, Sunderland, at Roker Park also had little or no effect as Leeds slipped to a 2–1 defeat. He picked himself again in a 2–1 defeat against Swansea Town in place of flu-stricken Bremner. Even though Revie got on the score sheet in a 3–2 loss at Kenilworth Road against Luton Town on 4 November, Leeds found themselves bottom but one.

For the rest of November there was an improvement in form. A 1–0 win over runaway leaders, Liverpool, on 23 December had been preceded by wins over Middlesbrough and Walsall. Despite this they were still perilously close to the bottom three, lying in 18th place.

A 4–1 defeat against Scunthorpe United on Boxing Day, 1961 left them only one point above the relegation zone. After only recording one win since the New Year in 1962, Leeds found themselves rock bottom after a dismal 3–2 loss at home to Plymouth Argyle on 24 February, level on points with fellow strugglers Charlton Athletic and Middlesbrough.

Thinking the club needed an experienced hand on the pitch, Revie named himself in midfield for the Yorkshire derby away to Huddersfield, but he struggled and clearly showed the passing of time. His legs could no longer keep pace with his footballing brain – he would be more use in the dugout from now on.

The game at Huddersfield would be the last time Revie appeared on a football pitch. The 2–1 defeat made it clear Leeds United needed a full-time manager and Revie now had to devote all his energies to keeping Leeds in the Second Division. He said, 'We were almost relegated in the first year and I was an untried manager. If it went wrong then no one will give you another chance because you are untried in the first place.'

As Leeds fought for their lives, the free-flowing style that marked Don's playing career gave way to the type of tactics that his later teams became renowned for. Jack Charlton was a revelation in those last few games as Leeds started closing teams down at the back. Just four goals were conceded in a nine-match run-in, with Charlton demonstrating more purpose and discipline than ever before.

Indeed, Revie was so impressed that he took Jack to one side for a supportive word. 'If you keep going like that you'll play for England. I mean it. If you "screw the nut." All the time, not just some of the time.' 'Screw the nut' meant being serious and focused about the game.

Despite this tough defending, Revie still couldn't buy a win. Two games against Bury were among five draws which saw Leeds close out a disappointing season. A 3–0 win away to Newcastle United at St James' Park on the final day of the season finally guaranteed Leeds' safety.

During that 1961–62 season, Leeds had drawn twice with Bury, once on Good Friday, 20 April, 1962. In itself, this was hardly earth-shattering, but what was to follow was. Sensational allegations of corruption against Revie made by Bury manager Bob Stokoe would hang over the Leeds manager for years to come.

It took Stokoe 15 years to sit down with a *Daily Mirror* journalist, in July 1977, and allege an attempt by Revie at match fixing. The match in question was the Good Friday game. Pulling into Bury's Gigg Lane car park an hour before kick-off, Stokoe said he noticed the familiar figure of Revie waiting for him behind the main gates. Struggling Leeds United were desperately in need of a win.

Stokoe claimed that as he walked towards the dressing rooms he was met by Revie who greeted him with the words, 'Can I have a word with you?' The alleged conversation that followed has been hotly disputed ever since but came to shape the public perception of Revie. According to the *Daily Mirror* in 1977, Stokoe alleged Revie said to him, 'I have £500 in my pocket for you, if you take it easy.' According to Stokoe's version of events, 'He was a very worried man at the time. I was staggered, amazed. I told him not bloody likely, I have only started in football. I would be a dead man.'

Stokoe, who turned down the £500, then alleged, 'He had the audacity then to say, "Can I have a word with your players?" which again made me extremely angry and more and more determined. I thought I must tell my directors that this particular thing had taken place. For me to be asked to go out and not try is like waving a red rag at a bull.'

Stokoe, fired up, went and told his players what had happened. 'From my point of view it backfired against them [Leeds United] because it made me more determined. I think in many ways the players supported me and [it] made them more determined that it was going to be harder for Leeds to get a result than it might have been because we didn't have too much at stake other than pride.'

Don and Stokoe would have been well-known to each other. Stokoe had spent almost his entire career at Newcastle United making 261 appearances before leaving to see out his career at Bury, where he made 82 appearances before spending a year as manager. In the 1955 Cup Final as the Magpies' centre-half he had been tasked with man-marking Revie. Derby County and Nottingham Forest manager Brian Clough remembered Stokoe calling him a cheat as he rolled around in agony in the muddy Roker Park goalmouth having sustained the knee injury that ended his playing career with Sunderland.

Billy Bremner would recollect Bob Stokoe as an extremely bitter man who had a personal vendetta against both him and Revie. To the point that every time they came into contact, Stokoe would never fail to make a personal barb against both Revie and Bremner.

Whilst Revie would very rarely talk about Stokoe, Bremner was left with the impression that Revie saw Stokoe as a loose cannon who was out of his depth, who could never reconcile with the fact he operated mainly in the lower leagues.

Just two years earlier football had been rocked by its first big football scandal since Sunderland stood in the dock accused of making illegal payments to its players. On 9 October, 1960, soccer was shocked to wake up to the headline: 'I fixed a match and picked up £500 cash from a manager's office.' For Manchester City it was particularly uncomfortable reading as the writer was none other than their 1956 FA Cup-winning captain, Roy Paul.

The glory days of Maine Road were now firmly behind the Welsh international. After failing to win a place in the squad for the 1958 World Cup in which Wales reached the quarter-final, only to go out to a solitary Brazilian goal from a 17-year-old Pele, Paul was now scraping a living in non-league football.

Throughout his career Paul had a reputation as a drinker and was now in the grip of alcoholism and desperately in need of money. Now he was sitting down with a journalist claiming while at Manchester City he threw matches with the help of a teammate. The footballing authorities looked on horrified.

Paul said, 'It was near the end of the season, every point was vital. I liked the lads and I liked the town and I'd have missed playing there if they had gone down. Because the local beer was good and the ladies gay, I'd always had a good time.

'No sooner had we arrived at the ground for this vital game, the other side's captain, an old pal, called me aside and said, "Roy there's £500 in it today for your boys if they lose. The money's in the boss' office already."

'I had a beer inside me, so I sweated the game out. I didn't do any obviously stupid things. I just didn't try too hard. If an opponent was going hell for leather for the ball, he got it. It was as easy as that.

'I collected the money from the manager's office and decided to split with just one other player. Over a few beers in a quiet little Manchester suburb that night we shared the money out.'

The latest allegations made by Paul were quickly dismissed as the rantings of another bitter footballer who had failed to adjust to life after his time on the pitch was at an end. At the time there was no hint to the identity of Paul's other teammate who helped him bribe players, either from Paul or the *Daily Mirror*. Revie was never asked about the allegations or linked to them.

...

An early tactical decision Revie made as Leeds United manager was to switch Jack Charlton from centre-half to centre-forward. Still only 26, he was already studying for his FA coaching badges and could not help being struck by the lack of professionalism he encountered at the club.

By his own admission, Jack was unsuited to leading the attack and was enraged when Revie bought Freddie Goodwin to replace him in the back four. Regular run-ins with trainers Syd Owen and Les Cocker meant things came to a head with Revie and Charlton.

Charlton wanted out and Revie was happy to put him on the transfer list. At first Liverpool were interested but Bill Shankly could not afford the fee. For a long time it looked as though Charlton was about to join his brother, Bobby, at Manchester United and went as far as to speak with Matt Busby. Initial interest died out after Manchester United went on a tour of North America and a few young prospects played well enough to make them think again about Charlton.

By this point Charlton, who had refused to sign a new contract with Leeds, had no option but to head back to Elland Road and promise Revie he would buckle down and change his attitude.

The man who would form a potent defensive partnership with Jack was also almost lost. The young lad from Gateshead had joined Leeds United in September 1958 at the age of 15, but looked about 12 and nothing like the formidable player who was to become known as Norman 'Bites yer legs' Hunter. He remembered being called into the manager's office after three years on the grounds staff at Elland Road.

'I was 17 and we were all getting called into the office to find out if we were getting retained, people were coming out of the office crying and some were coming out happy. I went in and it wasn't Don Revie back then, it was a guy called Jack Taylor [Leeds United's previous manager] who said to me, "You can't do this, and you can't do that but when you get the football you know what to do."

'There were better players than me but if it was just down to rolling up your sleeves then yeah, I deserved to be there. He could've said, "Off you go," but he said, "I'll give you another six months," and in those months he got the sack and Don Revie came in.'

Writing in Norman Hunter's testimonial programme, Revie remembered the meeting: 'So here we had a youngster of 17 from the North East, obviously willing to learn and even over-eager to try and make the grade. He used to come back every afternoon for extra training to try and improve his bad points. I remember that he was never particularly strong in the air, but the thing was, he was working hard to try and compensate.

'I took over as manager on a Friday and the following Monday morning I called young Norman Hunter into the office. He was probably expecting to be told the saddest of all decisions – that we were not going to keep him. But

Norman's eagerness and dedication had impressed us. Instead of letting him go, we signed him as a professional.'

Even though Revie had been club captain, Hunter had had very little to do with him. Over time the youngster would be teased by his teammates for being a second son to the manager. For Hunter, who had lost his own father at a young age, Revie would go on to be the father figure in his life.

Despite his first team potential, Hunter was still very much a work in progress. Remembering the diet of sherry and eggs that Johnny Duncan had prescribed for Revie when he, too, was a scrawny youth breaking through at Leicester, Revie told Norman to start each morning with a raw egg washed down with a glass of Harvey's Bristol Cream. Even though the concoction made the defender throw up on the odd occasion, Hunter did as he was told.

...

There had been rumours all season that John Charles was going to return to the place where it had all started for him. On 23 July, 1962, it was confirmed. The headline in the *Daily Mirror* told Leeds United fans, 'Charles bought back at £50,000.' On 28 July, *Daily Mirror* journalist Frank McGhee wrote, as he reported on John Charles' official signing ceremony, that, 'Elland Road no longer wears the sad air of a palace without a king.'

The re-signing of John Charles for a club record of £53,000 not only demonstrated ambition from a team that had finished fourth from bottom in 1961–62, but also addressed a pressing need. It was hoped Charles could fulfil the role as senior professional and reproduce the form which saw him score 157 goals in 297 games in his previous time with Leeds.

Not only would a top professional be able to bring the youngsters through in the way Revie had done with Billy Bremner, but it would also attract youngsters to the club who could play alongside their hero.

Life in Italy had been good to Charles. In the five years he spent in Turin, Juventus won three championships and two Italian Cups. Charles was Italian Footballer of the Year and played for the Italian League. In 1958 and 1959 he was one of the top three contenders for European Footballer of the Year. He scored 108 goals in 155 games for the club at a time when Italian football was renowned for its defensive tactics.

By the time club chairman Harry Reynolds met Charles, the player knew his time in Italy was coming to an end. He told Reynolds that his wife Peggy, who was from Leeds, was homesick and they both wanted their children to be educated in Britain. Juventus were aware Charles wanted to go, having only agreed to a year's extension on his four-year deal. The scene was set for the return of the king.

Even though the *Daily Herald* of 20 August, 1962, claimed John Charles had 'been tasked with inspiring Leeds to rise from [the] bankruptcy basement of the Second Division,' for those in the dressing room, the man who was going to change the culture of Leeds United was already there.

Back in March, 1962, Leeds United were rock bottom and Revie had just walked off the football pitch for the last time as a player. Desperately in need of a leader, he needed someone who could mould his young team into a crack outfit. Then he heard a rumour that Everton manager Harry Catterick was willing to let his captain Bobby Collins leave the club.

Everton historian Rob Sawyer, writing in his biography of Catterick, described Bobby Collins as, 'One of the most formidable and gifted players ever to don the royal blue shirt of Everton. His displays at inside-forward mixed skill, passing ability, goalscoring prowess and a vital nasty streak. He was also opinionated and strong-willed off the pitch – a natural leader whose diminutive 5ft 3in stature earned him the nickname, "Pocket Napoleon".'

Revie later remembered, 'A journalist tipped me off that Everton might be willing to let Bobby go, so after we got confirmation of this from Harry Catterick I travelled to Goodison the following morning with two of our directors to open negotiations. I spent an hour with Bobby after training and he told me in no uncertain terms that he felt that he still had a lot to offer as a First Division player and didn't fancy going to a club with one foot in the Third.

'We left it that he would think it over for a couple of days and get back to me. But as we headed home I decided to have another chat with him. I remember we arrived at his house at 2 p.m. and waited in the car no less than five hours before he turned up. We didn't leave until 2.30 the next morning but, by that time, Bobby had agreed to join us.'

Across Liverpool's Stanley Park, another manager had heard the same rumour – Bill Shankly also coveted the signature of Everton's midfield general. Don Revie would never know how close Bobby Collins came to being a Liverpool player. Had he been at home instead of at Elland Road, Bobby Collins may have picked up the phone to Bill Shankly. Despite ringing Collins on several occasions, Shankly never left a message.

As Collins made the trip to West Yorkshire, he was not aware of the interest from Liverpool, all he would have known was that Leeds were second from bottom in the second division with very few prospects.

Comparing the situation Leeds found themselves in to Everton, upon meeting Revie, Collins felt there was something about the club. Therefore, when Shankly did finally catch up with Collins over the phone, there was little the Liverpool manager could do, Bobby Collins was a Leeds United player.

Even though there was a last-minute concern from Bobby, namely that he did not want to uproot his young family from Aintree, the two clubs agreed a fee of £24,000 for the combative midfielder. Years later Revie said it was the best piece of business he ever did.

The transfer left a sour taste in Catterick's mouth as he had only let his club captain leave in his belief Billy Bremner would be coming the other way. 'Billy Bremner had played a handful of games for Leeds but had by no means established himself. I was interested in Bremner but Don Revie was very browned off with him. The lad had been homesick and going home to Scotland at weekends and not coming back until several days later. Don spoke to me about Collins and we agreed a fee of around £20,000. At the same time, I asked about Bremner and it was agreed that I could have him for the same amount. But Leeds had a series of matches coming up and they wanted to keep Bremner for a couple of weeks longer. I agreed the lad played for them. He did exceptionally well and the deal was off. The whole destiny of Leeds probably hung on that and you can imagine how I felt when I saw how Bremner developed.'

Unlike the good luck messages with which the *Yorkshire Evening Post* was inundated when John Charles put pen to paper in July 1962, when Collins signed there was no fanfare. However, his presence was felt straight away. Mick Bates, who was on the Leeds United ground staff when Bobby arrived, said, 'Up to that point Leeds were a very ordinary side; there were some good players but nothing exceptional. Then Bobby Collins arrived; he was the man who started it all. To me, Bobby was frightening – steel blue eyes, so competitive. I was only 15 but I feared him, he was a brilliant player.'

Speaking to Rob Sawyer, Everton historian, Mick Meagan, who played alongside Collins at Everton, said, 'Bobby was a brilliant signing by Revie – he gave Leeds an awful lot of backbone. I remember playing against Leeds' second team when Bremner, Hunter, Madeley and Reaney were all brilliant players but lovely lads – a pleasure to play against. A few years later we played them with Bobby in the FA Cup, and they had changed completely – the lovely lads had become rottweilers and I'm convinced Bobby Collins had a great influence on that. That's why Revie signed Bobby to give those lads a little bit of what was missing. Collins did wonderfully well for Johnny Giles who was a brilliant player but too nice – Bobby gave him his needle.'

When asked why he chose Second Division Leeds United, once he left FA Cup winners Manchester United in 1963, Johnny Giles, said, 'Two words sum up why I went to Leeds United: Bobby Collins. I thought if a professional like Collins thought Leeds were worth playing for then I was going to go there as well.'

In many ways Bobby was Revie's direct replacement on the field. He took up the inside-right position and wore Revie's old number eight shirt, but he was something much more. In Bobby Collins, Revie found a kindred spirit wanting to instil in the players a 'never say die' attitude.

On the pitch, Collins was to dictate things from the centre of midfield, with four upfront and wingers expected to track back and provide cover for the defence.

Up to the point Collins signed, Leeds had been using this system with little success. With the Scotsman ordering things on the field, Leeds were a team transformed with Collins constantly reminding them to keep their shape.

With Collins in the side there was a professionalism about Leeds. They were a team, and they had to stick together come hell or high water.

According to Johnny Giles, Bobby's effect on the club was immediate. 'Bobby was an experienced professional; he dictated to the players on the football pitch and at the training ground. His influence in the dressing room was there, too, so Don got rid of the players Bobby felt did not have the right attitude.'

If there was one positive to be gained from a season of struggle it was the style of play had to change if Leeds United were to have any chance of getting out of the bottom half of the Second Division and challenge for honours. As Norman Hunter said, 'Bill Shankly took Liverpool up in 1962, saying that to get promoted a team needed to claw its way out, it was so tough. We did that but were criticised for it ever since.'

At the start of the 1962–63 season the Leeds United faithful, so starved of success, were excited by the return of John Charles – so much so they were even willing to pay the extra Harry Reynolds had put on the price of a ticket to watch their hero. With a revitalised and focused Jack Charlton at the back, Bobby Collins commanding a midfield that included a young Billy Bremner, and legendary goalscorer John Charles up front, Leeds fans dared to dream.

The problem was Charles himself – he was a man in turmoil. Even though he told the press it was his Leeds-born wife Peggy who wanted to return to her home town, the truth was much more troubling. Long days on the road with Juventus had taken Charles away from his wife and, in his absence, she had found solace in the arms of a bathroom attendant.

If the emotional scars were not bad enough then the physical ones were even worse. A passion for Italian food had seen Charles' weight balloon to over 15 stone while the Italians' emphasis on skills over physical fitness, together with the slower nature of the Italian game, had made Charles woefully ill-equipped to handle the pace of the modern English game.

Speaking years later Charles said, 'I turned out for Leeds when I wasn't match fit, and every move I made was in the glare of publicity from television, radio and newspapers. Publicity is fine when you are doing well but I knew in my heart of hearts that I wasn't playing well.'

The style of play Revie favoured to get Leeds out of the Second Division did not sit well with the Gentle Giant: 'Football is played with players moving into spaces, moving close to the man with the ball. And it is not played at a breakneck speed all the time. For the first time in my life I worried about my football at Leeds. I realised that I just could not get used to it. And the more I worried, the worse I played.

'The style of play was nothing like that to which I had become accustomed. Italian football is slower with a more deliberate build up in midfield. I found it hard to adjust to the long-ball style with players scuttling around at 100 miles per hour.'

As August 1962 gave way to September, it was clear that the man who had been bought to score goals and bring the fans flooding back to Elland Road was struggling. He had only really shown his best when he had to drop back to centre-half to support Jack Charlton in a league match at Southampton, but it was not good enough and Don knew it.

Watching from the dugout it was not hard for Revie to see why the only other British competitor for Charles' signature was Cardiff City, who were eager to cash in on bringing the former Wales captain back to the land of his birth.

Charles said, 'I was very happy to come back, but things never went right. It wasn't the training – I got on with Syd Owen and Les Cocker alright. I had a bit of personal trouble at the time and that worried me. It was just myself – I couldn't settle back into it. Some people had said never to go back to a club that you'd been to before – people expect too much of you. At the end, I thought it was no good staying on. I was very sorry actually – I would have loved to play in the Revie side.'

Almost from the moment Charles had signed for Leeds, Italian clubs showed an interest in bringing *il Gigante Buono* – the Gentle Giant – back to those who had named him as their Footballer of the Year. Torino had already made a bid but when Roma came in for him with a bid of £68,000, Leeds decided to cash in and make £17,000 on the £53,000 it had paid out a few months ago. By the time of the Southampton game on 29 September, Charles was on his way back to Italy, having played just 11 games and scored three goals in his brief return to Elland Road.

The departure of Charles was the end of one era but three weeks earlier a new one had begun when three of the players mentioned in his programme notes in the 1961–62 season made their debuts in the first team against Swansea Town.

The team named on 8 September, 1962 – Gary Sprake, Paul Reaney, Cliff Mason, Eric Smith, Jack Charlton, Norman Hunter, Noel Peyton, Billy Bremner, Rodney Johnson, Bobby Collins and Albert Johanneson – was the first without Charles in the side but, more importantly, went on to form the nucleus of the Leeds team over the next few years.

Players like Norman Hunter and 22-year-old flying South African winger Johanneson would soon become household names, along with others, such as Eddie Gray. Meanwhile other clubs looked on with envy at the development of Billy Bremner.

Hunter said, 'Although we travelled with the first-team squad we didn't think we had a prayer of playing. As far as we were concerned we had gone along for the ride and to get some idea of what went on in the build-up to a first-team match. The first we knew of our inclusion in the side was just an hour before kick-off.

'The Gaffer took the four of us under the stand at the Vetch Field and dropped the bombshell that we would be playing that afternoon. I couldn't believe it. Neither could the others. I had been working so hard for this chance but I was staggered when he told me. I was very nervous.

'Revie took a big gamble that day especially as three of the four he brought in were defenders – a goalkeeper, a central defender and a right full-back. He didn't explain his reasoning to us but he did tell us that he had deliberately not warned us the night before the game that we would be playing because he didn't want it to prey on our minds. He wanted us to get a good night's sleep. "Get out there and just do what you're good at" were his words to us as we left the dressing room.'

The decision to put faith in young players and the progress Revie was starting to make did not go unnoticed. On 16 October, 1962, the *Daily Mirror* carried the back-page headline, 'After ten weeks' search – the FA face the awful truth! Nobody wants the England job!' The piece detailed the FA's fruitless search for a new manager in the wake of Walter Winterbottom's resignation after a disappointing 1962 World Cup in Chile. Written by sports reporter Bill Holden, it told readers, 'Graham Doggart, chairman of the Football Association, was given the go-ahead to approach a new short-list of "Mr Xs" in the search for a new England manager.

'The new names being whispered along the soccer grapevine last night as "possibles" – Bedford Jezzard, Fulham team manager; Jackie Milburn, one-time hero of Newcastle; and Don Revie of Leeds United. All are former England internationals.' When asked to respond to the rumours by the *Yorkshire Evening Post*, Revie dismissed them as 'ridiculous' and said his only focus was to put Leeds United 'on the football map'.

Besides, Revie was still learning on the job and wanted to reach out to others to share ideas. Just 18 months earlier, he had made a call to a manager across the Pennines. After his team was wiped out in the Munich air disaster, Matt Busby was in the process of re-building Manchester United.

Even though the club had won the league title in 1952, it was the team dubbed the Busby Babes that had won back-to-back league championships in 1956 and 1957, with an average player age of just 21, which had caught the public's imagination. Their deaths in the snow of a Munich airfield in February 1958 devastated not only the city of Manchester but the entire world.

Many of the players were well-known to Revie. Not only would they have been a familiar sight around Manchester when he was with City, but United captain Roger Byrne, striker Tommy Taylor and the most famous 'Babe' of them all, Duncan Edwards, lined up with Revie for England in his last international, a 1–1 draw against Northern Ireland in Belfast in October 1956.

Revie was so impressed with the young Edwards that he went on to say, 'You don't hear many professionals talk lightly of greatness because it is so rare, but that is what I saw in Duncan Edwards the first time I set eyes on him. He reached the same fabulous standard at left-half, centre-half, inside-left and centre-forward. He is the kind of player managers dream about.'

When he made the call to Busby, Revie was still a managerial novice. Revie's son Duncan said, 'Dad said to me one of the first things he did after taking over at Leeds was to ring Matt Busby at Manchester United and ask if he could spare an hour of his time one afternoon. Matt invited him across one day and was so helpful that dad ended up staying the whole day there.

'Dad always said the advice he got there was priceless and he never forgot what Matt Busby did for him. It meant in later years, when young managers such as Alex Ferguson and Lawrie McMenemy rang up, he would always spend time as Matt had done for him.'

The set-up at Manchester United was a world away from what he was working with at Leeds. The players were treated to the best hotels before games while the training was light years ahead of what was happening at Elland Road. However, the one lesson Don walked away with from his day with Busby was his belief that for a club to thrive it had to trust in youth.

That was easy for Busby to say. The glamour of Manchester United meant the club was always going to be in the running for the best young players. Midfielder Johnny Giles, who was with Manchester United from 1956–63, said, 'Manchester United would always have the pick of the best players, everyone wanted to play for them. Revie would have to rely on his personality and his powers of persuasion.'

Despite this obstacle, Harry Reynolds informed Revie that the £17,000 profit made from the sale of John Charles was his to be spent on players. Revie knew from bitter experience the transfer market could be very hit and miss. The big-money names would not come until Leeds United were firmly established as one of the best names in football.

It was to Scotland that Revie turned to pull off the first of his coups in 1962. Eddie Gray was one of the most promising youngsters in Scotland and, having heard other English clubs were interested, Revie drove through the night to secure his signature. While he was sitting in the living room almost pleading with Eddie's mother and father to sign their boy there was a knock on the door. Standing there was the familiar sight of Scottish-born manager Tommy Docherty, who was then building an exciting Chelsea side that included the likes of future stars like Terry Venables, Peter Bonetti, Ron Harris and Bobby Tambling. However Docherty was too late. By then Eddie Gray's mind had been made up, he was signing for Revie and Leeds United.

Eddie Gray said, 'When I looked in England you had the Manchester United team, the great Wolves teams of the late '50s, the Tottenham Hotspur team that won the double in the early '60s just before I came down to Leeds. Leeds United was not really a name that as a young Scottish boy growing up in Glasgow I had really heard of.

'The only thing that was in my mind when I first got asked to come down and have a look at the place in 1962 was that I had been to watch the Scottish schoolboys play the year before I played against England at Ibrox, and Peter Lorimer was playing.

'Don Revie told me I would be leaving school that day and he went into my headmaster's office and told him. Then he drove me to Leeds. I was 15 and I hadn't even taken my exams. It's a good job it worked out. He did great things for the club and the prestige helped the city. He looked after all the young players. He said we could always go to him with problems and we knew he meant it.'

Another boy who would bond with Eddie Gray, over a shared love of heavyweight boxing champion Muhammad Ali, was Mick Bates who later remembered how Revie charmed his father into convincing his son to sign for Leeds. 'I was born in Huddersfield, I didn't even know who Leeds United were. I had the opportunity to sign for Sheffield Wednesday but I couldn't take to their manager Vic Buckingham. Don Revie came to the house to see me and my dad I remember him saying, "Don't worry, I will look after him, I've got kids of my own." From that moment on, I was only heading to one place, Leeds United.'

Memories of the loneliness Revie felt when he first signed professional forms with Leicester City were still fresh in his mind as he sought to create a family atmosphere at the club. Sonny Sweeney, who followed Eddie Gray from the Castlemilk Estate in Glasgow a year after said, 'My mother loved him. When I first came down to Leeds, he made sure she stayed at the Queen's Hotel, was given tickets to the game and was made a fuss of. That was all the boss' doing.

'I remember every Christmas the club would put on a huge party for the apprentices. In my first year I will never forget the boss handed over a pair of silver cufflinks as a present.'

The Christmas parties were a huge part of the team building. Later on, Johnny Giles said, 'We would have parties at Leeds United, they would not even think of doing that at Manchester United. Then again, Don Revie was a lot more hands on than Matt Busby.'

Despite high hopes, Leeds lost three out of their first four games and shipped six goals home and away against Rotherham United. By 1 December, 1962, Leeds sat in 13th place, 14 points off leaders Chelsea.

There was more bad news. Two days later, at the AGM, the board reported a loss of £72,000 up to 31 July. The *Daily Mirror* reported Revie telling shareholders, 'I have made mistakes buying players, I'll make more but I'm learning. I'll do everything to put this club on the map and if I fail, I deserve the sack.' However, the losses did not stop the board sanctioning a bid of £18,000 for Rotherham striker Don Weston.

The big freeze that winter left Leeds without a game from 22 December, 1962, until 2 March, 1963, leading to a catch-up run of 22 games in just 78 days. When play resumed, Leeds beat Derby County 3–1. Their fifth round FA Cup match against Nottingham Forest on 19 March was their third cup tie in just under two weeks. Leeds fell 3–1, allowing the club to focus on an improbable promotion campaign.

By the time they arrived at The Valley to play Charlton Athletic on Monday 5 April, Leeds had climbed to 10th, their highest position under Revie, but still 18 points off top spot. The 2–1 win saw Leeds display the type of negative possession football that was starting to become a pattern, and which the Charlton crowd greeted with loud booing. The *Daily Herald* reported, 'The crowd were angry with Leeds' time-wasting tactics.' And according to the *Yorkshire Evening Post*, 'The crowd strongly objected to the way they taunted Charlton Athletic in the closing stages by rolling short passes to each other in midfield or putting the ball back to Sprake.'

In reply, Revie was enthusiastic about his team's performance. 'It's just making sure you keep possession by making safe, short passes and that accordingly you preserve the score with your team leading. It demands real skill, control and concentration by the players doing it – you can easily make an expensive mistake if you slip. But continental crowds cheer it when successfully done and rightly so in my opinion.'

A 3–0 win on 4 May, 1963, at Elland Road against Luton Town left Leeds United in fourth, only three points off second-placed Stoke City in an automatic promotion spot. The next day the *Daily Mirror* reported, 'Leeds end the season sniffing promotion and are stable and appreciative enough to offer manager Don Revie another three-year contract.'

Three losses in a row to Middlesbrough, Huddersfield and Southampton put paid to their promotion hopes. In the end Leeds missed out by just four points but a marker had been put down. They would enter the 1963–64 season as the favourites for promotion.

8

LEEDS UNITED (1963-64)

'Maybe we did not exactly endear ourselves to the soccer purists…
but we had to be realistic.'

Don Revie

As Don Revie settled down with his family in front of the TV to watch himself in a comedy skit with comedians Mike and Bernie Winters on ABC's *Big Night Out,* he could feel a sense of satisfaction. It was 31 August, 1963, and Leeds had followed up their resounding opening day 1–0 win at Elland Road over Yorkshire rivals Rotherham United with a thumping 3–0 win over Bury.

All summer long there had been a nagging rumour that any time soon Revie was going to cross the Pennines and be officially unveiled as the new manager at his old club, Manchester City.

The 1962–63 season had been dismal for Manchester City. Relegated to the Second Division they looked on with envy as their rivals, United, lifted the FA Cup. City's glory days of the mid-1950s seemed a long time past. There was little surprise when, with the board's encouragement, Les McDowall resigned from the manager's job. Within hours the press was speculating on his successor.

According to the *Daily Herald*, their prime target was Liverpool's Bill Shankly. When the tough-talking Scot made it clear he could not be prised away from Merseyside, attention turned to the man who was instrumental in gaining City's last piece of silverware, Don Revie.

The Leeds United board was concerned. Even though it had been announced in April that Revie had been offered a new three-year contract, he told the board he would not sign until his present one had run out, in March 1964. Revie was technically free to talk to other clubs.

The rumours all made sense – the Revie family still had friends in the Manchester area, City had a more storied history than Leeds and, crucially, City had funds to buy new players. However, even though Revie met with the Manchester City board, his potential appointment as manager was not unanimous.

It was only seven years since Revie had left the club and some on the board would remember how their old centre-forward had complained of unhappiness. Few would forget his constant requests for a transfer. In the end the board decided to shun the big names such as Revie, Ken Barnes of Wrexham and Jock Stein (then managing Dunfermline) and appoint McDowall's assistant, George Poyser.

With a strong youth policy and the backing of chairman Harry Reynolds, Revie then committed his immediate future to Leeds United. When Revie climbed in his car on 28 August to drive over the Pennines his destination was not Maine Road but Old Trafford. He had only one intention – to secure the signature of the final piece in his puzzle.

Despite being instrumental in two of Manchester United's goals in the 3–1 win over Leicester City in the FA Cup Final in May, Johnny Giles was unhappy. After playing in a 4–0 thrashing at the hands of league champions Everton in the Charity Shield at Goodison Park on 12 August, Giles found himself out of the team in the season opener against Sheffield Wednesday.

Being dropped was the culmination of a year of frustration for the young Irishman. Despite being able to operate on either wing or at inside-forward, and scoring on his debut aged 19 for the Republic of Ireland, Giles had a nagging feeling that Manchester United manager Matt Busby just did not rate him. 'I fell out with Matt or at least he fell out with me. We played the great Spurs team in the '62 FA Cup semi-final and I had a nightmare. I was up against Dave Mackay, Danny Blanchflower and John White.

'From that day Matt lost confidence in me. He never spoke to me; I was just out. I played in the final when we won the FA Cup the following year, but I was only in because Nobby Stiles was injured. I didn't think Matt was fair with me, I'd had one bad game.' Even the *Daily Mirror* weighed in on Giles, claiming after he requested a transfer, 'He does not have the pounding pace required to be a top-class winger.'

Having spoken over the phone with Busby, all Revie had to do when he arrived at Old Trafford was to convince Giles to sign. The midfielder did not need much convincing: 'I was faced with the choice of Blackburn Rovers and Leeds United. I would rather have joined an up-and-coming Second Division club than a First Division one on the slide. Besides, Leeds had just had a pretty decent season and Bobby Collins had signed. When I met Revie, I was very impressed by his determination and ambition. It was his personality that clinched it.'

Even though all eyes were on the new £33,000 signing, it was Bobby Collins who stole the show in Giles' debut, scoring the opening goal in a 3–0 win against Bury the following day. Writing in the *Yorkshire Evening Post* Eric Sangster wrote, 'Stop Collins and you stop Leeds, and they stay in the Second Division. But how? He gets in such out of the way places that he must be just about the hardest forward in the game to mark.

'The man who may one day succeed him as guide and mentor, Giles, had a steady, if not startling, debut on the right wing. He did many good things, few bad ones, quickly attuned himself to Collins' moves and will be all the better when he has got a better hang of United's style.'

Both Collins and Giles were named in the side that travelled to Millmoor, home of Rotherham United, on 3 September. With the game seemingly drifting into a non-descript 0–0 draw, a goal from Jack Charlton saw it burst into life. Two more goals from the home side and a late equaliser from winger Albert Johanneson had the crowd on the edge of their seats for the final 10 minutes as the score ended 2–2.

By the time Leeds travelled to Leyton Orient's Brisbane Road home the day after President Kennedy was assassinated on 23 November, 1963, Leeds were in the midst of a 20-match unbeaten run. So far, Manchester City were the only side to overcome an injury-depleted Leeds, on 7 September, coming out on top, 3–2, in a tough game at Maine Road.

The 2–0 win against Orient, with goals coming from Collins and Johanneson, was enough to take them to the top of the Second Division. By then they were being described by *The People* as 'tough and unrelenting'.

Much of this attitude was attributed to Collins and his will to win. Jack Charlton was to say, 'Collins set the standard that you could do anything to get a result, and it rubbed off on all of us. It was win at all costs. And why not?' Billy Bremner felt Bobby Collins was the closest thing he ever saw to a 'one man team' in his entire career.

Their unbeaten run was to come to an end at Roker Park on 28 December, 1963. Sunderland, managed by Revie's former boss Alan Brown, were pushing Leeds hard in second place. Reporting in the *Daily Mirror* the following day, Ken Jones said the 2–0 score line was of little consequence because 'the brutal promotion battle of Roker Park was a disgrace to soccer.'

Describing the game, Charles Summerbell, also of the *Daily Mirror*, wrote, 'It was as brutal as a sickening ring bout… a raw tangle in which skill was abandoned and only revenge counted. It was the most violent brawl I have ever witnessed.'

Writing in the *Yorkshire Evening Post* Eric Sangster said, 'I hope there are no more games like that at Roker Park on Saturday. It was so full of spite and malice that it did no credit to the 22 players, the referee or the huge crowd of 56,046. Where the tackling at Elland Road on Boxing Day was vigorous in the extreme here it overstepped the bounds.

'Thirty-nine free-kicks for fouls were given by Mr J A Cattlin of Rochdale – 11 against Sunderland in the first half; 10 against Leeds. Five against Sunderland in the second half, 13 against Leeds. I am loath to criticise referees whose job is difficult enough at the best of times but so many today fail to realise that control does not begin and end with the use of a whistle and notebook.'

As for Revie, he simply called the game a 'bad tempered affair'. Two days later the Sunderland board launched an enquiry into the conduct of its players; no such investigation was forthcoming from Leeds. Chairman Harry Reynolds told the *Daily Mirror*, 'There was no such discussion of the Sunderland game. We, on the board, know our professionals play the game hard. We also know Don Revie wouldn't stand for dirty play.

'Don as a former professional should be left to handle that side of the job without interference from us. If he sees fit to discipline a player that's up to him.' Revie would only add when asked about punishing any players in the wake of the game, 'I have never thought of such a thing.'

Going into the New Year the matter that concerned Revie most about the Sunderland game was the loss of points. Their lead over Sunderland was now just one, although they still had a game in hand over their rivals. Preston North End, 4–0 winners over Cardiff City, were level on points with Sunderland with Charlton Athletic three points adrift. With only two clubs getting promoted, Revie was worried Leeds would miss out again.

A trip to Cardiff in the third round of the FA Cup in the first week of January 1964 provided a temporary distraction. It was to be the first time former favourite John Charles would play for Cardiff after returning from an unhappy spell at Roma to join his brother, Mel, in his native South Wales. Even though both sides were reduced to 10 men, thanks to two players suffering broken legs, a 30-yard screamer from man-of-the-match Billy Bremner separated the two sides.

By 11 January it was clear only three teams were in the running for the championship. Leaders Leeds had beaten Manchester City 1–0, Sunderland were only a point off the pace and with third-placed Preston beating Southampton 2–1 a gap opened up between the top three and the rest. Charlton Athletic, who had mounted a strong challenge before Christmas, fell further back by losing to Newcastle.

Drawing league champions Everton at Elland Road in the fourth round of the FA Cup was a huge challenge for this young side. However, according to the *Liverpool Echo*, Leeds were something of an enigma on Merseyside, 'known only by their reputation'.

In a match Everton winger Alex Scott, who was a veteran of Old Firm clashes in Glasgow, described as the 'dirtiest game he had ever played in,' Leeds almost pulled off a famous victory. In the first 35 minutes Leeds were penalised 10 times, underlining Revie's assertion to the press, 'We play the game hard'. After going one up it looked as though Leeds were in control, but for a late foul in which Bremner clattered into Scott and the referee pointed to the penalty spot.

A mishit shot from Scott rolled harmlessly into the arms of goalkeeper Gary Sprake. Then came drama – the referee ordered the penalty to be re-taken. Among howls and catcalls from the home supporters and sensing Scott was affected by the crowd, Everton captain Roy Vernon stepped up to blast the shot past Sprake. With *The People* reporting, 'Even though Everton dominated the first half hour after Storrie scored for Leeds against the run of play it looked as though they shot their bolt.'

Goals in both halves from Everton separated the sides in the replay at Goodison Park three days later. Billy Bremner was again in the thick of the action earning him the man-of-the-match accolade and being described by Alf Greenley in the *Newcastle Journal* as 'terrier like who did not deserve to be on the losing side'.

Writing in the *Liverpool Echo* Leslie Edwards was impressed by the Leeds team. 'There was much to like about Leeds. They are a grand old side but a tough one. Both teams needed that quality last night.'

Though Leeds may have been disappointed by the result, the FA Cup was only ever a distraction – the real action was in the league and as they faced Cardiff at Elland Road on 1 February everyone was determined to get back to winning ways. John Charles and his brother Mel were in the Cardiff team. Those who watched the dour 1–1 draw with the Bluebirds would never have anticipated the fireworks in the tunnel after the final whistle.

As the players trudged off they were met with extraordinary scenes. Brothers John and Mel Charles found themselves struggling to restrain their manager George Swindin. His target was Leeds' trainer Les Cocker. 'You elbowed my player!' Swindin shouted, pointing at Cocker. Apparently while running on to the pitch Cocker had collided with Cardiff outside-left Barry Hole and, from his position in the crowd, Swindin swore it was deliberate.

Revie said it was accidental and believed the Cardiff manager's position made it look worse than it was. It was the second time in a week a Leeds official had been involved in an altercation, with reports of there being a confrontation after the Everton game. Commenting to the press Revie said, 'Look, I would defend them to the last drop if they deserve it but wouldn't if they did wrong things and I certainly wouldn't put up with them going this far, it was an accident.'

Once again, even though it was the team's conduct on the field that was making the back pages, Revie was more concerned with the dropped points. As Leeds and Cardiff were duking it out at Elland Road, Sunderland were smashing Swindon Town 6–0 and moving to the top of the table. There was no doubt there was a lack of firepower in the team – Leeds had not scored more than two goals since beating Southampton 4–1 on 26 October. The fix was obvious – buy a new striker.

Looking to his hometown of Middlesbrough, Revie set his sights on England centre-forward, Alan Peacock. But there was competition from Bill Shankly who was interested in adding Peacock to his forward line at Liverpool as they chased the First Division title. Peacock recalled, 'In the end it was between Liverpool and Leeds United. Obviously, Revie was from Middlesbrough, that was a major advantage and, due to illness in the family I needed to make regular trips back and forth to the North East. Leeds was closer and Revie told me I could have time off if I needed it – that was the clincher.'

More so than the signing of Giles or Collins, the £50,000 paid to secure the signature of Peacock was a statement of intent. In scoring 126 goals in 218 games for Boro, Revie hoped Peacock would replicate his form for Leeds. Scoring on his debut in a 2–2 draw against Norwich on 8 February, 1964, Peacock was an instant hit but again points were dropped, and Sunderland increased their lead at the top.

A 1–0 home win over Scunthorpe was followed by a 1–1 draw against Huddersfield. A 2–0 defeat to third-placed Preston on 8 March saw Leeds clinging to the precious second spot on goal average with Sunderland opening up a gap of three points at the top.

Four wins in a row against Southampton, Middlesbrough, Grimsby and Newcastle throughout March calmed nerves, especially as Leeds managed to find the net 10 times over those four games. It appeared that the Elland Road club was hitting form at just the right time.

By 28 March, when Leeds faced Derby County, they were back on top as Sunderland had dropped points in a 2–2 draw against Rotherham. A 1–1 draw broke Leeds' winning run but a 2–1 victory over Newcastle two days later left Leeds needing five points from four games to secure promotion.

A 2–1 win over Leyton Orient, which the *Daily Herald* described as a 'nerve-tingling game which showed Leeds as lacking the killer instinct' left them a point above Sunderland. As they travelled to Swansea, they knew that their fate was in their own hands. If they won their final three games they would secure the Second Division title, only the second piece of silverware in their history.

In the end, Leeds ran out comfortable 3–0 winners, with new signing Peacock scoring a brace and the other new boy, Giles, adding a third. With Preston and Sunderland both involved in scoreless draws they returned to Yorkshire from south Wales knowing they would be plying their trade in the First Division the following season.

At the final whistle Revie paid tribute to his team: 'We have a family spirit at Elland Road, everyone has been prepared to work that little bit harder and do that little bit extra. That has been shown on the field.

'The players have given 100 per cent effort in every game and no team, win, lose or draw, can do more than that. Their obedience to orders, tactical and otherwise, has been most gratifying and I know they have repeatedly lost the chance to make flattering headlines by making sure of victory or a point with unspectacular methods.'

Promotion was good but the championship would be the icing on the cake. Phil Brown reported in the *Yorkshire Evening Post*, 'Leeds United players are now determined to win the championship of the Second Division, as well as promotion. Team manager Don Revie told me: "We have the two matches left and so have Sunderland. We are two points ahead of them, 60 to 58, so we'll never have a better chance. It would ground the season for the club, and for me personally, if we can beat Sunderland to the title."

'Chairman Mr Harry Reynolds has been urging that United go for the title for months past, of course. He told me: "United have won so little that ranks in football. Ideally, I want them to win this season's title and we have a great chance but in all the years since the club entered the League in 1920 we have won but one honour – the Second Division championship in 1923–24, which is 40 long years back."'

Despite carrying a banner thanking the fans for their support, a nervous performance saw newly-promoted Leeds labour to a disappointing 1–1 draw against Plymouth Argyle. With nearest rivals Sunderland beating Charlton Athletic 2–1, everything was set up for a final-day shootout for the title.

On paper it looked as though the Wearsiders were favourites for the championship. On 25 April, Leeds faced fourth-placed Charlton, while Sunderland lined up to face relegation-threatened Grimsby. Sunderland's 2–2 draw, while condemning the Mariners to the Third Division, would have no impact on the destination of the title.

So exactly 40 years after securing their only Second Division title, Leeds would enter the top flight as champions after Alan Peacock fired in two goals in an emphatic 2–0 victory. The two goals meant that, per Peacock's contract, Leeds had to pay his old club Middlesbrough an extra £5,000 for securing promotion. But no one was complaining.

The two-point margin over Sunderland did not really do Leeds justice. They had not been outside the top two all season, had only lost three games and conceded only 34 goals – with Ian Lawson, who lost his place to Peacock, and winger Albert Johanneson coming in as top scorers with 15 goals apiece. Leeds' points tally of 63 was the highest in the Second Division since 1920.

As they proved in their FA Cup tie against Everton, Leeds could mix it with the best, although their functional style was winning few fans among the neutrals.

As Revie himself later reminisced, 'Our championship success that season was due to a defensive, physical style which made us probably the hardest team to beat in the league. Once we got a goal I would light a cigar, sit back on the trainers' bench and enjoy the rest of the game, secure in the knowledge that it would need a minor miracle for the other side to equalise. Maybe we did not exactly endear ourselves to the soccer purists in those days, but we had to be realistic.'

Writing in the *Yorkshire Evening Post,* Eric Sangster said of Leeds' success, 'The benefit of an overall team plan is that players can step from the junior side to the reserves and to the first team knowing exactly what is required of them. The club's style and general tactics are ingrained in them.'

Looking ahead to the 1964–65 season Revie felt he had a side that was more than equipped to compete with the best in English football, to the point where he refused to make new signings in the summer. He told the press, 'I intend to give the present team a run in the First Division and am very confident about them in that division.'

9

LEEDS UNITED (1964–65)

'We would point out that we have only had two players sent off at
Leeds in the last 44 years. We maintain that the dirty team tag which
was blown up by the press could prejudice not only the general public
but the officials controlling the game.'

Harry Reynolds, Leeds United chairman

When the coach turned up to take Leeds United to Wembley for the 1965 FA
Cup Final, the players were glad to get out of the Selsdon Park Hotel. What was
meant to be a relaxing few days of team bonding before the big match was
anything but as the manager had drilled the game plan into them.

A day earlier the boredom had spilled over into frustration. Jack Charlton
later recalled: 'We went to stay the few days before the cup final at a hotel near
London… I remember playing a little five-a-side game on the Friday. Norman
Hunter volleyed the ball and it hit Bobby (Collins) on the face, making his nose
bleed a little.

'It was clearly an accident, not deliberate or anything. Then the game
restarted, and when Norman got the ball Bobby just flew at him. It was obvious
Bobby meant to do him harm. I yelled, "Norman!" – and he looked up and
turned just as Bobby hit him in the middle with both feet. Bobby finished up on
top of Norman, punching him. I yanked him off and I had to hold him at arms'
length because he started trying to whack me. "Come on, Bobby, calm down,"
I said. "We've got a cup final tomorrow."'

Johnny Giles, the only player with experience of a cup final, in 1963, said,
'Players live for moments like the cup final, it's something you dream about, but
Don was nervous. I think it rubbed off on some of the younger players.'

Even before Leeds had left Yorkshire for the famous twin towers Revie was unhappy. The Leeds shirt delivered by sportswear company, Umbro, featured an owl while the Liverpool team they would face in the final had the famous Liverbird on their red shirts.

For as long as he could remember, birds had been an unlucky omen for Revie. 'He was extremely superstitious, as were the rest of the family. He was obsessed by gypsies and believed it bad luck if you ever turned one away from the door. For some reason he never liked birds or ornamental elephants,' daughter Kim later said about her father's obsessions.

'At the beginning of the season, a gypsy had knocked on the front door and told him he would fulfil his lifelong ambition in front of thousands, but he was not happy. He told mum about the gypsy's prediction and said, "I think she's wrong about that one!"' In the build-up Revie was incredibly tense.

Commenting on the inexperience of the Leeds side, which had an average age of 25, Bobby Collins would say, 'You've got little chance of winning at Wembley unless most of your players have played there previously and know what to expect. Leeds allowed themselves to be caught up in the hullabaloo surrounding the final and the youngsters especially found it very difficult to relax.'

Waiting for Leeds United when they pulled into the famous old stadium at 11.30 a.m. was former Spurs double-winning skipper Danny Blanchflower, now retired and working as a journalist. He had been tasked by the BBC to interview the players in the dressing room ahead of the kick-off at 3 p.m.

After sharing some words with Revie and his players, Blanchflower knocked on the door of their opponents Liverpool, only to find no answer. The room was empty. The traffic around Wembley and the throng of supporters who had followed them down to London from the North West had held up the team coach. A police escort alleviated fears the kick-off would have to be delayed.

This year Liverpool, who had won the league title in 1963–64, were appearing in their third final, having lost their previous two in 1914 and 1950. As their coach slowly made its way to the stadium they could be forgiven for believing they were travelling to a home game, such was the number of Scousers turning Wembley Way into a sea of red.

In fact, apart from Giles, only managers Don Revie and Bill Shankly had any experience of playing in a cup final – Revie with Manchester City in 1955 and 1956, while Shankly lost one with Preston North End in 1937, returning to win it with the same team in 1938.

At 2.45 p.m., with a threat of rain in the air, the two teams emerged from the tunnel. The 37-year-old Revie dressed smartly. A crisp, white shirt with a dark club tie, underneath a navy mohair suit, it was the same one he had worn in every round of the cup and thought it lucky. Just to be on the safe side he carried a rabbit foot in his pocket.

Behind him was his captain, the 5ft 3in Collins, smiling broadly. The yellowing old woollen socks his manager insisted he wore because they, too, were 'lucky' contrasted with the pristine white kit he and his teammates were dressed in.

Last but one to come out was his midfield partner, Billy Bremner, small and wiry, nonchalantly balancing a football on his mop of thick, red curly hair. Towering over Bremner at the very back was Jack Charlton, newly capped at centre-half by England, his face giving away no flicker of emotion as he looked around the famous old stadium. However, one player in the line was feeling the pressure more than any other.

Just moments before the buzzer sounded alerting the two teams they should be ready to walk out, Albert Johanneson had begged Revie not to play him. Already carrying an ankle injury from the final league game of the season, Johanneson was frozen with nerves. From the moment he woke up he had been suffering with sickness and diarrhoea.

Ever since he had become Revie's first signing for Leeds from South Africa on 5 April, 1961, he had been subject to racist abuse. According to Johanneson he was subject to monkey impressions on his debut against Swansea Town a few weeks earlier. Now as he waited to walk out in front 100,000, he worried about the reaction he would face. He did not have to wait long; all he could hear was monkey chants and other racist calls.

Even though Revie had told Johanneson to ignore the inevitable racist chanting and taunts and simply concentrate on using his speed to run at Liverpool, it fell on deaf ears. Close to having a meltdown, Johanneson wanted to be anywhere other than at Wembley that afternoon. Despite this the South African started the game.

The fixed grin Revie wore on his face masked a knot of nerves and tension. By contrast, the Liverpool manager looked ready for war. Shorter by a few inches than Revie, his slate-grey suit unbuttoned, head closely shaved and wearing a look that could turn a man to stone, Bill Shankly's swagger as he walked out alongside the Leeds manager resembled one of the movie gangsters he adored.

At 2.50 p.m. the teams lined up to meet the Duke of Edinburgh, alongside a delegation from the FA, who told Revie he hoped the game would not go to extra-time as he hoped to be in Windsor for a polo match at 6 p.m.

Having won the toss, Liverpool elected to kick off but it would not be long before referee Bill Clements was issuing a reprimand to the Leeds captain. Having dispossessed Liverpool striker Roger Hunt in the first attack of the match, Bobby Collins then clattered into left-back Gerry Byrne, breaking the Liverpool man's collar bone in the process.

Despite early pressure from Liverpool, a Leeds attack in the 18th minute saw the Yorkshire side grow in confidence and minutes later Collins had a chance, but his shot went wide of the Liverpool goal. A light drizzle began to make the game scrappy and cagey. The first shot on target came from Liverpool on 27 minutes, while Leeds forced a save from the Liverpool goalkeeper after a full 29 minutes of play as the rain fell harder, becoming torrential.

The *Sunday Mirror's* Sam Leitch said, 'Here were two sides locked in clumsy combat in the middle of the field between the two 18-yard goal areas. They square passed and back passed but avoided the simple art of shooting as if it were one of the seven sporting wonders of the world.'

The BBC commentator Kenneth Wolstenholme was not impressed with the action either, summarising, 'Both teams are so well organised perhaps they are organising each other out of the game? When one side produces an ace the other one trumps them.'

By the time the Royal Marines Marching Band, under the direction of Captain PJ Neville, came out to play for the 100,000 crowd at half time, the final remained goalless with both keepers only making four saves between them.

Midway through the second half and Liverpool were firmly in control. Both Jack Charlton, who had run into a pitch-side photographer, and Gary Sprake, who had been caught in a clash after a Liverpool attack, needed treatment.

Moving Bremner to centre-forward with Giles to replace him in midfield, and Johanneson switching wings, had little effect as fatigue caught up with the Leeds side. As the referee blew his whistle to signal full time, it was Liverpool who were frustrated they had not won the game in the 90 minutes.

Watching the match for the *Daily Mirror* Edgar Turner said, 'The nearest thing to a goal in 75 minutes came from Thompson. He sprang into life like a burst of sunlight splitting grey skies. He whipped in a fast, low shot from just inside the penalty area. The ball sprayed with water as it zipped along the ground and appeared set for the net just inside the far post.

'There was a green-and-white flash and by instinct more than anything else Gary Sprake flung himself full length to his left to finger the ball and inch it around the post.'

The *Sunday Mirror's* Sam Leitch also said, 'Their football did not win them many friends. Possibly it lost the game quite a few. Especially Leeds' sheer defensive tactics.' Regardless of the display, the FA Cup Final was going to be decided in extra time for the first time since 1947.

With his raincoat fastened up to his neck and a white towel draped over his head to keep him dry, Revie resembled a boxer who had reached the 11th round, given his all, but still had to fight the last round.

After such a long, tumultuous season Revie hoped, too, it would not go to extra time either. Now all he could do was close his eyes, say a silent prayer and hope the gods of football would smile on him and his players.

...

As Leeds United prepared to kick-off the 1964–65 season, Revie was fuming. The source of his anger was an article that had appeared in the FA's official journal in August 1964. Bemoaning the high level of foul play in the game, it published a league table of the clubs with the worst disciplinary records. At its top stood his Leeds team.

The article argued Leeds had more players suspended, fined or cautioned than any other side. Revie expressed his displeasure in an interview with Phil Brown of the *Yorkshire Evening Post*: 'We did not have a single first-team player sent off last season and we had only one suspended, Billy Bremner, after a series of cautions, which is a lot more than many clubs can say. Most of our offences were committed by junior second-team players or boys.'

Such was Revie's anger with the FA that he raised the matter at the Leeds monthly board meeting. To Revie the article was a stain not only on his reputation but those of his players. He wanted an official retraction from the football authorities and to this end he wanted a letter sent to the FA telling them in no uncertain terms that they were wrong.

The letter Harry Reynolds dictated to his secretary read, 'We would point out that we have only had two players sent off at Leeds in the last 44 years. We maintain that the dirty team tag, which was blown up by the press, could prejudice not only the general public but the officials controlling the game and, to put it mildly, could have an effect on the subconscious approach of both referee and linesmen, to say nothing of the minds of spectators, especially some types who are watching football today. It could lead to some very unsavoury incidents.'

For their part, the FA dismissed the matter out of hand, claiming the article was factual and was fair comment. It would not be the last time Leeds and Revie would cross swords with the footballing authorities.

There can be little doubt that Leeds could play hard but they operated in a world where every player had a hard man in their side. Johnny Giles said, 'In those days you had to commit grievous bodily harm to get sent off. There were other teams with players just as hard as us. There was Ron 'Chopper' Harris at Chelsea, Peter Storey at Arsenal and Ron Yeats at Liverpool. Every team had a hard man – you quickly learned to look after yourself.'

Talking about football of that era, Bolton Wanderers and England striker, Nat Lofthouse, amusingly said, 'There were plenty of fellers who would kick your bollocks off. The difference was that at the end they'd shake your hand and help you look for them.'

In his seminal 1968 book, *The Football Man*, Arthur Hopcroft devoted an entire section to 'Violent play – and refereeing', which summed up the state of football during the 1960s. 'The fierce, reckless tackle by which a tough defender clears a forward out of the path of goal in a desperate disregard of injury has been a feature of football for as long as I can remember… what gives concern is the deliberate assault that occurs, common lately, when the victim does not have the ball.'

George Best would express his hatred of playing Leeds United. Even though he preferred to play with his socks rolled down and no shin guards, he always made sure he wore a pair when he faced Leeds, such was the ferocity of the tackling he faced against the West Yorkshire club.

What made the experience even more uncomfortable, for Best, was the mountain of personal abuse he faced whenever he got close to one of the Leeds players, which could range from questioning his parentage to the morals of his close family. Best was not the only player who came to approach a fixture at Elland Road with dread.

Coming into the First Division, Leeds were something of a mystery. Those who did not attend games or own a TV would only know of the Yorkshire club through the newspapers. Rather than reporting on the sublime skills of Billy Bremner or Johnny Giles they would much rather report about their poor disciplinary records.

Besides, in most people's estimations, Leeds would soon be back where they came from – the Second Division. Johnny Giles said, 'We were expected to be the also-rans, everyone was talking about how well Sunderland was going to do. It was all about them, not us.'

Leeds' manager had other ideas. Striker Jim Storrie, signed by Revie from Airdrie for £15,650 in June 1962, scored 25 goals in 38 appearances, including two hat-tricks in his first season. He said of Revie, 'After winning promotion most managers would talk in terms of consolidation. He spoke in terms of finishing in the top four. We will come up against some world-class players but we will be the best team in the league. So, he had the optimists among the lads thinking we would win the league and even the pessimists thought we might finish halfway up.'

As Leeds headed into their opening match of the season against Aston Villa, there were few sides better prepared. There was advice on diet and a doctor was brought in to give the players regular check-ups. Central to the Leeds approach were tactical discussions based on dossiers Revie's backroom team had compiled on their future opponents.

Dossiers are now an accepted part of the modern managerial game but at that time it was as if Revie was indulging in sinister espionage. To Revie, the use of dossiers was nothing new as Sep Smith had used them on behalf of Johnny Duncan as Leicester City made their way to the 1949 FA Cup Final.

Revie said, 'Towards the end of the 1963–64 season I heard some good reports about a young player, so I sent Syd Owen along to run the rule over him. Well, the report that landed on my desk the following Monday was a masterpiece!

'I had never seen such a detailed breakdown of a footballer. Syd had left nothing to chance. He outlined how good the player was on his right and left side; the angles or lines along which he tended to run with the ball; the shooting positions he favoured, and so on. It struck us that a report like this would be invaluable if applied to the teams we met each week, and it all started from there.

'Each week either Syd, Maurice Lindley or I would watch our opponents for the following Saturday. The report was typed on the Monday morning and we would spend the rest of the week working on it with the players. On many occasions, we held practice matches in which the reserve players adopted the same style of play as the team in question and the first team lads had to try and break it down. For example, if the opposition did not read the game well at the back we would practise decoy runs designed to pull their defenders forward so that balls could be played over their heads for Leeds players to run on to. That type of thing.'

The reaction of the players to the dossiers and the in-depth team talks was mixed. Older heads like Jack Charlton and Alan Peacock would take little notice and inevitably the information so painstakingly compiled by the senior management ended up in the bin.

Norman Hunter recalled, 'I think we did pay the opposition too much respect. But whatever Don did at that time, you had respect for. Though looking back, I would never have a dossier to play against a team, I would have certain points. We analysed teams far too much.

'One thing Don never did was to change his routine. It went on up until the time he left. That was his way... and sometimes, even though you were 30-odd, you were sitting there through half an hour, three-quarters of an hour, talking about players you already knew. But that was his way.'

Billy Bremner added, 'I'd look at the dossier though I wasn't taking a lot in. But I thought I'd better pay attention because if he said to me "What was I saying there?" and I wasn't paying attention, he wouldn't be too pleased. Yet if we played Arsenal on the Saturday and then again on a Tuesday, three days later, we'd have the same dossier. The only time I would listen was when he was talking about continental players I didn't know.'

The dossiers were compiled by Revie's assistant manager Lindley and trainer Owen. They would have layers and layers of information.

Sometimes the players would be given these dossiers to read ahead of matches and then be quizzed by Revie to make sure they'd taken the information on board. Vital details would also be reinforced during the pre-match team talk.

An example could be seen in the 1974 ITV Yorkshire documentary *The Don of Elland Road*, where Revie talks ahead of a game with Liverpool. 'I have had Liverpool watched three times; each player is broken down and what we are going to do.

'One or two players have been really making them tick. Callaghan is a tremendous little professional, doesn't know when he's beaten. Keegan is very, very dangerous at coming off people and getting the ball. When he has his back into someone he is very tightly marked, one finger behind each other (holds up two fingers) like that. He can turn players like that and turn them out of the game.'

Giles said, 'When I was at Manchester United, I used to wonder what Matt Busby did. He was lauded for his man-management, but it passed me by. When I went to Leeds we did not have the same level of talent but there was desire, a hunger. Don's attention to detail was extraordinary, analysing and correcting what he felt went wrong on a Saturday.'

The sun was beating down on a very hot day as Leeds made their return to the First Division after an absence of four years. When the team ran out at Villa Park on 22 August, 1964, much of the crowd were either wearing sunglasses or holding up their hands to shield themselves from the glare.

Inside the dressing room the Leeds players were pumped up. Bremner said, 'When the whistle blew, we were like greyhounds let out of the traps.'

The Leeds team ran at Aston Villa. They dominated possession, until a goal against the run of play saw the Yorkshire side go in at half time 1–0 down. Revie calmly told his young team to stop running around like mad men and play calm football. Goals from Johanneson and Charlton made sure Leeds made a winning return to the top flight.

While Revie walked away pleased with the result at Villa Park he knew the real test lay on 26 August when league champions Liverpool would be the visitors to Elland Road. In many ways the Merseyside club were everything Leeds aspired to be.

Like the Yorkshire club they had stagnated in the Second Division for five long years until Bill Shankly was appointed manager in 1959, winning the Second Division title in 1962 and the league championship two years later.

Having put five past a poor Reykjavik side in their European Cup debut and a 3–2 win at Anfield against Arsenal, Liverpool had every right to feel they would be walking away from Elland Road with maximum points, even if they were without their main striker, Ian St John.

From the kick off it was clear Leeds were out to make a statement. With Collins marshalling the midfield, the use of the long ball saw the Liverpool defence pulled out of position. The first breakthrough came when a Johanneson shot clipped Liverpool captain Ron Yeats on the shoulder to put Leeds one up after 16 minutes.

The noisy 50,000 crowd was quietened eight minutes later when Roger Hunt equalised. Five minutes before half time, Don Weston made it 2–1 for the home side. Just 10 minutes after the break and Leeds fans were in heaven. In the space of two minutes, goals from Bremner and Giles had made it 4–1. 'We want five! We want five!' the crowd chanted as Leeds marched forward at the slow-footed Liverpool defence.

Even when Gordon Milne pulled one back for the visitors, Leeds were still in control. The final score was 4–2 and Leeds were only one of four teams to have won both of their opening games. Billy Bremner said, 'Don Revie told us to go out and prove that we were a match, and more, for them. His words inspired us and put us in exactly the right frame of mind for the task ahead. It was quite a task, of course, but we settled quickly and played the way we had performed in the second half against Villa.'

Another win, 3–0 at home to Wolves, was followed by a 2–1 loss in the return game against Liverpool at Anfield on 2 September, and a 3–3 draw three days later at Roker Park. Even though Sunderland had been tipped for great things, the club was in disarray. Their manager, Alan Brown, who had sold Revie to Leeds after a dressing-room bust-up, had resigned in July 1964. His destination was Sheffield Wednesday, a club once linked with Revie. By 14 September, Sunderland were bottom but one in the First Division, having failed to win any of their opening games. By contrast Leeds were fourth, just two points off leaders Chelsea.

On 16 September Revie travelled to Barnsley to visit his chairman Harry Reynolds who was lying in a hospital bed with 64 stitches in his face. Revie could have been lying next to him. He had been due to travel with Reynolds to watch a Rotherham v Portsmouth game, but was so angry with what had transpired at a board meeting that he had decided to watch Bradford Park Avenue take on local rivals Bradford City instead.

On the way back from Rotherham, Reynolds collided with a motorcyclist, hitting a wooden electricity pole and ending up in a ditch. He was lucky to be alive. Exchanging pleasantries, neither of the old friends broached the elephant in the room – Revie wanted to leave Elland Road.

Earlier that day, the *Newcastle Evening Chronicle* announced that Revie had applied in writing to be considered as the next permanent manager of Sunderland. The job was currently held on a temporary basis by one of Revie's childhood heroes, George Hardwick. When asked to comment from his hospital bed, Reynolds spluttered, 'Under no circumstances will Leeds United release Don Revie from his contract.'

Sunderland historian Rob Mason takes up the story: 'Historically, Sunderland are a bigger club than Leeds United, with a much bigger fan base. Football was only really beginning to get a foothold in a city which was traditionally dominated by rugby league, Sunderland was and is firmly a footballing town. Don, who played there, would only be too aware of the fanatical support the club enjoyed.

'At the beginning of the 1964–65 season Alan Brown had resigned on a point of principle. He had rebuilt the club since the illegal payments' scandal, he deserved to be recognised for that achievement. So, when the players all got bonuses or promotion and him and his management team were not offered any he was disgruntled.

'To add insult to injury, he had been living in a club house and was keen to purchase it. When the club turned down his offer, he felt he was left with no choice than to resign from a club which underappreciated what he had done for them.'

Brown was not the only one who was feeling undervalued by his board. Revie, who within three years had changed the fortunes of Leeds both on and off the pitch, hoped to secure his short-term career with a five-year deal. His children Duncan and Kim were settled into local schools and wife Elsie was enjoying teaching maths and PE at Leeds High School, but Revie knew his line of work was precarious. A run of bad results and that could be the end of him.

So he was extremely disappointed when the Leeds board could only muster a three-year contract when he had expressly asked for five. Even though he was rumoured to be the highest-paid manager outside the top flight with £4,000 per year, plus £10 per week expenses, he was hankering after job security. So once Leeds were in the top division he made a request to extend the contract.

The Leeds board had met on 14 September and a heated discussion resulted in two directors threatening to resign if the manager's contract was extended. Harry Reynolds, who had championed Revie, was bitterly disappointed with the attitude of his fellow directors, telling the press, 'I myself have fought to get Don's contract amended to five years. Other directors on the board are behind me, but we are not strong enough to carry it through.'

While the Leeds chairman lay in his hospital bed in extreme pain and uncertain about the future of his club, his Sunderland counterpart Eddie Collings could not have appeared more relaxed. Departing for a holiday in Majorca, he was confident they were going to get their man. At a three-hour board meeting there was only one subject of note in the minutes – the club wanted to appoint Revie as the new manager at the earliest opportunity and wanted to speak to him to agree terms as soon as possible. An official approach was to be made to Leeds in the morning.

Speaking to reporters at Newcastle airport, Collings said of the next manager of Sunderland, 'I have given the board a full mandate to negotiate in my absence and I have complete confidence in their ability to [do] the job successfully.'

Any hope of Revie's name being linked with the job being simply newspaper tittle-tattle was firmly scotched when a *Daily Mirror* reporter cornered Revie who confessed, 'I will not deny it, I have written to Sunderland.' The contract, worth £6,000 a year, was more money than Revie was on at Leeds and, crucially, the Sunderland board was willing to offer a five-year deal. Both clubs indulged in a tug of war – Sunderland determined to secure their former captain as manager and Leeds desperate to retain his services.

Meanwhile, Revie continued to prepare his team to take on Blackpool in a mid-week game at Elland Road. A spate of injuries that saw Giles, among others, out for a month with damage to his knee ligament, and Peacock needing a cartilage operation, meant Leeds played poorly as they were trounced 4–0 at Bloomfield Road on 7 September.

In the return game on 16 September, and with a strengthened side, a rampant performance led to a 3–0 scoreline that flattered the Seasiders, who were never in the game. Leeds were now in second place behind early pacemakers, Chelsea.

The anxious board of Leeds directors, without the chairman Harry Reynolds, was counting down the minutes to the end of the game. An emergency meeting had been called and its outcome would determine whether Revie would remain at Leeds or be sitting in the hot seat at Roker Park.

The most important result of the night came just before midnight at a deserted Elland Road. The vice-chair Percy Woodward, standing in for the hospitalised Reynolds, released a business-like statement: 'It was unanimously decided that Mr Revie will remain at Leeds United. Mr Revie is happy to do so. He will be given a five-year contract starting from last May at the salary he asked for.'

Speaking to the press the following day, Woodward elaborated on the position: 'Everybody is wonderfully happy and I personally am overjoyed that the question of Don's future has been amicably settled. Naturally we were all upset and rather surprised at the unexpected turn of events, but now everything has turned out all right and I am quite thrilled about it. Revie has got what he wanted – a five-year contract and the salary increase for which he asked and I am sure he is just as pleased as we are. He didn't really want to leave. We know that.'

In the end the contract would amount to more than Sunderland were offering as well as the increase on his term as manager. It was his fourth pay increase since he had been named as manager in 1961. Such was the board's desperation to keep hold of him, it had even agreed to a bonus should Leeds end the season in the top four. The whole saga of Revie leaving Leeds had been played out over 48 hours. It turned out not to be a bad bit of business.

To the press, who had been used to writing about Revie orchestrating various moves during his playing career, Revie made all the right noises: 'I am very happy that it has ended this way. Last night I was prepared to go to Sunderland but at the bottom of my heart I did not want to go.

'One sometimes says things in the heat of the moment that one regrets. I am very grateful to the Leeds board. I hope people do not think we have had a lot of differences, we haven't. The only one has been over the five-year contract.'

Although Revie was as good as his word and withdrew his application for the post the following morning, the dalliance with Sunderland left a bitter aftertaste in the North East. Writing the weekend Revie turned down the Rokerites, *Newcastle Journal* reporter Alf Greenley wrote, 'Are Sunderland AFC being taken for a ride?' Greenley then went on to cite Revie's application, 'In dispute with the board over the length of his contract, Mr Revie wrote to Sunderland asking for the manager's job there. Immediately Leeds announced he was under contract there and they would not release him. The point supporters and, I am sure, many others cannot understand is why applications have reached Sunderland, from people who must have known beforehand, that they were not in a position to take the post if it were offered.'

Referring specifically to Revie, he goes on to say, 'His contract was not to his liking. He applies to Sunderland and within 24 hours he has the contract he wants. Leeds and Sunderland are once again back to where they started. No one can begrudge anyone making every effort to better himself professionally and financially, but it is unfortunate Sunderland should suffer in the process.'

Despite whispers in some quarters that Revie had used the Sunderland vacancy as leverage in contract negotiations, Revie's official version for not taking the job was down to the simple virtue of loyalty to the club. 'I had landed the

Sunderland job and was walking into the locker room at Leeds to collect my kit when I came face to face with a group of newly-signed apprentices.

'Believe it or not, they had tears in their eyes when I told them I was leaving and that touched me. It might seem trite to say that I looked upon my players as sons but this is true. Most of them had been with the club since they left school and I promised their mothers and fathers I would look after them. I had repeatedly stressed the importance of loyalty to these lads and thought: "They've been loyal to you, so it's up to you to show the same loyalty in return."'

Back on the pitch wins against Stoke, Spurs, Burnley and Sheffield United meant Leeds won all their games in October. When they travelled to Goodison Park to meet Everton on 7 November, 1964, they lay in third place, just five points off leaders Manchester United and with a game in hand.

What should have been a routine league fixture cemented forever the label of Dirty Leeds. Lying in eighth spot, the Toffees were on a poor run of form, having lost their previous two games against Blackburn Rovers and Arsenal, and were in real danger of losing touch with the leaders.

Everton old boy Bobby Collins was particularly keyed up on his first return in the league to Goodison Park. After 15 minutes a Collins cross was met by Willie Bell, who headed into the net to give Leeds the lead.

Everton left-winger and former teammate of Bobby Collins, Derek Temple, said, 'Bobby was extremely aggressive. He had so many chips on his shoulder he could have had a fish supper. The atmosphere was frightening with the crowd heavily involved – it was so bad you felt it could go off at any given moment.'

After 36 minutes all hell broke loose. Scorer Bell collided with Temple who was knocked unconscious and carried off the pitch. As Temple was attended to coins rained down on Leeds trainer Les Cocker. The referee Ken Stokes, who had already dismissed Everton left-back Sandy Brown for throwing a punch at Johnny Giles, had had enough. In extraordinary scenes he ordered both teams off the pitch. The match resumed after 10 minutes and everyone was relieved when the final whistle blew.

The press were universal in their condemnation of the game, Jack Archer of *The People* called it 'a spine-chilling game'. Brian Crowther, match reporter for *The Guardian*, went further, blaming the players for their 'collective irresponsibility'; the fans for their 'disgusting behaviour'; and the referee for 'not being firm enough'. An 'unhappy day for English football' was how *The Observer's* John Arlott described it.

Even *The Times* weighed in: 'The front line of battle now was Merseyside. Goodison Park has already gained an unsavoury tribal reputation for vandalism. Leeds United, too, more recently have earned black marks for ill temper on the field. The marriage of these two dangerous elements sparked off the explosion.'

The chorus of disapproval that followed from all sides was all part of a plot to get at Leeds United, according to Revie. 'After the incidents of this weekend I must defend my club and my players after all the bad things that had been said about them. I feel it started last season when we were in the Second Division when we were tagged as a hard, dirty side by the press.

'I am disgusted by these attacks on us and I ask that we be judged fairly and squarely on each match and not on this unfair tag that we have got. We were wrongly labelled by the press and then by the FA. The result has been that opposing teams have gone on to the field keyed up, expecting a hard match. I think the number of opposing players sent off in our matches proves it.'

From the game at Goodison Park until a 1–1 draw home to Blackburn Rovers on Boxing Day, Leeds had lost only once, 3–1 away at Upton Park to West Ham United on 21 November. They had won every other game including victories against famous names like Arsenal, Manchester United and Wolves.

A 2–0 win at Blackburn's Ewood Park on 28 December and a 2–1 victory over a hapless Sunderland side on 2 January, 1965, meant they headed the table by four points over nearest rivals Chelsea. When lowly Southport visited Elland Road for the FA Cup third round, a 3–0 win over the Fourth Division outfit saw Leeds safely through to the fourth round.

Waiting for them there were Everton. In a highly-anticipated clash at Elland Road, Leeds went ahead through Jim Storrie only for them to be pegged back just over 20 minutes before the end with a Fred Pickering penalty. Jack Charlton recalled, 'Many believed that would have been it for Leeds in the replay at Goodison Park but they were soon proved wrong.' Goals from Charlton and Don Weston saw Leeds through without the fireworks of previous encounters.

In the fifth round Shrewsbury Town were dispatched 2–0 and a 3–0 win over Crystal Palace in the quarter-finals was again marred by a brawl in the middle of the pitch. In the semi-final, Leeds were drawn against a Manchester United side boasting the trio of George Best, Denis Law and Bobby Charlton.

Going into the tie, Leeds were full of confidence, as a week before the semi-final they had run out 4–1 winners at home to Everton, with Bremner and Peacock adding to Albert Johanneson's brace. That win left them top of the league, two points ahead of Chelsea and five in front of semi-final opponents Manchester United.

The game was staged at Hillsborough, home of Sheffield Wednesday, but neither team came out of it with any merit. Writing in the *Sunday Mirror*, Stan Halsley ran the headline 'What a disgrace!' claiming, 'The match would have been better staged at the Royal Albert Hall, Earl's Court or anywhere where people strive for success with a punch-up and gloves.'

After an hour Denis Law, who alongside Nobby Stiles was already in the referee's book, went after Jack Charlton. It was a big mistake because if Charlton relished anything, it was confrontation. It did not take much for the former miner from the North East to lose his rag and swing at the Scotsman.

The punches lit the blue touch paper in a game where tensions were high. Next thing, Bremner and fellow Scot and Manchester midfielder Pat Crerand were going toe to toe as the FA Cup semi-final descended into chaos. Several minutes ticked by before order was restored. For the football authorities it was a worrying sight. With the game ending goalless the warring sides would have to do it all over again on 31 March at Nottingham Forest's City Ground.

The next day the papers carried images of Law in a ripped and torn United shirt. The game did no one any favours, least of all Leeds who were already struggling with a reputation for being a hard team. The *Yorkshire Post* reported, 'Both sides behaved like a pack of dogs snapping and snarling at each other over a bone.'

Ahead of the replay Frank McGhee of the *Daily Mirror* offered this advice: 'For any fan of Nottingham Forest, the neutral club staging the FA Cup semi-final replay between Leeds United and Manchester United, who may be planning on taking a youngster along for a treat. Don't. This was X-certificate stuff, ferocious soccer that crawled out from underneath a flat stone to spread the ugly diseases of provocation, retaliation and revenge. This was football to make the two managers, Don Revie and Matt Busby, ashamed.'

With Liverpool beating Chelsea 2–0 in the other semi-final, the *Liverpool Echo* had this to say of Leeds: 'Which United will Liverpool face in the final at Wembley on 1 May? I think most people hope it is Manchester as the reputation of Leeds sinks lower and lower as the season progresses. However much manager Don Revie protests, his side is castigated as a dirty side; the facts speak for themselves.'

Perhaps with the criticism ringing in their ears, the replay was a much better game of football, although still a hard-fought one.

Just as the match was about to drift off into extra time a Giles cross found the head of Bremner who won it for Leeds after 87 minutes, sending Revie and the entire Leeds bench into raptures. Ken Jones in the *Daily Mirror* wrote, 'It was a case of the determination and discipline of Leeds United overcoming the instinctive skill of the Manchester United forwards.'

There were ugly scenes at the end when a Manchester United supporter ran on the pitch and rained punches down on the referee but nothing could mar the occasion for Revie.

'My proudest moment in my career was when the whistle went and Leeds United were in the final. Manchester played some absolutely scintillating football. What pleased me most was that Leeds kept their heads.' Just over four years after becoming manager, Leeds were in the FA Cup Final for the first time in their history and were on course for a remarkable double.

Three wins in nine days over West Ham, Stoke City and West Bromwich Albion left Leeds four points clear ahead of Chelsea when they welcomed their old rivals Manchester United to Elland Road on 17 April. Had the Red Devils lost, Chelsea and Leeds would have been left to fight it out for the title. It was not to be, a Tony Dunne goal separated both the sides as Manchester United came out 1–0 winners.

With Leeds conceding five goals over two games, home and away against Sheffield Wednesday, and Chelsea collapsing, Manchester United began an ominous run of form, winning six games in a row. A 3–0 win against Liverpool at Old Trafford and it looked as though the Red Devils were coming into form at the right time.

And even though Leeds laboured to a 3–0 win over Sheffield United, it looked as though the season was finally catching up with Revie's young side. But going into the final game all was not lost. Leeds were still in top spot by one point, albeit with an inferior goal average to Manchester United and having played one game more.

Leeds dropped a point in a 3–3 draw at relegated Birmingham City while Manchester United beat Arsenal 3–1 at Old Trafford. Even though the Manchester side would lose their final game to Aston Villa, their superior goal average meant they were crowned league champions even though both sides finished on the same points.

Leeds' points tally of 61 was another first, the highest recorded by a side finishing in second place and four points more than the 57 Liverpool posted on their way to winning the title in 1963–64. Coupled with an appearance in the FA Cup Final, it had been a remarkable season for a side no one was tipping back in August.

Naturally, to have come so close but not take the title was also disappointing, but there was still the FA Cup Final where they would face a Liverpool side that had meekly surrendered their league championship by finishing a mediocre seventh. With Liverpool finishing 17 points off the pace and having conceded 73 goals, heading into the cup final Leeds had every right to feel confident.

The last time Revie had made an appearance in an FA Cup Final he had been wearing the sky blue of Manchester City. Now after sacking manager George Poyser, Revie's old club hoped it could coax him back to Maine Road.

Just six days before the 1965 cup final, Manchester City made their move. Writing in *The People* Stan Liversedge told readers, 'Don Revie is wrestling with his own, personal problem. Should he part company with Leeds United and take over as boss of Manchester City? Last night Revie would only say, "I am happy at Leeds and I can make no comment."

'But I understand that City, one of Revie's former clubs, *HAVE* been in touch with the Leeds' boss. Only a few months ago Revie signed a five-year contract with Leeds after turning down the chance to take over at Sunderland on

£7,000 a year. Now Revie knows of City's intent he has only to pick up a phone and say "yes" to the Maine Road job.

'Revie tops City's list and they would be prepared to give him an even longer contract than his present one at the same salary.'

Revie had been told by his former Leicester City roommate Ken Chisholm that if he wanted to make serious money, he needed to keep moving clubs, so Revie was never afraid to agitate for a new club. He left Leicester for Hull as he was getting married, then went to Manchester City, and finally Sunderland, for a last big pay day. There was nothing to suggest he would not do the same thing now he was a manager.

The Leeds board, remembering the Sunderland episode just a few months earlier, began to get nervous. Refusing to grant permission to the City board to talk to Revie would not end the matter as Revie had connections there and was speaking to his old teammates Johnny Williamson and Ken Barnes.

After long conversations with his manager, Harry Reynolds knew Revie always felt he had unfinished business with Manchester City. Had they said the word when he was angling for a move from Sunderland in 1958 he would have gladly gone back there instead of Leeds.

City were not the only club chasing Revie as, just seven months after he had applied for the Sunderland job, the Rokerites were back trying to entice Revie to move to the North East. When Sunderland had failed to land Revie they appointed caretaker manager George Hardwick on a permanent basis. It had not worked out as hoped and the side finished the season in 15th place.

After meeting with the board, Sunderland chairman Sid Collings mulled over the idea. He was sure Revie could be tempted if there was enough money on the table but how would he get around the Leeds board?

Upon leaving for his holiday, Collings would tell the press, 'Sunderland have not approached Don Revie. If he cares to get in touch with us that may be a different matter.' When a formal approach was made, Revie's answer was the same as the one he gave to Manchester City – they would have to wait until after the cup final.

On the day of the cup final, as Leeds departed the Selsdon Hotel for Wembley, Reynolds visited Revie wanting to know what his plans were. After telling his chairman he was sorely tempted to return to his former footballing home at Manchester City, Reynolds asked Revie to name his price. The shadow boxing was over.

...

As the referee blew his whistle to signal the start the first half of extra time in the 1965 cup final Liverpool had been convinced by their manager that Leeds were on their knees and ran at their Yorkshire opponents.

After what many considered a drab 90 minutes, in just three minutes of extra time the game suddenly sprung to life. A cross from the injured full-back Gerry Byrne was met with a Roger Hunt header that put the Reds in front. Somehow Leeds dragged themselves off the floor and Bremner volleyed home a sharp equaliser from what was almost United's only chance of the game.

As the game seemed to be sliding towards a replay, Ian St John popped up to break Leeds' hearts with a winner in the second half of extra time. Edgar Turner wrote in the *Daily Mirror*: 'A header by Ian St John after 21 minutes of extra time gave Liverpool the FA Cup and climaxed a fantastic finish to a tame final. For 90 goalless minutes it was a match of too many Marlon Brandos and not one Sir Laurence Olivier. Too much method and not enough individual brilliance.'

The Times was slightly less critical of the match, reporting, 'In spite of much lateral method play it was a tense battle of human qualities.'

For Revie, all he would say to the press was, 'The better team won. It was tough luck, but Liverpool are a successful team with their European triumphs behind them. I am more than proud of what my lads have done in their first season back in the First Division. I thought Bremner played a fine game in defence and attack.'

Johanneson, who was largely absent in a game where so much was expected of him, had frozen on the big occasion. Hardly unexpected in the face of the vile racist abuse he faced every time he came near the ball.

Leeds had completed the unwanted double of finishing runners-up in both major domestic competitions. The only consolation was that Leeds would play in Europe for the first time in its history. It was still an incredible achievement for a club that just five years earlier had faced the real prospect of relegation to the Third Division and bankruptcy.

For Leeds' players there were a number of personal triumphs. Collins was named the 1965 Football Writers' Footballer of the Year, and Charlton and Bremner both won their first international caps for England and Scotland respectively. Peacock also forced himself back into the reckoning for England.

Charlton believed Leeds lost simply through lack of experience. 'I believe I'm right in saying that only Bobby Collins and myself had played at Wembley before – and my experience was limited to one game for England a few months earlier. Liverpool, on the other hand, had been in the big time [for] three or four seasons; they were hardened not only to the long grind of a 42-game First Division slog but inured to the atmosphere of games like the final, where emotional outbursts by the fans can have such a tremendous effect upon the players.

'The disappointing thing about the final, I think, was not that we failed to win – but that we lost so dully. Every player, I believe, wants to be associated with a classic final and our display was so out of keeping with our ability that it really hurt.'

As Revie and the team headed home from King's Cross over 200 supporters turned up to wave them off. By the time they arrived back from London, both Sunderland and Manchester City wanted an answer from Revie.

Remembering just how close they had come to losing the man who had raised them from the foot of the Second Division, the board meekly agreed with chairman Reynolds. For the fourth time in as many years, Revie had negotiated an extended contract and a larger pay packet.

A relieved Reynolds told the press, 'There has never been any danger of Mr Revie leaving the club. A contract is binding on both sides. We value his services. It is not our intention to part with our good players and the same applies to the management side.'

From Revie's point of view, the team of Sprake, Reaney, Bell, Bremner, Charlton, Hunter, Giles, Storrie, Peacock, Collins and Johanneson, which lined up in that final, had the makings of one of the most exciting teams in the First Division.

Liverpool manager Shankly had this to say of Leeds' perceived failures that season: 'Failed? Second in the championship. Cup finalists. Ninety per cent of managers would pray for "failures" like that.'

Revie said, 'It's a bit disappointing to finish second in both cup and league, but we have had a wonderful first season back in Division One, and I am very pleased with the team.' Collins echoed his manager's sentiments, 'We have had a great season, but lost both honours. We shall be having a go again next season.'

Looking ahead to the 1965–66 season and European football for the first time, Revie was determined his Leeds side would not be seen as one-season wonders.

10

LEEDS UNITED (1965–66)

'Our players will have to be perfect gentlemen this season. Last season
Leeds were unjustly labelled a dirty side and because of that I think a lot
of teams will play hard against us. My players are big enough to stand up
to this and I have warned them about retaliating.'

Don Revie

Watching as his team faded in the 1965 FA Cup Final, Revie was worried that
Bobby Collins, the man he had brought in to be a leader, was growing more and
more weary as the game wore on.

By his own admission, Collins did not have a good game at Wembley. Even
though he had signed a new four-year contract in April 1965, earning him £100
a week, both Collins and Revie knew that at the age of 34, the end of his playing
career was near.

The man who was to replace Collins was already in the side, Johnny Giles.
The Irishman would simply move from the right side of midfield into the centre
where Bobby was the general. 'It was always the intention that one day I would
replace Bobby in the middle of the park, we had been planning for that eventuality
after I arrived from Manchester United,' Johnny Giles confirmed.

The dilemma Revie faced going into the new season was, who was going to
fill the gap on the right? The answer seemed to be at the seaside, in the form of
Blackpool's Alan Ball.

Just days before his 20th birthday Ball had made his full England debut and
was firmly in contention for a place in England's 1966 World Cup squad. There
was little wonder that there was talk of Ball leaving the struggling Seasiders.

Like Bremner, Ball was flame-haired, had a massive heart and a temper to match. He had been mentioned more than once in Syd Owen's dossiers whenever Leeds played Blackpool. Revie had been impressed when he saw him up close on the touchline, telling Ball's fellow England international Norman Hunter to closely mark the midfielder – something Hunter, by his own admission, found almost impossible to do.

On 11 July, 1965, *The People* reported that Revie had made his move, bidding £90,000 for the diminutive midfielder. Despite talk of a transfer tug of war between Leeds, Tottenham and Everton, Blackpool manager Ron Suart told all suitors 'no deal would be done at this time.' To Revie, this meant Suart had left the door ajar and he would continue his pursuit of Ball throughout the coming season by fair means or foul.

As the 1965–66 season approached hopes were high. Ahead of their inaugural campaign in Europe in the Inter-Cities Fairs Cup chairman Harry Reynolds had pledged an investment of £500,000 to improve the ground at Elland Road, with a family social club that would be open seven days a week.

Heading into the opening day of the season Revie told the *Daily Mirror*, 'Our players will have to be perfect gentlemen this season. Last season Leeds were unjustly labelled a dirty side and because of that I think a lot of teams will play hard against us. My players are big enough to stand up to this and I have warned them about retaliating.'

After failing to land Ball, the Leeds side that ran out to face Sunderland for their first game contained no new names. The only real change was the addition of striker Jim Storrie on the bench, wearing the number 12 shirt – substitutes were allowed for the first time that season in case of an injury to a player on the pitch.

In front of a home crowd of 32,348, Leeds faced Sunderland on 21 August, 1965. Despite some early flourishes from Sunderland's big-name new signing, Jim Baxter from Glasgow Rangers, Leeds dominated possession but found it difficult to create chances. After Sunderland winger George Mulhall was sent off the fight seemed to go out of the Wearsiders with Leeds securing the points with a Norman Hunter volley in what was seen as a scrappy match. At Villa Park just two days later, Leeds were back to their dominant best with goals from full-back Terry Cooper and Alan Peacock earning a 2–0 win.

According to *The People*, even without their talisman Collins, Leeds never looked like being beaten by West Ham when they visited London on 28 August – until a sublime performance from Geoff Hurst took all the points. Despite going one-up with a goal from Peacock, Leeds were pegged back with a goal from West Ham's inside-right Martin Peters. The problem was the nervous display by goalkeeper Gary Sprake who could not handle crosses coming in from West Ham's Harry Redknapp, who was making his debut alongside Leeds' Peter Lorimer.

Even though Leeds did not deserve to lose, a virtuoso goal from Hurst sealed a 2–1 win for the Hammers, leaving Revie to rue that 'Upton Park seems to be a hoodoo ground for Sprake.'

It was Hurst's rival for England's number nine shirt, Jimmy Greaves, who was instrumental in the second defeat of the season, on 8 September. Greaves scored a brace as Tottenham ran out 3–2 winners, replacing Leeds at the top of the first division.

When Leeds met Torino on 6 October for the second leg of their Fairs Cup tie, Leeds were only separated from Liverpool at the top of Division One by goal difference. A 2–1 win over the Italians at Elland Road meant Leeds travelled to Torino knowing they needed only a goalless draw to make it through to the next round.

After a tight first half, Revie was feeling confident his players could hold the Italians and progress to the second round. Then five minutes into the second half Collins was scythed down by Torino left-back, Poletti, snapping his thigh bone in the process. Norman Hunter remembered the tough Scotsman writhing in agony on the floor: 'When I got to Bobby, his leg was waving around at the top because the bone was snapped high up the leg. It was horrendous.'

Upon seeing the Leeds captain cut down all hell broke loose. First on the scene was Bremner, red with anger and with tears welling in his eyes he screamed at Poletti, 'I will kill you! I will kill you!'

Standing guard over the stricken Collins, Charlton struck several Torino players who tried to bundle Collins off the pitch. He would not move until a stretcher came to carry Collins away. Upon seeing the extent of his captain's injury in the dressing room, Revie burst into tears.

Sensing Leeds were in a fighting mood, the Italians dispensed with the rough stuff. With substitutes still not allowed in European competition, a 10-man Leeds saw out a goalless draw to progress to the next round. When Leeds arrived home from Torino the following day, it was without Collins.

Overnight, under the guidance of world-renowned orthopaedic surgeon Professor Re, Collins had a 15-inch plate inserted into his leg to reset his damaged thigh bone. He would spend a fortnight in hospital before beginning a long period of rehabilitation but that night in Turin really brought his Leeds career to an end.

For Revie, it meant bringing his plans forward. Ever since Blackpool had turned down his bid for Alan Ball he had been secretly meeting with the player, under the cover of darkness. Over a pint in a pub near Saddleworth Moor Revie told the player how he foresaw a Leeds midfield of Ball, Bremner and Giles. So far, these meetings had come to nothing – and Revie needed to move fast.

At £30,000, Huddersfield Town's speedy winger Mike O'Grady was a fraction of the price of Alan Ball and did not take nearly as much coaxing to make the short move across Yorkshire to sign for the Whites. 'By 1965, Leeds was absolutely buzzing with excitement,' O'Grady later said about the club and the city. As compensation, Don Weston went in the opposite direction.

On 16 October, 1965, the new-look Leeds, with Johnny Giles as schemer in place of Collins, partnered by Bremner in the centre, with O'Grady on the left and striker, Jim Storrie, played out on the wing, met struggling Northampton Town. Charlton captained the side. Despite going a goal down early on Leeds ran out 6–1 winners with 18-year-old Peter Lorimer getting a brace.

The following week O'Grady got on the score sheet in a 2–1 win over Stoke City that meant that Leeds United were now back at the top of the First Division. But when Leeds lined up to face SC Leipzig on 24 November for the first leg of the second round of the Fairs Cup in communist East Germany, Giles and Co had been in patchy form.

A 2–0 win over Arsenal at Elland Road on 13 November, 1965, was the only highlight in a month that had seen Leeds lose 1–0 against Chelsea at Stamford Bridge and draw with Burnley and Everton.

Reaching Leipzig itself was an adventure. In 1965, the team had to catch a flight to West Berlin, take a bus through Checkpoint Charlie then transfer to another bus in East Berlin. Lorimer described the vehicle for the two-and-a-half hour drive on pot-holed roads to Leipzig as 'rust on wheels'.

When the players finally arrived at their destination the city was covered in six inches of snow. With no question of the game being postponed, officials packed the snow, drew blue lines on the pitch and played with an orange ball.

According to Peter Lorimer, knowing their footing would be unsure, Revie ordered all the players' studs be shaved down to expose the nails to improve grip on the ground. Knowing the studs would be checked, he put cardboard on each one to hide the nails. The plan worked and as soon as the players got on the pitch they removed the cardboard.

Peter Lorimer said, 'Within minutes blood was oozing from all of their players' legs and they were complaining furiously to the referee. Their protests fell on deaf ears, with the official insisting that he had already checked our boots.'

An evenly-matched game saw the tie remain goalless until the last 10 minutes when Lorimer and Bremner scored two in quick succession before a consolation goal from Leipzig centre-forward Frenzel. In awful weather conditions Leeds prepared for the return leg at Elland Road in a strong position.

The snow was coming down heavily in Leeds on 1 December as the East Germans battled in vain to level the tie. Despite them going close a few times the Leeds defence could not be vanquished. A goalless draw was enough to see Leeds in the hat for the next round of the competition in the spring.

The blanket of snow that covered most of Great Britain in December 1965 saw Leeds having to sit out the next two Saturdays as the conditions were deemed too dangerous to play. A superb 4–2 victory over West Bromwich Albion was the only game Leeds played before Christmas 1965.

The next time Leeds appeared in the league was on Monday 27 December – and there could have been no bigger game. Their opponents, Liverpool, were undefeated in eight weeks, winning seven of their nine matches and moving up from seventh to top spot – and opening an impressive lead, too. Leeds were unbeaten since 6 November but had played only three league games due to a succession of postponements. They had a massive four games in hand on the Reds.

The game took on the look of a two-legged cup tie, with the return match scheduled at Elland Road, the very next day. Although pressed back for most of the game Liverpool were unable to penetrate the defensive partnership of Charlton and Hunter. A counterattack from Leeds saw Peter Lorimer slot in from close range to separate the sides.

The gap between the two sides was now down to five points and a win at home the next day would make Leeds well-placed to challenge for the title in the New Year. In front of a crowd of 49,192, Liverpool got their revenge. This time it was Leeds' turn to fall victim to a counterattack, with a 48th-minute Gordon Milne goal winning the game for the Reds.

Still, heading into 1966 Revie had every reason to be optimistic. Leeds still had four games in hand over Liverpool in the league, were about to kick off their FA Cup campaign against Bury and had just drawn Valencia in the third round of the Fairs Cup.

On New Year's Day 1966 17-year-old Eddie Gray rewarded the faith shown him by Revie by hitting a 25-yard screamer into the top right-hand corner of the goal as he scored on his debut in a 3–0 win against Sheffield Wednesday.

Goals from Peacock and Giles from the penalty spot on 8 January secured a 2–1 win against West Bromwich Albion, which meant Leeds were able to stay in touch with leaders Liverpool. But progress again faltered with a pair of draws against Manchester United and Stoke City.

A ruthless display in the third round of the FA Cup on 22 January saw Bury hit for six with Peter Lorimer claiming a hat-trick. After Chelsea knocked out holders Liverpool on the same day, bookmakers offered odds of 6–1 of Leeds winning the cup, with Chelsea made second favourites.

If Revie thought the win over Bury was going to be the catalyst for a good run of form in the league he was sadly mistaken as Leeds looked a shadow of themselves when losing out to Sunderland, 2–0, at Roker Park. Of more concern was Peacock, who ruptured the ligaments in his knee and was ruled out for the rest of the season. It also meant he would not be considered by Alf Ramsey for the World Cup in July.

And for Revie it was nothing short of a disaster. From the start of the season Peacock had been in irresistible form, earning a recall to the England team.

Fighting for silverware on three fronts, Leeds would have to go into the final months of the season without their star centre-forward.

During this setback, Revie had to prepare his side for the Fairs Cup tie against Valencia on 11 February. The Spaniards had won the trophy in 1962 and '63 but, perhaps more ominously, they had never lost at home during a European competition.

Without a recognised centre-forward Revie agonised for days. His most obvious option was the inexperienced Rodney Johnson, a striker who had come through the ranks with Norman Hunter but whose first-team appearances were limited by Peacock.

Young Rod Belfitt was another option. A strong runner and graceful player, he was on the edge of the Leeds first team. Still not quite happy, Revie even debated putting Bremner up front.

In the end Belfitt was the only change to the familiar team Revie had been putting out since Collins was injured back in October. Leeds dominated the first half but struggled to find their rhythm. Against the run of play the Spaniards took the lead in the 16th minute.

After that, Valencia sat back and let the Leeds attack pound away at the them. A Giles cross found Lorimer, who hammered home early in the second half to level matters. From that moment, Leeds' tails were up as they piled on the pressure looking for the winner.

With 15 minutes to go the ball went out of play after a corner. Charlton, who had been captaining the side in the absence of Collins, started chasing the Valencia number five with his fists clenched. Having gone up to the Valencia penalty area Charlton claimed, 'One of my opponents slung a punch which would have done credit to Cassius Clay [Muhammad Ali].'

Very soon there was a melee on the pitch that involved players, stewards and police. Not for the first time in a Leeds match, the referee Leo Horn told the players to leave the field. When they were told to go back on Charlton was told to stay where he was. The referee had decided to dismiss him.

Charlton's only consolation was Valencia left-back, Vidagany, had also been told he need not return to the fray either. For his trouble, Charlton was fined £50 with £30 costs by the FA. After the match ended 1–1 referee Horn claimed Revie told him about Charlton, 'You cannot do this, he's an international!' Revie vehemently denied saying this.

The controversy surrounding the comments made by Horn about Leeds and their conduct meant the referee was another who would miss out on the return leg. His replacement for the second leg a fortnight later was Othmar Huber of Switzerland, who made it clear he would not stand for any of the nonsense seen at Elland Road.

In Spain and in sweltering conditions for February, Leeds played on the counter and 15 minutes from the end took the lead. Paul Madeley, wearing number nine but filling a holding role in midfield, put O'Grady free on the edge of the penalty area with a 30-yard pass over the full-back. The Spanish, thinking he was offside, pulled up, allowing the winger to pick his spot and fire a low cross shot into the net. Appeals to the referee were quickly waved away.

When the whistle blew Leeds had done what so many others had failed to do – beaten Valencia at home. They were now in the quarter finals. Revie went on to say, 'It was so superbly forged by a side of youngsters. I am fast concluding that there is just no end to their courage and fighting spirit. They were magnificent against a highly experienced club.'

Domestically, big wins against West Ham and Nottingham Forest, where they scored nine goals over two games, offset the disappointment of going out to Chelsea in the fourth round of the FA Cup. And after going out in the third round of the League Cup to West Bromwich Albion, Leeds were now free to concentrate on the league and the Fairs Cup.

It was Liverpool's defeat at Fulham on 26 February that saw Leeds close the gap on the league leaders after a dour 1–1 draw with Sheffield United. As March came around thoughts again turned to Europe, and Hungarian opponents Ujpest Dozsa. Watched on several occasions by assistant Maurice Lindley, who thought they were a crack outfit, in the end they were no match for Leeds.

Torrential rain had made the Elland Road ground resemble a mud bath rather than a football pitch as Leeds held the feet of their opponents to the flame. Scoring four times in quick succession, the tie was practically over before half time and the 4–1 score flattered the Hungarians.

In between the first and second legs of the Fairs Cup, Leeds contrived to lose 2–1 to strugglers Northampton Town, a side they had blitzed 6–1 at Elland Road earlier in the season. Just as in 1965, nerves were beginning to show. In what should have been a comfortable second leg in Budapest, Peter Lorimer later recalled, 'When we got over there, they absolutely pulverised us for half an hour. Gary Sprake was flinging himself left and right to make last-second saves, they were hitting the post, hitting the bar and missing by inches.'

A lone strike from Peter Lorimer saw Leeds safely into the semi-finals in a disappointing 1–1 draw. There was tension aplenty with a pair of 3–2 wins over Leicester City and Blackburn Rovers before disaster struck.

All season, Blackpool had looked like favourites for relegation so the two fixtures on 26 and 28 March looked like an easy four points for the Elland Road outfit. No one anticipated the 2–1 loss at home would be followed up by a 1–0 defeat in the return game. Unless something dramatic occurred, it looked extremely unlikely the league championship would be heading to West Yorkshire in 1966.

Still, Leeds kept on fighting, recording a 2–0 win against Chelsea on 4 April. A 3–1 win on Good Friday against Fulham raised hopes that the championship was not beyond them, when Liverpool could only manage a draw. All hopes of a maiden league championship were finally extinguished when the Cottagers visited Elland Road to secure a 1–0 win.

A 4–1 win over Everton lifted the team's sprits before they faced Real Zaragoza in the semi-final of the Fairs Cup. Winners of the competition in 1964, Zaragoza boasted a forward line dubbed the 'Magnificent Five'. To get past the Spaniards, Revie would have to call on all his tactical know-how.

In an outstanding defensive display Leeds were unlucky to lose to Zaragoza after an alleged hand ball in the penalty box by Bremner. There was an unpleasant scene near the end when Johnny Giles was sent off along with Zaragoza defender Violeta, who retaliated after claiming Giles deliberately kicked him.

Regardless of the incident, Don Revie was pleased with what he had seen, saying after the match: 'Get Zaragoza at Elland Road next Wednesday and I am sure we can take care of them, fine side though they are. They gave us a real stretching tonight but we held them as we planned and if only we could have scored from our three or four breakaways we might have done better than keeping this formidable side to one goal on their own pitch, and that goal a penalty.'

In an outstanding display on 27 April at Elland Road, Leeds ran the crack Spanish outfit ragged. Making up for his explosive behaviour in the earlier rounds, Charlton displayed the poise and calm that made him England's first choice to partner skipper Bobby Moore in the heart of England's defence in the World Cup.

Charlton made Leeds' first goal for Johanneson and scored the second, cancelling out an early goal by the Spaniards. When the captains came together to decide where the play-off game should be held, on a coin toss, Charlton called right and both the teams would return in a fortnight to Elland Road to decide who played in the final.

Although Liverpool secured the league championship on 16 April, 1966, the race was still on for the runners-up spot. Three wins in a row over Newcastle United, Arsenal and Burnley meant Leeds were perfectly placed as they readied themselves for action against Real Zaragoza.

The last call-out the local fire brigade expected was to Elland Road. When they arrived, they were not met with another inferno but by a smiling Revie. Knowing the Spaniards were used to hard pitches and remembering how Hungarians Ujpest Dozsa had been upset by heavy conditions ahead of the match, Revie asked the fire brigade to fire their water cannon on the pitch.

They did such a good job, and despite it being the middle of a dry May, the Elland Road pitch resembled a quagmire. However, Revie's plan backfired as it was Leeds that struggled in the conditions. Eddie Gray said, 'It was typical of Don to think of something like that, but on this occasion his scheming came unstuck. Real, far from being unhappy in deep mud, seemed to relish it.'

After being outplayed, all Leeds had to show at the end of 90 minutes was a consolation goal in a 3–1 loss. Dreams of European glory and silverware would have to be put on hold for another year. A resigned Don Revie said, 'We gave all we had but it was nowhere near good enough against a glorious side.'

Unable to lift themselves, Leeds lost 2–0 to Newcastle United on 16 May putting their second place at risk. Their final game, against Manchester United at Old Trafford, saw Norman Hunter and Jack Charlton rested at the request of England manager Alf Ramsey, who had also asked United not to play Bobby Charlton or Nobby Stiles ahead of the World Cup.

There were nerves aplenty among Leeds fans when David Herd put the home side one up. However, a returning Collins made his presence felt in his first game back from injury by beginning the move that saw Paul Reaney equalise to secure the point that meant Leeds finished runners-up for the second year in succession. More importantly, they had proved they were no mere 'one-season wonder'.

As Revie looked back over the season, he knew his young side could only get better. He reflected, 'In three or four years' time most of this current side will still be only 26 or 27 years old, and it is then I feel that we may be seeing them at their best.'

11

LEEDS UNITED (1966–67)

'For about half an hour after the final whistle, I felt completely numb.
But the remorse really began to hit me when I met my son Duncan
outside the ground. He was sobbing – and I felt like sitting down
and crying with him.'

Don Revie

On 15 August, 1966, after months of coaxing, cajoling and chicanery, Revie was
frustrated – the one player he prized more than any other had turned his back on
him.

Despite giving assurances to Revie that he would sign for him after the 1966
World Cup and allegedly accepting £100 delivered to his door anonymously by
a representative of Leeds every Friday night as an 'investment', Alan Ball had
decided his future laid with Everton and not, as Revie assumed, with Leeds.

After England's triumphant World Cup campaign, Blackpool quickly realised
they could not hang on to their best player any longer and Ball was up for sale to
the right bidder at £110,000. After all the groundwork he had laid, Revie had
been confident Ball would be on his way to Elland Road, once he met Blackpool's
asking price.

But Ball and his father had other ideas and even an improved last-minute bid
from Revie could not stop the World Cup winning midfielder from heading to
Goodison Park. For Revie it was a snub but he also had more pressing problems
to deal with.

After the final game of the previous season, Collins was back to full fitness
and desperate to reclaim his place in the first team. With Giles firmly established

in the centre of midfield, the question was, how was Revie going to accommodate Bremner, Collins and Giles?

An opportunity to experiment came when Leeds played a Glasgow Select XI on 10 August, 1966, but it was not a success. Despite Giles claiming a goal in a dour 1–1 draw, the *Yorkshire Evening Post* claimed both Collins and Giles were too alike to complement each other.

As in the previous two seasons, Leeds entered their opening game of the 1966–67 season without new signings. But unlike the previous two years, they had a long injury list. A strained hamstring sustained in the first 20 minutes against the Glasgow XI saw Jack Charlton join O'Grady, Peacock and Johanneson in the treatment room.

So in the opening game at White Hart Lane, Leeds had an unfamiliar look about them. Youngsters Rod Belfitt and Jimmy Greenhoff had been drafted into the side to play Tottenham Hotspur. On a muggy day in north London tempers were frayed with Bremner niggling a particularly irate Dave Mackay. Returning from a second broken leg, Mackay was upset with Bremner for kicking him in his bad leg, or so he claimed.

The resulting picture of Mackay grabbing Bremner by the shirt as the flame-haired Scot claims all innocence has become one of the most iconic photographs of English football in the 1960s. Mackay went on to say, 'Bremner was my pal, but when he pulled on his Leeds shirt he seemed to become a different man and for some reason he kicked me on my newly-healed bad leg.'

Another confrontation between the same two players moments later saw tempers really threaten to flare. Thankfully, the players calmed down and Leeds went a goal up through Giles, only for him to begin limping with a thigh strain.

The goal was the only highlight in the game for Leeds with the hugely fancied Tottenham side containing stars Jimmy Greaves, Alan Mullery, Alan Gilzean and Terry Venables taking control of the match and running out 3–1 winners.

Even though Giles was carrying an injury he was on the scoresheet in a 2–1 win at home over West Bromwich Albion a week later, which also saw Johanneson return to first-team action. At half time Collins was forced to stay in the dressing room, having picked up an ankle injury that would keep him out of the side for several weeks. With both club captain Collins and his deputy, Charlton, injured, it was Bremner who led the side out for the first time against Manchester United on 27 August, 1966. Back in his familiar role as playmaker, Giles flourished as goals from Reaney, Lorimer and Madeley saw Giles' old side crash to a 3–1 loss.

But the win over Manchester United was one of only three that Leeds recorded that September. A 3–0 loss away to Aston Villa saw Leeds languishing in a lowly 13th place. There were two main problems: an ever-growing injury list saw Revie lean heavily on youngsters, such as 19-year-old Lorimer, 20-year-old Jimmy Greenhoff and 18-year-old Eddie Gray. Added to that was the lack of a proven goalscorer. Despite expectations that Revie was going to sign a striker in the summer nothing had happened. Peacock said, 'Look, both Don and I knew my knee injury was bad and I was really struggling but he had always been fair with me and wanted to give me every chance. Not signing anyone was his way of showing he believed in me.'

One player Revie did look closely at was Aston Villa striker Tony Hateley but he baulked at the price, telling the press, 'I am not, as the club stands at present, going into the transfer market to buy big. I have no regrets about not getting Hateley, not at £100,000.

'I should not have served United well by having them pay a fee like that. If people get hot under the collar about it, well, they will just have to. I have my own reasons for not joining in the hunt for various other players, too, but they must remain private.'

A 3–0 win over Preston North End in the third round of the League Cup on 12 October settled nerves a bit, as did a 3–1 win over Arsenal three days later. An 8–1 aggregate victory over DWS Amsterdam in the Fairs Cup at the end of October saw fans dream of a repeat of last season's run in Europe. A hat-trick from Johanneson in a 5–1 drubbing of the Dutch at Elland Road raised hopes the South African was back to his very best form.

A 1–0 loss on 26 October to Southampton saw Leeds come back down to earth, but a Charlton goal saw them back to winning ways against Arsenal on 5 November. Then came the low point of the season. Revie watched his side get torn apart by a rampant West Ham side that put seven past a helpless David Harvey who was deputising for Gary Sprake in the fourth round of the League Cup.

Worse was to come just over two weeks later on 19 November when league champions Liverpool meted out a 5–0 thrashing in front of their home fans at Anfield. For many it seemed that after three seasons in the top flight, Leeds had finally been found out.

Writing in the *Yorkshire Evening Post*, Eric Sangster asked after the West Ham defeat, 'Was it a seven-goal wonder or does that thrashing at Upton Park mean that after three extremely successful seasons Leeds United are once more about to sink into the mediocrity which all too often has been their lot in the Football League?'

By the time of the AGM on 12 December, the fans were getting restless. A 2–1 win over West Ham on 26 November, followed by draws against Sheffield Wednesday and Blackpool had done little to placate them.

In heated exchanges, Revie and chairman Reynolds were asked why the team had just not clicked on the pitch. Revie cited injuries to seasoned professionals, pointing out that younger players needed experienced heads around them to develop.

Revie's comments led to questions as to why Reynolds had not opened his cheque book to sign new players as replacements. 'Don't assume that because we have not signed anyone we have not been trying, but the position is the same as if anyone came in for our players. They would get the same answer as we have received – we don't want to sell,' was the chairman's response.

From a financial point of view, things could not have been better with Reynolds announcing a profit of £59,028, taking the club out of debt for the first time in its 47-year history. In 1963 Leeds had owed a total of £250,000.

Over the previous 12 months gate receipts had risen from £277,519 to £312,398, though payroll costs had climbed substantially, up to a record £135,265. There were net transfer outgoings of £13,550, mainly down to the £30,000 purchase of O'Grady.

Wins over Tottenham on 17 December and a 2–1 win over Newcastle United on Christmas Eve were certainly welcome. An injury to Collins saw Bremner once again lead the team in the return at Elland Road on Boxing Day that saw Leeds come out 5–0 winners. This was followed by a goalless draw against league leaders Manchester United on 31 December that lifted sprits going into the New

Year. Leeds were now in sixth position, just four points off the top. Then a 3–1 win over Burnley put them only three points off the leaders. At this point, Leeds were yet to start their FA Cup campaign and were still in the Fairs Cup, although for the past month Giles had been out with a thigh strain.

But as so often happened in the early part of the season there was an unseen slip-up. This time it was at third-placed Nottingham Forest where Leeds went down to a solitary goal. Worse was to come when Bremner was sent off 17 minutes before the end for kicking the Forest goalkeeper while he was covering the ball on the floor. This dismissal resulted in a FA charge which saw Bremner banned for a fortnight and fined £100 with £20 costs.

In a repeat from last season, Leeds were once again drawn to face Valencia in the third round of the Fairs Cup. Despite missing three first-team regulars, Bell, O'Grady and Johanneson, a Greenhoff strike kept Leeds on level terms with the Spaniards at Elland Road. Since the previous season the rules had changed in European competitions and away goals now counted as double. This meant Leeds would go to Valencia with a distinct disadvantage.

The odds seemed tipped in favour of the Spanish when three weeks later, on 8 February, Revie received an injury list that included Reaney, Greenhoff, O'Grady, Johanneson, Peacock, Rodney Johnson and Terry Cooper. In the end, an early Giles goal, a determined defensive display and a decisive strike in the 87th minute by Lorimer earned a splendid 2–0 victory, which secured a last eight spot.

Between legs of the Fairs Cup, United had set off on the FA Cup trail with an easy 3–0 victory over Crystal Palace, then battered West Bromwich Albion 5–0. But their league form continued to stutter; a 3–1 hammering of Fulham was soon forgotten as Leeds contrived to lose 2–0 at Everton.

The exhilaration of their triumph in Spain inspired a comfortable 3–0 win at Elland Road against Stoke City on 11 February. The game was the last time Collins appeared in Leeds colours; 11 days later he completed a free transfer to Second Division Bury. It was hardly surprising as Giles and Bremner were established in midfield and by Collins' own admission were superb. Later, Revie was to describe Collins as 'his best ever signing'. Also on the move was Jim Storrie who was sold on to Aberdeen.

To many, selling two of his most experienced players when faced with an ever-increasing injury list seemed a strange decision, but Revie's faith in his young players was unshakable. To underline this, when Bremner returned from suspension he replaced Collins as club captain.

A 2–0 win over Southampton on 4 March put Leeds in the right frame of mind for their FA Cup fifth round clash at Sunderland. In a hard and bitter battle, both sides could not add to the first-half goals scored by Neil Martin of Sunderland and Jack Charlton. A 1–1 draw meant they had to do it all over again in a replay at Elland Road.

The replay could have been remembered for all the wrong reasons. On 15 March, some 57,892 crammed into an over-capacity Elland Road – many without a ticket. Thousands were left outside while some had even clambered on to the roof. It did not take long for crush barriers made of steel and concrete to give way.

It was estimated that when the Lowfields Road terracing collapsed over 1,000 people flooded on to the pitch resulting in the police asking for the game, which had only just kicked off, to be restarted. Over the stadium public address system, Reynolds asked the crowd to remain calm.

When the game restarted after only 17 minutes there were reports of 32 people with injuries but, thankfully, no fatalities – a major tragedy had been avoided. For many the game was secondary, but John O'Hare gave the Black Cats a 35th-minute lead, which was cancelled out by Giles. Heroics from Sunderland keeper Jim Montgomery meant Leeds were unable to find the winner, even after extra time. They would have to go to a second replay.

With the injury list still growing and an impending Fairs Cup tie against Italian side Bologna, another replay was the last thing Revie needed. The replay was scheduled for the same day as the Fairs Cup tie with Bologna, which meant that if there was another stalemate at Hull's Boothferry Park then Revie would face the nightmare of having to play Sunderland while sending out his reserves to Italy to play Bologna. Luckily the scenario never arose.

The second replay followed the pattern of the other two games – a goal apiece from both sides was followed by a long period where both sides were unable to break the deadlock. As the game seemed to drift towards extra time there was unexpected drama.

Just three minutes before time, in a controversial decision, referee Ken Burns ruled that Greenhoff was brought down by Sunderland defender Cec Irwin in the penalty area. The resulting penalty saw Giles calmly sweep the ball into the net, effectively deciding the tie.

All hell broke loose with referee Burns needing a police escort after dismissing Sunderland players George Herd and George Mulhall for arguing with him. Nearly five minutes of injury time was added as police struggled to keep Sunderland supporters from getting on the pitch but Leeds were in the FA Cup quarter-finals and could fully concentrate on their tie with Bologna.

Not only was the injury list a problem, so too was the fixture log jam. When Leeds played Bologna it was their fifth game in 11 days. They did well to pin the Italians down to scoring only once in a game where the home team looked weary.

Then it was back to winning ways as Leeds recorded five straight wins as they moved up the league in late March and early April. On 8 April they faced Manchester City in the sixth round of the FA Cup and, despite finding the Citizens in blistering form, it was a Jack Charlton goal that separated the two sides.

In the second leg against Bologna on 19 April, after Giles had levelled the aggregate scores with a penalty, the tie was decided by the toss of a coin. After holding his head in his hands and silently praying, Revie was relieved when Bremner called it right to ensure Leeds were in the Fairs Cup semi-final for the second season running.

After being all but written off after a poor start to the season, Leeds looked like serious contenders for three trophies. It had been a remarkable turnaround for Revie and his young side. However, as April turned to May, the Leeds bubble was about to burst.

In a brutal encounter, Leeds took on Chelsea at Villa Park on 29 April for a place in the 1967 FA Cup Final. From the off, the game was ill-tempered with goalkeeper Gary Sprake accused of kicking Chelsea's John Boyle in the face in only the seventh minute.

The first half continued to be tetchy with both sides dishing up crunching tackles but few chances. As the game headed to the interval, Tony Hateley, a former Revie transfer target, paid back some of the £100,000 Chelsea shelled out for him by heading the Blues in front. At half time, Revie pushed Bremner up front with Gray dropping deep. The ploy seemed to work as Leeds enjoyed most of the possession. With seven minutes left, a long Greenhoff ball found Cooper, who smashed it past Chelsea goalkeeper Peter Bonetti.

Just as the celebrations started referee Ken Burns ruled the goal offside. It was the referee's second controversial decision of that year's cup competition, having awarded Leeds a dubious penalty in the fifth round against Sunderland.

Seconds before the end, Bonetti was once again picking the ball out of his net after Peter Lorimer slammed in a shot after Giles passed to him from a Leeds free-kick. This time referee Burns disallowed the goal because the Chelsea wall had been infringed and ordered Giles to take the kick again. The second kick went nowhere and Leeds were out of the cup despite having scored twice.

According to Alex Montgomery of *The Sun* this was the game that changed Revie. He claims, 'From that moment on it confirmed what he believed was an anti-Leeds United agenda inside the game. He became more cynical and paranoid, like everyone had it in for him and his team.'

For Revie the result was devastating: 'We were sick – all football professionals should take these things in their stride I suppose, but let's face it, Wembley is their Mecca. It's terrible to lose your chance of playing there in such an unsatisfactory manner.

'For about half an hour after the final whistle, I felt completely numb. But the remorse really began to hit me when I met my son Duncan outside the ground. He was sobbing – and I felt like sitting down and crying with him.'

A 2–1 victory over Liverpool on 3 May gave Leeds an outside chance of securing the title but, as in 1965, Manchester United would not be denied. United's 6–1 win over West Ham on 6 May, on the same day Leeds United drew 2–2 with Chelsea, meant they were champions for the second time in three years.

A defeat at Manchester City on 8 May left Leeds unsure of their final place but a 2–0 win over Sunderland meant they finished in fourth place, and earned another crack at the Inter-Cities Fairs Cup.

All that was left of the 1966–67 season was a meaningless Yorkshire derby with Sheffield Wednesday on 15 May, which they won 1–0, and the first leg of the Fairs Cup semi-final against Scottish side Kilmarnock, in which they came out on top, 4–2. Rod Belfitt played the game of his life to score a hat-trick and effectively kill the tie stone dead.

A trademark defensive display saw a goalless draw in the second leg in Scotland on 24 May. The Leeds players headed off for their summer holidays knowing they were in the final of the Fairs Cup.

The competition had run so far behind schedule that the first leg of the final would not be played until 30 August when the 1967–68 season would have already kicked off. Revie would have to wait and see if this was the season when Leeds could finally secure some meaningful silverware.

12

LEEDS UNITED (1967–68)

'There were few dramatic moments in a Wembley final which will
go down as one more memorable for Leeds breaking their big-time
jinx than for the 90-minute play.'

Sam Leitch, Daily Mirror

The caption to the picture printed in the *Liverpool Echo* could have summed up
how Revie was feeling as Leeds United entered the 1967–8 season. Looking
pensive as his team lined up in the background on 18 August, 1967, it read,
'Caught off guard by the cameraman the Leeds United manager shows in this
Elland Road training picture what a worrying and harassing life it is.'

All summer Revie had been worried. Despite Leeds recording a profit of
£64,174, Revie had still to put that money to any use and he knew he needed
new firepower. With the exception of Giles, who top-scored with 12 goals, not a
single Leeds player had managed to get into double figures. Injuries had been a
problem with Revie only naming the same side in two matches all season. Still,
he had failed to add anyone to his squad.

After going so close in three major competitions, Revie knew there was a huge
amount of expectation on him to deliver a major piece of silverware. If Revie
needed reminding about his shortcomings, the *Leicester Chronicle* ran a piece about
the merits of so-called 'method football' whereby teams used a tightly packed
defence looking to hit teams on the break. Describing Leeds as the greatest believers
in the system, readers were quickly reminded Leeds had failed to win any honours.

Adding to his woes was the knowledge that chairman Harry Reynolds, the
man who shared his vision for Leeds and backed him both morally and financially,
was going to retire.

Reynolds, now 67 and increasingly using crutches to get around due to arthritis, had told Revie over the summer that now he had got the club on a sound financial footing he would retire at the beginning of the season.

With this going on in the background, Leeds opened the 1967–68 season with a 1–1 draw with Sunderland before falling to defeat against champions Manchester United, then Wolves. So going into the first leg of the 1967 Fairs Cup Final against Dinamo Zagreb they were rock bottom of the First Division (albeit having only played three games) and had scored only one goal.

Played out in oppressive heat in Yugoslavia, Revie selected semi-final hat-trick hero Rod Belfitt as the lone striker. Giving a good account of themselves, it looked as though Leeds would go in level at half time. That was until the 39th minute when Zagreb took the lead. Forced to chase the game, Leeds fell further behind on the hour mark, returning to Elland Road without the precious away goal.

On 4 September, Reynolds formally announced his retirement as Leeds chairman. According to the *Coventry Evening Telegraph* the boardroom upheaval meant Revie was now the favourite to replace Jimmy Hill as manager at Highfield Road. All Revie had to say was he knew nothing about any approach, was focused on the second leg of the Fairs Cup and was happy to see out his contract.

Despite having to score three times to win the return leg of the final at Elland Road, many of the players, such as O'Grady and Lorimer, were critical of Revie's defensive stance, and claimed he was too negative and overfilled their heads with opposition tactics. Leeds paid for their caution. Unable to break the deadlock, they were once again the bridesmaids and missed out on a major trophy as Dinamo Zagreb lifted the cup.

Such was the worry about being seen as 'nearly men', Bremner was compelled to write in *Shoot!* magazine, 'Make no mistake – Leeds United will not always be the "bridesmaid". All right, I know we have disappointed ourselves during the past three seasons by failing at the death in the FA Cup, the league championship and now the Inter-Cities Fairs Cup and the sum total of all our efforts during this time, in terms of trophies, has amounted to nil.'

After a 1–1 draw with Southampton, a 3–1 victory on 13 September over Luton Town opened the League Cup campaign in some style. But a defensive

1–0 win over Everton on 16 September again underlined the lack of firepower in the Leeds ranks. For once, Revie was not concerned.

Under the radar, Revie had been tracking Mick Jones of Sheffield United. At 22 years old Jones was a full England international and had scored 63 goals in 149 games for the Blades. After having several enquiries about Jones knocked back by Sheffield United manager John Harris, on 22 September Revie made his move, paying £100,000 for the striker's services.

Jones said of his decision to move: 'I really wasn't sure I wanted to leave Sheffield United. Then I met Don and he said to me, "Are you ambitious?" I already had a high opinion of him, good footballer and great manager, after talking to him for five minutes I said to him, "I would love to play for you."' At the time Revie told the press, 'We have been missing a lot of chances lately and Jones is just the man to stick them in.'

Making his debut in a 3–2 win over Leicester on 23 September, Jones scored his first goals for the club in a 9–0 drubbing of minnows Spora Luxembourg in the first round of the 1968 Fairs Cup. For the fans who felt robbed of goals it was a welcome bonus.

The arrival of Jones meant the departure of Peacock, who knew his injuries were becoming chronic. 'I knew I was near the end and Don came to see me and said he had spoken to the Plymouth manager and they agreed a £10,000 fee for me. He also arranged a nice signing-on fee for me. I was very grateful to him.' Also leaving the club was Willie Bell who, frustrated by the lack of first-team opportunities, went to Leicester City for £40,000.

When Chelsea travelled north on 7 October, they were a shadow of the club that had knocked out Leeds in last season's FA Cup semi-final. After a summer of dismay Tommy Docherty resigned as manager and Leeds compounded their misery by knocking seven past them in a dominant display. Bremner was involved in five of the goals before scoring with a spectacular overhead kick.

In the next game, Collins arrived at Elland Road with his new side Bury for the fourth round of the League Cup. It was an unhappy return for the Scot as Charlton, Greenhoff and Johanneson got on the scoresheet in a 3–0 win.

The dismissal of Bremner in an earlier game at Fulham cost Leeds dear. For arguing with the referee Bremner earned another FA charge, which resulted in a

28-day ban. With the club captain in such great form, the ban could not have come at a worse time.

A 7–0 win over Spora Luxembourg and a 2–0 win over Newcastle United were bookended by away losses to West Bromwich Albion and Manchester City. A 3–1 win over Arsenal saw Jones claim his first league goal on 4 November, while a 1–0 win at Manchester United saw Leeds firmly in contention for the league championship. However, a loss at Sheffield United on 11 November was the third game in the season where Leeds failed to win on the road.

The hoodoo was broken in the next game at Roker Park where Leeds recorded a 2–0 win over Sunderland to progress to the fifth round of the League Cup.

On 29 November, United resumed their European campaign with a visit to Partizan Belgrade. Leeds went into the first leg without Sprake, Giles, Jones, Johanneson and O'Grady but took a surprise lead in the 24th minute through Lorimer. Belfitt added a second goal eight minutes after the break, shooting home after Charlton headed a corner across goal. The wheels almost came off in the last ten minutes when Mick Bates was dismissed and Belgrade managed to grab a consolation goal.

With vital away goals in the bag, Leeds were guilty of taking the win for granted in the return leg. When Peter Lorimer put them one up in the 56th minute, Leeds took their foot off the gas and allowed Belgrade to score on the counterattack. A largely defensive display allowed a nervous Leeds to progress to the next round of the Fairs Cup.

For Sprake, the game against Liverpool on 9 December would be remembered for all the wrong reasons. With Liverpool leading 1–0 and spraying the ball around magnificently, Leeds were looking to hold on till they could regroup at half time. They never had the chance. A minute before the break, Sprake advanced to the edge of his area to collect a back pass. Looking to quickly recycle the ball, he shaped to throw it to left-back Cooper but instead the ball slipped out of his control and flew into the far corner of the net.

Whether he changed his mind mid-throw – as Cooper was being pressurised by Ian Callaghan while Roger Hunt was sniffing around the area – or simply lost his grip has never been fully explained.

At the time it was no laughing matter. Years later Revie was to say with a smile, 'I remember when Gary Sprake threw the ball into the net at Anfield. As soon as he did it the public address system started playing *Careless Hands* by Des O'Connor and the crowd quickly joined in!' Unfortunately for Sprake, the name was to stick.

A 2–0 win over Stoke City four days later put Leeds in the quarter-finals of the League Cup. Good form in cup competitions continued as Leeds earned a 1–0 win over Scottish side Hibernian ahead of their Fairs Cup second leg on 10 January, 1968.

They completed the year with a pair of wins, both home and away, over Yorkshire rivals Sheffield Wednesday, leaving them in a strong position going into the New Year. They lay third in the league; were in the semi-finals of the League Cup; looked forward to an FA Cup third-round tie at home to Derby County; and held the upper hand in their upcoming Fairs Cup tie.

If 1968 was shaping up to be a memorable year, then the omens looked good at Craven Cottage on 6 January. Everything just clicked as Leeds ran out 5–0 winners in what was widely seen as one of the most complete performances by a Leeds side. Even Revie was moved to say, 'In all the seven years I have been associated with them, Leeds United have never played as well as they did at Fulham. It was terrific.'

A Charlton header cancelled out an early Hibernian goal in the second leg of the Fairs Cup tie, ensuring safe passage in the competition, even if the intense pressure from the Scottish side made for uncomfortable viewing from the Leeds bench.

With a dominant 5–0 win over Southampton, Leeds were set up nicely for their League Cup semi-final clash against Brian Clough's Derby County. It would be the first of three games between the two sides in early 1968 – a two-legged semi-final and an FA Cup third-round tie.

In the League Cup match at the Baseball Ground on 17 January Derby gave Leeds a stern test. The away side needed a classic performance and a second-half Giles penalty to secure the win.

Just 10 days later, Leeds repeated the feat with a 2–0 FA Cup victory at Elland Road. Charlton and Lorimer's second-half goals secured a scrappy victory.

On 7 February, the trilogy was completed with the second leg of the League Cup semi-final. Leeds took the lead and never relinquished it, running out 3–2 winners. In a TV interview alongside Revie after the game Clough was left to rue: 'I felt we were put through the Leeds United machine today.'

For the first time in three years Leeds were back at Wembley with another opportunity to put the 'bridesmaid' tag to bed once and for all – but first came games in the league. Lorimer grabbed two goals in a 2–1 win over West Ham on 10 February. After a largely negative performance in the FA Cup fourth-round win over Nottingham Forest on 17 February, Leeds were ready to make the trip to Wembley to face Arsenal in the League Cup Final.

On 2 March, 1968, in only the second League Cup Final to be played at Wembley, Revie led out his Leeds United side. Both sides were desperate for silverware – Arsenal had not won anything for 15 years since becoming First Division champions in 1953, while Leeds, despite going close in recent years, had won nothing.

Unusually, the Leeds players found Revie in assured mood, telling them that winning this cup would be a springboard to even greater success. Bremner also boasted to the press, 'We are so confident of winning this one, I am only concerned we may be over-confident.'

Despite Charlton and Giles carrying injuries, Revie was able to name a full-strength side, with the only change being Paul Madeley coming in for a cup-tied Jones. Even though Arsenal were also at full strength, by common consent they had been going through a lean period.

Before the match, Ken Jones of the *Daily Mirror* tipped Leeds because of the maturity the experiences in the Fairs Cup had given them. Citing the leadership of Bremner, the brilliance of Revie and competence of the entire Leeds first XI, Ron Wylie of the *Sports Argus* joined Jones in his belief that it would be Leeds who lifted the cup.

The skies above Wembley were overcast with a light wind. From the first whistle, Leeds took the game to the Gunners launching wave after wave of attacks. When Cooper struck in the 19th minute to give Leeds the upper hand, Arsenal, under the leadership of Frank McLintock, seemed to be getting a foothold in the game.

After that, Leeds played a cautious game and made little or no attempt to score again, with their only threat coming from Eddie Gray. Drama came midway through the first half when keeper Sprake was heavily challenged by McLintock, resulting in an ugly melee among the players in the goalmouth.

Writing in his autobiography Sprake said, 'There were a few unsavoury incidents but nothing major – even the incident with McLintock was nothing really, just a few handbags. However, the tension between the two teams was genuine and was like the hostility that had developed between us and Chelsea.

'The London press hated us, and this certainly created a North/South divide. Revie really stoked us up to put one over the London clubs every time we played them.'

Even though Arsenal kept pressing, they still only managed to stretch Sprake to one save in the second half in what was described by *Goal* magazine as 'one of the poorest (if not dullest) big games at Wembley'.

When the final whistle blew, a young girl reached out her arms to be lifted over the barriers by her father, 'We did it, pet!' Revie said as he hugged his daughter, Kim. After four years of trying Leeds were finally able to put some silverware into their trophy cabinet. While the Leeds fans danced and taunted their rivals with chants of 'dirty Arsenal!' in response to heckling from the north London crowd throughout the game, neutrals would have switched off in their droves after another dull performance at Wembley.

Goalscorer Cooper reckoned, 'The most important thing about that success was that it broke the ice as regards winning something. Up until then we had been regarded as the bridesmaids, always coming runners-up in the League or losing cup semi-finals and finals.

'We didn't pick up as many trophies as we should have but after that win against Arsenal we went on to some big things. Our side wasn't far off its peak then. All the players were there and it was just a pleasure to play in that team.'

Sam Leitch, writing in the *Daily Mirror*, commented, 'There were few dramatic moments in a Wembley final which will go down as one more memorable for Leeds breaking their big-time jinx than for the 90-minute play.'

A cautious Revie later said, 'Before the final, I was seriously thinking of goading the lads by opening an empty trophy case and telling them: "This is what you have to show for all your sweat and toil in recent seasons!" I hate to think what might have happened had Leeds lost this one, too. You can only take so many disappointments.'

Goal reported, 'By winning the second League Cup Wembley final, Leeds United finally achieved success after so many seasons of finishing runners-up in one major competition or another. But it was the way they triumphed on the day that won few friends.'

The criticism did not affect Revie who told Ken Jones of the *Daily Mirror*, 'Now we have won this trophy, we feel that a great weight has been lifted off our shoulders. At last Leeds has cast away that champion runners-up tag – and are now in a good position to win more honours.

'I am positive we will take another title before the end of the season. Our best chance must be the FA Cup, but the league championship is still my real goal.' Alongside the story was a picture of a beaming Revie, cradling the newly-won League Cup.

After the highpoint of Wembley there was controversy in the very next game, a week later, on 9 March, in the fifth round FA Cup tie with Bristol City. Goals from Jones and Lorimer in the 11 minutes before half time put United in a commanding position, but the game finished with ugly scenes as Gary Sprake was sent off. Chris Garland brought Billy Bremner down and as referee Arthur Dimond rushed over to book him, all hell let loose with Sprake punching Garland after he allegedly spat in Sprake's face. Peter Lorimer was forced to keep goal for the dying minutes of the game which saw Leeds win 2–0.

Three straight draws followed in the league yet those points were enough to take Leeds top. They were level on points with Manchester City and Manchester United but ahead on goal average.

Leeds now faced second-placed City in a crucial match played in front of a crowd of 51,818, Elland Road's best of the season. A 2–0 win added to an unbeaten run which stretched to 22 games as Leeds prepared to face Glasgow Rangers in the fourth round of the Fairs Cup, on 26 March. This was another cagey, goalless performance leaving everything to play for in the return at Elland Road on 9 April.

A goal from Madeley against Sheffield United was enough to see Leeds through to the semi-final of the FA Cup for the second consecutive year, while a 3–0 win a week later against the same opponents saw them maintain their title charge.

A handball from a certain Alex Ferguson led to a penalty against Glasgow Rangers in the Fairs Cup return leg at Elland Road. After Giles duly converted, Lorimer made sure of a 2–0 victory. So Leeds United found themselves in their third semi-final of the year, where they would face Scottish opposition again in the form of Dundee.

The Easter period kicked off in unpromising fashion at Tottenham. Leeds conceded their first goals in seven games to see the end of a 26-game unbeaten run. The same day Manchester United regained the First Division leadership by beating Fulham 4–0 at Craven Cottage. Manchester City closed in on third spot by beating Chelsea, though fourth-placed Liverpool surprisingly lost 2–1 at Anfield against Sheffield United.

But Leeds were still in a strong position and two 1–0 wins, away to Coventry and at home to Spurs, left them well-placed. A 3–1 win at home to West Bromwich Albion kept up the momentum, although Manchester United retained supremacy with a 1–0 victory over Sheffield United. With Manchester City dropping a point at Wolves, it looked like the title would go to either Manchester United or Leeds.

Leeds had the chance to regain top spot on 23 April as they played their match in hand away to a Stoke City side that was second bottom of the table. It looked like an easy two points. But goals from Charlton and Greenhoff were not enough as relegation-threatened Stoke City, fighting for their lives, pulled out their best performance of the season to come out as 3–2 winners. The loss to Stoke was the catalyst for a late-season Leeds collapse.

The following week in the FA Cup semi-final Gary Sprake had one of his momentary lapses of concentration and kicked a weak ball straight into the path of Everton striker Jimmy Husband, whose shot was only stopped from crossing the line by the hands of Charlton.

Everton left winger Johnny Morrissey converted the ensuing penalty to unceremoniously dump Leeds out of the FA Cup. A 1–1 draw in the semi-final of the Fairs Cup was the only highlight in a barren May that saw Leeds lose their last three games, against Liverpool, Arsenal and Burnley. Much to everyone's relief, a Gray goal put Leeds in the final of the Fairs Cup for the second year running. Their opponents would be Hungarian side Ferencváros.

After watching his team fade away at the end of the season, Revie was glad the two-legged final would be played on 7 August with a return in Hungary on 11 September. Having been in pursuit of four trophies all season long, the Leeds players were glad of the rest. All in all, it had been a tough but rewarding season and Revie could finally call his boys winners.

13

LEEDS UNITED (1968–69)

'After the disappointments over the past four years, when we got into
those final few minutes, my heart nearly stopped beating. Every minute as
the final whistle drew near seemed like an hour.'

Don Revie

With the first leg of the Fairs Cup scheduled for 7 August, Revie had called his
players back early for pre-season training. Standing on the centre spot of Elland
Road as the players gathered around him Revie stated his intent for the coming
season, 'You are going to win the championship this time, lads, and what's more
you are going to do so without losing a single league match!'

What's more they were going to do it in style with Revie telling a press
conference in July, 'Next season we intend to open up and play attacking football
away from Elland Road. We feel this will give us the edge we need to lift major
trophies.

'Only two teams scored more home goals than us last season but now we
have established ourselves in the First Division. Now, the players have the
knowledge and experience, we feel we can be more adventurous away from
home. From now on we intend to let the players off the leash.'

Looking ahead to the new season in the pages of the *Sports Argus* Revie was
confident enough to tip his own side for the league championship, writing,
'Providing we can maintain our usual fine home record we should at least win
either the championship or FA Cup. Last season we made the mistake of a draw
when we should have gambled for victory.'

In an interview in *Goal* Norman Hunter echoed the comments of the boss:
'The championship is the thing we are after now. We've been so close before; it

must be our turn this time. It gets tougher every year, of course, but with the team getting better all the time, it doesn't worry us too much.'

If any of the 25,268 spectators who turned up at Elland Road for the first leg of the Fairs Cup final against Ferencváros of Hungary were expecting an exciting, free-flowing game of football they were sorely disappointed. A scrappy game ensued that was marked by roughhouse tactics from the visitors, with the only goal of the game coming from Jones poking the ball home from two yards in the 41st minute.

Reporting for the *Daily Mirror* Ken Jones wrote, 'The reputation of Ferencváros as a team of glowing quality was lost last night as they succumbed to the cynicism of European football.

'For Leeds, on the threshold of a season when they have promised to play with more ambition, it was a frustrating experience. Without a better-than-fair share of the breaks on the return in Budapest on 11 September, a one-goal lead is unlikely to be enough.'

The problem for Leeds still seemed to be the lack of a recognised goalscorer, something Revie had still not addressed as Leeds readied themselves for their opening league match against Southampton at the Dell on 10 August.

The omens did not look good when Leeds found themselves 1–0 down after 90 seconds when a misdirected header by Charlton slipped past the immobile Sprake. Enthused by their early good luck, Saints surged forwards only to be caught on the break as Peter Lorimer grabbed an equaliser from 20 yards.

Just five minutes before the break Mick Jones put Leeds in front. The second half was all the away team with substitute Terry Hibbert, who had come on for a hobbling Bremner, making it three after 63 minutes. Apart from Bremner's torn muscle it had not been a bad day out in Hampshire.

A 4–1 win at Elland Road against Queens Park Rangers got the home fans cheering. The 2–0 victory against Stoke on 17 August meant that, after only three games of the new season, Leeds were the only undefeated side in the First Division.

After opening a 2–0 lead through Belfitt and O'Grady at Portman Road there were jitters when newly promoted Ipswich pulled level at 2–2 before

Hibbert popped up in the 78th minute to secure the win with his third goal of the campaign.

As Leeds headed to the City Ground, home of Nottingham Forest, at the end of August, Leeds were the in-form side and stood proudly in top spot. In a preview of the game, *Goal* magazine carried the headline, 'Leeds ready to set fire to Forest'. At half time Revie was not happy. Being held 1–1, the manager felt Leeds could have made more of their chances. As Revie waxed lyrical, keeper Sprake tried to motion to the boss that smoke was coming from under the dressing room door. On several occasions he was told to keep quiet because Revie was talking.

Kim Revie said, 'The stand was burning overhead but dad was concentrating so hard on the game he paid no attention to what was going on.' Over 30,000 people were evacuated as fire ravaged the main stand turning it into a smouldering mess. After a conference with the referee Revie was left with no choice other than to agree to postpone the match.

Luckily no one was injured. However, the Leeds players lost valuables such as cash and rings, with Revie telling the press the club had arranged for players to return to their homes wearing their kit.

In their following game, on 28 August, Leeds dropped their first point of the season in a disappointing home draw with Sunderland, while the last day of the month brought a vital battle against title rivals Liverpool, also at Elland Road. For this game both Giles and Madeley were on the injured list, giving opportunities to Belfitt and Hibbert. A goal from Mick Jones in a 1–0 win saw Leeds pick up maximum points.

After a good 2–1 victory against Wolves the following Saturday, Leeds boarded the plane for the second leg of their Fairs Cup final against Ferencváros in the Nep Stadium, on 11 September. Considering Sprake had been labelled 'careless hands' the previous season, the goalkeeper more than repaid Revie's faith in him with a superb display in Budapest.

Despite repeated onslaughts from a desperate home side the Leeds defence held on to become the first British club to win the Fairs Cup. More than that, they had now held their nerve in two major finals. Frank McGhee in the *Daily Mirror* claimed their success in Hungary put paid to their reputation as football's perennial bridesmaids. He wrote, 'Leeds have at last fought their way into British football's Hall of Fame – the small select group of clubs who have won a major European title.

'If anyone tries to deride them after this as soccer's champion runners-up, they can point to a trophy every club in Europe would be proud to possess – the gleaming silver Fairs Cup that was carried round the Nep Stadium here tonight by Leeds skipper Billy Bremner.'

At the end of the match Revie commented, 'After the disappointments over the past four years, when we got into those final few minutes, my heart nearly stopped beating. Every minute as the final whistle drew near seemed like an hour. It was a real team effort here tonight. Ferencváros pressed very hard, particularly in the second half when they attacked all the time. The way the boys kept their heads and their cool play was really tremendous.'

Just a week after winning the 1967–68 Fairs Cup, and having drawn 1–1 with Leicester City in the league, Leeds were back in European action for the 1968–69 competition against Standard Liege at their Stade Maurice Dufrasne home. Leeds reverted to type, keeping it tight in a goalless draw and setting themselves up nicely for the second leg at Elland Road.

Back in the league, Leeds played Arsenal on 21 September. Even though there had already been a civic reception in the city to celebrate the Fairs Cup, Revie sent two junior players out onto the pitch with the League Cup and Fairs Cup to show the fans, as Revie put it, 'what our hard work has achieved'.

Whether this was genuine sentiment or just mind games from Revie, the ploy seemed to work as Leeds battered Arsenal into submission in a fantastic 2–0 win. When the Gunners arrived at Elland Road they were top, now they trailed by goal average.

After a pretty straightforward 2–1 win over Bristol City in the third round of the League Cup, with Giles finally returning after a long layoff, Leeds arrived at Maine Road, home of the champions Manchester City. It had been a disappointing start for the Citizens and Leeds were expected to show their own championship credentials by vanquishing their rivals.

In the end, Revie was a helpless spectator as his dream of going all season unbeaten went up in smoke. In a stunning game, City oozed class as they ripped pretenders Leeds apart with Colin Bell scoring two goals. Shaking his head with disappointment, Revie claimed too many players were out of sorts.

Single-goal victories at Newcastle and Sunderland at the beginning of October took Leeds back to the top of the table as Liverpool dropped a point in the Merseyside derby, and Arsenal drew at Manchester City. Goals from Lorimer and Giles secured a 2–0 win against West Ham in a bad-tempered clash on 12 October, with Hammers winger Harry Redknapp being dismissed for kicking out in retaliation.

Much worse was to come: four days later Leeds surprisingly lost 2–1 at Crystal Palace in the League Cup, meekly surrendering the trophy they had been so proud to win the previous March. That was as nothing, though, to the hiding that they took on 19 October at Burnley. A young Turf Moor outfit won 5–1, the worst defeat Leeds had suffered since they lost 5–0 at Anfield two years previously.

They had to rely on a Bremner goal two minutes from time to see off Standard Liege in the second leg of the Fairs Cup first round after the Belgians had taken a two-goal lead at Elland Road. Such shaky performances led many critics to question whether the rot had set in, but United stabilised matters with a return to defensive basics, resulting in three successive goalless draws.

A fantastic 2–0 win over Napoli at Elland Road in the second round of the Fairs Cup on 13 November, with two goals from Charlton, seemed to point to an improvement in form. A reversal of the same result in Naples saw the clubs level on aggregate and Bremner managing to call right on the toss of coin to ensure safe passage to the next round.

In between the two legs, it was back to winning ways as Coventry City were dispatched 1–0 on 16 November and Everton 2–1 four days later. A 1–1 draw with Chelsea after their European excursions was followed by a 2–0 win over Sheffield Wednesday on 7 December and a 1–1 draw at Upton Park against West Ham.

Beginning with a 5–1 win over Hannover 96 on 18 December, Leeds smashed in 13 goals in three games. This included gaining revenge over Harry Potts and his Burnley side with a rampant 6–1 win on 21 December, which for Revie was the perfect early Christmas present. A 2–1 win against Newcastle

United on Boxing Day left Leeds perfectly placed to challenge league leaders Liverpool for top spot in January. When the game against West Bromwich Albion was postponed because of severe frost Leeds ended 1968 in second place, two points off Liverpool with two games in hand.

But there was disappointment when Leeds, despite being among the favourites for the FA Cup, crashed out to Sheffield Wednesday, 3–1, in a third-round replay in front of their own fans on 8 January, 1969, having been held to a 1–1 draw at Hillsborough four days earlier. For the first time, Leeds were now only pursuing two trophies and had all their key players available for selection.

There was crowd trouble when Leeds met Manchester United at Elland Road on 11 January. The 2–1 scoreline was largely forgotten about as missiles were thrown resulting in about 50 spectators needing hospital treatment.

On 18 January Leeds won a point in a hard-fought goalless draw at White Hart Lane but the result was overshadowed by the leg break suffered by Spurs full-back Joe Kinnear. And what looked like a routine visit to Loftus Road on 24 January was anything but. Queens Park Rangers, who were bottom of the table, took the fight to Leeds from the off, going close in the first minute.

A goal from Jones provided brief respite as Rangers continually attacked the Leeds defence. At full time Leeds were lucky to hold on and walk away with two points. Captain Bremner later said it was the hardest game of the season. Writing in *Goal* magazine he said, 'Without any doubt the toughest of all for us was that Friday night in January against Queens Park Rangers at Loftus Road. Rangers threw everything at us and never stopped coming forward. Believe me, we were relieved to hear the final whistle that evening.'

A torn thigh muscle kept Giles out of the 3–0 drubbing of Coventry City on 1 February and, three days later, Leeds finally finished off Hanover 96 to gain passage to the quarter-finals of the Fairs Cup for the third consecutive season.

In the middle of a snowstorm they met Ipswich Town at Elland Road on 12 February. Despite playing in the most appalling weather conditions, goals from Jones and Belfitt saw Leeds carry off all the points in a 2–0 victory. More significantly, Leeds deposed Liverpool at the top of the league, leading by a point after 29 games.

Snow and frost were still on the ground when Chelsea came to visit on 15 February. Having kicked the game off at 3.15 p.m., a quarter of an hour later than everyone else, after 75 minutes they knew their nearest rivals Liverpool had lost 2–0 to Nottingham Forest. Leeds were content to hold on to the 1–0 lead Lorimer had given them after 58 minutes and were now three points clear with 12 games to go.

Revie, though, struck a note of caution in his weekly column in the *Sports Argus:* 'Liverpool must be the team I fear most because of their remarkable consistency and ability to play well under extreme pressure. This latter attribute can only be attained through experience and I have had enough evidence this season to feel confident that Leeds United now possess this quality. It was particularly evident when we beat Chelsea.

'One could sense the tension building up in the United players as they battled to overcome the problem. The most encouraging feature was that they did not allow this tension to interfere with the normal tempo of their game.

'They continued to attack patiently and skilfully and reaped the reward when Peter Lorimer scored the winning goal. In previous years we would probably have panicked if we had failed to score earlier on and fallen into the trap of hammering high balls into the Chelsea goalmouth.'

The weather got the better of the game between Leeds and Sheffield Wednesday on 22 February, with a frozen pitch postponing the match. Any hopes Liverpool had of closing the gap in their game against West Ham were dashed when they could only manage a 1–1 draw at Upton Park.

The rescheduled match with Nottingham Forest caused by the fire earlier in the season saw Jones and Lorimer register a 2–0 win as Leeds stormed into a commanding four-point lead at the top of the league with a game in hand over Liverpool.

With Liverpool in FA Cup action it was the turn of Leeds to strengthen their hand in the league when Southampton came visiting from the south coast on 1 March. There were nerves a-plenty as the sprightly Saints pushed a jittery Leeds all the way in a 3–2 win. Even though Revie was angry a crowd of only 33,000 had turned up to watch the league leaders, the gap between the top two had opened to six points with only ten games remaining.

After so many glory nights in the Fairs Cup, Revie was disappointed by his team's performance against Hungarian side Ujpest Dozsa on 5 March. Well beaten by a classy side who had mastered the counterattack, the 1–0 win flattered Leeds somewhat.

Normal service in the league resumed on 8 March when Leeds ruthlessly destroyed Stoke City in front of their home fans at the Victoria Ground, leaving England goalkeeper Gordon Banks to pick the ball out of his own net five times in a 5–1 rout. With Liverpool out of action – their game against Arsenal was postponed because the Gunners had eight men out through sickness – Leeds stood on top of the league a full eight points clear.

Then illness ravaged the Leeds team that travelled to Budapest on 5 March to play the second leg of their Fairs Cup tie against Ujpest Dozsa. Reaney, Charlton and O'Grady were all left at home with flu with Bremner, Madeley, Cooper, Jones and Hunter all unwell on arrival. There was little hope of winning the tie. Leeds, with Bremner at full-back, were lucky to hold out until the 62nd minute, eventually going out 2–0. Revie claimed that if he had had a full team he would have won.

With the Fairs Cup now gone too, Leeds could focus their full attention on winning the league. On 29 March, after a frustrating goalless draw with Wolves, Leeds had their lead cut as Liverpool ran out 2–1 winners at QPR.

Another 0–0 draw, this time with Sheffield Wednesday on 1 April, was only offset by the 1–1 draw from the rearranged Liverpool-Arsenal game. On 5 April, Liverpool's drab 1–0 win over Wolves was offset by Leeds' equally dull 1–0 win over Manchester City.

As the gap narrowed further to five points, Liverpool were due to play their game in hand against Stoke City on 8 April. Win that and the gap would be only three points. With Liverpool's easy-looking game against relegation-threatened Leicester City coming up on 12 April, Leeds had to go to Highbury and get something out of third-placed Arsenal. But a goalless draw at Stoke City left Liverpool manager Bill Shankly rueing the fact that his side only managed one shot on target.

With the Whites' lead down to four points, Liverpool kept up the pressure in their next game, recording a 2–0 victory at Filbert Street, Leicester. Things were not so smooth at Highbury. After just four minutes Arsenal striker Bobby Gould was left sprawled on the floor by a left hook from Leeds' goalkeeper Sprake. Apparently, Gould had 'kicked him in the nuts' and called him a 'Welsh so and so'. Even though both Sprake and Gould were booked, many observers felt Sprake was lucky to stay on the pitch.

Just over 10 minutes later Jones took the lead for the visitors, only to be pegged back by a George Graham volley on 34 minutes. Just before the interval Giles regained Leeds' advantage earning a 2–1 win. The gap stayed at three points with only four games to play.

With Leeds beating Leicester 2–0 and Liverpool hammering Ipswich 4–0 on Saturday 19 April the gap was still three points. Leeds only needed four points from three games but they involved trips to Anfield and fourth-placed Everton.

On 22 April Liverpool were at Coventry while Leeds travelled to Everton. With a potential title decider coming up at Anfield six days later, Liverpool were desperate for a win. In the end both sides came out of their respective matches with goalless draws.

Of the two managers, Shankly and Revie, it was the Leeds man who had more to be happy about. Leeds had only two games left, one at Anfield and then the other two days later, at home to Nottingham Forest. A win or a draw at Liverpool would guarantee Leeds the title. Even a defeat would mean that Leeds could still win the title if they beat Forest at Elland Road.

The eagerly anticipated Anfield clash played on 28 April, 1969, failed to live up to its billing. Very few people had watched such an important match where so few chances were created. The game resembled a relegation battle as both sides worked hard not to concede a goal. With so much at stake the press was expecting fireworks but just like the cup final four years earlier, they got a damp squib.

Liverpool's midfield players couldn't build up anything as the ball was being repeatedly hit backwards and forwards over their heads. The more the game went on, the more people were convinced Leeds wouldn't lose.

The goalless score line was unimportant, as the result meant Leeds United were league champions. At the end of the 90 minutes Revie encouraged Bremner to take his team on a lap of honour. When the players stood before the Kop end they were at first met with silence. Then a lone Scouser started chanting

'Champions! Champions! Champions!' as the 53,000 Leeds and Liverpool fans came together to salute Revie's team.

Giles remembered, 'It was a fabulous moment, a fabulous feeling to be taking the applause of this truly great crowd. There was a lot of respect between Leeds and Liverpool, we had many big matches with them back then, played in the best spirit. Bill Shankly was gracious too, and typically funny when he came to congratulate us. Shanks got on well with Don.

'Apparently he would ring up Don about 11 o'clock on a Saturday night to talk about the events of the day in football – and frankly I doubt if they spoke about any other subject in all the time Shanks was making those calls. So Shankly came into the dressing room.

'We all went silent, waiting for his verdict. He thought about it for a moment. "The best team drew," he said. And through laughter we had a fair idea who the best team was in his estimation. But it was done with humour and style and it makes the memory of that wonderful night just a bit warmer.'

That night on Merseyside the transformation of Leeds United into an English superpower was complete. Just eight years after being so broke they were forced into taking a risk with an untested, young manager, Leeds had swept all before them.

Over 46,000 fans went wild when Leeds United wound up the season on a record-breaking note. Already crowned champions, they beat Nottingham Forest 1–0 at Elland Road to smash the 38-year-old First Division points record for a season by taking their total to 67. And in doing so they went through the entire year unbeaten at home.

It was a night of joy and tears as Revie and his players showed off the championship trophy, but it needed a great late goal to snatch that record. It was Giles who kicked off the party when he volleyed home a superb winner six minutes from time against Forest.

At the final whistle thousands of fans poured on to the pitch, some crying, some cheering, but all unashamedly worshipping their heroes. It was a night to treasure for the two men hugging that precious trophy who had done so much to make it all possible – manager Revie and skipper Bremner. Revie, near to tears himself at one stage, said, 'This is the happiest day of my life, truly. I think 67 points is a fantastic achievement, but it might be beaten. I don't think the record of only two league defeats in a season will be.'

Two days later there were more honours for Revie when he was named Bell's Whisky Manager of the Year. He won 15 of the 16 votes of a panel of sports writers who decided the award.

Winning the £1,000 award, he followed the previous two winners, Jock Stein and Sir Matt Busby, as he prepared for the coming season. He hoped to join them in the exclusive club of being a European Cup winner. Based on the past season no one would have bet against him.

14

LEEDS UNITED (1969–70)

'We should have won it. I have never seen the lads play better.
I don't know where they got their energy from.'

Don Revie

The 1969–70 season was still six weeks away but that did not stop Revie from setting down a marker for the coming year. On 23 June word had got to Revie that Allan Clarke of newly relegated Leicester City wanted to leave. He wanted to play for England in the 1970 World Cup and the only way that was going to happen was if he was playing regularly in the top flight.

Just a year earlier Leicester had signed the marksman for a British record fee of £150,000. In order for Revie to get his man Leicester manager Frank O'Farrell told him in an early-morning phone call he would have to beat that, but he had to be quick because Chelsea, Everton, Liverpool and Manchester United were all interested.

Instantly Revie offered £166,000, which was quickly accepted. Now all he had to do was convince the player himself. Within hours Revie and his wife had arrived in Leicester. Elsie was going to spend the day with her sisters while the Leeds manager was going to drive the short five-mile distance from the city centre to secure the signature of Clarke. When Revie arrived at Clarke's house he was greeted by the player's wife Margaret with the news that Clarke was ill in bed with gastroenteritis.

What Revie did not know as he waited in the dining room for Clarke to come down was the striker had secretly been hoping Leeds United would come in for him. Two years earlier he had turned down a move to Manchester United from Fulham simply because they had not met him at the train station. Groggy and ill, Clarke was impressed Revie had travelled to his house to convince him to sign for Leeds.

'He came to my house and it was obvious he'd done his homework when he met me in my dining room. Leicester were paying me £100 a week and he asked me how much it would take to get me to Leeds. God's truth, I asked for £10 a week more and he wouldn't give it to me. He said all his players were on the same wage. Who was I to disbelieve him?

'I signed a two-year deal at Leeds for the same money. Do you think any players would do that today? But I wanted to play for Leeds and the rest is history. It was only when I got there, I realised I had been told a bare-faced lie. There were players on more. But I didn't go knocking on his door. I thought right, I'll show you how good I am.'

Although this did not mean there were doubts about how Clarke would fit in, Bremner said, 'I had played against him and knew what his ability was like, but he also had a reputation for being the sort of person who kept himself to himself and didn't have much to do with the rest of the squad.'

Within 24 hours, Clarke was a Leeds United player and the fee made him the most expensive player in league history. Even though the board had no hesitation in sanctioning the fee for Clarke, Revie was worried about money with Leeds reporting a loss of £45,682. Most of their money had been spent on ground repairs and payroll.

Finances was something which was always on his mind. As Revie explained in a radio interview, 'You take it when we won the title in 1969. I went to the directors and said, "Now we have won the league, the players are going to want better wages, more money, bigger bonuses, can we get a big company to put their name across our shirts?"

'The directors thought it was a good idea, so I said why don't I arrange a meeting with Alan Hardaker, the secretary of the Football League? The directors thought it was a good idea so I went over to meet him at his office in Lytham St Anne's.'

The meeting between Revie and Hardaker began cordially enough – that was until Revie broached the subject of a sponsor emblazoning their name across the Leeds United shirt. 'What's this?' the curmudgeonly football administrator said to the league championship manager. 'Are you trying to turn this game into a circus?'

The conversation quickly descended into a full-blown argument with Revie telling Hardaker prophetically, 'One day it will come to pass that every team in the country will have a big company written across their chests.' Just as English clubs would accept European football, so would sponsors' names become a familiar sight at football grounds around the country.

Long before he lost the battle over shirt sponsorship, Revie's son later remembered a conversation with his father long before he had enjoyed any success with Leeds United. 'I remember him taking me on to the pitch at Elland Road in 1963 or 1964 and it was a tip. It was just like a slag heap.

'There was a shed at one end, there was a kop at the other. The pitch was awful, and dad just pointed around and said, "One day son there'll be boxes here, there'll be people coming for lunch at 12, not coming at five to three. There'll be sponsorship on the shirts. There'll be television worldwide and it will be a complete revolution." I looked at him as if he was mad, but everything he said has happened.'

From a personal point of view Revie was in a good place financially. First, in May, a week after winning the championship, Italian club Torino came in with a bid for him. The *Daily Mirror* reported that the salary was to be three times as much as Leeds were paying. It got as far as Torino officials making the trip to the UK to discuss terms with Revie. Not to be outdone, their city rivals Juventus came in with their own offer of £30,000 a year.

In the end the Leeds board reacted the way they had always done in the past, by offering Revie, who was still in the middle of a seven-year contract, an extension that would keep him at Elland Road until 1975. It was reported that Revie was now the highest-paid manager in the league on £15,000 a year, far higher than his nearest rival, the now-retired Matt Busby who had only been earning £10,000.

Revie was focused not only on winning the European Cup but also dominating English football going into the 1970s. He set out his stall when speaking to his players ahead of their first appearance in the 1969 Charity Shield at Elland Road. Revie said, 'We lost only twice on our way to the league championship last season. This time, we don't want to lose at all.'

Reporter Ken Jones wrote in the *Daily Mirror*, 'Such ambition in a European Cup season suggests that Leeds are aiming for the impossible and that their rivals will benefit from it during the hard slog ahead. But recent history shows that the improvement of Leeds has been consistent.'

In the Charity Shield game on 2 August against cup holders Manchester City, Leeds showed they intended to start as they had left off in May, blending flashes of individual brilliance with the functional excellence of their team play.

Goals from Charlton and Gray put Leeds two up and they never looked in danger of relinquishing the lead, although a late Colin Bell goal served as the consolation for City. The *Daily Mirror* reported, 'Teams should realise when Leeds go two up, they very rarely fail to close the game out.'

If Tottenham thought there was going to be any change in the champions' winning mentality when the clubs met for their opening game on 9 August they were sadly mistaken. Bremner opened the scoring after only 15 minutes. And showing no signs of nerves from carrying such a hefty price tag, Clarke, partnered by Lorimer for his league debut, nodded home on 57 minutes to endear him to the Elland Road crowd. A goal from Jimmy Greaves for Tottenham came against the run of play before Giles put matters beyond any doubt from the penalty spot.

A goalless, ill-tempered game against Arsenal four days later saw 12 minutes of injury time added at the end and Leeds extending their unbeaten run to 30 games, overtaking a record Burnley set in 1921. After missing the first two games through injury, Jones partnered Clarke for a visit to Nottingham Forest's City Ground. In a 4–1 win, the two players just clicked, adding an extra dimension to Leeds.

There then followed three consecutive 1–1 draws with Arsenal, Newcastle United and Burnley before they faced Everton at Goodison Park. At one point Leeds were 3–0 down before storming back with goals from Clarke and Bremner, but in the end it was too little, too late and their unbeaten run was over.

A 1–0 win against Third Division Fulham in the League Cup third round on 2 September was their first win in five games, although they were lucky not to get beaten in a 2–2 draw at home to Manchester United – only a spectacular bicycle kick from Bremner saved the day late on.

Once again there were worries about Sprake after a poor performance against Manchester United but Revie stuck with the goalkeeper for the 2–1 victory at Sheffield Wednesday on 13 September. Thrashing SK Lyn Oslo 10–0 at Elland Road on 17 September in their inaugural European Cup tie was a statement of intent in the competition that Revie valued higher than them all.

A 2–0 win over Chelsea in the league on 20 September was a much-needed boost but the 1–1 draw against the same side four days later in the third round of the League Cup caused a headache. The replay was scheduled a day after Leeds met SK Lyn Oslo in their return leg. Revie declared that he would pick completely different sides for the two games, but in the end arrangements were made with the Football League and the Chelsea replay was delayed by a week.

There were injury worries when Leeds beat Coventry City 2–1 at Highfield Road on 27 September with Clarke, Hunter and Giles all picking up knocks. None of the trio featured in the return leg with SK Lyn Oslo on 1 October as Leeds ran out 6–1 winners.

It needed Giles to convert penalties in both halves to secure the points against Stoke City in a 2–1 win at Elland Road on 4 October and with several players out there were few tears shed when Leeds lost their League Cup replay with Chelsea 2–0 on 6 October.

After a pair of 1–1 draws against West Bromwich Albion and Crystal Palace, both away from home, Clarke was back in the side to nick two goals against Derby County in a 2–0 win at Elland Road. On 29 October, Lorimer grabbed a hat-trick as Leeds hammered a hapless Nottingham Forest in a midweek game at Elland Road.

For the third consecutive match away from Elland Road, Leeds could only manage a drab goalless draw with Sunderland. Indifferent away form was usually followed up with a sparkling performance at Elland Road and this was the case on 8 November when Ipswich were dispatched 4–0.

Heavy rain lashed down when Leeds welcomed Ferencváros to Elland Road on 12 November. A muddy pitch favoured the home side, who put three past the Hungarians with no reply. The scoreline was repeated in the second leg on 26

November, seeing Leeds through to the quarter-finals of the European Cup in the New Year.

The *Yorkshire Evening Post* reported that, as reward for gaining a place in the last eight of the European Cup, the club had bought their manager a five-bedroom house, Three Chimneys at Aldwoodley, at a cost of £18,000 in the exclusive Sand Moor area of Leeds. The house had originally been owned by board member Manny Cussins. As soon as the article appeared Revie reacted with anger accusing the paper of invading his privacy and disputed the sums of money involved.

Shortly after moving in Revie invited all of Elsie's family to move in with him. Daughter Kim said, 'Mum's family that dad brought from Scotland to live with us in Leeds were my gran, two great aunts and one great uncle who were in their 70s and 80s. Four of the greatest characters you could hope to meet and the love between them and dad was tangible. They are part of virtually every recollection I have of growing up.'

Another draw on the road at the Dell against Southampton on 15 November was the fifth time Leeds had failed to win away from home. A 2–0 win at home to Sunderland and a 1–1 draw with Liverpool on 22 November kept them within touching distance of league leaders Everton but even at this relatively early part of the season they were already six points behind.

Their poor form away from home came to an end on 29 November with a fine 2–1 win against Manchester City at Maine Road. From there they won three in a row against Wolves, Sheffield Wednesday and West Ham, before facing Newcastle United at St James' Park. Before Leeds could compose themselves they were 2–0 down and despite Giles giving some hope with a 25-yard screamer, Leeds left the North East on the wrong end of a 2–1 score line.

The following day was the eagerly awaited top-of-the-table clash with Everton. If there had been charges of complacency when facing Newcastle on Boxing Day, a fired-up Leeds completely dominated the side who hoped to replace them as champions. A Jones brace put them 2–0 up and they were unlucky to concede a late goal against the run of play.

Being married to a Scot, Hogmanay was always a huge occasion in the Revie household where the Leeds manager would often play the master of ceremonies,

ABOVE: Revie in action for Leicester City during his first full season as a professional, in a goalless draw against Brentford in the FA Cup, 25 January, 1947.

RIGHT: The injury jinx strikes. Having suffered a nasal haemorrhage, Revie listens to the 1949 Leicester City v Wolves FA Cup Final on the radio in hospital.

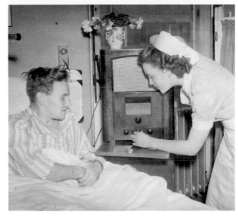

BELOW: Revie's surprise switch to Hull City in November 1949 was front-page news in the *Sporting Mirror*.

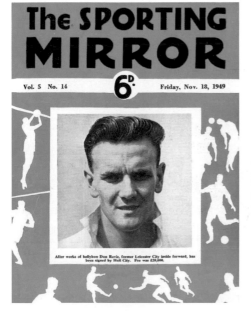

ABOVE: Revie poses uneasily with the legendary Raich Carter, Hull City's player/manager, on Boxing Day, 1949. Revie's time at Hull was not a success.

LEFT: Revie smashes home the first goal for his new club, Manchester City, in their 2–1 win over Fulham on 3 November, 1951.

BELOW: Disappointment for Manchester City as they lose 3–1 to Newcastle United in the 1955 FA Cup Final. However, Revie went on to be named Footballer of the Year that season.

ABOVE: Training at Roehampton with the England squad ahead of their famous 7–2 win against Scotland on 31 March, 1955, in which Revie scored.

RIGHT: Revie at home with his wife, Elsie, and son, Duncan, in 1955. Elsie was the niece of Revie's first manager, Leicester City's Johnny Duncan.

BELOW: Revie's sixth and final England cap came in a dismal 1–1 draw against Northern Ireland in Belfast on 6 October, 1956.

ABOVE: Manchester City captain Roy Paul, on Revie's shoulders, lifts the 1956 FA Cup after beating Birmingham 3–1. Revie was named Man of the Match.

ABOVE: It has long been assumed that it was Revie who changed the colour of the Leeds strip when he became manager in 1961, when in fact they began playing in white shirts in September 1960, under Jack Taylor.

ABOVE: Revie leads out Leeds United alongside his great friend, Liverpool's Bill Shankly, for the 1965 FA Cup Final. Liverpool won 2–1 after extra time.

ABOVE: Winners at last! Revie embraces Leeds trainer Les Cocker at Wembley, after beating Arsenal 1–0 in the 1968 League Cup Final.

ABOVE: There was a rapturous reception in Leeds after the League Cup win, which was the club's first major trophy under Revie.

ABOVE: Revie addresses the Leeds
United players at the start of the
new season, 1 August, 1968.

RIGHT: Leeds United celebrate
winning the 1968–69 league title,
breaking several records along the
way, including those for the most
wins (27) and fewest defeats (2).

RIGHT: A dramatic 1–0 win against
Arsenal in the 1972 FA Cup Final
saw Billy Bremner lift the cup for
the first time in the club's history.

LEFT: Les Cocker, Revie and Mick Bates look relaxed as Leeds cruise to a 3–0 victory in the 1972 FA Cup semi-final against Birmingham City.

ABOVE: Revie and Sunderland manager Bob Stokoe lead out their teams for the 1973 FA Cup Final. Second Division Sunderland pulled off a shock win.

LEFT: Revie poses with Billy Bremner and actor Paul Luty after winning the 1973–74 league title.

ABOVE: Revie and his players at Elland Road, celebrating the league win in 1973–74. Revie had already agreed to replace Sir Alf Ramsey as England boss.

RIGHT: Revie's energy and ideas impressed both the FA and the press, making him a popular choice as England manager.

BELOW: The England team training for the 1974–75 Home Internationals. England won the tournament, but cracks were beginning to show.

ABOVE LEFT: A worried-looking Revie walks away after England's 1–0 defeat against Wales at Wembley on 31 May, 1977.

ABOVE: Revie and Elsie at the High Court in London, where he overturned the FA's 10-year ban on him taking part in football. It was a hollow victory.

LEFT: Back home. Graham Ibbeson's sculpture of Revie was unveiled at Elland Road in 2012. Revie was one of English football's greatest-ever managers.

making everyone get up and do a turn with such favourites as *Strollin'*, *Underneath the Arches* and *Bye, Bye Blackbird*.

This year there was something extra special to celebrate because in the Queen's New Year's Honours List it was announced that Donald George Revie would be made an Officer of the Most Excellent Order of the British Empire. It was a world away from the cobbled streets of his youth. It was another step towards his acceptance into the middle class, which had begun when he was initiated into Leodiensis Lodge No.4029 in 1965, joining the likes of Sir Alf Ramsey and Ron Greenwood as Freemasons.

Two days later it was back to business when Swansea City visited Elland Road for a third-round FA Cup tie. As at Newcastle eight days earlier, Leeds were sloppy and complacent, nearly becoming a victim of FA Cup giant killing by falling behind after 24 minutes. After the Swansea captain Mel Nurse was dismissed for laying out Clarke, Leeds dominated. A penalty from Giles calmed nerves before Jones struck to win the game 2–1 and save any blushes.

Leeds made a mockery of league places on 10 January, 1970, by thrashing third-placed Chelsea 5–2, while a 3–1 victory over Coventry saw them take top spot by a single point. Even when Leeds were putting Sutton United to the sword, 6–0, in the FA Cup fourth round, Everton failed to capitalise. Being held to a draw at Newcastle meant Leeds were leading the table by goal average when they drew 2–2 with Manchester United at Old Trafford on 26 January.

But a 1–1 draw for Leeds against Stoke City on 31 January meant it was Everton who took the lead on goal average going into February. There was never an upset on the cards when Leeds cruised past Mansfield 2–0 in the FA Cup fifth round on 7 February. A commanding 5–1 win over West Bromwich Albion opened a gap of two points over rivals Everton.

Even when Leeds were in action in the FA Cup, the Toffees still could not seem to make hay. When the West Yorkshire side beat Swindon Town 2–0 to reach the FA Cup semi-final, Everton could only manage a scoreless league draw with Coventry.

When Leeds lined up to play Standard Leige in Belgium on 4 March in the European Cup, they were coming off a 2–0 win over Crystal Palace that maintained their two-point lead at the top of the league. When a Lorimer goal separated the two sides in the European match, it looked as though a historic treble could be on the cards.

Back in the league, a goalless draw with Liverpool cut their lead to one point with Everton holding a game in hand. A jittery Leeds struggled into the European Cup semi-final when Giles converted a penalty to see off Standard Leige just four days later on 11 March.

When Leeds faced Manchester United on 14 March in the FA Cup semi-final, they were one point behind Everton who had won their game in hand against Tottenham. Against Manchester United, both sides were unable to break the deadlock, it was the same story in the replay on 23 March when even extra-time was unable to produce a goal from either side.

Three days later in the second replay, Billy Bremner proved why he had been recently elected 1970 Footballer of the Year, when a display of individual brilliance resulted in a goal which finally separated the two sides at Burnden Park, Bolton.

The three games left their scars on Leeds in more ways than one with Bremner, Reaney, Jones and Cooper all missing for the game at Southampton on 28 March, where a lethargic looking Leeds lost 3–1 to the Hampshire side.

When Leeds failed to turn out six of their first-team players for a league game against Derby on the following Monday other managers were extremely unhappy, especially those caught up amid a relegation battle. Crystal Palace manager Bert Head, who was fighting relegation alongside Southampton, said, 'I was angry to see they had pulled six out of the team for a match equally important to the relegation battle, and I think Leeds should remember that others are involved in different league battles and those two points considerably help Southampton.'

Matters were not helped when newly promoted Derby County, with their outspoken boss Brian Clough, managed to vanquish the seemingly unbeatable Leeds 4–1. To the press he said, 'They could have played their third team as long as we won.'

Revie's answer when questioned about his team at Derby was: 'What is the point of employing the services of a fully-qualified medical officer if you don't take his advice? Our doctor declared that the players concerned were thoroughly tired, mentally and physically, and that if they carried on there was no knowing what damage might be caused. So we had no alternative but to take the steps we did. After all, the health of the players must be the first consideration of any club.

'By the end of the second replay at Bolton, the strain was obvious and the doctor expressed his views which we accepted. But it is quite wrong to say that we took a dive and wittingly sent out a weakened side. If similar circumstances arose again, I should do the same thing. I think most people understand our predicament, and I imagine that quite a few clubs would have done the same thing in our position.'

From Revie's point of view he was protecting his players, claiming he had advice from a doctor who warned him his players were on the verge of burn-out. Besides, the following day, Scottish champions Celtic would be visiting Elland Road for the first leg of the European Cup. Including the two FA Cup replays with Manchester United, Leeds had played eight times in 15 days. With an FA Cup Final against Chelsea to look forward to Revie effectively conceded the league to Everton.

There was retribution for fielding a weakened team, despite Bob Russell writing in the *Daily Mirror*, 'Considering the fantastic demands on Revie's team, I believe the football league will dispense with a fine and deliver a small rebuke.' Such speculation could not have been more wrong. The league decided to fine the club £5,000 and threatened to kick them out of European competition.

On 2 April Leeds United welcomed Celtic to Elland Road for the first leg of the European Cup semi-final. Up until now Leeds had not conceded a goal in the competition and were confident they could push aside their Scottish rivals.

No one could possibly have visualised such drama so soon. Leeds were caught by one crucial error in defence. Madeley, playing in place of Hunter, failed to head away a speculative lob on the edge of the penalty area. After Celtic had gained possession the ball went to George Connelly and his shot spun off Charlton's body and bounced tantalisingly out of reach of Sprake into the corner of the net.

It could not have been a worse start for Leeds and there were other problems when Bremner was hurt in a duel with Celtic captain Billy McNeill and had to go off in the 68th minute, to be replaced by Mick Bates. The blow on the head had left him concussed.

Despite looking particularly weary Leeds battled on and did well to stop Celtic from scoring again but the Glasgow team went to Hampden Park on 15 April with a precious away goal. Meaningless league games followed against West Ham and Burnley before Leeds travelled south to Wembley for the 1970 FA Cup Final.

The game was played unseasonably early on 11 April. With England hoping to defend their World Cup in Mexico in June, the domestic football season was finishing early so players could go and acclimatise to the South American heat. Just a week earlier the ground had been ripped apart by the Horse of the Year Show and the playing surface was one of the worst seen at Wembley.

The players had already been out to inspect the pitch and there was general agreement that it was already a mud bath, and the sand used by groundsman had failed to help matters. The pitch had been spray painted green to give the illusion that the final was to be played on something resembling grass.

Allan Clarke, who was playing in a second consecutive final after being on the losing side for Leicester City against Manchester City in 1969, remembered his studs sinking into the boggy pitch as Revie, decked out in his lucky blue suit, led out his team. Both Bates and Giles had the same experience.

Bates said, 'The pitch was in a terrible state. There was not a sign of the normally immaculate turf which everyone associates with Wembley. The pitch had been sanded – but you found yourself almost ankle deep in mud and sand at times – and if Wembley's once lush turf was stamina-sapping, I can tell you that the pitch on which we played destroyed the energy of the players as the game wore on. The pitch didn't run true – the ball came at you from awkward angles, bounced and bobbed about as you tried to play passes with precision.'

Giles added: 'In 1970 my mind may have been elsewhere, thinking about the state of the pitch which had been destroyed by the Horse of the Year Show. We knew that the pitch had been in a poor state for the League Cup Final in which Manchester City had beaten West Brom, but it was only when we walked out on to it an hour before the match we realised the extent of the damage. It was just a big field of compacted mud, with almost no grass on it, nowhere near the great arena of green turf that would normally be such a novelty at the end of the season. Yet the terrible state of the pitch is probably one of the things that made the final so distinctive, so memorable.'

All week Revie had been talking up how Leeds were going to play attractive, aggressive and adventurous football as soon as the game kicked off against Chelsea. There was only 20 minutes on the clock when Charlton ran away from the Chelsea goal with his arms aloft – Leeds pressure and the Wembley pitch had combined to see his header crawl over the line. Four minutes from half time and it was Leeds' turn to succumb to the uneven pitch as a shot from Chelsea's Peter Houseman slid under the body of keeper Sprake.

Later Frank McGhee of the *Daily Mirror* wrote, 'No team can surely ever again, dominate as much of two hours' football with so little luck – the only ingredient that was missing from a Leeds' display of all the skills and strength that make football the greatest game in the world.'

Leeds had hit the woodwork three times and there were now only eight minutes left on the clock. Playing with a freedom not seen since the turn of the year, Leeds were totally dominant. Surely, they were not going to be robbed by bad luck again. Then it happened, after a goalmouth scramble Jones' left-foot shot hit the post before ending up in the net.

Those in the Leeds dugout went wild – all except one man. All afternoon, Revie had sensed something was not right with his Leeds team. Rather than running to the pitch to celebrate, he had instructions for his players but found his way blocked by several policemen. Giles said, 'When Jones scored, the boss leapt off his seat near the touchline and tried to move nearer the pitch to tell Bremner, "Make sure the lads close up the game now, and do not lose their concentration." Unfortunately those bobbies barred his way and the message didn't get through; afterwards he would blame those policemen for losing the cup final.'

Any suspicions Chelsea would come back at Leeds were proved right as an Ian Hutchinson diving header for Chelsea levelled things in the 86th minute. Eddie Gray said, 'When you score with only five minutes to go you expect to have won the cup. We were unfortunate.'

For Revie it was hard to hide his disappointment, 'We had the chances to win and I thought we murdered Chelsea. We should have won it. I have never seen the lads play better. I don't know where they got their energy from.'

As the teams went on a joint lap of honour after extra time failed to settle it, a replay, even if it was at Old Trafford, was not what Revie needed.

The team would have to travel to Glasgow for the European Cup second leg, hoping to overturn the 1–0 deficit from the first. This was the first season when drawn matches in Europe would not be decided by away goals. Like his fellow Scot Bill Shankly, Celtic manager Jock Stein was quick to capitalise on any chink in his opponents' psyche telling the Scottish press, 'Leeds have shown us so much respect that it has cost them the league.'

Just four days after the Wembley mud bath, Leeds turned out to face the Scottish champions at Hampden Park. Despite being disappointed by his team's showing in the first leg, Revie went into the tie in a confident mood. Of his regular first team only Paul Reaney was out with a broken leg.

'Celtic were the better side on the night but we are still not out of it. Anything can happen when we play the return game at Hampden Park. We are keener than ever to win the FA Cup and the European Cup now for Paul's sake. I would give a year's wages to beat Celtic,' Revie told the press ahead of the game.

On big occasions some players were aware of Revie's nerves. Mick Jones remembers Revie as 'always blinking before a big game', while Gordon McQueen said you could 'see the tension in his body language when he gave his team talks. I think sometimes it rubbed off on his players.'

An early strike by Bremner inside the first quarter of an hour gave hope to Leeds but goals from John Hughes and Bobby Murdoch just after the break eliminated them from the competition. It meant that after finishing as runners up in the league and being knocked out of the League Cup – ironically by Chelsea – losing out in Europe now left the FA Cup as the only hope of silverware for Revie's team.

After the European Cup exit Revie said, 'That was a bitter pill to swallow but I like to think, and I do believe, that we at Leeds took our knock out in the right spirit. We congratulated Celtic and we meant it when we said we hoped they would bring the trophy back to Britain.

'I wasn't really feeling like receiving visitors though just before we left Glasgow for home it was a surprise to me when a local minister called in to wish us all the best for the replay against Chelsea. But when he told me that he intended to point to my example in his Sunday sermon, I just had to smile.

'The minister, it seemed, had been impressed by my attitude in defeat; by the way I had taken the disappointment of the past few weeks seemingly in my stride. He was basing his sermon on my attitude "as a model of how to accept life's disappointments". He was sincere when he said this and yet I had to smile. No one had seen me, tossing and turning during the night, as I went through the game, and the despair of that defeat. And I told him, "Don't let it fool you. It's all on the surface. Inside, I'm sick." And I was.

'But if I was sick, I was also proud, proud of the Leeds United players who had given all and were prepared to go on giving all, so long as there was something left to fight for.

'Celtic were much too good for us over those two matches but I'll never stop wondering what the result might have been had we been fresher.'

However high the stakes had been in the FA Cup they would now be even higher, when the teams met again in the replay at Old Trafford on 29 April.

Most pundits agreed that Leeds had been the better side in the first game and with Gray dominating Chelsea's David Webb on the Yorkshire club's left flank, only the woodwork had denied them victory.

If the first game was rough, the replay took that to a whole new level. To illustrate the level of violence in what has become known as one of the most notorious games in English football history referee David Ellery, at the time considered one of the country's top officials, later watched a replay of the game and concluded that the teams should have received six red and no fewer than 20 yellow cards between them.

In the first action of the game, David Webb cluttered into Eddie Gray, leaving stud marks in the Scotsman's left shin. Just 12 minutes later Webb would be in the thick of it again, this time a late, two-footed lunge, this time on Allan Clarke deep in the Chelsea half.

Further seemingly clear offences came and went without punishment – Billy Bremner sent spinning from the field by Peter Houseman, Hunter and McCreadie coming to blows.

In the 31st minute Chelsea goalkeeper, Peter Bonetti, suffered a painful knee injury in a fiercely contested aerial duel with Leeds forward Mick Jones – one that required lengthy treatment and prompted BBC commentator Kenneth

Wolstenholme to comment: 'This almost deserves an X-certificate.' He emerged after half time heavily strapped and unable to take goal-kicks.

As the game wore on Peter Osgood fouled Jack Charlton, who immediately jumped up, kneed and headbutted the Chelsea man to the floor. The only booking of the game came on the 85th minute when Chelsea's Ian Hutchinson shoved Billy Bremner to the floor. After that all hell broke loose with both sides seemingly wanting to kick each other off the pitch.

Just as in the first game, Leeds dominated, going ahead through Jones, only for Peter Osgood to score with a header to bring the teams level and another 30 minutes of extra time. It was the irony of ironies that Webb, who had been thoroughly outplayed in the first game, should get on the end of an Ian Hutchinson long throw to send Chelsea into the lead for the first time in the tie, eventually taking the trophy back to west London.

Norman Hunter said afterwards, 'Not one of us wanted to take any credit from Chelsea but we knew that we had not only done enough to win the trophy, we had done enough to earn it. Morally, we had been the victors each time.'

As the depressed players sat in the Manchester dressing room after the game, Revie knew he had to put his own disappointment aside. Looking at each of them he told his players to lift their heads up. What was past was past; the league championship, FA Cup, even the European Cup – all gone. There was nothing they could do about it – they all had to look to the future.

Reminding them of where they were, he told them of Manchester United's trials and tribulations after the Munich air disaster and how it had taken them 10 years to claw their way to European glory. He said Leeds had only just started. Forget tonight, he told them, there would be more glory ahead.

Both Giles and Hunter later said that while they were not exactly laughing and dancing at the end of Revie's speech they had been shaken out of their gloom and were determined to come back stronger than ever next season.

Speaking to the press after the match Revie expressed pride in his players: 'If I were given the chance to have last season all over again, I would not reverse the decisions which were taken at Elland Road. We had our moments of bitterness, of sorrow, of extreme disappointment and drama, and sheer, heart-stirring emotion.

'We could not have done other than go for that magical treble, even if we did know that we were asking for a miracle. You cannot be a winner every time out, but you have got to try to win 'em all. And Leeds United's players made their manager a proud man, even during disappointment.'

Lessons would be learnt from this season and, in many ways, this would be a turning point for Revie. If anything, this season was the beginning of the siege mentality for which Leeds United became renowned.

15

LEEDS UNITED (1970–71)

'I cannot mention names but I have a little book with two names in it
and if I get the chance to do them I will.'

Jack Charlton

Looking ahead to the 1970–71 season, Revie thought only Everton and
Manchester City could challenge Leeds for the league title. And Frank McGhee
of the *Daily Mirror* agreed, saying both Liverpool and Manchester United were
fading forces, going through a transitional spell.

The bookies also agreed, making Leeds United favourites for the title at 7–2
and current league champions Everton 4–1. Even as early as August journalist
Ken Jones predicted it was going to be a two-horse race between last season's two
top-placed sides.

When McGhee asked Revie whether his Leeds side were going to be affected
by the events of 1970 when the side came so close to the treble but only had a
place in the European Fairs Cup to show for their efforts, Revie was defiant.

'Over the years the bigger the disappointment the more fiercely our lads have
responded. Last year was perhaps the biggest disappointment of all and that is
the reason why I feel sure we will do well this time.'

To many, the reason why Leeds finished up empty-handed was because they
had simply played too many games. To Revie, there was no question his side were
going to forfeit any cup competition to focus on the league championship and
another crack at the European Cup. It came down to economics.

The summer had seen updates – a newly-laid pitch, a grandstand and office
accommodation. It was estimated that the new building work would eventually
cost more than £1 million. As Revie said to McGhee, 'We cannot exist without

them [cup competitions]. With the class of player we must pay and the money we need to live our weekly bill is about £7,000. To get that through the turnstiles we need gates of 37,000 which means a place in the top four all the time to survive. We need the extra competitions to provide the profit for all this.'

Despite Leeds seeming to be everyone's pick for the championship, the start to the season could not have been tougher. They visited Manchester United at Old Trafford on 15 August, Spurs at White Hart Lane four days later, then Everton at Elland Road on 28 August.

For Billy Bremner it was vital the team got off to a strong start, 'The competition is fierce. That means teams which do not start well will find themselves struggling for top prizes, but where do you find an easy start? We have Manchester United, Spurs and Everton in our first three games. If we fail in these matches then we can forget about it.'

Despite having lifted the European Cup just two years earlier, Manchester United were not the same side. Both Bobby Charlton and Denis Law were ageing, George Best was losing interest and Sir Matt Busby had retired, leaving Wilf McGuinness in charge.

Even without Jack Charlton, Terry Cooper, Allan Clarke and Norman Hunter, who were all rested, having featured for England in the 1970 World Cup, Leeds were dominant. A Mick Jones thunderbolt after 22 minutes against Manchester United settled things between the sides in a game marked by the running and precision passing of Bremner and Giles.

Both Giles and Eddie Gray were on the scoresheet as Leeds walked away with an impressive 2–0 victory over Spurs. In their next game against champions Everton the Whites had to come from behind twice before a late winner from Bremner saw them claim all the points. A pair of 3–0 wins over West Ham and Burnley saw Leeds close out August with five straight wins.

The run was ended with a 0–0 draw with Arsenal at Highbury on 1 September, but there was joy in the capital four days later when a Clarke goal got the win at Stamford Bridge against Chelsea. A loss to Sheffield United in the second round of the League Cup was not as worrying as the ankle injury sustained by Charlton, who joined Giles in the treatment room, Giles having suffered a similar injury at West Ham.

A strangely off-colour Leeds suffered their first defeat in the league at the Victoria Ground against Stoke City on 12 September. The game took a bizarre turn when Peter Lorimer had to don the goalkeeper's jersey for eight minutes after Gary Sprake went off for treatment. Upon Sprake's return, Stoke City added to their two first-half goals to complete a 3–0 win.

Revie then had to prepare his team for a trip to Norway, where they would play Sarpsborg in the first round of the European Fairs Cup on 15 September. An understrength Leeds, depleted by injuries, struggled for 75 minutes against a team that wanted to play with a nine-man defence. It was a Lorimer strike that saw Leeds finally get the precious away goal.

The Southampton match on 19 September at Elland Road was a match of two penalties, the first missed by Saints' striker Ron Davies, the second converted by Giles, in the 38th minute. The game was marred when Southampton's Jimmy Gabriel headbutted Clarke leaving them both sprawled on the ground. Gabriel later claimed he only retaliated after being kicked in the back and punched on the jaw.

For his trouble Gabriel was stretchered off. It was only when referee Ray Tinkler would not allow Southampton to use their substitute did anyone realise the Saints' man had been sent off. As if to prove it was a particularly hard game, Gray, Clarke, Hunter, Cooper and Giles all reported injuries.

The only thing to come out of the 0–0 draw with Nottingham Forest on 26 September was a fractured cheekbone for Giles that kept the Irishman out of the side for the next six games.

The 5–0 win in the return leg on 29 September over Sarpsborg was not the only thing worth cheering about. Paul Reaney, having recovered from a broken leg sustained in April, came on at half time to mark his return to the side.

But injury worries were beginning to mount up again. Giles was out and Revie was aware that Bremner was playing through the pain barrier and then Gray limped off after 15 minutes of the 2–0 win over newly-promoted Huddersfield Town on 3 October.

There were catcalls and jeers every time Charlton touched the ball when Leeds rolled up at the Hawthorns to play West Bromwich Albion. Earlier that day, an interview recorded on 3 October with Fred Dinenage of Tyne Tees

Television had been shown nationally in which Charlton was quoted as saying, 'I cannot mention names but I have a little book with two names in it and if I get the chance to do them I will.

'I do not do what I consider to be the bad fouls in the game such as going over the top. That is about the worst foul in the game, but I will tackle as hard as I can to win the ball, but I will not do the dirty things, the really nasty things.

'When people do it to me I do it back to them. Because I am not noted for doing so people don't do it to me, but there are two or three people who have done it to me, and I will make them suffer before I pack this game up.'

The comments caused widespread condemnation and resulted in the FA writing to Leeds to tell them they intended to act against the big defender.

For Revie it was a fuss over nothing, and he told the press, 'I think more people have contacted me over this than tickets for the cup final. I have watched the tape and cannot see what he has done wrong.' The issue would not be resolved until December. Meanwhile, the game with West Brom ended in a 2–2 draw meaning Leeds maintained their lead at the top of the table with Arsenal, Spurs, Chelsea and Crystal Palace just behind them.

Indifferent form continued with a 2–2 draw with Manchester United on 17 October before Leeds had to rely on the away goals rule to get past Dynamo Dresden. The day before the United game the *Daily Mirror* reported that Leeds had signed a complete unknown in the shape of Morton's Joe Jordan. Just 18, Jordan had played only six first team games for Morton but was recommended to Revie by Bobby Collins, who was by then plying his trade with the Scottish club.

The £15,000 capture of Jordan was Revie's first signing since Albert Johanneson departed for York City for £4,000 in the close season.

A pair of 2–0 wins over Derby County and Coventry City saw the start of an unbeaten run throughout November and December. So impressive was the form of the Elland Road club that when Harry Miller of the *Daily Mirror* asked all the top managers on 13 November where the title was likely to end up, names such as Bertie Mee of Arsenal and Brian Clough of Derby County were moved to say, Leeds United.

Likewise, Liverpool's Bill Shankly said, 'I was impressed with Tottenham when they played us, they were methodical and careful, but Leeds, despite a lot of injuries, are still top and are my favourites.' Chelsea's Dave Sexton agreed: 'Leeds, because of their experience. They have done it before; they are always up there and they will be there again.'

When asked, Revie had moved away from his pre-season pick of Manchester City or Everton and went with Tottenham, although those close to the manager knew he secretly agreed with Shankly and Sexton.

Wins over Manchester City on 28 November and a 9–2 aggregate victory over Sparta Prague in the third round of the Fairs Cup underlined the scintillating form Leeds were in. Only draws against Liverpool on 5 December, and Ipswich the following week, stunted progress. Leeds rounded off 1970 with a dominant 3–0 win over Newcastle United on Boxing Day.

On the morning of 2 January, 1971, Don Revie's latest column appeared in the *Sports Argus* in which he wanted to address two issues. The first was the rumours linking him with the now-vacant manager's job at Manchester United. After failing to make his mark on the job, Wilf McGuinness had suffered the humiliation of being demoted to reserve team manager with Matt Busby back in the hot seat, but looking for a big name to replace him. The two names most bandied about were Sir Alf Ramsey and Revie, with the *Daily Mirror* speculating that if Ramsey did take the job then Revie would replace him at England.

In his column, Revie was quick to rule himself out of the running for the United job, writing, 'I expect loyalty from the Leeds playing and administrative staff and they expect loyalty in return. That's why I am not interested in becoming manager of Manchester United, or any other club for that matter. It is my ambition to remain at Elland Road for the rest of my career.'

Revie then moved to the issue he had first discussed with Frank McGhee in August: 'The business of spectator amenities is a thorny problem. Most grounds are out of date and have little hope of improvement under the system by which the few profitable clubs are heavily taxed.

'A curious anomaly is that a club is forced to pay 45 per cent corporation tax if it spends its profits on ground improvements, but none if it is spent on new players. All-seater stadiums MUST come eventually if soccer is to survive as a booming spectator sport.

'The innovation cannot be achieved while the government continues to adopt such a narrow-minded attitude towards soccer supporters. Clubs are also to blame for the fans' raw deal. I believe they should provide pre-match entertainment for the crowds.'

That afternoon Revie's words were almost prophetic. There was a crush among the crowd at an Old Firm game between Rangers and Celtic at Ibrox Park. Crush barriers collapsed as thousands of fans made their way out of the stadium. The Ibrox disaster caused 66 deaths and more than 200 injuries. Up to that point it was the worst incident in British football history.

Frost had seen the scheduled FA Cup third-round tie on 2 January with Third Division Rotherham United postponed. A further bout of bad weather saw the rescheduled game called off again a few days later. So Leeds' first game of the New Year came on 9 January, 1971, against Spurs at Elland Road.

From the moment Spurs' Martin Chivers scored after 10 minutes, Leeds were always on the back foot and not even an equaliser from Allan Clarke on 18 minutes could fire up the home side. It was Chivers again who decided things after 72 minutes and, with that, brought an end to the West Yorkshire club's unbeaten home record.

Finally, Leeds got around to playing their tie with Rotherham at their Millmoor ground. What should have been a routine game was anything but with Rotherham, roared on by a capacity crowd, holding their illustrious opponents to a goalless draw. For Revie it was just a blip, as normal order would surely be restored in the return at Elland Road two days later. But more bad weather, fog this time, saw the replay called off.

Then finally, in yet more terrible weather, this time lashing rain, Leeds played Rotherham again. Making a mockery of their respective league positions the visitors led the tie 2–1 at one point, before Lorimer and Giles ensured passage to the fourth round.

Any doubts over form were put to rest with an easy 4–0 win over Swindon Town in the FA Cup fourth round five days later. Then came a superb 2–0 league win over third-placed Manchester City, which confirmed that the Elland Road club were favourites for the title with the bookmakers offering evens on Leeds being crowned champions.

Over the previous two years, Revie had had doubts about keeper Gary Sprake. On big occasions the Welshman could be suspect. With David Harvey, the Leeds-born Scottish international reserve goalkeeper agitating for a move for more first-team football, and with his well-known admiration for Leicester City's Peter Shilton, Revie knew things would soon come to a head with Sprake.

Among others, Billy Bremner was hugely critical of the Welsh goalkeeper, citing a lack of concentration in big games. Even when offered help, Bremner claimed Sprake was not interested, doing the same things repeatedly, much to everyone's frustration.

For Bremner, even though everyone recognised Sprake as a liability, he only kept his place because of a misplaced sense of loyalty from Revie. Something which would cost them in the long run.

When Sprake fumbled an innocuous shot from Liverpool's Phil Boersma on 6 February into the path of John Toshack after only two minutes, all those fears about Sprake came to the surface. The fact the keeper blamed Paul Reaney for the incident only added insult to injury.

Later that week Revie went on record in the *Sports Argus* to deny interest in Shilton and talk up Sprake's qualities, claiming, 'People have criticised Gary for a couple of mistakes, yet he plays blinders week after week and nothing is said. You won't find any of the lads criticising him because they know that Gary has saved the team on many occasions.' Years later Revie would contradict his column and claim had he not been so loyal to Gary Sprake, and had a better keeper been available, then Leeds would have been a lot more successful.

Despite the anger directed towards Sprake from fans after the Liverpool game Revie named him in the team to face Colchester United in the fifth round of the FA Cup. With Bremner and Gray injured and Clarke running a temperature, Leeds were under strength. In one of the great giant killings the FA Cup sometimes throws up, Colchester United beat Leeds 3–2 at Layer Road. Amazingly, the Essex team went in at half time leading 3–0.

The two home defeats led Denis Hill-Wood, chairman of second-placed Arsenal, to claim Leeds were 'creaking like a rusty gate'. Leeds responded in the most emphatic fashion by destroying Wolves 3–0 at Elland Road on 20 February, then Ipswich 4–2 at Portman Road.

Speaking after the Ipswich game Revie told *Shoot!* magazine, 'In fact the defeat against Colchester was just the spur we needed. The boys were back to their brilliant best against Wolves and Ipswich. Leeds United can only be judged by the standards they've set over the last six years. We've never finished out of the top four and I'll back us to win the title again this season.

'The competition at the top is ferocious and neither Arsenal nor us can afford to slacken. Arsenal are a great side and have games in hand, but the pressure is on them now. They must try and catch us.'

A Lorimer goal was enough to secure victory at Coventry on Friday 26 February and take United seven points clear of Arsenal, though the Gunners now had three games in hand. They squandered one of those opportunities the next day, losing 2–0 at Derby.

The Fairs Cup resumed on 10 March with Vitória de Setúbal of Portugal the visitors for the quarter-final. Despite Gary Sprake having recovered from a badly-gashed hand sustained in the loss against Colchester, it was David Harvey who kept goal. Also in the side that day was Joe Jordan.

There was an early shock when the Portuguese side took the lead after 90 seconds but it was not long before Leeds began to control the game. A goal from a Lorimer free-kick and a penalty from Giles and Leeds would travel to Portugal in charge of the tie.

Points were dropped three days later in a dull 1–1 draw at Bloomfield Road where relegation-threatened Blackpool worked hard to shut out Leeds. But there was a double celebration on 20 March when Leeds visited the capital to beat Crystal Palace 2–1 and on the coach back Revie cracked open a bottle of champagne to mark his 10 years in charge of the club. Paying tribute, *Shoot!* magazine carried an editorial which read, 'Don Revie celebrates 10 years as manager of Leeds next week. In those years at the Elland Road helm he has built a mountain called Leeds United and changed a mood of stagnant depression into buoyant confidence.

'In order for that to be successful, the Revie record at Elland Road is unparalleled. Leeds United have dominated the last decade. Today they are respected as one of the finest teams in Europe, if not the finest. For that they can thank one man, Don Revie.'

Even Manchester City manager Joe Mercer was moved to say of his rival, 'Don Revie's achievements at Leeds have been fantastic in such a competitive profession. He has made an incredible contribution to modern football. His record as a manager couldn't be bettered.'

A 1–1 draw with Vitória de Setúbal in the second leg of their Fairs Cup tie set up a fascinating all English semi-final with old rivals Liverpool.

Although Leeds were six points clear of Arsenal, the Gunners still had those three games in hand. Four goals from Clarke in a dominant 4–0 win over Burnley eased nerves somewhat but there was very little Leeds could do about Arsenal beating Chelsea and Coventry to close the gap.

There were more dropped points in a 1–1 draw with Newcastle on 10 April. Things did not improve in a goalless draw with Huddersfield two days later, Easter Monday. At the same time Arsenal won all their matches, reducing the gap to two points with Leeds preparing to meet Liverpool at Anfield on 14 April for the first leg of their Fairs Cup semi-final.

In dramatic fashion, Bremner returned from injury to pop up to score the only goal of the game to beat Liverpool 1–0 and take a vital away goal back to Elland Road.

Three days later, on 17 April, Revie was raging. For the first time since he had become the manager of Leeds he felt the need to run on to the pitch and remonstrate with the referee. The incident came after 69 minutes when Leeds, already unexpectedly 1–0 down after 20 minutes against West Bromwich Albion, were pushing for an equaliser. Hunter brought Leeds forward but his misplaced pass was intercepted by Albion's Brown who raced forward with it. The linesman's flag was instantly raised as West Brom midfielder, Colin Suggett, yards offside and the only man in the Leeds half apart from Sprake, ran forward into the empty space. Brown pulled up, seemingly knowing the game was up, and United's defenders hesitated.

But referee Ray Tinkler waved play on, ignoring the flag and insisting that there was no offence. Brown, realising his good fortune, picked his way towards the unguarded area and the oncoming Sprake.

As the goalkeeper advanced, Brown slipped the ball to big striker Jeff Astle, who was also looking suspiciously offside. The centre-forward obliged with a simple tap-in as Reaney sought vainly to catch him.

The ground was a sea of chaos as it became clear that Tinkler was going to allow the goal to stand. Revie was frantic with anger, ushering the linesman over to intervene with the referee. Tinkler consulted with his assistant but would only confirm his original conclusion – the goal was good!

Leeds' Mick Jones said, 'None of us could believe the goal had been given but the referee was adamant: the goal stood. The crowd was also incensed and several of them raced on to the pitch; they were so frustrated. What riled them so much was that after my goal was unluckily chalked off, a blatant offside goal was given. I managed to stop one person as he raced towards the referee. He was so angry, if he'd reached him, I hate to think what he'd have done. I'm convinced that if my goal had stood, we'd have gone on to win the game, but the decision knocked us back.'

In the centre of midfield, Billy Bremner was getting more and more irate at the way Tinkler was conducting the match. Being particularly harsh on Leeds while ignoring heavy challenges from Albion players.

When the captain remonstrated with the referee, he was told to go away, while Albion continued unabated with the rough stuff. The controversial goal left Bremner incandescent with rage, something which would stay with him for years whenever he was asked about the match.

There had never been scenes like it before. With fans on the pitch, coins and other things were thrown, ironically striking the linesman who had flagged for offside. Included in the throng was the Leeds United manager.

Bremner added, 'I saw the boss get up from the dugout. He rarely moved during a game so it must have been something exceptional.'

Commentating on the match for the BBC, Barry Davies said, 'Don Revie is on the pitch, the linesman is going to talk to the referee.' Eventually Revie trudged off – bizarrely he was still carrying a tartan travel rug under his arm – shaking his head, with Davies concluding, 'Don Revie, a sickened man. Look at him looking at the heavens in disgust. So many fans on the field being taken off and more police on the field than players.

'And the Yorkshire spirit is really coming to the fore. There's a wrestling match going on in the centre circle but, when all is said and done, the goal is going to stand. But what a cruel goal. Listen to the crowd going mad.'

Speaking later in a BBC interview Davies said, 'I remember that the delay was so long between Tony Brown going clear and the referee waving him on. It cost Leeds the league, absolutely. It also cost Ray Tinkler the FA Cup Final. I really think he would have got it. After the game when Don Revie came out, against all journalistic decorum, I sent him back. I suggested he return to the dressing room to have a moment to think, otherwise he would have got himself into trouble.'

In his eventual comments Revie seemed to condone the pitch invasion by saying, 'I have never been so sick at heart. The ref's decision on Suggett was the worst I have ever seen and, boy, was wrong, and it wrecked nine months' hard work here. We must have professional referees. I regret the crowd scenes like anybody else but I can understand why they cut loose.'

About 50 police tried to quell the mob. Others formed a barrier in front of the stand to prevent more fans from getting onto the pitch. There were 23 arrests made. At the end of the match Tinkler was escorted from the pitch through a hail of coins and other missiles. There were ugly scenes outside the ground and a glass door at the main entrance was shattered.

Revie said to the waiting press, 'It could have been a riot and it would have been on the referee's head. The referee's decision was unfair. A man like that can destroy you. There must be an enquiry.'

Even when Revie spoke on *Match of the Day* later that evening he had still not calmed down, 'If anything I feel stronger about it now. I'll put one thing right though, I didn't want to suggest those spectators who came on to the pitch were right to do so. I said they had a right to get angry and I'll say this too, if the incident had happened at one or two other grounds then there might have been a riot.'

Leeds chairman Percy Woodward backed his manager up, saying about Revie, 'Here we have a man who has worked so hard with such a loyal team and has had 12 months' work destroyed by the act of one man. It's deplorable!'

But Ian Johnson, the editor of the *Sports Argus*, a publication Revie regularly wrote a column for, was damning about Revie: 'Revie's outburst after the Jeff Astle goal which helped Albion beat Leeds 2–1 was wrong, completely wrong. "Thanks very much for ruining nine months of hard work" – that is the caustic comment of a man in charge of a brilliant team who promised so much but achieved so little in the way of trophies. Certainly not a rational statement.'

Goal magazine was more sympathetic when it said, 'Goal verdict: sheer tragedy for Don Revie and Leeds.' Even Arsenal's Bertie Mee said, 'I feel damn sick about the whole issue.'

Despite the anger and sense of injustice, the title could still be won. A 3–0 win at the Dell over Southampton on 24 April sent out a powerful message to Arsenal that Leeds were true to their motto and were going to keep on fighting.

On 26 April Arsenal travelled to West Yorkshire for a mouth-watering clash with their nearest rivals Leeds. A win and the Gunners would secure the title and a loss would not be catastrophic as they still had a game in hand. For Leeds, nothing but a victory would do. In a tight, tense and scrappy match Charlton scored a late winner. Ironically, all claims from Arsenal players for offside were waved off by the referee.

Leeds now entered the second leg of their Fairs Cup semi-final a point clear of their London rivals but had played one game more. They were now reliant on Arsenal dropping points.

A largely defensive display from Leeds saw the Elland Road club just edge out Liverpool in a dour Fairs Cup goalless draw. With the European final to be played over two legs on 28 May and 3 June, Leeds' attention turned to the final game of the league season at Elland Road against Nottingham Forest.

In the run-up to the game Revie told the press, 'It is essential we play patiently. We mustn't let the importance of the situation blind us to the fact Notts Forest are a First Division side who can score goals. We must create our chances in the usual way and ensure we keep a clean sheet to help our goal average.'

In July 1977, Gary Sprake sat down with the *Daily Mirror's* Richard Stott and, for a fee of £7,500, claimed Revie had sent Bremner into the Forest changing room. It was alleged that a few words with the Forest players would produce the right result.

Sprake began his tale: 'In the Leeds dressing room Revie mentioned to Bremner about going into the Forest dressing room. Billy was not changed and still in his suit. I then saw Billy leave our dressing room.

'About five minutes later Billy came back and although I cannot remember the exact words he used it was clear to me he had been in the Forest dressing room. I think he said he'd been to see a few of the lads, or words to that effect.'

In time, the allegations would make Sprake a black sheep among Revie's former players. He was never welcome at Elland Road and excluded from the players' reunions. For one, Billy Bremner would never forgive Sprake, speaking only with contempt of his former teammate. Never the biggest fan of the Welsh goalkeeper, Bremner felt the decision to sell his story to the tabloids was another mistake in a career littered with them.

In a dominant performance, Leeds beat Forest 2–0 with goals from Bremner and Lorimer but the news when they got to the dressing room at full time was not good. Arsenal had beaten Stoke by a single goal. Even though Leeds had closed out the season leading the table by a single point, they had to hope Spurs would do them a favour in two days' time.

Things were looking good for 88 minutes with both Spurs and Arsenal failing to find the net. Just when it seemed as though the title was heading to West Yorkshire, Arsenal's Ray Kennedy headed past Pat Jennings to secure the title for the Gunners and the first half of a remarkable double for the Highbury side.

In defeat, Revie was gracious: 'Obviously we are sick but good luck to Arsenal. It was a tremendous feat to succeed at Tottenham. It has been a tremendous tussle and the fact the championship was so close indicates the standards that have been set over the past few years.'

The Fairs Cup final would be the last before it was replaced by the UEFA Cup in 1971–72. Whoever won between Juventus and Leeds would then go into a challenge match with the first-ever winners to decide who could keep the trophy permanently.

The first attempt to play the match on 26 May was ruined by heavy rain rendering the pitch unplayable, although they got to half time before the match was abandoned. It looked as if the terrible weather might lead to both legs being played in Leeds but eventually the skies cleared and the match was restaged at the Stadio Communale on the Friday evening.

Juventus twice took the lead before being pulled back, first by a goal from Madeley and then one from Bates. The 2–2 draw gave Leeds a clear advantage for the second leg at Elland Road a week later.

In the return leg at Elland Road on 3 June, Clarke gave them an early lead only for Juventus to level. From that point on both clubs retreated into their defence shells. When the final whistle blew it was Leeds lifting the Fairs Cup for the second time in four years.

Despite the smiles and plaudits, Revie brooded. He was still not over the Tinkler affair and he could not help but think that if it had not been for a poor refereeing decision the club would be parading the league championship trophy as well as the Fairs Cup through the city centre. Feeling the world was against him and his team, things had to change in the coming season.

16

LEEDS UNITED (1971–72)

'Every time Leeds touched the ball the crowd would cheer. I think it was
the first time I heard the call "ole!" every time a pass was made.'

Jeff Powell, Daily Mail

It was 10 June, 1971, just over a week after the Fairs Cup triumph, and Don
Revie was on holiday. But there would be no rest and relaxation in the sun. Back
home, an FA disciplinary commission had been convened to discuss the actions
of Leeds United in the game against West Bromwich Albion on 17 April.

In Revie's mind the referee Ray Tinkler had cost him and his players the
1971 league championship and now, as he agonised and waited for the verdict,
he was sure he was about to lose the 1972 race before a ball had been kicked.

The commission's outcome was damning. In an official statement it said they
were satisfied there had been disorder by certain spectators; the pitch invaded;
the referee molested; and the linesman struck by a missile.

The commission was also of the opinion 'that the attitude of some of the
players of Leeds United FC was a contributory factor in the invasion of the pitch
by spectators.'

The punishment? To close Elland Road for the playing of all matches from
14 August to 4 September, 1971 inclusive and a £100 fine. Further, Leeds were
to compensate any visiting club for the loss of revenue in those matches and it
was estimated this would cost them in the region of £30,000.

Even though both Revie and chairman Percy Woodward had apologised for
their outburst against Tinkler, they were both reprimanded and warned about
their future behaviour. Leeds fans greeted the verdict with outrage and Eric
Carlile, secretary of the Leeds supporters club, called the decision 'diabolical'.

In the *Daily Mirror* Sheila Kay, the mother-in-law of up-and-coming Leeds midfielder Terry Yorath, asked, 'Why is it that when Leeds are involved in any kind of trouble, they are always seen to be dealt with more harshly than anybody else?'

Alfred Rawlings, a pub landlord from Harrogate said, 'I have spoken to dozens of fans who are shocked and appalled. I think it is disgusting to think the FA can hand down treatment to a club with no previous of this kind of thing.'

While Paul Dacre of Beeston, near Leeds, claimed, 'If almost any other club but Leeds, certainly a London club were involved, I don't think the punishment would be so hard. The football authorities appear to go out of their way to be unhelpful to Leeds. Now I think they have been victimised again.'

Even though the Police Federation was concerned there had been too many incidents of this nature, it was clear Leeds United were far from the worst offenders. After considering the verdict with his board upon his return from holiday, Revie decided to accept the punishment. There would be no appeal.

Instead, to circumnavigate the ban, Leeds tried to re-arrange the affected four games of the season. The Football League Commission was firm there would be no postponements with president Len Shipman telling the press, 'First, Leeds would have to get agreement for postponement from the opposing teams and if they did that it would be a difficult and embarrassing problem for the league committee.

'While I can't anticipate the minds of the eight committee members, the fact is there are three members who are also members of the FA disciplinary commission who of course imposed the shutdown penalty on Leeds.'

Instead of wallowing in self-pity, Revie was going to use the handicap of playing away from Elland Road as motivation for the coming season, telling the press, 'We just say to ourselves that if we could win the championship with this sort of problem it will be the greatest championship. It will be harder than it was last season. There will be six or seven clubs in the running from the start, but I feel that two of them will break away from the pack.'

There was some support for Arsenal, Chelsea, Spurs, Everton and Manchester City in the press when asked to pick the champions. However, as in 1971, Leeds were the odds-on favourites to lift the championship with Peter Cooper of the

Daily Mirror summing up the mood on 10 August: 'Ask anybody realistically, in or out of football, why Leeds might, can and probably will win the league championship then stand back.

'Otherwise you will be pinned to a wall before being given a brief rundown of Leeds United's assets which could take up an hour; or be frozen with a look which asks in turn where you have been for the past five or six years.'

The only dissenting voice was Martin Chivers of Spurs who claimed, 'Leeds do not look as strong at the back as they have done in the past, [and] it's no secret Don Revie has spent the summer scouring around for a goalkeeper and centre-half.'

While it was well-known Revie had his doubts about Gary Sprake, reserve keeper David Harvey looked like a ready-made replacement. The real concern going into the new season was Charlton who, at 36, was not getting any younger and injuries were catching up with him. Sooner or later, Revie would have to draft in a replacement.

As Leeds prepared to open the season at Maine Road on 14 August there had been no additions to the side. After failing to live up to his early promise, Terry Hibbitt had been offloaded to Newcastle United.

In a new crackdown by referees on rough play, both Manchester City and Leeds found it difficult to break each other down. It was only a strike from Lorimer on 72 minutes that separated the two sides.

Three days later Leeds conceded two sloppy goals in the last three minutes at Bramall Lane to give Sheffield United a flattering 3–0 win. As per the FA ban, the following two fixtures, which should have been played at home, were played at Leeds Road, Huddersfield, where Leeds United drew 0–0 with Wolves, followed by a 1–1 draw with Tottenham at Boothferry Park, Hull.

Then came three victories in a row – 2–0 against Ipswich at Portman Road, a thumping 5–1 win against Newcastle at Hillsborough, and a 2–0 victory over Crystal Palace at Leeds Road. By the time they faced Derby County for the second round of the League Cup on 8 September, Leeds were in second place behind early league pacesetters Sheffield United.

After a disappointing 2–0 defeat to reigning champions Arsenal, Leeds got ready for their first UEFA Cup tie against Belgian side Lierse SK. Chris Galvin, in for an injured Clarke, scored alongside Peter Lorimer in a 2–0 win. As Revie travelled home to Leeds he could be happy his side had two away goals to carry into the home leg at Elland Road.

The club finally played at their real home again on 18 September and faced old adversaries Liverpool. As always, the game was tight and hard fought with a Lorimer goal giving Leeds the spoils, keeping them in touch with the leaders.

On 25 September Leeds travelled to Spain to play Barcelona for the right to own the Fairs Cup trophy outright. Leaving without Cooper, Clarke, Jones, Madeley and Gray, Revie did not hold out much hope of winning the trophy in what was ultimately a glorified friendly.

After Barcelona took the lead, Jordan quickly equalised and Leeds did well to hold Barcelona deep into the second half. It was not long before the Catalans struck again to ensure the Fairs Cup would go on permanent display in the Nou Camp.

There was more discomfort on the way when a pair of goalless draws against West Ham in the league and League Cup were followed by a poor 3–1 defeat against Coventry City at Highfield Road on 9 October. Leeds were now lying in eighth place in the championship. All Revie could do was bemoan the bad luck of having Clarke, Jones and Gray all out at the same time. So depressed was Revie with the result he took himself off on an impromptu holiday with Elsie to Jersey.

Both Jones and Clarke were back for the 3–0 win over Manchester City on 16 October and the 1–0 defeat after extra time against West Ham in the League Cup was not that painful. Form picked up in the league with three wins in a row.

On 6 November Leeds were getting ready to run out against Leicester City with their new £177,000 signing Asa Hartford in the side. That was until the doctor told Revie that Hartford had a heart defect and the transfer from West Bromwich Albion was off.

Mick Jones said, 'I was in the dressing room with Asa when the news came through, the lad was devastated. There he was already to run, his kit hanging up and suddenly he was gone. It's fair to say we were all in shock.'

According to midfielder Chris Galvin, who was then on the fringes of the first team, the aborted attempt to make Asa Hartford a Leeds United player set Revie on the way out of Elland Road. 'There was something different about Asa

Hartford, he was 21 and Don was looking to replace players who were ageing. He was devastated when the transfer failed to go through. Things were never the same after that.

'Players were meeting and questioning his tactics. I remember him saying once if that's the way you feel then pick the team yourself. That was so unlike Don. In Asa I think he wanted to rebuild a new team; after that incident he gave up.'

For Clarke, this view was premature. 'Even after Asa, Don stayed for another three years. He was the most wanted manager in the league – if he really wanted to go, there would have been no shortage of offers, absolutely no doubt about that.' The affair would cause a rumpus in the press for a few days but did not affect the league form.

A run of six wins in seven games between 23 October and 4 December was only interrupted by a 2–1 loss to Southampton at the Dell on 13 November. A draw against Chelsea on 11 December brought the run to an end before two dominant performances, beating Derby County 3–0 on Boxing Day and Liverpool 2–0 on New Year's Day, saw Leeds hit top form, starting January 1972 in third place.

On 15 January, Bristol Rovers were the visitors to Elland Road for the third round of the FA Cup. Unlike in the previous year's spluttering cup campaign Leeds made no mistake, winning 4–1.

A Clarke header in a 1–0 win over Sheffield United on 22 January took Leeds to the top spot for the first time in the season. But losing 1–0 to Spurs at White Hart Lane was not the type of performance Leeds needed as they prepared to face Liverpool in a crunch fourth-round FA Cup tie at Anfield on 5 February.

A tight goalless draw meant the two sides had to do it all over again four days later on 9 February. A dominant performance with two goals from Clarke guaranteed safe passage to the fifth round against Cardiff City on 26 February, where two Giles goals knocked the Welsh club out of the competition.

Any designs Manchester United may have had on the league title were quickly smashed to pieces as Leeds dissected a poor United side 5–1. It got so bad for the 1968 European champions that the Leeds players were inviting the United players to attempt to win the ball.

On 4 March, Southampton were the visitors to Elland Road. Johnny Giles recalled, 'In a game immortalised in *Match of the Day's* highlights of our 7–0 destruction of Southampton we decided to showboat. There were flicks and back heels and all sorts of trickery and we kept possession of the ball for 40-odd passes, each one greeted with acclaim from the crowd at Elland Road.'

Watching as a reporter for the *Daily Mail* Jeff Powell wrote, 'Every time Leeds touched the ball the crowd would cheer. I think it was the first time I heard the call "ole!" every time a pass was made.'

Revie was finally giving this talented team the type of freedom it craved. Speaking in 1984 he said, 'I let them off the leash in the last three to four years I was there, it was my fault, I didn't realise their talent. When I came there, they were bottom of the Second Division, so I spent most of my time drilling them and getting them to play the way I wanted. In the end they played some of the best football I had been privileged to have ever seen.'

The sixth round of the FA Cup saw Spurs travel north on 18 March to a different type of Leeds. After trying to convince Spurs' manager Bill Nicholson of the advantages of public relations, sports artist Paul 'The Beaver' Trevillion was introduced to Revie, who liked the comic illustrator's ideas.

One of the innovations on show that day was the Leeds players emerging before kick-off to warm up and boot footballs into the crowd. Eagle-eyed fans would have seen Leeds wearing sock tags which the players autographed and handed out at the end of the game. Both ideas were the work of Trevillion.

Regardless of the PR, Leeds ran out as 2–1 winners to book a place in the semi-final of the FA Cup for the first time since 1970. There then followed a dour 0–0 draw against Leicester before Leeds ripped apart one of the so-called top teams 3–0 on 25 March. The unfortunate victims this time were the reigning champions Arsenal. Leeds were now second, two points behind Manchester City and with a game in hand.

A dropped point from a 2–2 draw against West Ham on 31 March saw the race for the title tighten up with only a few points separating Manchester City, Leeds, Derby County and Liverpool. Two days later an injury-ravaged and fatigued Leeds lost 2–0 at the Baseball Ground to third-placed Derby County. Revie was left to rue playing two vital games in three days.

A 3–1 win over Huddersfield on 5 April, and a 3–0 win away at Stoke City three days later settled nerves. An easy 3–0 win over Birmingham City in the FA Cup semi-final had Revie dreaming of emulating Arsenal's double of the previous season. However, it was back to earth with a bump on 15 April when Leeds lost 1–0 to Newcastle United.

A Johnny Giles penalty beat West Bromwich Albion on 22 April but Manchester City wound up their season by beating Derby County 2–0, leaving them top of the league. However, Leeds, Liverpool and Derby all had superior goal difference and, crucially, games in hand.

Going into the game against Chelsea on 1 May it was still difficult to predict where the league championship was going to end up. Two goals from Jones and Bremner gave Leeds victory.

At the same time, it was Derby's turn to wrap up their season with a win over Liverpool. Like Manchester City they, too, finished their season top of the league, one point ahead of their nearest rivals Leeds and Liverpool, who both still had a game to play. With the FA Cup Final on 6 May Revie was moved to tell the press, 'The double must be on now.'

It was 100 years since the staging of the first FA Cup Final and such was the pomp and circumstance of the occasion the Queen, never the keenest football fan, handed the cup over to the most consistent team in the land.

The 1–0 scoreline had flattered Arsenal. From the first whistle Leeds were totally dominant, moving Frank McGhee of the *Daily Mirror* to write, 'Arsenal could have tried for another 100 years and still would not have had a serious chance of beating Leeds in the centenary FA Cup Final at Wembley. Not on this form, the mood and the manpower seen in this match.'

In his column Charlton, wrote, 'Arsenal? They never bothered us a lot. In fact, their forwards had very little to say during the game. I thought we found our way through their defence easier than they did at our end. We should have knocked in more goals, but I never had the feeling we would lose. Indeed, the boys have never been so sure and confident of winning a trophy as this one.'

Despite all the disappointments in the past, Revie was still all about winning, which is why his team did not attend the traditional post-match banquet and instead headed straight to the Mount Hotel, Wolverhampton, to prepare for their date with destiny at Molineux.

The Leeds team had every reason to believe the double was on – the title would be theirs if they avoided defeat at Wolves. Mathematically, a draw might allow Liverpool to finish above them by virtue of goal average but they would need an 11–0 victory against Arsenal at Highbury.

If Leeds lost, a Liverpool victory would see them win the title. Table-topping Derby County would be champions if the Reds failed to win. When Leeds kicked off against Wolves the Rams manager, Brian Clough, was enjoying a family holiday in the Scilly Isles, hardly the actions of a man who expected to be celebrating his first title win.

The Leeds team arrived in Wolverhampton late on the Saturday night. Speaking to the press it was clear Revie was determined to see the double through. 'Leeds United must go all out for victory. This might appear illogical since we need only a draw to finish ahead of Derby County and Liverpool, but I reckon it would be soccer suicide to adopt a defensive style of play. Attack really is the best form of defence against Bill McGarry's team, because they possess the ability to swamp opponents like a tidal wave.

'It is vital to stop Wolves defenders and midfield players from supporting the likes of Derek Dougan, John Richards and David Wagstaffe up front. The best way to do that is to keep them under pressure. Wolves prefer opponents to play defensively, because it means that their own flaws at the back are not exposed.

'Although Wolves have only an academic interest in the championship and are in the middle of a two-leg UEFA Cup Final with Tottenham, this will not make our task any easier. Teams can always be relied upon to raise their game against us and this should be particularly true in Wolves' case, considering the tremendous atmosphere that can be expected at Molineux on Monday.

'I can't recall a team being forced to play a championship decider so soon after appearing in a Wembley cup final. But I am convinced that there is sufficient character in this Leeds team to accept the challenge and emerge triumphant.'

Leeds' fixture pile-up was compounded by England facing West Germany in the second of their European Championship qualifiers on 13 May, meaning they could expect some of their players to be called up for the national side.

When asked if he would make the Wolves game, striker Clarke said, 'It's better playing with pain to get the double than not playing at all. But I must admit I really felt pain towards the end of the match. I will decide myself before the kick-off whether I can play. I do want to be there and want to go with England to West Berlin next Saturday.'

The club appealed for the Wolves fixture to be delayed until the middle of May, but there were several issues with this, not least the circumstances of the clubs they faced. Chelsea were unwilling to co-operate because they had arranged to leave on a tour of the Caribbean on 13 May, while Wolves themselves were scheduled to play Spurs in the UEFA Cup Final on 3 and 17 May.

For Alan Hardaker, the Football League secretary, it seemed country won out over club when it suited him. He said, 'I have not seen one suggestion of a better solution to the problem. If Leeds United wish to play Wolves on 9 May they are quite free to do so as far as the league is concerned, but they will have to play without their England players unless the FA agreed to release them.

'Similarly, if Wolves will agree to play Leeds on 19 May, two days after the UEFA Cup Final and the FA would release their international players, the league would not object. Nor would the league object if Leeds suggested dates to play without their England players.

'It seems to me that for years the press has been saying that country must come before club, and yet when it comes to criticising the league for a decision that had to be made, the England v West Germany matches have been very carefully overlooked.'

Johnny Giles said, 'Leeds made a request to the FA to postpone the Wolves game until the Wednesday. The extra two days' rest would have made all the difference. But the Home Internationals between England, Scotland, Wales and Northern Ireland were due to start in a week, so the FA said that if Sir Alf Ramsey agreed, it was all right for them. And Alf, the cute old bugger, agreed, that Leeds could play on Wednesday night but with one important stipulation – he wanted the England players Norman Hunter, Allan Clarke and Paul Reaney in Wales no later than midnight on Monday. Which left us with no option but to play on Monday.

'Alf had no intention of doing Don any favours. The club managers held the power at the time to decide whether a player would report for international duty. And Alf remembered with resentment the way Don had persuaded some of the England players to pull out of games, on the pretext of illness or injury. Alf had a long memory.'

Striker Clarke recalled Revie telling him to feign injury when called up for England. He said, 'I was called up by England and Don told me to tell Alf I had a knock. I said, "I am perfectly fine." Don responded by saying, "Tell him you are injured." Again, I said to Don "I am not." To which Don replied, "Remember who pays your wages."'

The night of the Molineux game was already full of high tension and drama. After the excitement of the cup final Leeds had to dig deep to find something inside. It was confirmed centre-forward Jones, who had dislocated his elbow in the closing seconds of the final, would not be taking part in the title decider.

Several other players were carrying injuries. Clarke and Giles had painkilling injections before the game and Gray and Clarke both played with heavy strapping. All three had treatment at nearby West Bromwich Albion on Sunday. Jones' place was taken by Wembley substitute Mick Bates, who played in midfield with Billy Bremner, but was now in the unfamiliar position of leading the attack that night.

A crowd of more than 50,000 packed behind gates that were closed long before kick-off. During the match, more than 70 people suffered injuries when crush barriers gave way. One man sustained a broken leg and nine others required medical attention. Journalist John Helm described the night as having something of the surreal: 'It was a weird night, you had the feeling that anything could happen.'

There was no doubt that on that evening of Monday 8 May, 1972, Leeds United were facing a date with destiny. They could become champions for the second time in three years and would be only the third team in the 20th century to win the double. As important as the match was, it would have far reaching consequences and would define the way Leeds and Revie would be perceived for years to come.

The UEFA Cup finalists Wolves, in 10th place in the league, were keen to spoil the party and the Molineux atmosphere was at its boisterous best.

The first key moment came when referee John Gow turned down an appeal for a penalty after a blatant handball by Bernard Shaw in the 23rd minute. The second came when Frank Munro closed in on the far post for a right-wing corner and slipped the ball past Paul Reaney for the vital first goal.

Then the second goal came in the 67th minute from Derek Dougan, who took a pass from John Richards and calmly slid the ball past the advancing keeper David Harvey for his 24th goal of the season.

Then the game seemed to explode and Leeds went on the attack. Bremner slammed a pass from Madeley into the roof of Wolves' net to keep his hopes of the double alive. In the last few minutes Leeds, looking very weary, pressed hard and got a late corner. Yorath was on target with his header until Wolves' Gerry Taylor bobbed up to head it over the bar and away to safety.

The frantic pace continued. Even though Leeds came desperately close to snatching the crucial equaliser Wolves clung on to prevent Leeds from taking the championship. Leeds had given everything they had, but on the night, they caught Phil Parkes in exceptional form and Wolves played far above themselves.

On the same night another of the title challengers, Liverpool, failed to beat Arsenal at Highbury leaving Derby County, whose players were already on holiday (like their manager), champions for the first time in their history.

Unlike his sporting statement congratulating Arsenal the previous year, Revie made no mention of Derby winning the championship, only rueing bad luck and poor refereeing decisions: 'Naturally we are bitterly disappointed after all the hard work of the last nine months.

'But what can you do when the decisions go against you? We could have had three penalties. The first incident was a penalty and if anyone has the picture on TV, they will see that Bernard Shaw touched the ball with both hands.

'The second looked equally blatant when Phil Parkes brought down Allan Clarke and lay on top of him and I also thought there was another handling offence.'

There was a sense of sour grapes in his column for the *Sports Argus* on 13 May when under the headline 'You did not deserve it Derby' Revie wrote, 'Congratulations to Derby County on winning the championship but, deep down, I cannot accept they deserved to snatch the title from Leeds United's grasp. However, it would be dishonest for me to say that Derby won this gripping championship race because they were the best side.'

Revie then went on to blame the Football League for scheduling the Wolves game two days after the FA Cup Final and the decisions of referee Gow in the match itself. The bitterness in Revie's words masked one thing: for the first time in the history of Leeds United the FA Cup was at Elland Road. It was scant reward for a man who increasingly believed the world was against him.

17

LEEDS UNITED (1972-73)

'One defeat doesn't mean the bottom has fallen
out of the season for us.'

Don Revie

In July 1972, Don Revie celebrated his 45th birthday. A month earlier he had been named the Bell's Manager of the Year for the third time, having won the prize in 1969 and 1970. Despite claiming it was his intention to win the league in 1973, then the European Cup and the World Club Championship, Revie knew time was running out for him and Leeds United.

When he put pen to paper in 1971, taking his contract with Leeds up to the 1978–79 season, he knew it would be his last. 'Dad had no desire to continue in management beyond the age of 50,' said Kim Revie. As a nod towards the future Revie had already agreed to take up a five-year consultancy role with Leeds once his contract came to an end.

Things were changing on the home front as well. After 20 years as a teacher, Elsie Revie told Leeds High School she intended to retire at the end of the school year. Revie's son Duncan, 18, was at Cambridge University reading law, and daughter Kim, 13, was developing an interest in music.

On the playing side, Revie was approaching the time when he would have to make some tough decisions. As was pointed out in the *Liverpool Echo* on 19 August, 'Revie's remarkable record has been achieved with just one team. In 1965, newly-promoted Leeds missed the First Division title on goal average. Last season they got within a goal of the league and cup double; nine of the Elland Road players played in both campaigns.'

It was true the only real additions to the side were strikers Clarke and Jones and, looking at the team, Revie had failed to find an adequate replacement for central defender Jack Charlton, who was by then 37 years old.

In midfield, Giles was soon to be 32 and captain Bremner would celebrate his 30th birthday in December. Hunter was only a year younger. Very soon Revie knew he would have to find replacements for them all. The *Liverpool Echo* saw one stumbling block in rebuilding the side – 'sentimentality'.

Those closest to Revie knew breaking up the side was going to be a huge wrench for the manager, as his wife Elsie told the *Liverpool Echo*, 'Relationships with Don are always intense. He is terribly loyal to his staff and players.

'He feels things deeply. He is fiercely protective. Anything said about his players is said about him. This is the strain. I know he hides it well from the world, but he is a very warm man, a very sensitive man.'

Even Revie himself was to cast doubts about building a side as good as his present one, telling Frank McGhee of the *Daily Mirror*, 'I realise that during my period as Leeds manager it is unlikely so many outstanding players will be available to build a side as good as this one.'

As the 1972–73 season approached it seemed as though the rebuilding had begun with the addition of 24-year-old Trevor Cherry, bought for £100,000 from relegated Huddersfield on 8 June. Signed as a long-term replacement for Hunter, in the short term he was to provide cover for Terry Cooper at left-back, who had broken his leg at Stoke City in April.

In August, with Bremner, Hunter, Clarke, Jordan and Galvin facing FA disciplinary committees for a variety of offences, Revie was forced back into the transfer market by going back to Huddersfield for 29-year-old centre-half Roy Ellam, bought for £30,000.

At the same time, Revie was keeping close tabs on 20-year-old St Mirren centre-half Gordon McQueen but the fee of £80,000 was felt to be extortionate. The Scot would eventually sign for £30,000 in September.

As Leeds prepared for a trip to Stamford Bridge for the first game of the season on 12 August against Chelsea, Clarke was suspended alongside Norman Hunter. David Harvey was preferred to Sprake in goal and Lorimer started up front with Jones. Cherry and Ellam made their debuts alongside Madeley and Reaney in an unfamiliar-looking back four.

Then after 25 minutes disaster struck as Jones and Harvey had to go off after sustaining injuries. This meant Lorimer had to play in goal for the rest of the game and, just before half time, Chelsea went one-up, before knocking in three unanswered goals as Leeds suffered a heavy defeat.

In the next match, Charlton returned to the side in place of Ellam who Revie deemed nervous and unsure of himself in his first game at the heart of the Leeds defence. Jordan stood in for the injured Jones.

An assured 2–0 win over Sheffield United at Brammall Lane got Leeds back to winning ways. In the first home game of the season, Charlton retained his place in the side and, back from suspension, Clarke opened the scoring before a Giles penalty saw Leeds secure a win in front of their home fans.

An exciting 3–3 draw at Elland Road against Ipswich Town on 23 August saw Leeds go in front three times with a brace from Jordan and a penalty from Giles, only to be pulled back every time.

A 2–0 win over Norwich in the league on 2 September was followed by a 4–0 win over Burnley in the second round of the League Cup on 6 September. It looked as though Leeds were back to their dominant best. However, there were more concerns about defensive frailties when Leeds allowed Stoke City to come back at them for a 2–2 draw, having taken a 2–0 lead at the Victoria Ground on 9 September.

An understrength Leeds drew 1–1 against Turkish outfit Ankaragücü in a rough-and-ready European Cup Winners' Cup match in Turkey, then it was back to winning ways against Leicester City at Elland Road on 16 September.

However, there was no reporting of the game in *The People* the following day, which focussed on something much more sinister. In an exclusive, Wolves full-back Bernard Shaw claimed he was telephoned 24 hours before the league decider the previous May by a man who suggested he sell the game. Shaw was quoted as saying, 'He was not connected with Leeds and has no connections within the Leeds team. But I am not prepared to say what offer was made. My first reaction was to inform the manager Bill McGarry, but I was unable to get in touch with him until the morning of the game.'

When asked for his reaction McGarry said, 'From what Shaw said I immediately called the players together to inform them of the approach to Shaw asking them to sell the game.' According to *The People,* other Wolves players were targeted, too – Frank Munro and David Wagstaffe.

Revie, who called the allegations 'ridiculous' defended his players. 'There is no need for me to speak to the players. I will not be seeing them before Wednesday anyway, but I have no intention of speaking to them specifically on these matters. There is a board meeting on Thursday. I have nothing further to say until we have discussed this at the meeting.'

But the FA secretary Denis Follows told the *Daily Mirror* on 19 September, 'Unquestionably the matter will have to be investigated.'

When the Leeds players arrived for training on Wednesday, they found themselves called into the manager's office one by one to be asked about what went on before the Wolves game. To a man, the players denied any knowledge. The statement from Manny Cussins, who had replaced Percy Woodward as chairman of the club in the summer, placed the blame on what he called 'gambling types'. They would now await the outcome of the FA investigation.

Showing no signs of being affected by events off the pitch, Leeds battled hard on 23 September against a resolute Newcastle United at St James' Park. A Jones goal in a 1–0 win over Ankaragücü at Elland Road saw Leeds safely through to the next round of the European Cup Winners' Cup on 27 September.

It was then the turn of league leaders Liverpool to visit Elland Road on 30 September. An early Jones goal gave the home side hope, but again defensive issues let Leeds down as Liverpool ran out 2–1 winners, handing Leeds their first home defeat for 18 months.

A dull, defensive 1–1 League Cup tie against Aston Villa in Birmingham saw a replay at Elland Road on 11 October, which they duly won 2–0.

There could be no doubt the loss of the league title to Derby County in 1972 still niggled. Since winning the title there had been criticism from some quarters that their manager Brian Clough was more interested in being a television celebrity than football manager. In early October he had been handed a reprimand from the FA for some of his more controversial comments.

On the pitch, Derby had got off to a horrendous start and when they travelled to Elland Road on 7 October, they were lying 14th in the table.

Jack Charlton made his feelings about Derby known in a joint interview with their centre-half Roy McFarland in *Goal* magazine. 'Well Roy,' said Charlton, 'Cloughie and you can say what you like, but Derby never won that title last season. We lost it and if you win it this time with all the pressure you'll be under, then you really will be the best team and Cloughie can accuse me of being a know-nothing.

'But frankly I don't think you will be, judging by your terrible start to the season. Europe is a different thing. I'm not saying you won't win the European Cup, although I doubt that too.'

With Leeds playing with a point to prove, the champions were never in the game, smashed to pieces 5–0, with two goals from Giles, before Clarke, Bremner and Lorimer also got on the score sheet.

A 2–1 win against Everton on 14 October then a disappointing 1–1 draw with Coventry City on 21 October were indicative of the patchy form Leeds were showing before they headed to East Germany for a goalless draw against Carl Zeiss Jena in the European Cup Winners' Cup second round, first leg.

Back home, a 2–0 win over Wolves, which was billed as a grudge match in the press following the match-fixing allegations, was followed by a hard fought 2–2 draw in the League Cup against Liverpool.

United took the lead at Ipswich on 4 November through Charlton, but had to settle for a 2–2 draw, with Peter Lorimer scoring his 100th league goal to tie the game up in the second half.

Four days later, Leeds reached the quarter-final of the Cup Winners' Cup when they defeated Carl Zeiss Jena, 2–0 at Elland Road.

Two days before Leeds faced Sheffield United on 11 November the FA announced, having received statements from both clubs, that they would be reporting the match-fixing allegations in the Wolves v Leeds game back in May to the police. Welcoming the news, Revie told the press he looked forward to his players having their names cleared.

There would also be no further progression in the League Cup as Liverpool dumped Leeds out in a battling 1–0 victory at Elland Road on 22 November.

The 5 December home game against Manchester City seemed to be drifting into a goalless draw before Cherry, Clarke and Lorimer struck in the last 20 minutes to make it 3–0.

In the past, December was the month when Leeds began their title charge but a 2–1 home loss to Arsenal was a blow, before normal service was resumed with a 1–1 draw with Manchester United being the only blip in a five-game unbeaten run that saw wins over West Ham, Birmingham, Newcastle and Spurs between 9 December, 1972, and 6 January, 1973.

It had been over 10 years since Spurs had won back-to-back FA Cup victories, in 1961 and 1962, and on 13 January, 1973, Leeds began their quest to emulate them, facing Norwich City in the third round. Even though the Canaries were in the League Cup Final very few expected them to trouble the mighty Leeds. A pair of 1–1 draws in the FA Cup on 13 and 17 was then followed by another tight game against the same opposition in the league at Carrow Road that Leeds edged 2–1 on 20 January. Complaints from Norwich City boss Ron Saunders that Leeds were interrupting his side's rhythm by feigning injuries and slow play riled Revie and his players.

Claiming Saunders had gone down in his estimation, Revie used Saunders' verbal attacks to motivate his players, who finally showed their class in their second FA Cup replay with the Canaries, played at Villa Park on 29 January. Clarke was in scintillating form, claiming a hat-trick in a resounding 5–0 win.

The man known as 'Sniffer' because of his prowess at snapping up half-chances was again on the score sheet four days later as Leeds saw off Plymouth Argyle at the first time of asking to make their way to the fifth round of the FA Cup. There, a Clarke brace would see off opponents West Bromwich Albion on 24 February.

In the league, a terrible 2–0 loss to Leicester at Filbert Street, followed by a frustrating draw at Chelsea on 17 February, saw Leeds slip further behind Liverpool. Even though they were still within touching distance of the top, as March came around it looked unlikely the title would be heading towards Elland Road.

One place the championship was not going this year was the Baseball Ground. By the time Derby played Leeds at home on 3 March their only chance of glory was the European Cup or the FA Cup, their title defence having never really recovered from a poor start.

Already there was tension in the air. Perhaps frustrated by his team's inability to repeat the performances of the previous season, things came to a head with Brian Clough on 28 January at an awards night organised by the Variety Club of Great Britain at the Queen's Hotel, Leeds, to name Lorimer as Yorkshire Sports Personality of the Year.

After keeping guests waiting for his speech, among other things, he insulted Lorimer and alluded to Leeds as being cheats and a dirty team. Despite being told to sit down and shut up, Clough was defiant, claiming they should be grateful as he had come to the event at his own expense on his day off. Yorkshire Television cut his comments from its programme. Later, Clough claimed that half the audience was against him because they were Leeds fans who could not accept that Derby had won the league championship in 1972.

When Clough's and Revie's sides next met it was an ill-tempered affair with Hunter receiving his eighth booking of the season, McQueen playing the entire second half with damaged ribs, and Reaney hobbling off. Leeds had to come from behind twice to win the game 3–2 and silence the controversial Clough – for the time being.

The quarter-final of the European Cup Winners' Cup was next, on 7 March, with Romanian side Rapid Bucharest the visitors to Elland Road. Any thoughts they may cause an upset were quickly forgotten as a rampant Leeds ran out 5–0 winners in their first leg. A 2–1 win over Everton at Elland Road kept fading league hopes alive but now the focus was on retaining the FA Cup and winning the European Cup Winners' Cup.

It was Revie's turn to take a swipe at Clough before their FA Cup quarter-final clash. On 10 March, a week before the game, Revie wrote in his column for the *Sports Argus*, 'It must be abundantly clear to most soccer followers that Derby County manager Brian Clough and myself are not exactly the best of friends. As our relationship stands now, he is the last person with whom I would wish to be stranded on a desert island, and no doubt he feels the same way about me.

'Why? From my point of view it all boils down to the fact that I dislike the way Clough repeatedly knocks other personalities in the game – especially rival managers. I think it is wrong to criticise your colleagues as Clough does because the job is difficult enough without any of us slitting each other's throat. I find it surprising that he should appear to be so indignant about teams going in hard for the ball. No matter what he might say to the contrary, you can take it from me that Derby are as physically intimidating as anyone when the need arises.

'This was shown last Saturday when Leeds overcame Derby 3–2 at the Baseball Ground in a match littered by no less than 55 fouls – 26 of them by Derby players. Therefore, Derby can be classed as one of the most rugged and fiercely-combative sides Leeds have met this season.'

The scene was set for a real FA Cup battle at the Baseball Ground. Anyone expecting fireworks was sadly disappointed in a game played in bright sunshine. Despite a positive start from Derby, Leeds dominated the match and it was perhaps poetic justice – after Clough ruined his night in late January – that a Peter Lorimer goal in a 1–0 win should dump Derby out of the competition. After finishing off Rapid Bucharest, 3–1, on 21 March, Leeds now found themselves in the semi-finals of two cup competitions.

Their winning run came to an end when they were held to a goalless draw in the league on 24 March by Wolves at Elland Road, and they dropped another point when they failed to win at West Bromwich four days later.

Going into their match with Manchester City on 31 March they were lying in third place, six points behind leaders Liverpool with two games in hand. A win at Maine Road and they would force themselves right back into the title scene. It was not to be, despite Manchester City being unsettled by the departure of Malcolm Allison to take charge of Crystal Palace. The Citizens ran out as 1–0 winners.

But that was not the end of their league ambitions. Leaders Liverpool and second-placed Arsenal both failed to press home their advantage. This meant Leeds had to win their games in hand, and a 1–0 league win over Coventry at Highfield Road gave them some hope going into their FA Cup semi-final against Wolves.

In the semi-final, just as he had done in 1965 and 1970, Bremner scored the only goal of the game to take Leeds to Wembley for the second year running.

A Clarke goal against Hajduk Split of Yugoslavia at Elland Road in the first leg of the European Cup Winners' Cup set Leeds up nicely for the second leg as once again they found themselves chasing three trophies in April. A 1–1 draw with West Ham on 14 April left Leeds six points behind Liverpool with two games in hand. They simply had to beat Manchester United at Elland Road on 18 April. An out-of-sorts Leeds, with McQueen and Yorath at the back, lost 1–0.

At the end Revie was philosophical, 'We are disappointed but this is how it goes. It was an exciting match and we don't have any grumbles. Liverpool are now in the enviable position at the top but we'll have to press on and hope for the best.

'One defeat doesn't mean the bottom has fallen out of the season for us. Don't forget that we are in the FA Cup Final, the European Cup Winners' Cup semi-final and have an excellent chance of making the final in that competition.'

Two days later, a 4–0 win at relegation-threatened Crystal Palace gave Leeds a confidence boost going into a league match against Liverpool at Anfield. Revie knew only a win would do.

Watching Anfield's new star Kevin Keegan have a hand in the first goal and score the winner in a 2–0 Liverpool victory must have got Revie wondering why Doncaster-born Keegan was wearing the red of Liverpool and not the white of Leeds United. Keegan was one of several local youngsters Leeds were beginning to miss out on.

At the end of the match, and remembering the very sporting gesture Liverpool afforded Leeds when they won the title in 1969, Leeds returned the favour by clapping the champions-elect Reds off the field.

A goalless draw against Hajduk Split, which took Leeds into the final of the European Cup Winners' Cup, was the only high point in April as Leeds suffered defeats against Birmingham and Southampton in their next two games. With Arsenal doing so well, the highest place Leeds would be able to finish was third. It was hardly great preparation for the 1973 FA Cup Final against Sunderland.

Even though Leeds arrived for the final as overwhelming favourites, on present form they were struggling. After going so close to the championship in the previous three seasons, a third-place finish was a dismal return on a season which promised so much. Their opponents Sunderland, on the other hand, were riding a crest of a wave. Ever since Bob Stokoe took over midway through the season they had risen from third-from-bottom in the Second Division to finish sixth by showing the type of form which, in any other season, would have seen the side pushing for promotion.

And Sunderland's run to the cup final was a fairy tale. In the quarter-final they had dispatched title contenders Manchester City then shocked observers who were expecting a repeat of the 1972 FA Cup Final by stunning Arsenal in the semi-final. The relative unpopularity of Leeds and the avuncular image portrayed by Sunderland's manager ensured they were many neutral's favourites in the final.

To people like Clough and Revie, who had played against Stokoe, nothing could be further from the truth. As Clough writhed around in the mud in the Sunderland goalmouth after suffering a career-ending injury on Boxing Day 1962, Stokoe playing for Bury would stand over him screaming at the referee that he was play acting.

Ever since that Good Friday meeting 11 years earlier Stokoe had become bitter and plotted revenge against Revie. Speaking to the *Daily Mirror* in 1977, in which he alleged a match-fixing attempt, 'I have respected his success but I have always felt very, very strongly because he was prepared to destroy me before I had even started by tempting me to take something I shouldn't.

'I felt if I could pull this one off, it would be more than I could ever hope for. To kill it on this occasion would be a measure of revenge.'

Jeff Powell of the *Daily Mail* wrote, 'Bob fell out with both Don and Brian Clough. He was angry they seemed to have chances he did not. Bob always saw himself as a manager who was destined for the top. Unfortunately, his record did not warrant that.'

In later years, while managing Fulham in the 1980s, former Newcastle hero Malcolm Macdonald remembered an incident when Stokoe was the opposing manager for Carlisle: 'I was sitting in the dugout at Craven Cottage and could hear Stokoe shouting to his players, "Break his fucking leg". After about an hour I had enough and went over to him and said, "You tell your players to break anybody's leg and I'll break your legs. Got it?" Stokoe said nothing and was quiet for the rest of the game.'

By the time Revie, dressed in his lucky blue suit, and Stokoe, in his distinctive red tracksuit and few strands of hair swept over to cover his bald head, walked out into the light rain neither said a word to each other. The distrust between the two men started years before when Stokoe, then manager of Blackpool, refused to sanction a move by one of his players to Leeds United.

According to journalist Ken Jones, 'He [Stokoe] was reluctant to agree a deal with Leeds for the talented Scottish international inside-forward Tony Green, who eventually joined Newcastle United. "I tried to get Liverpool interested," he told me. "When Bill Shankly asked me why I was set against the offer from Leeds I told him about the thing with Revie at Bury. Bill went silent. I don't think he ever again saw Revie in the same light."'

Whatever the reason, there was always bad blood between Revie and Stokoe, whether it was jealousy or something much deeper, no one quite got to the bottom of it. Least of all Billy Bremner, who was shocked by some of the critical comments that some of the Sunderland players had made about Leeds United in the run-up to the final.

The most stinging was the one attributed to Bob Stokoe, who claimed Leeds United were unable to finish the job in the latter stages of competitions. While the response from Bremner, 'at least we reach finals regularly' seemed petty, it did nothing to quell the jitters of a team who were expected to overrun the perceived mediocre team from the second division.

Just like the finals of 1965 and 1970, it seemed luck was not on the side of the side from West Yorkshire. From the off, Sunderland established their tactics immediately and refused to be intimidated by their more illustrious opponents, tackling fiercely and defiantly. Leeds looked anxious, lacking their usual composure. The match itself was decided by two crucial moments that would be talked about for years to come.

After 32 minutes Sunderland took the lead. A corner from Sunderland's Billy Hughes was hit at the far post where danger man Dave Watson was waiting, with Madeley and Jones ready to compete with him. In the eventuality, the ball beat all three of them and went on to bounce off the chest of the incoming Vic Halom.

It fell nicely for Porterfield in a space in the centre of the area. He cushioned it on his thigh and stroked a lovely volley that eventually ended up in the roof of the net past a stricken David Harvey.

A shocked Leeds battled back with predictable determination, but Sunderland's goalkeeper Jimmy Montgomery was outstanding, defying Leeds with a string of fine saves and preserving his team's lead.

The turning point of the match came midway through the second half. Montgomery dived to palm away a close-range header from Cherry. It fell into the path of Lorimer who blasted goalward from 10 yards but Montgomery managed to divert the ball on to the underside of the bar, and Malone scrambled the ball clear.

Writing in the *Sunday Mirror* the following day Ken Jones said, 'Bob Stokoe's beaming, tearful face told it all at Wembley. The triumph was complete. Sunderland from the Second Division, and the very depths of improbability, had won the FA Cup.

'The whistle had barely died on an astonishing upset when Sunderland's manager sprinted from the bench towards the goal his team had defended so heroically throughout the second half. It was in that goal that Jim Montgomery had performed a football miracle with two super reflex saves inside two seconds from Cherry and Peter Lorimer just when it seemed Leeds had broken through at last.

'Montgomery already engulfed by delight was swept into Stokoe's arms. Leeds – every professional's choice as the best team in Britain and probably Europe too – had been beaten.'

What should have been a celebration at the Savoy Hotel had turned into a wake. Called on to speak Revie was unable to muster any words and with tears in his eyes he just broke down. The only words which came out were to say to his vanquished team, 'I feel that our players have done enough in 10 years to walk on to your applause even without the FA Cup. We never tried to cheat. We tried to be honest and we would be less than honest if I did not ask you to salute the most consistent side that ever lived. This season we still have the European Cup Winners' Cup to play for. Lads, you've had a terrible season again.'

Looking at a team with an average age of over 27 and his two midfield kingpins, Bremner and Giles, now into their 30s, Revie had the nagging feeling he had taken the club as far as he could go.

Giles said, 'Everyone was very depressed after the Sunderland match. We had a banquet and Don was in tears. Soon there were rumours Don was leaving, the players picked up on that. We went into the European Cup Winners' Cup Final not knowing whether Don was going to stay.'

Bremner added, 'I think everything about the FA Cup final of that year has already been said. It always fucking well hurts. It would have been great to win it two years in succession but Sunderland had lady luck with them that day and we really didn't do ourselves justice. Afterwards, I went to congratulate some of them on their win and got told to "piss off". They really did enjoy beating us and rubbed it in.'

The following Monday Frank McGhee of the *Daily Mirror* claimed it was the end of an era. 'Sunderland smashed the most consistent team of the last decade. This was such a shattering blow to pride, composure and self-respect the cracks will not be easily repaired even by Don Revie, the manager who has hauled them up from the floor so often in a past studded with second places. It may well be that Leeds cannot recover this time and bring the club back to where they were or what they used to be. It could well be one of the great teams of our time is breaking up.'

There had been disappointments before, but this was different. The previous summer Revie had agonised over when to start rebuilding his team but had hesitated because he believed his side had another two or three years at the top. On the evidence of the cup final he would have to start breaking up the side in the summer to come.

However, he looked to the examples of his peers. It was only now, a full seven years after his last title win in 1966, that Shankly had a side to challenge again for top honours at Liverpool, and there was a seven-year gap between Harry Catterick's two title wins with Everton in 1963 and 1970. Even the great Sir Matt Busby had to wait five years for his second title win with his Babes in 1956 (after his first in 1951) and it would not be until 1965 that he won the championship after the Munich air crash in 1958.

Then there was Stan Cullis, dismissed at Wolves in 1964 only five years after his team had won back-to-back titles in 1958 and 1959. Even Bill Nicholson, a double winner in 1961 with Spurs, had now gone 12 years without the championship.

There was no time to waste. Revie desperately wanted to win the European Cup and if he could not do it with Leeds perhaps there was another club with more resources that could help him achieve his ambition. For the first time in 12 years, Revie was contemplating life away from Elland Road.

First, though, he had to lift his players for the European Cup Winners' Cup against AC Milan. It would have been difficult enough but harder still when Revie could not pick himself up off the floor.

18

LEEDS UNITED (1973-74)

'We've got to win four games, show character and pick up three or four points away from home and that will be the championship wrapped up.'

Don Revie

The lads who had been with him throughout the years could hardly believe what they were seeing. There was the boss, the man who had come to dominate their lives, openly weeping. Ever since they had lost the FA Cup Final against Sunderland, Revie had been quiet and not even a thumping 6–1 win over Arsenal to round off the season on 6 May could lift his spirits.

When the players arrived in Athens ahead of the European Cup Winners' Cup Final on 16 May they found Revie distracted and lost in thought. Rather than socialising with the team, Revie preferred to spend his nights locked away in his hotel room.

'From the moment we arrived in Greece something was not right. At first I thought the boss was unhappy at losing the cup final but there was something more to it than that,' Norman Hunter later recollected.

Arriving after the others, having played in an international for the Republic of Ireland, Johnny Giles saw that something was amiss from the moment he got to Greece.

'When I got to the hotel, straight away I thought it was odd that he wasn't there to meet me. Normally he'd be waiting for me; to see how I was. He'd be anxious about any injuries I might have picked up on international duty which was the bane of his life.

'Instead, a couple of the lads – Norman Hunter and Mick Bates – were waiting for me. And they looked anxious, for reasons that I would soon discover.

'But first, I went to find Les Cocker to tell him about an injury I had picked up playing for Ireland. When I had told him I couldn't play, I was surprised that he didn't say something like, "You'd better see the boss." It would be completely uncharacteristic of a man with Don's obsessive attention to detail not to want to know everything as soon as it happened, always.

'It was Norman and the lads down in the lobby who provided the explanation. "There are big rumours that the boss is leaving and going to Everton," Norman said.

'I looked at Norman and Mick Bates, who had been at Leeds with Don since they were lads. They were shocked, dispirited, confused. I had great difficulty myself, trying to take it in. I felt that the first thing we needed to do was to find out exactly what was happening, from the only man who really knew.

'The best thing we can do, I said, is go to his room now, and just ask him straight out if he's going.

'So Norman, Mick and I went up to Don's room. He was sitting on the bed. I knew I had to ask the hard question but I already knew what the answer would be. The fact that Don still hadn't said anything about my injury said it all.

'There are rumours you're going to Everton and obviously the players are unsettled,' I said. "Yes, I'm going," he replied. And then, just as he had done at the Savoy, he broke down and cried.

'We appreciated his honesty. We knew he wasn't going to fob us off in that situation and he didn't. Don said that the only reason he hadn't told us already was that he hadn't wanted to upset the players before the game. He had planned to tell us afterwards. And, anyway, the deal with Everton wasn't done yet.

'But the lads were devastated. They'd grown up at Leeds participating fully in the family atmosphere which Don had created, and which had formed such strong bonds of friendship and solidarity when the going got tough.'

When Everton won the 1970 league championship they boasted a midfield of Alan Ball, Colin Harvey and Howard Kendall. The way they had left the likes of Leeds, Liverpool, and Arsenal in their wake on their way to taking the first division title had many tipping them as the team of the '70s.

It was the second title for their manager Harry Catterick, to go alongside the one he had won in 1963. At one point, Catterick could claim to be the most successful manager on Merseyside as Bill Shankly struggled to rebuild his Liverpool side in the late '60s and early '70s.

Then, almost overnight, it went wrong for Catterick and Everton. The rot set in when the Everton manager decided to offload his prize asset Ball to Arsenal. Even though the Toffees managed to double their money, at 26, Ball was in his prime.

Whereas Everton's sale of Bobby Collins to Leeds 10 years before came out of a need to build a younger side there was no direct replacement for World Cup winner Ball. The following season, as Arsenal won the league and cup double, Everton slumped to 14th in the league and went out in the quarter-final stage of the European Cup.

It got worse for Catterick. When travelling home from Sheffield on the second day of the year in 1972, he suffered a heart attack. It took him out of the game for two months. His eventual return was not enough to save a dismal season as Everton slipped to 15th, scoring only 37 goals. By April 1973, the Everton board had decided to move Catterick on.

The *Liverpool Echo* was clear, Revie was Everton's man. After approaching Bobby Robson of Ipswich and Jimmy Armfield at Burnley, Everton had focused their attention on the Leeds manager.

With the European Cup Winners' Cup final just a few days away it would have been usual for Revie to be poring over every detail with his backroom staff. Instead, he was driving around the Liverpool suburb of Formby looking for the home of Everton chairman and Littlewoods Pools millionaire John Moores.

The house was about a quarter of a mile away from Freshfield station. Totally lost and confused in a strange part of the city he did not know that well, Revie made a mistake of asking two people he had stopped for directions.

They wasted no time in ringing the *Liverpool Echo* to tell them the Leeds manager, or someone who looked remarkably like him, was driving around Formby asking about the whereabouts of John Moores.

The local paper delved further discovering that Revie would not be meeting up with his team at Leeds but at Manchester Ringway Airport to fly out to Salonika, Greece.

Unlike with earlier approaches from Sunderland and Manchester City, the *Daily Mirror* was confident enough to announce on the eve of the cup final that Revie was to be named as Everton manager at the end of the match.

When asked to comment on the story by the *Liverpool Echo* former Leeds chairman Percy Woodward told the paper, 'I have heard nothing about this. How can a man sign for another club when he is contracted to us until 1978–79 and for five years after that as a consultant? The board will have to discuss the matter first.

'There can be nothing signed, and no decisions taken, until next Monday when the board meets at 4 p.m. I can't intervene until I have information, and I can't see any information coming that is authentic until it comes before the board.

'I spoke to Mrs Revie last night after she had been in contact with Don. As far as I am concerned, this is all rumour and speculation now. There is nothing we can do until the board meeting on Monday. We are not stupid at Elland Road. We don't let managers walk in and walk out just like that. There must be a reason, but who's to say the reason can't be overcome? We have had no discussion about this at all and nothing can be done before Monday's meeting.'

The only comment Revie would make was to say he was to stay in Greece for a two-week holiday after the final to contemplate his future. Giles said, 'There was bitter disappointment of the defeat to Sunderland and his breakdown at the Savoy. There was also the plain fact that Don had never been on more than £15,000 a year at Leeds, which played its part in the open disdain for the chairman and the directors throughout his time at the club and his eventual decision to move on.

'But in a complex way, I think that Don's personal feelings for the players also influenced his desire to move to Everton. I wonder if he had formed the view deep down that maybe the critics were right for a change, that some of the lads really were finished, and that we wouldn't be able to stay at the top level with this particular team.

'He loved those lads and the feeling was mutual and in the mood of despair after the cup final, I think he saw a day coming when he would have to tell some of them that it was time to go. And he couldn't face that.'

Heading into the Athens final there were other rumours which reached the ears of the Leeds players. Giles added, 'We'd heard rumours before the match about the referee, one Christos Michas. And when AC Milan went ahead after five minutes with a goal by Chiarugi, who scored direct from an indirect free-kick, it seemed as if Michas had that result on his coupon. A good goal of ours was disallowed, a penalty wasn't given to us for a blatant handball and Norman Hunter was sent off.'

Giles' fears seemed well founded as the game progressed. The final was nothing short of a sham. In the game the referee turned down three strong appeals from Leeds for a penalty, in what were obvious fouls. Every decision went the way of AC Milan, Bremner felt it was almost as though the Italians were playing with an extra man.

When the final whistle blew and AC Milan were declared winners, their celebrations were cut short. After collecting the trophy, what began with jeering from the largely Greek crowd turned into shouts of shame, and when coins and bottles began raining down on the Italians they had to beat a hasty retreat to the dressing room.

The referee was placed under investigation by the Greek Football Association on suspicion of bribery, and although the allegation was never proven, he received a lifetime ban from UEFA and never refereed another international game again.

In March 2009 Richard Corbett, Labour MEP for Yorkshire and the Humber, launched a campaign in the hope of reversing the result. He set up an online petition to pressurise UEFA into a new investigation. Corbett wrote to all the surviving members of the Leeds team asking them to sign up, along with the 12,200 others who did so.

Corbett said, 'The match has always stuck in my mind as one that ended with a grossly unjust result, due largely to the dubious refereeing performance of Christos Michas whose performance was so poor he was banned from officiating a European game again.

'There has long been cause to suspect Michas was bribed and the match fixed. Match fixing and bribery in sport is clearly unacceptable at any level. If football in Europe is to retain its integrity UEFA must show its commitment to fair play and reverse the results where there is evidence matches have been fixed.

'When I spoke to officials from UEFA with a view to overturning the result they were very sympathetic but the law of statute was such that it was out of time. Leeds were robbed once again.'

Corbett travelled to Geneva to deliver his petition. He met Peter Limacher, UEFA's head of legal affairs and compliance, and revealed, 'They told me they were staggered at the response to the petition, particularly as it dates to a game so long ago.

'I and others were amazed that so many signed it in a short space of time. But UEFA have told me that the only way the matter could be resolved would be for it to go to court and that the courts would shoot it down, not least because UEFA cannot re-investigate cases dating back more than 10 years. Put simply, their hands are tied by the courts. Considering what I have been told it appears, sadly, as though there is little or nothing we can do.'

After their Greek tragedy the Leeds board had to move fast as the day after their board meeting Revie and family would be heading back to Greece for a holiday.

The Leeds board had been completely blindsided by Revie. This was the third time they had met to discuss Revie's future. The previous tactic of a pay rise and contract extension, so effective at warding off potential suitors in the past, seemed to fail this time. When Revie and his wife boarded the plane back to Greece his future was still uncertain.

The board was in disarray. Chairman Manny Cussins was in the south of France and, to all the world, it looked as though once he was back from his holiday, Revie would be announced as the new manager at Everton.

...

On a blistering hot day, a luxury yacht cruised on the waters of the Aegean Sea. As the family dived off the side of the boat, the north of England seemed a long way away. They were on the yacht as guests of Nikos Goulandris, president of Athens team, Olympiacos. The club was dominant in Greece, winning the double and breaking records on their way to the league championship. Now Goulandris wanted the European Cup for his beloved club.

Anyone who had witnessed the run up to the Cup Winners' Cup final knew Revie was unsettled. Now Goulandris, who had been impressed by the way Revie had pulled Leeds up by their bootstraps, wanted their manager. As a shipping magnate he was used to getting what he wanted.

He made his move just as his staff was clearing up the plates after lunch. The offer was a lucrative £20,000 a year tax free and it matched the offer the Greek Football Association had also made Revie to make him their national team boss. When another Athens club, Panathinaikos, offered £28,000, also tax free, it looked as though Revie's future was going to be in Greece, one way or another.

Then when all hope of keeping Revie at Leeds was lost, Woodward received a call: 'Mr Revie telephoned me from Greece to tell me that he will be staying with us as manager. Naturally if the conditions are to be the same as they were previously, I will be more than delighted.

'The board will be meeting Mr Revie on his return from holiday and we shall then learn the truth of the newspaper reports we have been reading. I am hoping that the matter will be concluded to the satisfaction of both parties when Mr Revie returns. If it is, the better it will be for football and for the club.'

Kim Revie said, 'He was certainly flattered [by other clubs] but, in the end, Everton would have taken a few years to build and he would have been leaping into the unknown with Greece.'

When he arrived back in the UK on 4 June, under the headline 'Revie Stays', the *Daily Mirror* announced, 'Don Revie flew into London from a Greek holiday last night declaring he would stay manager of Leeds, despite an offer of a five-year contract worth £100,000, plus a lump sum from Greek club, Panathanaikos.'

There was a quick golfing holiday to Ayrshire to celebrate his birthday and take in the British Open at Royal Troon in mid-July before it was back to work and a disciplinary hearing in London at the end of the month, which had been delayed for a year and could not be put off any longer.

The charges related to on-field discipline stretching back two years. Despite several warnings in 1971 about conduct on the field, the disciplinary record of

Leeds going into 1971–72 had not improved. In the 1972–73 season there were 40 bookings among first-team players. Going into the new season, defenders Yorath and Cherry, and striker Jordan, were already suspended.

As Revie travelled on the 10.25 a.m. Leeds–London train on 25 July with chairman Cussins there was speculation Leeds could be fined upwards of £5,000. It was not the fine that was the only worry for Revie. The FA was quite clear it had the power to suspend the manager if it saw fit.

After a 90-minute hearing, Leeds were found to have 'persistently violated the laws of the game and brought the game into disrepute', receiving a suspended fine of £3,000 as punishment. The FA promised to waive the sanction if United's record were to show 'a substantial improvement'. The only comment a beaming Revie would give the press was that the team would 'continue to play hard'.

There were two departures in the summer. After failing to land a regular first-team place, Galvin moved on to Hull City for a fee of £25,000.

The other player of more significance was Jack Charlton who, despite an offer of an extra year as a player, decided to take the manager's job at Middlesbrough. Writing in his autobiography he said, 'When I told Don I wanted to retire, his initial reaction was that I had still something to contribute to the team. He offered me a two-year contract and I think he had an idea that I might finish up on the staff at Elland Road. But he didn't push it too hard. Typically, he told me that his phone line was always open if I needed any advice after leaving the club. That was an invitation I appreciated.'

Despite knowing the team needed rebuilding, there were no new signings. Instead, there was innovation off the pitch. When the players reported back for pre-season training they were subjected to a battery of tests by specialists at Leeds Royal Infirmary to look at ways of improving their fitness.

Further to this, when the team ran out to face Everton at Elland Road on 25 August, it would look different. Just four years after being embroiled in an argument with Football League secretary Alan Hardaker over his refusal to allow Leeds to carry sponsorship on their shirts, Leeds had signed a deal with Admiral to provide their kit.

Thanks to the 1968 Design Copyright Act, companies such as Admiral would be able to design a shirt, copyright it and legally own it exclusively. From that moment Bert Patrick knew football would never be the same again.

His company, Cook & Hurst Ltd, which traditionally manufactured woollen hosiery and underwear under the brand name Admiral, had recently diversified into football shirts and wanted to speak with Revie.

Patrick said, 'At our first meeting in his office at Elland Road I sold Don Revie my dream, a swish new kit designed by Admiral in a new lightweight fabric. His players would look so good in it, the Leeds fans would want to wear it to emulate their heroes, too. And crucially Admiral would pay Leeds money.

'Don was interested, but wary. It had never been done before. There was no way he was going to allow us to redesign the very successful home kit… as a marketing man myself, I could see that Don Revie himself was switched on to marketing ideas.'

As part of the deal a new 'smiley' Leeds United badge would be introduced. Patrick takes up the story: 'The idea behind "smiley" was introduced with the express intention of attracting support from outside Yorkshire. The Leeds manager told me he wanted to create a family ethos with the players and staff that could sit comfortably around his youth policy.'

The original contract was based on a £10,000 fixed payment that would be offset by a 5 per cent royalty for the club against sales of the club's Admiral clothing. In addition, Admiral would pay extra bonuses for success, for instance if the club won the FA Cup or were finalists, or won the First Division or were runners-up. The same applied to the League Cup.

A Leeds tracksuit was produced in time for Christmas 1973. This comprised a white jacket with blue-and-yellow rings on the sleeves and yellow trim neck. Blue trousers had yellow stripes down the sides. The Leeds team of stars was photographed at Elland Road in their new tracksuits with their names on the back of the jackets and Admiral across the front.

At the same time Peter Fay was appointed as a Public Relations Officer. The thank-you letters to fans, the new access to players and the warm relationship with the press was part of a public relations campaign Revie had been pushing for the past two years.

A quarter of an hour before kick-off the team came out to form a line either side of the centre circle and would wave to the four corners of Elland Road. It was all part of an attempt to change the image of 'Dirty Leeds' into 'Super Leeds'.

At the beginning of the season Revie gathered the team together and challenged them to remain unbeaten. Striker Clarke said, 'The gaffer said, "Right, lads, we've been the best team for the last decade. I know we haven't won as much as we should have, but that's in the past." Then like in 1969, he challenged the team to go through the whole season unbeaten.'

What looked on paper like three difficult opening games against Everton, Arsenal and Spurs were anything but. Looking rejuvenated after the previous season's disappointments, Everton, under new manager Billy Bingham, were beaten 3–1 on 25 August.

At Highbury on 28 August, goals from Madeley and Lorimer secured a 2–1 win against the previous season's runners-up, Arsenal, and a 3–0 win at White Hart Lane on 1 September meant Leeds left the capital with full points.

It was not until 22 September, after Leeds had beaten Wolves home and away, plus Birmingham and Southampton, that Leeds would drop any points. A goalless draw with a struggling Manchester United side was disappointing but normal service resumed the following week when a Giles strike was the only goal of the match in a 1–0 win at Norwich's Carrow Road.

The European campaign began on 19 September with a 1–1 draw in Norway against amateurs Strømsgodset Drammen in the first round of the UEFA Cup. It was the last time Sprake kept goal for Leeds United. On 2 October Revie accepted a record bid of £90,000 from Birmingham City for the Welshman, who had not been a regular in the side since April 1972.

Revie said of the error-prone keeper, 'Gary has been a great servant to the club and I am sorry to see him go. He has grown up with the side we have built so successfully at Leeds and was one of the family. I fully understand his point of view of wanting first-team football.'

On the day Sprake left, 6ft 2in Scottish under-23 goalkeeper David Stewart was signed from Ayr United for a fee around £30,000. The following day a 6–1 win at Elland Road in the return against Strømsgodset Drammen underlined the brilliant early season form Leeds found themselves in.

A sub-standard performance against Stoke City produced a 1–1 draw on 6 October before a weakened Leeds lost their 100 per cent record in a 2–0 defeat to Ipswich two days later at Portman Road in the second round of the

League Cup. With the league and qualification for the holy grail of the European Cup now a top priority, few tears were shed on the trip back from Suffolk.

As good as their start had been, they still only led the table by two points with league champions Liverpool scheduled to visit Elland Road on 20 October. In a demonstration of excellent passing involving Clarke, Bremner and Lorimer, Jones fired in the only goal of the game, giving Leeds the precious points and extending their lead at the top.

Perhaps with a nod to the importance of keeping his players fit for the league campaign, Revie rested McQueen, Hunter, Giles and Gray for the UEFA Cup tie with Hibernian four days later. United were below par and were outplayed by attack-minded opponents but achieved a goalless draw.

A late goal from Bates after 76 minutes snatched victory at Maine Road in the league on 27 October and Bates was again among the scorers in a resounding 4–1 win over West Ham on 3 November.

Key players were rested for the UEFA Cup return leg against Hibs. The game reached the end of extra time without a goal, sending the tie to penalties. It was Bremner, who always seemed to perform at key moments, who kept his composure and scored the decisive spot kick that sent Leeds through to a third-round clash with Portugal's Vitória de Setúbal.

There was a strange atmosphere at the Baseball Ground on 24 November when Leeds faced Derby County. The absence of Brian Clough, now replaced as manager by former captain Dave Mackay, took the bite out of the clash as both sides lacked imagination in a colourless 0–0 draw.

A Cherry goal on 71 minutes gave Leeds a 1–0 lead over Vitória de Setúbal in the first leg of the third round of the UEFA Cup on 28 November. That lead could have been doubled had the Vitória goalkeeper not saved a Lorimer penalty in the 76th minute. In the end, 1–0 was not enough of a cushion so when the team travelled to Portugal for the second leg on 12 December they rued that Lorimer penalty miss by being on the wrong end of a 3–1 scoreline.

The loss to the Portuguese was the only blot on the copybook during December, with Ipswich, Norwich and Newcastle all beaten. Birmingham City halted the run with a 1–1 draw on 29 December.

As Leeds prepared to face Spurs at Elland Road on New Year's Day 1974, they were eight points clear and unbeaten in the league for 22 games. That was extended to 23 after a hard-fought 1–1 draw.

Leeds then opened their FA Cup campaign on 5 January against Wolves at Molineux and a penalty taken by Lorimer, in place of a rested Giles, took the tie back to Elland Road for a replay.

Watching the two teams battle out a stalemate for 82 minutes must have given Revie a sense of deja vu after the anguish Norwich City had given them last season. He was thankful when a Jones header settled things in the 85th minute to put Leeds in the fourth round. This was also a game where David Stewart made his debut in place of the injured David Harvey.

A 2–1 win over Southampton at Elland Road on 12 January kept the gap over Liverpool at eight points. A goalless draw a week later at Goodison Park had no effect on standings as Liverpool failed to capitalise, only managing a 1–1 draw at Stoke City.

Lowly Peterborough United were easily cast aside in the fourth round of the FA Cup with a brace from Jordan joining goals from Yorath and Lorimer in a resounding 4–1 win away from home. A 1–1 draw against Chelsea reduced Leeds' league lead to seven points but they were now unbeaten in 27 matches.

It was back to winning ways with a 3–1 defeat of Arsenal and a 2–0 win over relegation-threatened Manchester United four days apart, on 5 and 9 February. But the Manchester United win was the last time Leeds would record a victory throughout February. The dismal run began with a 1–1 draw in the FA Cup fifth round against Bristol City at Ashton Gate. Despite being tipped to win the replay at Elland Road, Leeds went out 1–0 in one of the great cup shocks.

Dreams of an unbeaten league season were destroyed when Leeds squandered a two-goal lead to lose in their 30th league game at Stoke's Victoria Ground on 23 February. An inspired home team hit back with three goals to come out on top, 3–2, in a thrilling game.

Nerves had clearly set in for the next two matches when Leeds could only muster 1–1 draws against Leicester City and Newcastle United. There was another jittery performance against Manchester City but a Lorimer penalty was enough to give Leeds a 1–0 win in their first victory for a month, on 9 March.

It was the wrong time to go to Anfield and face Liverpool, who were the form side. Unbeaten in 16 matches since Boxing Day, the Reds were confident they could pull off a morale-boosting win as they chased down the West Yorkshire club's lead at the top. A tight, nip-and-tuck game saw Liverpool nick a 1–0 win. The pressure was now on.

Ahead of the game against Burnley on 23 March Revie let the cameras into his team talk for a Yorkshire Television special, *The Don of Elland Road*. Looking at the players and addressing them before they went out Revie said, 'In the last four or five matches things have not gone well but you don't lose ability. Don't forget you've played 38 matches and you've lost two but the main thing I'm looking for today is that confidence to accept responsibility.

'Whenever a team has gone through a patch like you have then it's up to everybody to accept responsibility. When there's a player in white on the ball I want every player to hold the ball, I want confidence, I want you to feel 10 foot tall when you go out there today.

'Always remember there's nobody better than you and fitter than you. Ability-wise and experience-wise we've been playing European football, FA Cup football and today we can't afford to lose any points. We've got to win four games, show character and pick up three or four points away from home and that will be the championship wrapped up.'

'I don't want you to worry about Liverpool. I don't want you to even mention their name, but all you've got to do is worry about what we've got to do. What you do really counts so let's go out there and take this team apart.'

The game was a disaster, in front of the home fans Burnley made a mockery of the form guide ripping Leeds apart 4–1. Sitting in front of the cameras after the game with a plate of steak and chips and a pint of dark ale Revie, dressed casually in an open-necked shirt and V-neck pullover, was left to rue, 'It hasn't been a good week. Lost to Liverpool 1–0, lost 4–1 to Burnley today but I always think it takes tremendous character to start again on Monday morning after disappointments and start all over again. We have had to do this for the last 10 years at Leeds United. You need to be good winners but our players have an in-built ability to cast disappointment aside and possibly go out and win the championship.

'I do believe they will give every ounce they've got – even when they were four down today. Burnley took their goals very well but we gave away some silly goals.

'It is the first time since I became manager that we have conceded four goals at Elland Road but this is the worst part of the job. You don't enjoy your steak, it ruins your weekend but on Monday morning, and it takes me till Monday to get over it, when I see the lads again I get lifted in the same way they do.'

There was another setback at Upton Park in the very next game on 30 March where, despite taking the lead early through Clarke, Leeds ended up losing 3–1. There was now a real fear that they could, yet again, squander a great chance of winning the title. Although Leeds were still four points clear, Liverpool had three games in hand and if they won those and their remaining matches they would retain the championship.

A 2–0 win over Derby County at Elland Road was welcome but Leeds were now dependent on Liverpool slipping up. In the following week, Liverpool lost at Sheffield United then drew 1–1 with Manchester City on 12 April, giving Leeds hope. Going to Highfield Road, home of Coventry City, Leeds were three points ahead of Liverpool, who still had a game in hand. A good win would put Leeds in the driving seat but all they could muster was a goalless draw.

Alarm bells were ringing loud and clear now as Leeds failed to score for the second consecutive match, this time a 0–0 draw with Sheffield United at Elland Road on 15 April. At the same time Liverpool put four past Manchester City. A win finally came in the return game against Sheffield United at Bramall Lane on 16 April.

Leeds only had two games left to Liverpool's four but maintained a critical four-point advantage and a superior goal average. Both sides had home games on 20 April, Leeds against third-placed Ipswich Town and Liverpool facing Merseyside rivals, Everton.

Leeds kept up the pressure with a 3–2-win, made even better by a 0–0 draw in the Merseyside derby. This left Leeds five points clear. Liverpool had three games to play but a superior goal average meant that Leeds only needed one point at Queens Park Rangers on 27 April.

Entering the Queen's Hotel in Leeds on 21 April, Revie did a double take. Liverpool boss Bill Shankly and striker Kevin Keegan were there but why? 'Football business,' was all Shankly would say.

Most Sundays, the Queen's Hotel was the venue for the Leeds United social events. Admiral's Bert Patrick said, 'I was often invited to club social events by Revie, usually on Sunday evenings and usually at the Queen's Hotel, where the whole squad was expected by the manager to attend.

'I remember one charity occasion when Revie, whom I always sat next to, stood up and said he wanted to raise money for a Sunshine Bus for the disabled. "How much do you want Don," shouted a wealthy Leeds businessman. "Sixteen thousand pounds," replied Don.

'The man took out his cheque book, asked who the cheque should be made out to and said, "Now you have it, for goodness sake let's get on with the evening's entertainment." That was just typical in those heady days of the '70s. Leeds United was top of the pile.'

Although disturbed by the presence of Shankly, Revie got on with the night. At the top of the table, out of the corner of his eye, he could see someone approaching him. There was nothing untoward in that, Revie was often approached at these dinners by autograph hunters.

This one was different. Someone slipped his arm around Revie's back and said the immortal words, 'Don Revie, this is your life.' As Eammon Andrews related Revie's life from Middlesbrough to Leeds it was good to see people such as Bill Sanderson tell viewers how Revie got started in the game and it ended with Revie's old mentor, Sir Matt Busby, proclaiming him as one of the greatest football managers of all time.

For the days leading up to the airing of the programme Revie's mind was elsewhere. Even as Revie was being honoured and Liverpool manager Shankly was expressing kind words about his rival, the canny Scot could not resist playing mind games. Looking to the coming week, the Liverpool manager said, 'We have to pick ourselves up and beat Arsenal on Wednesday. Then next Saturday Leeds go to Queens Park Rangers and I don't fancy their chances. Rangers are very tough to beat on their own ground.

'If Leeds lose and I think they will, all we have to do is win our last two matches.' To underline how seriously Shankly took the Arsenal game, he told the assembled newsmen he was leaving Leeds immediately after the dinner explaining, 'I've got important business. I am training with the lads on Monday morning to build them up for the clash with Arsenal.'

For Revie, an invite to go and eat with his neighbours while they all watched *This is Your Life* seemed a good way to break the tension. Besides, as Revie told Elsie as they got ready, every time he had gone over to his neighbours when a game was on he got the right result.

In between courses, Revie broke off to listen to the radio. A tense and tight encounter was broken by a 55th-minute strike from Arsenal's Ray Kennedy. Any pretence of trying to enjoy the evening was scuppered as the battle at Anfield entered the final minutes. After what felt like an age, the final whistle blew. Leeds United had done it! England's most consistent team of the past decade had won the championship without even kicking a ball.

Shankly, the man who was so confident the title was heading back to Merseyside for the second consecutive season, was left to regret missed chances: 'Without us Leeds would have run away with the whole thing and what annoys us is that we've lost our home record, though we created more chances than in our last five games.

'I feel sorry for the lads who have played brilliantly throughout this season. But few people will deny Don Revie, so often the bridesmaid in the championship, his right to the big one.'

At this moment of his greatest triumph, there was only one group of people he wanted to share the moment with. Everyone went back to Revie's house where the champagne had been kept on ice, just in case. It was not long before the telephone was ringing.

The press wanted his comments and Revie was effusive in praise of his team: 'I'm fortunate enough to be manager of the greatest squad in the world. This is the greatest night of my life. We faltered near the end of the season. But all sides have spells where nothing goes right.

'All credit to Billy Bremner and the lads for coming back after Easter when deep down I thought our chance had gone after three defeats on the trot. That is the mark of true champions and our record of only four defeats in 41 outings speaks for itself.

'I feel as though someone has come along and lifted six tons of coal off my back. It's a great feeling. I feel as though I am walking on air. Tonight, I am going to go out and have a good time at last.'

At last, after so many disappointments, Revie could now chase his dream of being crowned champions of Europe. On this night everything seemed possible. Revie was going to make people finally acknowledge Leeds United as the best club side in the world. What could possibly stop him?

19

LEEDS UNITED (1974)

'Leeds gave me the chance to start my managerial career and we have had our ups and downs, but everybody in the club, the directors, coaching staff and, in particular, the players, have stood by me through thick and thin.'

Don Revie

As Revie celebrated the league championship with family and friends, Sir Alf Ramsey was harbouring a secret. No one who watched him present the Texaco Cup to Newcastle United captain Bobby Moncur at St James' Park on 24 April would think there was anything out of the ordinary in the England manager's demeanour.

Just two days earlier, a special sub-committee of the FA, which had been formed to examine and report on the future of international football, had met in a secret session. One of its conclusions was that Sir Alf Ramsey had failed in one-too-many important matches.

The criticism was co-ordinated by Professor Harold Thompson, a 66-year-old vice-chairman of the FA Council, and Oxford don, who had failed to establish any form of relationship, personal or professional, with the England manager.

It was now six months since the fateful night on 17 October, 1973, when a 1–1 draw against Poland at Wembley saw England fail to qualify for the 1974 World Cup finals in West Germany. But Ramsey had found sympathy and support – every First Division manager, when asked, thought he should stay in post. Even Football League secretary Alan Hardaker, not known as one of Ramsey's most vocal supporters in the past, was reported as saying, 'The England manager's job is the one job in football I would not want, you just cannot win.'

By the time the sub-committee reported its findings to the FA Executive on 22 April, 1974, Ramsey could have been forgiven if he thought he had weathered the storm. Since the World Cup debacle he had led England in a narrow 1–0 defeat against Italy in November 1973 and had travelled to Portugal for a 0–0 draw on 3 April. He had even picked the squad for the forthcoming Home Internationals and a summer tour of Eastern Europe, a total of seven games.

The outcome was brutal. Ramsey, 1966 World Cup winner, was to be replaced as England manager. On the night Leeds won the league championship, Ramsey was given five days to clear his desk at the FA's Lancaster Gate headquarters. An era had come to an end.

For all the plotting and scheming to eject Ramsey from his position, the sub-committee had not discussed who was going to replace him. So desperate were they to keep their deliberations secret they had given no consideration to who was to be the next manager.

In the short term, the FA appointed former Manchester City championship-winning manager Joe Mercer. An affable and popular man, Mercer made it clear he would act as caretaker for seven games, then no more. Once the qualification for the European Nations Cup began on 30 October against Czechoslovakia a new permanent manager would be leading England out.

Once it was officially announced on 1 May that Ramsey had been removed from his position, speculation was rife as to the identity of the man who would become the first new England manager in 11 years.

If the FA chiefs at Lancaster Gate had consulted the newspapers on who to choose they would have found no shortage of advice. 'Revie's the man,' trumpeted the *Daily Mail*; 'Take it Milne' advised the *Daily Express*; 'Greenwood and Big Jack for Alf's job,' said the *Daily Mirror*. *The Sun*, although not coming out strongly for any one candidate, seemed to lean toward Revie, telling the FA they needed to appoint the most successful manager out there.

The bookmakers were just as confused, making Queens Park Rangers' manager Gordon Jago 7–4 favourite with Coventry's Gordon Milne at 9–4, Ipswich's Bobby Robson at 4–1 and Revie at 5–1. The outsiders were Brian Clough and Jack Charlton at 12–1.

The advertisement that appeared in *The Times* on 3 May was blunt and to the point. It read, 'The Football Association – England Team Manager' and encouraged applicants to send their CVs to the recently-appointed FA secretary Ted Croker, who had replaced the retiring Denis Follows, care of Lancaster Gate.

Although there was no mention of desired experience or wages, within days hundreds of applications had come in. But one name was not among them – Don Revie.

No one expected Revie to apply anyway. The consensus in the press was even though the FA would want someone of the calibre of Revie, he would be too expensive. And besides, he had made it clear that what he really wanted was the European Cup.

In his column for the *Sports Argus* on 4 May all Revie would say was, 'Had England beaten Poland to qualify for the World Cup finals, Sir Alf Ramsey would still be manager. Indeed, the fate which has befallen him this week would have been unthinkable.

'All of which shows that NO manager in British soccer, no matter how highly rated, can feel certain of keeping his job. It is a chilling thought for soccer managers everywhere that, despite Ramsey's remarkable record over the last 12 years, his job hinged on those 90 minutes against the Poles.

'I have mixed feelings about Ramsey's dismissal. It can be argued that you can be in a job too long. As is so often shown at club level, a change of manager tends to have a stimulating effect. However, whoever the FA choose to succeed Sir Alf has my sympathy.

'It is no secret that Sir Alf and I have clashed at times. I've always found him a very difficult person to get to know. Even so, I have the highest regard for him as a manager. His record speaks for itself – and I find it impossible to visualise anyone doing better.'

On 7 May, the day after Revie and his players paraded the League Championship trophy after Billy Bremner's testimonial against Sunderland at Elland Road, the *Daily Mirror* reported that Revie, building up for his tilt at the European Cup, had bid a massive £300,000 plus a player for Southampton striker, Mick Channon. Revie was quoted as saying, 'Channon is a great player, far too good to be in the Second Division.' It was speculated that the Leeds player involved in the deal was Mick Bates. If this was the case, then Channon's value was closer to £400,000.

Now, Revie needed to recharge his batteries. With no cup final to prepare for this year, Revie and his family looked forward to an extended holiday in Portugal where he could enjoy leisurely days on the golf course with Elsie.

It was a chance to reflect. He had been at Leeds as player and manager for 16 years and he had always been quite vocal about leaving football completely by the age of 55. So, when Elsie told him perhaps it was time to get off the treadmill, Revie thought she had a point.

In the Portuguese sunshine the vacant England job looked tempting. There would be no weekly grind, less travelling and, crucially, he would have access to the best players in the country. Before he left for his holiday he had penned a column where he thought out loud about what he would do had he been in Ramsey's shoes, name-checking Sheffield United's Tony Currie and Birmingham City's Trevor Francis as potential England internationals.

As soon as he touched down in England in late May Revie had made his mind up. When the FA switchboard put Revie through to Croker he was surprised to hear from the Leeds manager. Like everyone else, Croker thought Revie had ruled himself out of the running for England but was told, 'I am very interested in the England job and I'd like the opportunity to talk to you about it.'

Explaining he had no wish to apply for the position in the normal way, he simply asked that Croker put his name before the six-man selection committee. The only sticking point at this stage was money. Revie knew Ramsey was on a paltry £7,250 a year, while Revie was getting £15,000 from Leeds. He would expect somewhere in the region of £20,000 if he was to become the new England manager.

For the sub-committee, the news Revie was interested was a welcome relief. Ever since its formation the members had regretted the decision to dismiss Ramsey without a successor lined up. Names like Jago, Milne and Jimmy Bloomfield of Leicester City, who had all applied for the job, were unlikely to capture the public's imagination. There were even voices in the FA that were prepared to lobby Joe Mercer to take the job on a permanent basis. Now, with Revie's interest, all that was about to change.

Conscious of Revie's previous flirtations with other clubs, the FA was determined to ensure he really was interested. So in the first week of June, FA chairman Andrew Stephen and his counterpart on the international committee, Dick Wragg, travelled north with Croker to interview Revie.

The man they met was determined to make a good impression. Revie wanted the job and the FA delegation told him they would not have made the trip to Leeds had they not wanted to give it to him. After talking through some of the changes Revie would make, Croker walked away with the belief that Revie understood how the FA worked and would thrive in its structures.

In terms of salary, Croker had long believed Ramsey had been underpaid. Convinced the FA had found their man, he was prepared to go before the FA sub-committee and tell them if they wanted the best manager for the job then they had to pay him the best wages.

At the conclusion of the 45-minute meeting Revie was, in all but name only, the new manager of the England national team. There were now a few hurdles to overcome before the appointment could be made official.

On 27 June the FA committee had to ratify Revie's appointment, with Stephen and Wragg in agreement that this would be a mere formality. Only then would an official approach be made to the Leeds United board who would want compensation for being deprived of their championship-winning manager.

To those who were not party to the negotiations, life went on as normal. On 25 June, Revie met with Maurice Lindsay, who was tasked with a 10-day trip to the World Cup finals to look at players Leeds could potentially face in next season's European Cup. Bayern Munich were the holders and Revie told Lindsay to pay close attention to the German pair, Franz Beckenbauer and Gerd Müller.

Having finalised the travel arrangements for Lindsay's trip Revie got in his car and drove north of the border for a two-day visit to Scotland where he would meet with scouts to discuss targets and watch a few potential players in pre-season friendlies.

While he was in Scotland the FA met. Croker told the press this was simply a routine meeting but on the agenda was one item of business – the appointment of the England team manager. Members were informed there was only one outstanding candidate for the job, Don Revie.

It was then agreed a letter was to be sent to the Leeds board asking them to allow the FA permission to speak to their manager. Even though members were asked to keep this information confidential, the news leaked out.

Following the meeting, Croker was happy to tell the press there was somebody in line for the job but no specific approach had been made yet. Croker went on to say, 'I believe that this man can be numbered among the best in the country and quite obviously we must expect to pay the scale of salary current among the big-league clubs. It will certainly be more than Sir Alf received.'

On the question of compensation Croker would say, 'We will tackle the question of compensation as the clubs do. The question has not been considered now but it would be subject to negotiation if the matter arose.'

Reacting to the rumours that the mystery man was Revie, Leeds chairman Manny Cussins claimed that his manager was 'very happy at Leeds, I do not think he will go, in fact I am certain he would not go.' When the press tried to elicit a comment from the man himself, Revie curtly replied that he did not comment on speculation.

Writing in the *News of the World* Frank Butler was clear the FA must, 'Buy the world champs,' claiming, 'Cash can't stand in the way so the FA should appoint the best manager in the world. Don Revie is that man.'

Later in the same paper, Don Evans reported that Leeds had ruled out suggestions the club would be willing to share Revie with England on a short-term basis to groom his successor at Leeds. Cussins was quoted as saying, 'I don't believe such an arrangement would be satisfactory for the club and I doubt the FA would want it.'

On 1 July, even before Leeds United board members had had the opportunity to digest the contents of the letter from Lancaster Gate, the news was out: 'Revie to follow Sir Alf – he takes England job,' screamed the headline in the *Daily Mirror*.

The article went on to claim Revie would earn £20,000 a year, appoint Les Cocker, Revie's right-hand man at Leeds, as his England assistant and Johnny Giles would be his replacement as Leeds manager. A delegation from the FA would meet with Leeds' directors on Wednesday to finalise the deal.

As the Leeds board waited to meet the officials from the FA on 4 July it seemed the only way to stop Revie from becoming England manager was the salary. Cussins was quoted as saying, 'Sir Alf Ramsey was on a pittance, a shocking salary. After the end of the present wage freeze, there'll surely be some pay restraint. We don't know what terms the FA could or would offer.'

If Croker was expecting negotiations with the Leeds board to be straightforward he would be sadly mistaken. After arriving at Elland Road on the morning of 4 July the same delegation of Croker, Stephen and Wragg, who had met with Revie in June, now came to thrash out terms with the Leeds manager. Over the course of two hours it was agreed Revie would become England's new manager on a five-year contract with a salary of £25,000.

The news was not greeted with much enthusiasm by the Leeds board, which was firm in its demand that it wanted compensation of £250,000 for their manager. The stalemate carried on for 90 minutes with neither party budging. The delegation from the FA would have to come back again the following day. Revie would meet with the board at midday before the FA would try again at 2 p.m.

Finally, at 4 p.m., in front of a tired and frustrated press, Croker was able to read the statement confirming that Leeds United would release Revie from his contract to become the new England manager. For Revie, it was the chance of a lifetime: 'I am delighted to be given the chance to manage England. This must be any manager's dream. I also have a feeling of sadness after 13 years as manager of Leeds. I have tried to build the club into a family and there must be sadness when anybody leaves a family. The first result I will be looking for on a Saturday night will always be Leeds United's.

'Leeds gave me the chance to start my managerial career and we have had our ups and downs but everybody in the club, the directors, coaching staff and, in particular, the players, have stood by me through thick and thin. I was in contact with the players about leaving them. They all understood and said the England job was a little bit special in their minds. They would have been upset if I had been going to another club.'

At the same time, Revie signed an agreement with Leeds that once his stint with England was at an end, he would take on a consultancy role. However, not everyone was happy about the way Revie left the club. For many it left a bitter aftertaste.

Long-standing trainer Syd Owen said, 'I was disappointed that having been at the club all that time, having been a loyal servant to Don, having played a great part in the development of some of the players, he didn't give his staff the security in football he was looking for himself in the future; that he didn't make sure all the coaches and physios who had served him had been made more secure with contracts.

'I was at that club all those years and put in all those hours but when I wrote a letter of resignation, all I got was what I had worked for. I understand Don had made a signed agreement that he would come back to the club as a consultant. Having done that, I would have thought he would also have looked after his loyal servants.'

The only thing Revie left behind was a recommendation that Giles be appointed as his successor. Giles was to say of his former boss, 'I firmly believe that they could have easily persuaded Don to stay at Leeds. They could have made him an offer he couldn't refuse, certainly a lot more than the £15,000 a year he was getting. And I'm convinced he would have taken it. In fact, they made a settlement of in the region of £100,000 with his successor, which I'm sure Don would have found more than acceptable.

'But in truth the board wasn't sorry at all to see Don going. After 14 years, Don was nowhere near being financially secure. So, when this far-more lucrative offer came from the FA, and when it became clear that Leeds had no intention of matching it, he was left with no option but to leave.'

Norman Hunter said, 'He left Elland Road on a high because we bagged the league championship that season, holding off a strong challenge from our old adversaries, Liverpool, to win the title and qualify for another crack at the European Cup. Revie longed for that opportunity to come his way again and I think he always felt he would get the chance, so many people were surprised he succumbed to the pressures from Lancaster Gate to take the England job. I wasn't one of them.

'The chance of attempting to win the European Cup with Leeds would obviously have weighed on his mind but when you are asked to manage your country it is a great honour and one you really cannot turn down. He had proved himself a very good manager at club level with Leeds and to me he was the ideal man to take over as England boss.'

Instantly the city of Leeds went into mourning. It was difficult to imagine life without the man who had dominated the city for so long. Peter Jackson, who grew up in Leeds and went on to play for Newcastle United, remembers the day Revie left: 'It was like a passing in the family. I was still at school and all my mates were in tears; we thought he would never, ever leave. It was never the same after that. Don was the manager when I went to Elland Road for the first time; it was hard to believe someone else would be in the dugout.'

It was the end of an era for both Leeds United and Revie. By any stretch of the imagination, it was a remarkable record. When Revie took over as manager in 1961 Leeds United faced near bankruptcy. Nearly relegated in his first full season in charge, over the next decade he had moulded a team of youngsters into one of the most formidable clubs in Europe. Together, they had won two league championships, two Fairs Cups, an FA Cup, and a League Cup. As Allan Clarke was to say, 'There will be good sides in the future, of that I am sure, but not one as great as ours.' When Revie woke up on 6 July, all that was in the past. England, and the glory of the World Cup, were his future now.

'Any Englishman that is worth his salt would want to manage the England team.'

Don Revie, at his unveiling as England manager in 1974

'Although Revie never moaned about it publicly… he found it [hard] to understand the lack of technique and professionalism in players from clubs who hadn't organised like he had in his 13 outstandingly successful years with Leeds.'

Frank McGhee in the Daily Mirror, *1977*

'I know people will accuse me of running away, and it does sicken me that I cannot finish the job by taking England to the World Cup finals in Argentina next year, but the situation has become impossible.'

Don Revie in the Daily Mail, *1977*

PART THREE

20

ENGLAND (1974–75)

'After the West Germany match, I felt more convinced than ever we were really on our way. I think it was as good a side as England had produced since the 1970 World Cup finals.'

Alan Ball, after captaining England to a 2–0 win over World Champions, West Germany, in 1974

For as long as Revie could remember, the week leading up to the first game of the season had been one of pressure and worry. Now, as his Leeds United team ran out to face Stoke City at the Victoria Ground on 17 August, 1974, somebody else would be sitting in the visitors' dugout going through the gamut of emotions the first game of the season brings.

Just a week earlier Revie had been at the Charity Shield match. Now televised live and played at Wembley it had become the annual showpiece to kick off the season. Invited as a guest by the FA, Revie watched from the Royal Box as Bill Shankly led out Liverpool for the final time with his captain Emlyn Hughes carrying the FA Cup won three months before.

To Shankly's left was the familiar sight of Billy Bremner carrying the League Championship trophy, his curly, mop of red hair now receding rapidly at the temples. Also in the line-up was the man Revie recommended to the Leeds United board to replace him, 34-year-old Johnny Giles. It was hoped Revie would lead his team out for one last time but he was adamant – Brian Clough was the new Leeds manager now. It was *his* job to walk out in front.

For once Revie was simply an interested bystander to an ill-tempered game, which saw Allan Clarke carried off and Giles booked for throwing a punch at

Kevin Keegan. It was another Giles punch after 60 minutes that saw Keegan explode and start brawling with Bremner in full sight of the referee.

Upon being dismissed from the pitch both players stripped off their shirts and threw them down to the ground. The full-time 1–1 deadlock was broken by a penalty shootout that Liverpool won 6–5.

As Sir Stanley Rous handed the Charity Shield over to Hughes, Revie could be forgiven for breathing a sigh of relief. For once it would be Clough rather than him who would have to deal with Clarke's injury and Bremner's inevitable suspension.

As Revie was to tell Ken Jones of the *Sunday Mirror*, 'It got through to me at Wembley, there they were; people who had occupied such a large part of my life but it was no longer my team. It was someone else's.'

As Clough prepared his Leeds players and Bob Paisley began life as Liverpool boss without Shankly, Revie took himself off to Sunningdale for a spot of golf. As he sliced his way around the course, finding it almost impossible to sink a putt, the publicity could not have been better with the *Daily Mirror* reporting that 80 per cent of correspondents backed his appointment as England boss. In particular, they supported his view that schoolboys should be allowed to enjoy the game and develop their skills.

All week a peculiar sense of calm had enveloped him. There were no early-morning rises, no meetings with the training staff and no reports to pore over. Even Elsie had noticed a difference because the last season with Leeds had been tough. In all the years Elsie had known Revie she had never seen him so tense and anxious as he had been that last season.

Watching as the usually ultra-competitive Revie laughed off his poor form on the golf course, Elsie was sure he had made the right decision to take the England job. Having been at the grindstone of club management for 13 years, it was time for a more relaxed way of life. For Revie his season would not kick off for another two months, when England faced Czechoslovakia on 30 October for the opening fixture of the European Nations Cup.

The change in gear between Leeds and England was stark. Whereas before he was involved in 60 club matches a season, by his own reckoning Revie thought he would now be lucky to be involved in 12 matches of major importance over the course of his whole contract.

The differences in the two jobs was something Revie talked about in an interview with the *Daily Mirror's* Jones on 17 August. He said, 'When you are a club manager and things have gone wrong, you can take immediate steps to put them right, but there are usually long gaps between international matches and so it gets difficult to get points over.

'It is why I hope to get potential England players together as often as possible. I am aware of the problems in that direction. There aren't that many spaces in the English season. I hope to gather about 50 players on a Saturday night so that we can have a serious discussion the following morning. I want them to know what I expect on and off the pitch and what England will be looking for in the way of performance.'

About a month later Revie would head to Manchester to meet the players he felt would be in his plans for the 1978 World Cup – a meeting termed a 'talk-in'. Over the coming weeks he would watch the players who were invited. On 28 August he was in the crowd for Liverpool's 2–0 win over Wolves to cast his eye over central defender Phil Thompson, and on 7 September it was Ipswich against Sheffield United to watch defender Kevin Beattie.

Without any games to prepare for, watching matches was one way of killing time as England manager. Future England boss Kevin Keegan said, 'As England manager, there are a lot of meetings which frankly I found boring. You want to be out on the field but there is not a lot you can do on a day-to-day basis. Most of the time I found myself watching games when I knew the players really well or going to games where there was a chance I was going to cap the player even if I never intended to.

'In Don's day we didn't have the transport links we have now. So, if you wanted to move around the country you could be spending a lot of time on back roads. I do wonder if he found that part of the job difficult especially when he was so used to being hands on at Leeds.'

Despite setting the pace of watching a match every week and drawing up plans for a tour of South America in the summer of 1977 to acclimatise ahead of the following year's World Cup in Argentina, it was Leeds that suddenly came back into Revie's life in the first week of September.

For the past few years since giving up the chairmanship of his beloved Leeds, Harry Reynolds had been enjoying his retirement. Still interested and an avid spectator, on 4 September while watching Leeds' reserves in a Central League game at Elland Road, Reynolds suffered a massive heart attack and died. He was 73.

The death hit Revie particularly hard with the England boss telling the press, 'Mr Reynolds was the man who gave me my chance. Without him there would be nothing.'

Within the club itself there was deep unhappiness. Despite putting his name to an article in the *Sunday Express*, on 5 August, 1973, calling Leeds United the dirtiest club in Britain and calling on them to be relegated and fined because of their poor disciplinary record, the club had appointed Brian Clough as Revie's successor, sending shockwaves through the football world.

To no one's surprise, the experiment had not worked. Struggling to bond with players he had once held in contempt, Clough cut an increasingly isolated figure. After being outplayed 3–0 away to Stoke City on the opening day of the season, and in response to claims he'd made that Leeds United would lose fewer games under him than Revie, Clough quipped, 'Leeds would have to win the next 41 games to beat the previous season's record of 29 wins without defeat.'

By the time Leeds arrived at Leeds Road on 10 September for the second round of the League Cup against Huddersfield Town, they lay in 19th place after just one win from their opening six league games, and only four points from a possible 12. Looking on in the crowd, Revie watched his former team struggle against a dogged Huddersfield managed by former Leeds captain, Bobby Collins. Leeds were lucky to walk away with a 1–1 draw.

Two days later, in a replay of the sacking of Bill Lambton in 1959, the Leeds players met in the dressing room to discuss the future of their manager. The message delivered to the board was simple – Clough had to go. A little over six weeks – 44 days to be exact – after accepting what he termed the biggest job in the country, on 12 September Clough was relieved of his duties as manager.

Speaking to the press after the sacking and with Clough next to him, Leeds' chairman Manny Cussins was scathing: 'What has been done is for the good of Leeds United: the club comes first and the happiness of the players. Nothing can be successful unless the staff are happy. They (the players) seem to criticise the tactics, the training and so forth of Mr Clough.' The chairman then went on to say, 'We have been spoiled by Don Revie.'

From the outset Clough had been making digs at Revie. It had begun almost immediately with Clough alleging in a Yorkshire Television interview on 1 August that Revie had left behind 11 contracts with senior players, which were unsigned.

Revie was so incensed at the accusation that he was moved to ring up Yorkshire Television and ask for a transcript of the interview. It was rumoured in the *Daily Mirror* that Revie had engaged the services of a solicitor to investigate a potential case of libel.

In the same call, Revie had asked for a right of reply and on the evening of 12 September he got it. In a *Calendar* TV programme special called *Goodbye Mr Clough,* Revie and Clough went head-to-head in an interview chaired by Austin Mitchell.

With legs crossed and his body turned away from Clough, Revie tried to remain calm as Clough attempted to get under his skin. The interview sparked into life when Revie questioned Clough about why it had taken him so long to meet the players, telling Clough he had held a cocktail party for 70 people from the FA to introduce himself. Clough snapped back at Revie, calling him a cold person. Revie lost his composure and there ensued nothing short of a slanging match. It may have made for extraordinary television but meant nothing. Revie was still England manager.

It was the evening of 21 September and Revie was exhausted. He had left Leeds for Liverpool that morning to watch their 3–0 win over Stoke then travelled back to Manchester in anticipation of the 'talk-in'.

The Piccadilly Hotel, where Revie waited to greet 79 English footballers, was 14 storeys of modernistic concrete overlooking the central bus station in Manchester. Among those invited was England skipper Emlyn Hughes and 1966

World Cup winner Alan Ball. Also included were Everton's £350,000 striker Bob Latchford and Peter Taylor of Third Division Crystal Palace. From Leeds came Clarke, Madeley and Hunter.

From 6 p.m. until 11.45 p.m. Revie stood in the foyer of the hotel to personally greet each player as he arrived. Of the 84 invited, five dropped out for personal reasons. They were Keegan, Thompson and Kevin Beattie, the inaugural PFA Young Player of the Year and Ipswich centre-half, plus Sunderland's David Watson and Derby's Colin Todd. There was slight embarrassment when Nottingham Forest's John Robertson was invited, only to be told he was ineligible because he was born in Scotland.

The only straggler was Queens Park Rangers' Stan Bowles who was late, according to Revie, because his wife was ill. It was past midnight before Revie finally got to his room for a meal before a 7.00 a.m. start, when he put the finishing touches to his opening remarks.

Even though Shankly was broadly sympathetic to the idea in the *Liverpool Echo,* not all journalists were supportive. Writing in the *Daily Mirror,* Mike Langley wrote on 22 September, 'Make no mistake, Revie's opening assembly as the new England manager is principally a public relations job. He knows better than anyone, that England doesn't contain 84 real international class players. He's invited seven men who have been sent off in the past 12 months, exposing all the hopes of a better-behaved England as pie in the sky.'

At 9.00 a.m. over breakfast, Revie began his remarks by telling all the players assembled, 'You are all part of my plans for the future. If any of you don't want to play for England say so now.' There was not one dissenting voice.

Telling the players his sole aim was the 1978 World Cup, Revie then outlined his plans. There would be a £5,500 bonus per man for winning the European Nations Cup and £5,000 each for qualifying for the 1978 World Cup. There would also be an increase in appearance fees with £200 coming on top of the usual £100 fee for a win and £100 for a draw.

In response Hughes stood up and told Revie in front of the assembled players he did not play for England for the money but for the glory. Later while appearing on the BBC's *Match of the Seventies* he was to say of Revie, 'I think he was virtually money ruled.'

Hoping to build a family ethos, Revie told the players there would be complimentary tickets for wives and girlfriends, and VIP treatment for the players. This meant the best hotels and limousines to transport the players back home after international games.

To improve the image of football England internationals would be expected to go into schools and work with youngsters on their skills. Plans were already being formulated between the English Schools FA and the FA Director of Coaching to bring this about.

After his 55-minute talk Revie was to tell the press, 'I made it clear that I don't mean to waste my time with anybody who is going to say that he doesn't want to go to South America for the World Cup. I want responsible players and totally dedicated players.

'We want to be sure that they are playing for their country because they are proud to be Englishmen.' On pay, Revie said: 'I cannot be specific yet because the facts and figures have to be passed through committee but there will be a new wage structure and a bonus scheme. Professional footballers have a short life and they should be well paid.'

Hughes was not the only one who found the Manchester 'talk-in' an underwhelming experience. Newcastle United striker Malcolm Macdonald observed, 'Biggest lot of nonsense. We were banned from going out on Saturday night. To me it was a load of bollocks; nothing inspirational at all. Afterwards I drove all the way back to Newcastle just to find out I was not in the squad.'

The public relations offensive continued a month later on 24 October when Revie addressed journalists at a public lunch that had been arranged for Revie to give his thoughts on the future of international football.

Knowing the reporters were desperate for a story Revie was more than obliging. Over the course of his speech he revealed he had met with the Football League Secretary Alan Hardaker and it had taken him six hours to convince him to help England's cause.

'I asked him specifically if Saturday matches could be postponed so that I could have my squad for a full week before important World Cup qualifying games. I think it is vital that it can be arranged. My suggestion was received sympathetically but Mr Hardaker made some conditions which I am not going to go into now. Sir Alf only had his squad from the Saturday before the vital game against Poland. It makes a hell of a difference if the players get together the previous Wednesday.'

Writing in *The Times* Geoffrey Green reported Hardaker was unable to respond immediately because of a throat infection but 'by yesterday the trouble had apparently cleared rapidly; sufficiently at least for the League Secretary to frame a sharply-worded statement calculated to put Revie in his place like some little schoolboy.'

That statement read, 'I have seen my name mentioned on numerous occasions by Mr Revie concerning possible postponements of league matches. These are unauthorised statements and if Mr Revie wishes to reveal all his business with me to the press then I wish it to be known that I cannot co-operate.

'It is true we met in my office, together with Mr Wragg, chairman of the International Committee, and Mr Croker, Secretary of the FA, and discussed future co-operation. I promised Mr Revie the same co-operation that I gave his predecessor but made it quite clear that I have no authority to postpone league matches.

'This is the prerogative of the clubs and the management committee. I resent any suggestion made in public that I have promised to undertake such action. In any event, premature statements of this nature will only serve to make the job more difficult.'

To Green, the statement brought home 'some of the difficulties experienced by his predecessor, Sir Alf Ramsey, during his 11 years at the helm. I well remember asking Ramsey in a BBC broadcast the day he was appointed how he proposed to surmount some of the problems that lay ahead of him. His reply was, "What problems?"

'He discovered in due course just as Revie will. As always it is a case of club versus country in these islands with our priorities the wrong way around. Other countries postpone their league programmes before international games considered of prime importance. Why not us? Is the league the be-all and end-all?'

Just two days earlier Revie had named his 23-man squad for the opening tie of the European Nations Cup on 30 October. Out of the side were 1966 World Cup winners Ball and Martin Peters. Surprisingly, in-form Newcastle striker Macdonald was also omitted.

There were six new caps in the shape of Beattie, Stoke's Alan Hudson, Middlesbrough's Willie Maddren, Queens Park Rangers pair Gerry Francis and Dave Thomas, and Birmingham's Trevor Francis. Unavailable were the Derby centre-backs Roy McFarland, suffering from a broken leg, and Colin Todd, who had a groin injury. There was a doubt over Hunter but Revie felt he would be ready for the game.

Commenting in *The Times* Geoffrey Green said of the squad, 'This list is predictable in the main. One of the more interesting selections is Thomas of whom Revie said three or four years ago, "This boy could be one of the finest players in all of Europe." Of the new men, Maddren has little chance while one of the Francis players might make it, but about Thomas, I have an open mind. I hope Mr Revie sticks to his dictum that England will play constructive attacking football.'

Heading into the first game, Revie was cautious in his comments: 'It is not going to be easy. I would have liked five or six games before facing a competitive match. The Czechs have been together a long time. I have seen them twice and they are a well-balanced, skilled side who know each other's play. They get behind the ball and make it very difficult to score. The England side has not only got to win but got to do it in a style which will excite people.'

So England, under Revie, began their attempt to regain their place among the elite of world football. A few hours after the England game Muhammad Ali entered the ring in Zaire to win back the world heavyweight boxing crown from George Foreman. The parallels between the two fallen giants attempting to regain former glories would not be lost on the British press.

As the fans flooded through the turnstiles at Wembley they were handed a thank-you letter from the new England manager. On the back were the lyrics to *Land of Hope and Glory*. When England and Czechoslovakia walked out for the first time under the new regime, it was hoped Wembley would resemble the last night at the Proms.

Controversially, the pristine white England shirts were replaced by a new red, white and blue design courtesy of Admiral. For the first time, England supporters would be able to purchase replica shirts so they could wear the same strip as their heroes. No one had seen the new strip before the team captained by Hughes ran out at Wembley in October 1974.

For Revie, the 1966 win was a missed opportunity. 'If the Football Association had cashed in after 1966, then they could have benefited football at all levels from schoolboys upwards. When I took over at the FA they were paying for all the kits and the footballs. They never asked for quotes and were paying top dollar for it all. So, when I came in, I said to Ted Croker, "Why don't we get companies to pay to provide our kit?" And Croker liked the idea.'

When the idea of a new England kit was discussed, the first call Revie made was to Bert Patrick of Admiral who later said, 'The FA had no formal arrangement with a kit supplier, although through the 1960s they wore Umbro without any distinguishable embellishment other than the much-venerated Three Lions.

'Consequently, I met the FA International Committee to negotiate the first commercial kit contract. I made it clear that it would have to include the Admiral logo on the chest opposite the Three Lions and include a new exclusive, copyrighted design. The existing plain white England shirt was not available to the public with the Three Lions badge.'

The new shirt was met with mixed reviews. A collar returned to the England shirt for the first time in two decades. For the first time there was red and blue striping on both collar and sleeves along with the famous badge.

Former England forward Jimmy Greaves said the new strip looked like a set of pyjamas. The new shirt was worn with blue shorts in a lighter shade than the traditional navy blue and had white-and-red stripes down the sides. White socks also had red and blue stripes at their top.

The shirt manufacturer's insignia also appeared in a prominent place on the England shirt for the first time. As Croker explained in his autobiography, the colourful shirt design and the presence of the manufacturer's logo were the result of a new commercial arrangement under which the manufacturers paid royalties to the FA for the first time for the right to promote and sell replica England uniforms.

Croker, who became an entrepreneur after his playing career ended and brought a strong business background to his FA post, wrote, 'The FA was criticised in the years following my appointment for allowing a company, Admiral of Leicester, to market and sell the England kit in return for royalty payments. It was said that we were exploiting youngsters and allowing them to be ripped off.'

The deal was highly lucrative. A five-year contract was signed with Admiral for a starting payment of £15,000 a year, or a 10 per cent royalty, whichever was the greater.

Finally, after four months in the job, the Don Revie era kicked off. In front of 86,000 enthusiastic fans, England lived up to the pre-match hype, attacking brightly, creating three chances in the opening quarter of an hour. But from that point on, frustration set in.

With the Czech players crowding out the penalty area strikers, Frank Worthington and Mick Channon found it almost impossible to get on the end of anything meaningful, to send the sides in 0–0 at half time. By the 70th minute, the game seemed to be drifting into an unforgettable stalemate. Even the crowd, so vocal in the first 20 minutes, seemed subdued.

Then Revie made a double substitution and the whole complexion of the game changed. Thomas and Trevor Brooking came on for Worthington and Martin Dobson, and it was Thomas who created the first goal when his cross was headed in by Channon.

Two more goals followed in the next nine minutes. Channon found Colin Bell with a superb diagonal pass and he steered it into the net with a well-placed shot. Then the inspired Channon crossed the ball for Bell to head in the third goal that sent choruses of *Land of Hope and Glory* thundering around Wembley.

Afterwards Revie told the press, 'Naturally I was disappointed at half time that we had not scored with so much of the play and I thought it may sneak away from us like another Poland. The use of two subs at the same time was a gamble and I could have been in trouble if we had an injury after that. I could never be satisfied but I thought they did well considering the short time they have been together with me.'

In response, the manager of Czechoslovakia Vaclav Jezek said, 'I am not so disappointed because we have been beaten, for England were the better team and my players are so young. I hope we can play better in the return match in Bratislava for home is home and we want to do well.'

Writing in the *Daily Mirror* the following day Harry Miller was fulsome in his praise of Revie, 'England transformed Wembley from an arena of hope into one of glory as Don Revie's reign opened on a winning note last night.'

With the first game out of the way Revie could feel confident England would be well placed to achieve a dominating position in their group. If they beat the Portuguese at Wembley on 18 November, they would have four points under their belt with games to be played home and away against Cyprus, both of which should have been easy wins.

Geoffrey Green of *The Times* reckoned, 'To reach the quarter-finals round of this competition should give them what they need for the future and confidence to qualify for the final stages of the next World Cup in 1978, wherever it should be held should Argentina, given a year to prove their capability, fail to come up to scratch.'

On a personal front Revie was feeling more settled. Since his appointment he had been living in a hotel room but now he had taken a lease out on a bungalow in Tunbridge Wells, Kent, so at least Elsie could make regular visits when he was on England duty.

Announcing his team ahead of the game against Portugal at Wembley, Revie left out four of the men who started against Czechoslovakia. Worthington, Keegan, Dobson and Hunter were now out in the cold, with Todd coming into the side.

The *Land of Hope and Glory* anthem that rang out for Revie's first game quickly descended into boos and jeers as England struggled to make any impact against a disciplined and resolute Portuguese defence. Terry Cooper, recalled by his old Leeds United club boss after three years in the international wilderness, broke down with a nagging injury. There was a lack of understanding between the midfield and the front line with a procession of passes going astray on the rain-sodden surface. The 0–0 result was not what Revie had hoped for.

A disappointed Revie said at the end, 'It was a bad pitch but I'm not looking for excuses. I accept the boos I got as part of the job. The crowd must have been as disappointed as we were.'

For Revie there had been too many individual failures. Allan Clarke, so dependable for Leeds, had failed to perform in an England shirt and Thomas, so devastating against the Czechs, found his dribbling and acceleration going nowhere on the night. Bell, Brooking and Gerry Francis failed to come to any understanding in midfield.

The frustration was reflected in the morning headlines with *The Times* running, 'Revie told how hard the going can be,' and the *Daily Mirror* with the more devastating, 'What a load of rubbish.' England now had three points from two matches with games against Cyprus in February and April 1975, and then two away games against Portugal and Czechoslovakia. Revie knew they had made it hard but they had no one to blame but themselves.

On 6 December Revie travelled to Cyprus with Croker to inspect the facilities. For weeks the political situation on the island had been deteriorating and there had been a doubt whether the game would be played.

After visiting the ground in Limassol, Croker was happy to declare, 'Providing there is no further deterioration in the situation then the European Championship match against Cyprus will go head on 5 February.' However, anti-British rioting in the following weeks would lead to the game being postponed until 11 May. The next time England would run out would be against world champions West Germany on 12 March, 1975.

Once again, with an eye on public relations ahead of the meeting with the West Germans, Revie decided to make Alan Ball, the last survivor of the 1966 England World Cup winning squad, captain for the game.

On the night England ran out to face the world champions it seemed as though the tide was turning in Revie's favour. The Football League took the decision to postpone the game between Arsenal and Coventry, which was due to be played the day before the West Germany game. By doing so, Ball was free to captain the side.

The *Daily Mirror* reported it was the first time that the Football League admitted international football was more important than their fixture programme.

The League told the paper the game could have been played but would have instructed Arsenal to release Ball for the game. For Revie, it was an even more significant victory than the one on the field over the Germans.

The England team left the dressing room after a rousing speech by Revie who told them, 'Remember what they did to our homes in the war.'

In the midfield, Ball was partnered with Bell and Hudson against a German side that boasted the likes of Beckenbauer, Berti Vogts and Sepp Maier, stars of the team that a little over a year before had paraded the World Cup around the Olympic Stadium, watched by Revie.

It was Bell who gave England a 25th-minute lead with a deflected shot, following a Hudson free-kick. Malcolm Macdonald, whose pace was always a problem for an experimental German team, scored his first goal for England in the 66th minute when he raced to the far post to head in a cross from Bell. It was also the first victory England had registered over their great rivals since the famous July afternoon some nine years earlier.

At the end of the 2–0 victory Revie was full of praise for his team, complimenting its balance, arrogance and skill. He said it was the best performance since he had taken over as England manager three games earlier. The huge cheers at the end were in stark contrast to the boos and jeers that had followed the goalless draw in the previous game against Portugal.

Even Ball felt England had finally turned the corner: 'After the West Germany match I felt more convinced than ever we were really on our way. I think it was as good a side as England had produced since the 1970 World Cup finals.'

The *Daily Mirror* claimed, 'England beat, outclassed and at times even frightened the life out of the reigning world champions at Wembley last night. They cannot claim the world title because of that but they can claim the type of skilful player and adventurous football needed to challenge for the most important soccer prize of all.'

In the dressing room, Revie thanked all the players individually for their performance. All except one – goalscorer Macdonald. 'He went around the dressing room saying "good match, Alan; good match, Kevin" and so on. Then he completely ignored me. He told me a few days earlier he only put me in the side because the press told him to.

'Actually, in a funny sort of way that helped as I knew I would be playing in the side. I was determined to show him I was worthy of a place.'

Midfielder Hudson, who was praised by the press for a majestic performance, was later to comment, 'I was picked for the Germany match and never wished good luck by the man in charge; but that only helped me to prepare for the biggest match of my life with more determination than ever before.

'If I had not been up to the test, or played badly, I would have been cast off and labelled as not being up to international football by Revie and all the buzzards who had been waiting to swoop. Even to this day I know it would have stuck but instead, the question most asked of me is, "Why did you only get one more cap after such an incredible debut?"

'I was playing against West Germany and Leeds United rolled into one. How many people could have made their England debut under such circumstances? Oh, how sweet success can be! Not only did I put one over on the Germans, but Revie as well.'

Just a few weeks after the West German victory Revie sat down to put pen to paper. His intention was to set out for vice-chairman of the Football Association, Sir Harold Thompson, the activities he had been undertaking in the post. As the successor to Ramsey, Revie would have been all too aware of Thompson's reputation as a dictator and autocrat. He was largely blamed for the dismissal of England's only World Cup-winning manager.

Setting out how he had attended games at all levels from under-21s, to youth and schoolboys as well as corporate commitments, Revie also told Thompson of the various commercial activities he had been working on with Croker, such as suits for the England squad provided by tailors Austin Reed, sponsorship contracts with textiles giant Courtaulds, and talks with the Milk Marketing Board, Stylo football boots and the travel company Thomas Cook.

The reply to Revie's letter from Thompson, who was a year away from becoming the FA Chairman, was cordial. 'I thought that I lived a mad hectic life, but I think yours is even more gruelling and complex. At any rate, I am sure that everybody is grateful for the effort you are putting in, and I hope in due course it will be properly rewarded.'

After the West Germany match England had to get down to serious business. Minnows Cyprus had only played one previous European Nations Cup match and were drubbed 7–1 by Austria, in 1968. They did not expect to qualify from a group also containing Czechoslovakia and Portugal – but England most certainly did.

More than 68,000 fans turned up at Wembley for this one on 16 April, 1975. Just like the game against West Germany, the famous pitch was muddy and full of divots. Once again, Ball was to wear the captain's armband.

Pleased to be back in the side, Malcolm Macdonald was eager to prove his performance was not a one-off. He was surprised to be confronted by the England manager who said, 'Look Malcolm, I do not rate you. Score tonight or else I will never pick you ever again.'

The striker recalls, 'Upon hearing of this Alan Ball told me not to worry. He then went over to Mick Channon and Colin Bell and said this man is going to break records, he will score six tonight. After my run-in with Revie it really picked me off the floor.'

At the end, the Wembley scoreboard read: 'Congratulations – Supermac 5 Cyprus 0.' Revie headed off down the tunnel with his head buried in his jacket lapels and his hands in his pockets. Macdonald pointed at the scoreboard and shouted after him, 'Read it and weep, you bastard.'

Just like the West Germany game, Revie congratulated all the members of the team except Macdonald. According to Macdonald, the only time Revie spoke to him was to tell him to get out of the bath and change because the press and BBC TV wanted interviews.

Allegedly Revie then led Macdonald to the BBC room. The five-goal striker said, 'Usually the press and television do everything in their power to make you feel relaxed, not on this occasion. Tony Gubba, who I always got on well with, was extremely cold towards me that night. When the interview started Gubba began, "Malcolm, you might have scored five, but what about the two you missed?" Again, when Revie took me to the press, the mood was cool.'

The following season, Macdonald discovered why. He said, 'Upon bumping into BBC director of sport, John McGonagle, who was at a game I played which was featured on *Match of the Day*, I extended my hand, but he would not shake it. "I don't know how you've got the cheek," said McGonagle.

'I was bewildered and told him that I was yet to receive the standard £25 fee for the post-Cyprus interview. McGonagle exclaimed: "I've already paid you!" Evidently Revie had said I would not come unless he was given £200 in cash, which was raised through a collection among the sound man, lighting engineer and so on, but never passed on.'

A month later, on 11 May, England finally played their postponed game in Cyprus. On his earlier visit Revie expressed concerns about the state of the pitch, calling it patchy and bumpy, but as Keegan struck in the sixth minute there were hopes of a huge score.

The bumpy pitch led to many England passes missing their target in a scrappy match during which goalkeeper Ray Clemence was hardly tested. Kevin Beattie, winning his second cap, limped off with a groin injury just before half time, and Manchester City's Dennis Tueart came on as a 73rd-minute substitute for Thomas.

The following day the *Daily Mirror* reported how a lifeless England flopped to a one-goal win in the sun with Revie telling the press, 'The main thing is we got the points.' Coming out of the game England were still in control, topping the group with seven points from four games. Czechoslovakia were second on four points after three matches, and Portugal on one point having only played twice.

Six days later, on 17 May, England were ready for the opening game of the Home Internationals against Northern Ireland. There was tension in the air. Against the backdrop of 'The Troubles', England would be visiting Belfast for the first time in four years. Then the FA received a specific threat from loyalist paramilitaries against one of their players, Keegan.

Deciding against the offer of withdrawing, Keegan bravely played in a dour 0–0 draw that saw heightened security around the England team. The only positive to be drawn from the game was England equalling their record of a sixth consecutive clean sheet.

After suffering the stress of playing with his safety on the line, Keegan was upset he had apparently been dropped from the next game against Wales on 21

May. Afterwards, having waited in his hotel room until 6.00 p.m. for an explanation from Revie, Keegan decided to check out and drive home. Once he got there, he took the phone off the hook so no one could get through to him.

Despite telling the press, 'I don't want players at the World Cup who go running to the airport when they are excluded for one match,' Revie sought out the Liverpool man. Finally, after a couple of hours of trying, he got through to Keegan, telling him he had not been dropped for the match but was simply being rested for the game against Scotland and that he had not found time to explain the changes to him. He then went on to invite Keegan to rejoin the squad, which he did.

Later Revie told the press, 'If anybody did this twice to me there is no way he would be included in any future internationals. There is no question of any disciplinary action being taken. This little fellow has done so much for me. Nobody puts more into training sessions and he is the last person I would have expected to run away.'

Keegan said of the affair, 'If Don had not made that phone call, I would never have come back. He was the one who convinced me I had a future and was part of his plans.'

The Wembley game against Wales was another disappointment, although Ipswich Town's David Johnson made a memorable debut, scoring both of England's goals, including an 85th-minute equaliser that stole victory from a spirited Welsh team.

The next match was the performance for which England fans had been waiting ever since Revie had been appointed manager. On 24 May, England vanquished Scotland 5–1. England scored twice in the first seven minutes; the opening goal from Gerry Francis was a spectacular shot that rocketed into the net from 25 yards. Scotland never recovered from this shattering start despite some superb play by Kenny Dalglish.

On 40 minutes, Bell made it 3–0 before Bruce Rioch pulled one back from the penalty spot in the last minute of the half. Ball, Bell and Francis were in unstoppable form and it was Francis who made it 4–1 in the 63rd minute with a deflected shot, after Ball had pushed a free-kick through Bell's legs into his path. Johnson steered the rebound into the net to complete the rout of a dispirited

Scottish side. Despite being pelted with beer cans from Scottish fans as they left the pitch, Revie beamed as he told the press, 'This was the best England performance since I took over.'

Ken Jones reported in the *Daily Mirror*, 'The victory was so complete that thousands of shame-faced Scots refused to suffer until the end. They fled the famous stadium banners dragging, their sprits broken by the crisp effectiveness of England's football.'

The crushing win over Scotland meant England had won the Home International Championship by a single point and, more importantly, had gone through the tournament undefeated.

If anyone felt he was established in the England side it was Ball. Having impressed in the win over West Germany and led England in the thumping 5–1 win over Scotland, he started imagining an England swansong in Argentina. Then an unexpected letter arrived in the post.

The letter on FA notepaper, informing Ball he was not only being removed as England captain but dropped from the team completely, was not even signed. It simply stated 'team manager dictated by Mr Revie and signed in his absence'.

Even though Ball had been transfer-listed by his club Arsenal and was not in the first team, it was a bitter blow for the World Cup winner. Ball's wife, Lesley, called Revie a disgrace. All Revie would say was, 'I suppose I shall have to wait until they become managers before they appreciate what I had to do. I haven't had time for sitting on the fence and postponing unpleasant decisions.'

On 3 September, England moved into a new era with Gerry Francis donning the armband for a friendly against Switzerland in Basel.

It was Keegan who opened the scoring from close range in the eighth minute and had a penalty saved three minutes later. In the 19th minute, David Johnson laid on a second goal for Channon and England looked on course for a comfortable victory.

But the Swiss were allowed back into the game after sloppy marking had allowed Kudi Müller the freedom of the penalty area for a headed goal in the 30th minute. England's defence was often at full stretch in the second half but the best scoring chances fell to the feet of substitute Macdonald who missed the target twice in the closing stages.

The game against Czechoslovakia on 29 October came almost a year to the day after Revie had led England out for the first time. It had all the ingredients for an explosive encounter – an Italian referee, a hostile crowd and a side desperate to win.

The team England faced was different to the one they had played at Wembley. Since losing 3–0 they had gone undefeated, and trailed England by only a point in the qualifying table and had a game in hand. On 28 October, the England party flew into the grey city of Bratislava.

Touching down, Revie told the assembled press he was bubbling with excitement and had assembled a side that was going flat out for victory. Speaking to Frank McGhee, Revie told the *Daily Mirror* reporter that this was one of the most important matches of his England career. 'If we qualify, we get a whole range of competitive matches against top-class opposition, the quarter-finals, maybe the semis; even the final.

'And we all know that the only way a good team can be built is playing a lot of matches and spending time together.' Adding to his confidence was the recall of Leeds players Madeley and Clarke.

However, all was not well in the England camp. Before England flew out, Revie handed out the 11-page dossier on Czechoslovakia that his assistant, Les Cocker, had compiled. At Leeds, the players expected these dossiers but they came in for ridicule by some England players who were not used to the Leeds way.

Ball claimed he did a crossword on the back of his while Macdonald called them a 'load of shit'. He said, 'You take the West German game; we are given these dossiers on players we had all seen in the previous summer's World Cup. What's he going to tell us about Franz Beckenbauer? The Cyprus one I was given contained players who weren't even on the pitch. They did nothing for me.'

Channon later said, 'Eventually with Revie your mind was full of too much – you could end up a nervous wreck. Some would take the dossiers seriously, though to others they were a joke. Revie should have just said they were there if we needed them – that's the way he meant them, to be fair to him. He was misunderstood. Players aren't really that intelligent. They didn't need all that. They just want to play football.'

For Keegan they were an innovation: 'Most of the players took them seriously but the press only want to listen to the ones who could not get on with them.'

Over the next few days, bad weather moved in. As befitting the lead up to Halloween, a ghostly mist descended on the city. By the time the game kicked off, the fog was so thick it was impossible for spectators to pick out the players.

A perfectly good goal by Macdonald was ruled offside but there were no complaints when the referee decided to abandon the match after 17 minutes. However, Revie had liked what he had seen and was confident England would come out on top when the match was restarted the following afternoon.

When the game was replayed the Czechs trailed 1–0 to a Channon goal after 26 minutes, but the clever Masny laid on an equaliser a minute before half time and then a winner in the opening minute of the second half.

England were unsettled by the no-holds-barred, physical approach of the Czechs and started to retaliate with reckless tackles of their own in a game that was often brutal. The only player ordered off by a lenient referee was the Czech reserve goalkeeper who was sent to the dressing room for disputing a decision from the substitute's bench.

It was the general view that at least two Czech players should have followed their teammate for an early bath because of tackles that were out of the chamber of horrors.

It was the first time Revie had been beaten as England manager and the defeat could not have come at a worst time. It meant the fate of the team was out of his hands. Even though England now needed to beat Portugal and hope Cyprus did England a favour, Revie refused to give up hope.

Speaking to the press ahead of boarding the plane home, Revie said, 'I honestly don't think we deserved to lose and on reflection it was a terrible pity that the first game was fogged off. The result makes it desperately difficult for England to qualify for the quarter-final stages of the tournament.

'I haven't given up all hope. It would be a terrible shame if England should go out after playing as we did. I am shattered about the result but I still can't feel too disappointed because we played so well.

'My players did everything I expected, apart from giving away the goal Czechoslovakia scored just before half time. It was a hell of a time to give a goal away. It gave the Czechs a tremendous lift and I have to say their second goal was a beauty. I have never known a team as ready to go as England were on Wednesday night. Certainly, I have never prepared a team as well or in such detail for a match.'

For Revie, the problem lay squarely at the door of the Football League which had put on a full league programme the weekend before the most important match England had played in over two years. This led two players to withdraw through injury but, most crucially, it left Revie with only one day with the squad before they flew out.

Revie and Cocker were booked on a flight to Portugal and they hoped against hope that the Portuguese would conjure up the type of magic in their home match against Czechoslovakia last seen the heady days of 1966 and a World Cup semi-final. England desperately needed the Portuguese to beat the Czechs.

It had been a frustrating few weeks. Another hard league programme had forced Revie into making changes to his injury-ravaged side, prompting the England manager to write, 'Compared to other countries we have an amateurish outlook but we expect professional results at international level.

'I know the problems of managers and clubs but it is most important that there is much time for preparation, especially when it comes to qualifying for the World Cup. If we could get the co-operation right down the line I could have no complaints if we didn't qualify for the final stages of the World Cup, and frankly I wouldn't deserve anything.

'The ideal situation is to have players 10 days before a match and the games on Saturday involving England players should be put off. Then there wouldn't be this continual worry about injuries and certainly the players would be less tired. I must say I have had great help in private discussions with Alan Hardaker and the Football League. I have been offered a ray of hope and my pleas don't seem to have fallen on deaf ears.'

But the England manager could only look on with envy as the Czechs cancelled all fixtures to prepare for international commitments and the Portuguese put their national team into camp before facing them. The game ended in a 1–1 draw and now England had to find a way past the Portuguese.

The England players were under intense pressure going into the Wembley game against Portugal, not only on the pitch but also financially. It was estimated that failure to qualify would cost the FA somewhere in the region of £1 million. When England failed to qualify for the 1974 World Cup it was estimated it had cost £500,000, speeding up the exit of Sir Alf Ramsey.

The make-or-break game was a damp squib and things got off to a terrible start. England went a goal down in their final European Nations Cup qualifier to a 16th-minute free-kick by Rodrigues that swerved viciously on its way into the net from 25 yards.

The Portuguese missed two easy chances before Channon equalised with a free-kick that deflected into the net off a defender three minutes before half time. England needed a victory to boost their fading chances of reaching the European quarter-finals but they kept running blindly into an offside trap and had to settle for a draw. The result left the Czechs needing only a draw in Cyprus to qualify ahead of England and, unsurprisingly, they did more than that with a 3–0 away win.

The game was broadcast live on ITV and at full time the England manager was in no mood to talk to anyone. Unlike the league, where Revie could regroup and start again, at international level it could be years before there was a chance to make amends.

Once off the pitch Revie, dressed in a brown suit and tie, narrowed his eyes as he rounded on his perceived critics: 'A lot of people like to pick the team and ram a thousand players down my throat. But a lot of people like Jimmy Hill and other managers who are talking have never won a trophy yet.

'When they start winning something and they start doing something at their own clubs, then they can criticise me. But I think it's part of the England manager's job to be criticised by the public, the press, television but I've always made up my own mind about situations and players and teams and I'll continue to [do] that because I think if you start listening to everyone in sight you don't know where you are.'

For the third time in a row England had failed to qualify for the final stages of a major tournament. More so than ever, the pressure was on for England to be at the 1978 World Cup finals in Argentina and as Frank Butler wrote in the *News of the World*, 'If any one man can inspire the side to rise above themselves it is Don Revie.

'A superb professional, he admits the pressure on him and the team will almost be unbearable but every man is prepared to have a go or burst in the attempt. Yet while Revie remains our best manager, he can't work miracles. England will stand or fall on ability with luck going either way.'

21

ENGLAND (1975–77)

'I have done more and given a lot to the team, and five defeats out
of 26 matches is not a failure at any level, but I will be if we do
not get to Argentina.'

Don Revie

On 20 November, a tired and dejected-looking Revie was photographed
leaving Lisbon airport. Failure to qualify for the European Nations Cup meant
England would not be seeded for the qualifying draw of the 1978 World Cup.

Back home, Revie had been subject to another petty attack by Alan Hardaker
who had labelled Revie's build up to matches as 'amateurish', before going on to
accuse the England manager of 'trying to buy everyone'.

Brushing aside the disappointments of Europe and ignoring the outrageous
attack by Hardaker, Revie was relieved to hear that England had to battle with
Italy, who were in the process of re-building after going out in the first round of
the 1974 World Cup Finals. Making up the group were Finland and Luxembourg
to achieve his dream of qualifying for the 1978 World Cup.

Within the next few days, Revie would fly off to Paris to meet representatives
of Group Two qualifiers to sort out fixture dates. The group would be played on
a home-and-away basis and had to be completed between 1 January, 1976, and
31 December, 1977.

Breathing a huge sigh of relief Revie told the press, 'This will be a vital
meeting with the dates all important. I am hoping that we, Italy, Finland and
Luxembourg can sort it out between us in one happy meeting rather than have
to go to FIFA for an independent decision. If we are still in disagreement, then
it will be down to the toss of a coin and no one wants that.

Although Finland and Luxembourg were being written off as no more than cannon fodder, Revie was quick to emphasise the importance of balancing the games against them with the two important deciders against the powerful, seeded Italians. 'You only have to look at results in the European Nations Cup to see how many small teams have upset the big ones,' said Revie. 'West Germany struggled against Greece while East Germany had a terrible time against Iceland. These games have got to be won and won well.'

Nevertheless, it was double World Cup champions Italy who presented the major obstacle. Negotiations were at an early stage for England to get a quick test against Italy as both countries, along with Brazil, had been invited to compete in a tournament in New York in May 1976 to celebrate the American Bicentennial. Revie was to comment at the time, 'Negotiations for this are still in [the] very early stages but it certainly sounds an attractive and useful proposition.'

The Football League Secretary was not the only one who was quick to stick the boot in. It was almost inevitable that Brian Clough would have something to say for himself. Declaring himself a candidate for England manager when Revie retired, Clough told Vince Wilson of *The Mirror* on 23 November, 'Football, like a marriage, is all about a good relationship and Revie hasn't found one. The England team is not playing for him. I'm not saying they haven't tried, I believe they have, but the chemistry isn't right.'

On the same day, Mike Langley of the *Daily Mirror* came up with a half-baked idea of a United Kingdom team to compete in the next World Cup, inviting readers to write in with their views, as well as who they would like to see manage the team.

Reporting back the following week, Langley said that had it been left to *Daily Mirror* readers, the England manager would not even be in the running for the mythical job. Langley wrote, 'Revie has worked for a year polishing his image and will be rocked by an almost unanimous view, he is "an excuse maker", "manager of robots" and "distrustful of flair".'

Responding to criticism in his column for the *Sports Argus*, Revie was to say, 'As England have only lost one out of 11 matches they have played, I don't find the criticism levelled at me now difficult to take. It is fair to say that England weren't exactly riding a crest of a wave when I became manager. Considering how long it can take to build a successful team, I suggest people are judging too early.'

On 9 January, 1976, Revie wrote to 28 players telling them to set aside any plans for the summer as they were now officially on standby international duty. Included in the 28 were so-called mavericks such as Charlie George of Derby County, Alan Hudson of Stoke and Stan Bowles of Queens Park Rangers. There were also call-ups for Derby's Colin Todd and Roy McFarland.

One player who was not impressed was Alan Ball. Now fully restored as captain to the Arsenal side, the diminutive redhead was still smarting at the way his England career was brought to an end in such brutal fashion at the hands of the England manager.

In an exclusive interview with the *Sunday People*, Ball described training sessions as 'farcical', some of the players as 'donkeys' and 'too thick' to understand tactical instructions. Ball claimed the reason England failed to qualify for the European Nations Cup was simply because Revie had picked the wrong players.

According to Ball, 'The first thing Revie looks for in a player is obedience. If you say, "Yes, Mr Revie, no, Mr Revie, three bags full Mr Revie," then you are halfway to being in the England team.' In response, Revie claimed Ball's attack was a 'kick in the teeth'.

Apart from a Welsh Football Association Centenary Celebration game on 24 March, the next competitive game would be the Home Internationals between 8 and 15 May, followed by the tournament in the United States that featured games against Italy, Brazil and a United States Select XI, from 25 to 31 May. These dates would mark the longest period Revie would have spent with his players since he had been appointed England manager.

Heading into the game with Wales, he was still unsure of his best team. By now he hoped he would have 20 England players ready for the World Cup qualifying matches against Italy, Finland and Luxembourg at the end of the year. Instead, he had about 12, and only Kevin Keegan, who Revie said was his player of the year in 1975, and Mick Channon had shown any consistency.

So when England ran out to face the Welsh at Wrexham's Racecourse Ground, Revie was still experimenting with his best line-up. The team included seven new caps: Trevor Cherry, Phil Neal, Phil Thompson, Mike Doyle, Phil Boyer, Ray Kennedy and Dave Clement, in a team that included five players from Liverpool.

It was Ray Kennedy who gave England the lead after 70 minutes, before Peter Taylor, from Third Division Crystal Palace, on as a 46th-minute substitute for Mick Channon, doubled the score 10 minutes later. Alan Curtis grabbed a consolation goal for Wales in the final minute.

On 8 May, England were back in Wales, this time Ninian Park in Cardiff for the opening tie of the Home Internationals. Once again, Peter Taylor was on the scoresheet in a scrappy match that England were lucky to win 1–0. Eight of the players only had 10 caps between them with Tony Towers, Stuart Pearson and Brian Greenhoff making their debuts as Revie chopped and changed again.

The contrast in the atmosphere after the games between Wales and Northern Ireland on 11 May could not have been greater. Revie and his players were in party mood. Northern Ireland had been comprehensively beaten 4–0 and everyone had been invited back to Revie's suite at the Esso Hotel near Wembley Stadium, where the England team stayed before the game. Playing an impromptu gig at the piano was the new chairman of Watford FC.

Gathering around for a sing-along was Kevin Keegan. 'After the match we all went up to Don's suite and who was there? Only Elton John. Don admired talent whether it was on the football pitch or in any other world. We had just beaten Northern Ireland and we had a great time.'

Whilst Elton John enjoyed entertaining the players, he had another reason for being there – he wanted to speak to Revie about the Watford job. The two men had actually been firm friends for years. Kim Revie said, 'Elton was due to stay the weekend with us and I was in school. To save my father the trouble of getting me back to Leeds, Elton offered to pick me up. Well Elton turned up in his big Rolls Royce and all these schoolgirls were hanging out of the windows to look at him. That weekend Elton and my dad played tennis together. They looked a sight, Elton every inch the rock star and dad dressed in his England tracksuit.'

With Watford just failing to get out of the Fourth Division, Elton decided he needed a change. Even though he was a lifelong fan of the Vicarage Road club, by his own admission he knew very little about the lower divisions. When he became chairman, it was not just for show. His ambition was to take his beloved club into the top flight and Europe.

Travelling regularly with Revie and the England team, Elton was used to rubbing shoulders with star names and there was none bigger than the England manager himself. He had the money, now all he had to do was to convince the man who had created the legend of Leeds United to do the same in Hertfordshire.

Kim Revie said, 'There was no doubt about it, Elton told dad, "I want you to manage Watford, just name your price." Dad replied he was very flattered but there was no way he could manage the club, but he offered to cast his eye over anyone Elton had in mind.'

The man Elton wanted to bring Watford up from the Fourth Division was World Cup winning captain, Bobby Moore. Only Revie had other ideas and, according to Kim, told Elton: 'The man you want is Graham Taylor at Lincoln City, he's the best young manager in the country.'

So Taylor, who had just won the Fourth Division title with Lincoln City, visited the singer's home in Old Windsor to formally accept the job as Watford manager.

Taylor was the latest in a long line of people that Revie had recommended. Lawrie McMenemy credits the England manager for recommending him to the Southampton board: 'I got to know Don at Lilleshall when he was still at Leeds he made a point of coming over and sitting with us at lunch, to chat with us about our thoughts on the game. When I was coach at Sheffield Wednesday, he would invite a few of us down to watch coaching sessions. I got to know him well so when the Southampton board asked about me, Don was only too willing to help.'

Even future Leeds United manager, Howard Wilkinson, was grateful for Don's advice: 'I was studying for a degree in physical education at Leeds University when I wrote to Don asking if I could have a chat with him about his methods. He said he could give me an hour and asked if I could meet him at the Queen's Hotel.

'Instead of giving me just an hour, he spent an entire afternoon with me over tea and sandwiches giving me his view on the state of the game.'

Back on the pitch, it was on to Hampden Park and the Home Internationals decider on 15 May. Both Roy McFarland and Mick Channon linked up well to give England the lead on 11 minutes before Bruce Rioch's powerful header from an Eddie Gray corner put Scotland back on level terms six minutes later. A Ray Clemence mistake, where he managed to let a weak-looking shot from Kenny Dalglish through his legs on 49 minutes gave Scotland a 2–1 win and the British Home Championship.

From there, England flew out to Los Angeles for the opening game of the USA Bicentennial Cup. Those watching the coverage on the BBC on 23 May could be forgiven for thinking that England were robbed when a last-minute goal by substitute Roberto gave Brazil a 1–0 victory. A disappointed Revie said, 'It was heart-breaking to lose so late in the game. I am sure that any neutral observer would say that England deserved at least a draw.'

If the roar of the crowd was anything to go by in a hot and humid New York City, Italy could have been playing at home. And no one was under any illusion that the game was being played in a baseball stadium – the diamond, marked out by sand, was very clear, even if Yankee Stadium had been marked out for a football game.

Not that it mattered to the crowd – the Bronx boasted one of the largest communities of Italian-Americans and they were out in force to cheer on the Azzurri. Both teams had only been invited to take part in the American Bicentennial Soccer Cup by way of failing to qualify for the European Nations Cup.

It was hoped the presence of three World Cup-winning teams, and a select Team America, would further promote the game in the US, which already saw the likes of George Best, Pele and Franz Beckenbauer turning out on a weekly basis for teams in the North American Soccer League.

For Revie, the game was only a warm-up for the real business. A month later, England would venture to Helsinki to begin their World Cup campaign. Revie knew he had been given the benefit of the doubt after England had flopped out of the European Nations Cup. Another disaster and that would be that – he fully expected to be sacked if England did not reach the World Cup finals in Argentina.

The tension Revie was feeling was not helped when England went two goals down against Italy inside the first 20 minutes, but they struck back to win with three goals in the opening seven minutes of the second half. Both teams played open and enterprising football. Channon was in inspiring form as captain, his two goals coming either side of a header by Phil Thompson. Chelsea's Ray Wilkins also made his debut that day.

Watching that day was the new FA Chairman, Sir Harold Thompson, the man credited with sacking Sir Alf Ramsey, who was also on the trip. Admiral's Bert Patrick, who was travelling with the team, remembers an incident with Thompson that was to cast a shadow over the tour: 'I travelled extensively with the England team and began to sense there was an unpleasant atmosphere developing between manager and chairman.

'On one occasion… Don was having a conversation with me in the team hotel, when Sir Harold Thompson, chairman of the FA, interrupted our conversation. He rudely demanded of Don Revie the team sheet. He was told in no uncertain terms that, when he as manager had selected the team, it would not be shown to Thompson first!

'I thought they were going to come to blows. It was most embarrassing in the middle of the hotel reception area. On that same summer tour, Revie told me later that during a meal Thompson said to him, "When I get to know you better Revie, I shall call you Don," to which Revie flashed back, "and when I get to know you Thompson, I might call you Sir Harold."'

On 31 May, England rounded off the tournament against Team America, effectively a training match. The American side included Bobby Moore, Tommy Smith and Pele who were all plying their trade in the North American Soccer League. The game, in which Keegan scored a brace along with one for Gerry Francis, resulted in a 3–1 win for England.

Despite this morale-boosting tour, the real action was to come two weeks later, on 13 June, when England would host Finland at Wembley. After all the plotting and scheming, now it was serious – every game was vital in the quest to reach the 1978 World Cup finals in Argentina.

Sitting down with *The News of the World*'s Terry McNeil, the tension was clear: 'This is my most important match in 16 years as a manager. I felt something like this when I was at Leeds and we were away to a Third or Fourth Division side in cup ties.

'But… so much depends on England's getting through. I believe qualification would lift everyone at home and I even believe it could help the country's exports as well.'

Much of the tension Revie felt heading into the Finland game was his inability to decide on his favoured first XI. For example, he could never settle on his first-choice goalkeeper with both Peter Shilton and Ray Clemence sharing the duties.

For FA Secretary, Ted Croker, Revie had broken the golden rule of international management, do not make changes. By the time the Finland game came about, Croker claimed of the 81 players who had attended Revie's 'talk-in' in Manchester in 1974, nearly all of them, had been capped. One of the many regrets Croker was to have about Revie's tenure as England manager.

Writing in his autobiography, *The First Voice You Will Hear Is…* Croker claimed Revie had fallen into the classic trap of wilting to the weight of public opinion, being particularly swayed if a player had been championed in the press or had performed well when he had gone to watch them at a match. Things had not been helped when injuries to key players had disrupted his plans meaning Revie had to make unforeseen changes.

Having watched Revie at close quarters, Croker believed ultimately, the England manager, thrived on the day-to-day contact with players. Seeing himself as something of a father figure to them. When Revie attempted to play this role at England, Croker felt events went against him and he was unable to build the type of rapport he enjoyed with the players at Leeds United.

Not seeing players for months on end deeply affected Revie leaving him almost as an administrator, for as Croker pointed out, Revie had all the skills to succeed in club football but was found wanting on the international stage.

As Croker wrote for an international manager, a key skill is diplomacy, something Revie was sorely lacking when it came to the various public spats he had got involved in with Alan Hardaker, who as the secretary of the Football League, would have been instrumental in postponing league matches before England internationals.

For Croker, it was not just the lack of inter-personal skills which most concerned the Football Association but the absence of any paper qualifications, namely a full FA coaching badge. Holding only a preliminary coaching certificate, as Revie did, was not a problem for Leeds United.

However, to Croker and the Football Association, appointing Revie as England manager with his lack of coaching badges made a mockery of the FA coaching system. Further to this, there was disappointment Revie had put people like Gordon Banks and George Eastham in charge of the under-23s, both of whom lacked coaching experience. Whilst greengrocer Ken Burton, who had never managed in the Football League, oversaw the youth team.

All these things led Ted Croker to believe only six months after appointing Revie as England manager, the Football Association were indeed as Alan Hardaker claimed 'Off their heads' even offering Revie the job in the first place.

According to Croker even though, Revie's position was coming under increasing scrutiny and there was some antagonism towards him from some people on the international committee, there was never any suggestion they did not have the right man for the job, or he should be replaced. With World Cup qualification still on the cards it was in no one's interest to remove Revie from his job just yet.

Looking back years later, Revie said, 'I should have done what Sir Alf Ramsey did, decide on my best players and stick with them. Instead, I kept looking for something that was not there. Billy Bremner was a Scotsman and Johnny Giles was an Irishman, I should have given more players more time rather than looking around for those same players.'

In the press Revie was upbeat, telling Terry McNeil, 'The players are ready in mind and body, they know they will have to battle, be patient and accept that Finland won't give them any room. But they must go out there and do it. This is the big one.' But behind the scenes he was still fretting. Without daily contact with the players, he had a lot of time on his hands and he filled that up with worrying.

If there was one player who emerged as a superstar under Revie it was Keegan. Against the Finns he was simply outstanding as England got off to a flying start. He laid on the first goal in the 14th minute for Stuart Pearson, who returned the compliment after the Finns had forced an equaliser against the run of play. Mick

Channon made it 3–1 in the 57th minute before Keegan wrapped it up three minutes later with a superb solo goal. The only downside of the performance was that England missed a procession of simple chances against the team that were the whipping boys of their group.

'We're on our way!' claimed the *Daily Mirror*, who praised the courage and confidence of the performance in the face of some heavy tackling from the Finns. Frank McGhee wrote, 'It really is beginning to look as though he is putting a team together at just the right time in just the right way. It isn't perfect yet.

'The defence had some distinctly dodgy moments against the Finnish amateurs. But the midfield men, Gerry Francis, Trevor Cherry and Trevor Brooking, looked a balanced blend and the three front players, Kevin Keegan, Mick Channon and Stuart Pearson, took their scoring chances well.'

'It is a result that will cause anxiety in Italy, the nation that presents the biggest menace in England's qualifying group.

Speaking afterwards, Revie said, 'I am more than pleased with the way it went. The Finns made it difficult for us to play, pulling lots of people back, behind the ball. I would have settled cheerfully for this score before the game because it is nice to get a good start in our qualifying group.'

There was a reunion of sorts when England lined up to play the Republic of Ireland at Wembley on 8 September, with both teams presented to Leeds United president and past FA chairman, Lord Harewood, before the game.

The Irish, managed by former Leeds midfielder Johnny Giles, were unlucky to fall a goal behind when Stuart Pearson steered a Kevin Keegan cross into the net from close range a minute before half time.

The Irish equalised through Gerry Daly from the penalty spot following a foul on Steve Heighway. And they were the more inventive side, too – England were lucky to escape with a draw. For the first time, Kevin Keegan, skippering the side in place of Gerry Francis, tried his best to lift his teammates. Words were exchanged between Charlie George and Revie when George, who was out of position, lasted just over an hour before he was substituted by Gordon Hill.

It was then back to the business of the World Cup as England entertained Finland at Wembley on 13 October. All was going according to plan when

England raced into the lead with a third-minute goal from Dennis Tueart but an inspired Finland equalised early in the second half before Joe Royle headed a 52nd-minute winner from Mick Channon's centre.

The chant of 'what a load of rubbish' went up as the players trudged off the Wembley pitch. Their manager, in his now familiar long winter coat, knew England had made it hard for themselves.

In the post-match interview, Revie was almost grovelling, 'We didn't play well, and I told the team I would apologise on their behalf for the way we played. We lost our passing and our positional sense and our thinking. We worked on finishing for six solid days but when it mattered, we didn't do it, we will just have to work harder.'

At Craven Cottage, fans were being treated to an Indian summer, as fresh from the USA, George Best and Rodney Marsh were treating the long-suffering Fulham supporters to some exhibition football. Speaking on the radio in Sheffield, Marsh had lost none of his gift for controversy: 'I don't want to be too cutting but Don Revie isn't good enough to be England manager. You have a man in charge for two years and three months to pick his team and system and he's no closer getting them than he was all that time ago.'

Two weeks later, Patrick Collins, writing in the *News of the World* said, 'At a time when the Don Revie Supporters' Club could hold its annual meeting in a telephone box, the England manager may take some comfort from messages drifting up from the south coast: "The fellow was at Leeds all those years and they won everything in sight. He takes over the England job and suddenly everyone tells you he's a bad manager. I'm sorry but I don't believe it," says Alan Mullery. And if those of us who have found it difficult to see Revie as the answer to a nation's prayer are unconvinced by that little act of faith, Mullery's next proposition is difficult to contradict.

'"I'll tell you the real test," he says. "Let Revie pack in the job tomorrow. Then see what offers he gets. There'd be half a dozen First Division clubs waving contracts at him within the hour, no danger."'

It was not supposed to be like this. The Finland game was supposed to give the English players a boost ahead of their visit to Rome on 17 November for the crunch game against Italy.

This was no Roman holiday. Hotels had been vetted, quiet bedrooms were found, food had to be up to scratch, and training facilities were the very best Italy had to offer. It was these minute details that Revie thrived on.

Over 70,000 packed the Olympic Stadium in Rome while those back home in England had to wait until *Sportsnight* that evening to watch the action – authorities worried that if the game was shown live at 1.30 p.m. on a Wednesday afternoon, people might skip work. David Coleman was in the commentary box for the BBC.

To further add to Revie's woes, Alan Hardaker was once again grumbling about the postponement of fixtures ahead of an international match telling the *News of the World*, 'There are many people who have been annoyed by this season's mucking about of fixtures. Quite honestly it hasn't proven a success. I think it will be altered next year, we must certainly look at it.

'In future we might have to let players train together but go back to their clubs on the Saturday before rejoining the England squad.' Revie claimed such a move would be a backward step as he awaited news of the fitness of Stan Bowles.

The inclusion of Stan Bowles seemed to be another sign of Revie pandering to the press when it came to his selection. As a player for QPR, Bowles could be brilliant when in form but lacked consistency and was not the type of player Revie would have brought into Leeds.

Revie made six changes from the side that had beaten Finland at Wembley, completely refashioning his back four by bringing in Dave Clement, Mick Mills, Roy McFarland and Emlyn Hughes. After being overrun at times in the middle of the park by the Finns, he filled his midfield with grit and determination by selecting Trevor Cherry, Brian Greenhoff and Trevor Brooking. His biggest gamble however was up front where the mercurial Stan Bowles, who was recovering from flu, was chosen to play alongside Mick Channon and Kevin Keegan in a three-man forward line.

England were comprehensively outplayed. A settled Italian side, containing Roberto Bettega, Dino Zoff, Claudio Gentile, Marco Tardelli, Franco Causio and Fabio Capello totally dominated the match. Giancarlo Antognoni's 20-yard shot and Bettega's diving header saw off England 2–0.

Emlyn Hughes later recalled that, 'They murdered us 2–0'. Trevor Brooking, who stood forlornly up front for England during the game, reflected, 'I think even coming off the pitch it wasn't a great surprise to have lost, because going out there you were hoping it was going to happen for England but you didn't quite have that belief.'

For his part, Revie was left to tell the press, 'I believe, because I've got to believe it, that England can still make it to Argentina by our own efforts. We must concentrate on building up big scores in both matches against Luxemburg next March and October. We've got to really thrash them. That way we can hope to put some pressure on Italy before they come to Wembley for the rematch next November. It will be up to us to beat them.'

On the Finns, who Revie hoped would do England a favour, 'They can look at the league table in our group and believe themselves [to] still have a chance of qualifying. Any success they have against Italy will be a bonus for us, but I am putting that out of my mind.'

What was meant as a gesture of support only served to embarrass the England manager even more. In an interview with the *Daily Express* Dick Wragg, the chairman of the International Committee, said, 'In Don Revie, England possess the best manager in the business, I believe that. My colleagues on the International Committee believe that – and we are backing Don 100 per cent. He will remain England manger whether we go to Argentina or not…

'I'm very close to Revie and he has never intimated to me that he would resign if we didn't make the finals. And there is certainly no question of him being fired. Why should we sack the best manager there is?'

Behind the scenes, Revie knew things were very different. There were rumours. Apparently, the FA were talking to the Cobbold family, owners of Ipswich Town, about the availability of their manager, Bobby Robson.

Nigel Clarke from the *Daily Mirror* said, 'It was quite well-known during that period. The FA were looking around, a new manager and a new start. Bobby Robson was the favoured choice, a far more malleable and amiable character than Don.'

Things were not helped by Thompson, FA chairman. Croker said: 'Don obviously got the impression that Sir Harold didn't think too much of him. You could say that Thompson referring to Don as "Revie" might have been a typical schoolteacher thing, but it wasn't, for he didn't call everybody by their surname. He chose to do that to Don and it was undoubtedly derisory. But it was public knowledge I didn't get on with Sir Harold either. He certainly was opinionated... he simply didn't have the capacity to get on with people.'

Rudeness was one thing but interference in Revie's management was another. Thompson would think nothing of trying to meddle in team selection. 'The classic one,' Croker recalls, 'was when Thompson told Don he shouldn't play Malcolm Macdonald after Macdonald had a particularly poor game. It puts a manager in a very difficult position. There is no way after that match that Revie would have played him.

'Yet he would think, "If I don't play him, Thompson's going to think I'm listening to his advice."' Afterwards, Croker reprimanded Thompson. 'I said, "Please don't ever make comments to the England manager about selection because it's just not fair." Things were critical at the time.'

Italy and England were both on four points at the top of the group. However, the Italians had a game in hand and had a superior goal difference over the English. It was as the *Daily Mirror* said after the match: 'Wembley or bust!'

Those around Revie were getting worried he was staring into space, lost in thought, and was beginning to wear a defeated look. The Christmas period would give some respite and a chance to recharge his batteries. As family and friends gathered around for Revie's annual New Year's Eve party, they found him in better spirits than they had for months.

If Revie really was looking for a way out, then an opportunity presented itself in January 1977. With Everton slipping down the league, manager Billy Bingham was dismissed on 11 January. John Moores had drawn up a shortlist of just two men – the first, Don Revie, and the second, Bobby Robson.

On 18 January, Moores made his move. Having called Revie and expecting to be knocked back he was surprised the England manager had agreed to meet him. He told Moores the England job was his top priority but he would be interested in the vacancy after the game against Italy in November. Unwilling to appoint a caretaker manager and fearful of being messed around by Revie again, the Everton chairman passed on him and pursued Robson instead, also unsuccessfully.

Instead, Revie concentrated on the upcoming friendly with the Dutch. Writing when he was appointed England manager, Revie was fulsome in his praise of both the Netherlands and West Germany teams following the previous World Cup: 'Overall, I was disappointed with the teams in the World Cup. I didn't think the standard was exceptionally high in any way. I thought England — who in my opinion were desperately unlucky not to qualify — would have reached the semi-finals at the very least.

'But the Dutch and the Germans did impress me with their open, attacking football. And what really caught my eye was the way that their defenders played. They weren't afraid to move up into attack and leave the back vulnerable. More often than not this left a one-against-one situation if the opposition broke forward.

'Neither side conceded a lot of goals and both entertained. They were the most successful teams in the tournament, finishing first and second!'

After the winter break, Revie concluded that what both he and England needed was a morale boost. This time he would not listen to the press who were clamouring for the return of Malcolm Macdonald or the claims of this player or that player. He would decide on his best XI and stick with them.

Beating the Dutch and their Total Football philosophy would send a powerful message to his bosses at the FA that he was the best manager in the business. Against the backdrop of industrial turmoil in the UK, the national team were going to lift the nation's spirits. As Revie relayed in a New Year message: 'Our destiny is in our hands.'

Revie, who had been drilling the players all week, felt sure the side he sent out on 9 February, 1977, could nullify the World Cup runners-up in much the same way they had done against West Germany.

But the Netherlands produced what many considered the finest display at Wembley by a visiting team since Hungary beat England 6–3 in 1953. Johan Cruyff and Johan Neeskens dictated the pace and pattern of the match and it was Jan Peters, playing in only his second international, who nipped in for two goals in 10 minutes in the first half.

The reports of the time summed up the mood of despair from the journalists who witnessed the game. Brian Scovell for the *Daily Mail* said, 'Johan Cruyff dominated last night's match as no great player has ever dominated Wembley before. He had 61 touches of the ball and of his 50 passes, 30 were positively forward balls. He switched play with some stunning 40-yard passes which left the crowd and England's defenders gasping. Unlike some stars, Cruyff also worked hard, often appearing in his own penalty area. By comparison, England's new striker, Trevor Francis, had only 21 touches – well below average.'

Jeff Powell of the *Daily Mail* weighed in by writing: 'England joined the rest of the second-raters in the gutter of world football last night. The last dregs of self-respect drained away to the accompaniment of Wembley's new theme tune, "What a load of rubbish." To be one of 90,000 Englishmen in this once impregnable stadium was a demoralising experience, as even manager Don Revie bore unhappy witness. For England were not merely beaten for the first time by Holland [the Netherlands]. They were torn apart.'

Kevin Beattie said, 'They ripped us to pieces that night. I only played nine times for England but that was easily the worst game. Cruyff was unbelievable. They just passed the ball so quickly, all the way through the team from back to front.

'We couldn't get near them and even Don Revie afterwards admitted they had played some smashing stuff. It was Total Football and, although on [the] one hand it was just awful, you really had to admire it. I've no idea why I'm flat out for the goal. I must have been having a lie-down. I'd been marking Robbie Rensenbrink and he'd tired me out.'

Sitting down over a cup of tea with the *Daily Mirror*'s Frank McGhee, Revie gave the impression of being a broken man. Claiming it would take 15 years to build a team ready to take on the world, he criticised all levels of English football from schoolboys upwards. In the two years he had been in the job he had accepted he had failed in his task.

He and Elsie sat in their lounge, night after night, talking after failing to get to sleep. Revie could never escape the reality. He did not have 15 years, nor 15 months, he had to get results soon. If England did manage to somehow get to the

World Cup finals, they would have to get past teams like the Netherlands in order to win it. And that seemed highly unlikely.

Then out of the blue came an unexpected phone call. It came from Qasem Sultan, general secretary of the United Arab Emirates (UAE) Football Association. Sultan informed Revie he was acting on behalf of UAE ruler, Sheikh Zayed bin Sultan Al Nahyan, who identified the England manager as the man he wanted to take to head up a root and branch reform of the game in the country.

Eammon O'Keefe, who became the first English footballer to play in nearby Saudi Arabia, said: 'Even in the '70s, the Arabs could not get enough of English football. They would have been all too aware of Don Revie and what he had done at Leeds United. Money would have been no object.'

Like the other offers which had come Revie's way the answer was a polite thanks but no thanks. However, the Arabs would not take no for an answer. As the pressure mounted in the England job Revie became more and more intrigued by their offer. It would not be long before he would be taking their overtures seriously.

There were very few men Thompson would defer to. However, by virtue of being the Queen's cousin, Lord Harewood, president of Leeds United and past president of the FA, was part of the aristocracy, an exclusive club Thompson would never be invited to join.

Harewood had admired the way Revie had pulled Leeds United up by their bootstraps to become champions of England and, as a close friend, had been worried about Revie's general disposition for weeks.

He was also the one who told Revie that the FA had been sniffing around Bobby Robson. It was in the oak-panelled boardroom at Portman Road, when Leeds played Ipswich there in early 1977, that John Cobbold first told Harewood about the FA approach for his manager. Over a whiskey, Harewood listened incredulously as Cobbold told him that Dick Wragg, publicly loyal to Revie, had been anything but behind his back.

There was certainly tension in the air in the weeks after the Dutch debacle. To have any hope of qualifying for the World Cup England had to produce a cricket score against Luxembourg. While Revie agonised over getting the best out of the players in the dressing room below, high up in the stands in one of the executive boxes, the champagne was flowing among the members of the International Committee.

Excusing himself from the room, Lord Harewood headed for the toilets. On the way he noticed the hunched over figure of Thompson. Seeing the chairman, Harewood greeted him with a smile and a 'Let's hope for a good win tonight.' The FA chairman gave the peer a cold look and muttered, 'Or a loss, which would settle it all.'

To Harewood it was clear that Thompson wanted England to lose so it would make dismissing Revie easier. What Thompson nor Harewood knew at that stage was that Revie was planning his exit. Talks with UAE officials had reached the stage where Elsie had booked tickets to fly out to Dubai and, if all was well, Revie planned to join his wife to thrash out the terms of a contract to become the new national coach of the United Arab Emirates.

It was the four goals in the last half hour that just about kept England's faint hopes of qualifying for the 1978 World Cup finals alive. Kevin Keegan had given England a 10th-minute lead, but then the team became anxious against the Luxembourg part-timers. John Gidman also made his debut at right-back, while Paul Mariner got his first taste of international football as a substitute for Joe Royle.

On 28 May, England kicked off their Home International against Northern Ireland. It was the Northern Irish who took a fifth-minute lead through Chris McGrath against an England team weakened by the absence of Liverpool players, who had won the European Cup just three days earlier.

The increasingly reliable Mick Channon equalised in the 27th minute. There was yet another debutant when Brian Talbot of Ipswich Town replaced Ray Wilkins in the 65th minute. A Dennis Tueart header from a Brian Talbot cross in the 86th minute eventually gave England a victory they barely deserved.

Clambering onto the flight home, Thompson, already smarting after England had crushed Luxembourg 5–0, hissed at his manager, 'Well, that was rubbish wasn't it?'

Revie now had only three days to get the team ready for Wales' visit to Wembley. Wales had never won at Wembley and would have to go all the way back to 1936 to find a win against England. It should have been an easy match.

The tension in the Revie household was palpable. Having already told the family he was going to resign, Revie was naturally still anxious to avoid the sack. 'With mum having agreed to head to Dubai, all dad could think about was plans for her trip. During that period dad was totally distracted, his mind was only focused on an offer from Dubai and the future,' Kim Revie recalled.

By the time Wales earned their first victory in England for 42 years and their first ever at Wembley, Revie was past caring. It was Leighton James who scored the only goal of the game from the penalty spot a minute before half time, after Peter Shilton had pulled him down following a mistake by Emlyn Hughes.

On 8 June, 1977, England were due to play Brazil as part of their week long tour of South America – the trip had been years in the planning. All being well with Elsie's visit, Revie wanted to see Dubai for himself and he wanted to do it soon. Delaying his journey to South America under the premise of watching World Cup rivals Italy play Finland in Helsinki would provide the perfect cover.

As usual, the beer and wine were flowing at the Esso Hotel, although the manager's suite now resembled a wake. The journalists were sharpening their pencils, ready to write Revie's obituary as England manager. Jeff Powell of the *Daily Mail* said: 'I spoke with Don and told him the FA had already approached his successor, I had already been tipped off that he had been offered the job with the Arabs. I knew he had turned them down initially but knew there was more to it.'

That was all the confirmation Revie needed. Unlike the times he was offered jobs away from Leeds United, Revie felt no pull for him to stay. All he wanted to do was to get through the Home Internationals and then the South American trip and he would be gone.

If Revie wanted to fuel the rumours he was going to leave the England job for another in the First Division, his comments to the press would only add fuel to the fire: 'I will probably be considered a success if England reach the Argentina finals. If they do not qualify, what happens to me rests with the FA.

'You have to be big enough to stand up and be counted. If you are doing well as a manager at any level, then you are walking on thin ice. I must admit I enjoyed it more as a club manager simply because I preferred to work with players all the time instead of having them for short periods as you do at international level.

'When you are an international manager you have to live with your last result. I know if we win against Scotland and then do well on the tour of South America people will start saying, "He's not so bad."

'I have done more and given a lot to the team and five defeats out of 26 matches is not a failure at any level, but I will be if we do not get to Argentina.'

Les Cocker, the man who had stood by Revie's side ever since he was appointed at Leeds United, looked at the England manager and was worried. The tension was now etched into Revie's face. 'You are taking too much stick, don't worry about the Brazil game, go to Helsinki and watch the Italian game. I will take the team to Rio.'

Straight after the Scotland game on 4 June, Revie would join Elsie, who was already in Dubai, and talk about taking over as UAE national team manager. From there, Revie would travel to Helsinki to watch the Finns take on the Italians before heading to South America. Telling the press, 'I'll be at the game with fingers and toes crossed,' there was no hint of what was to transpire.

So, on 4 June, 1977, nearly 100,000 fans packed Wembley Stadium to watch the annual Home International football match between England and Scotland and it seemed as though the Scots had invaded London.

Gordon McQueen – one of Revie's defenders while at Leeds – and Kenny Dalglish scored for Scotland, while a late Mick Channon penalty was only a consolation for England. The game ended 1–2. Chaos then ensued as the Scottish fans, including singer Rod Stewart, invaded the pitch, tearing down the Wembley goal posts. It was another shameful day for football.

Embarrassingly, England limped home in third place, a point above Northern Ireland, two points behind Wales in second and three off Scotland, who won the Championship for the second year in a row.

Days later on 5 June, after weeks of talking on the phone, Revie finally sat down face to face with Qasem Sultan, the Secretary of the UAE Football Association. Revie was honest with him. Revie believed England would beat Italy at Wembley, but they would not qualify for the World Cup on goal difference.

Stalling, he asked the Arabs to wait until November, when he would be able to join them. However, that was never an option as the Arabs were keen to make an appointment and had other candidates in mind.

Upon Revie's arrival in South America, Norman Fox of *The Times* would comment Revie looked noticeably depressed. Revie sought out Dick Wragg, where he repeated how he was not sleeping at night, the depression caused by the poor performances and the press coverage, and how much he wanted out.

According to Wragg, Revie offered to resign right there in the hotel room, if the FA would pay out the remainder of his and Les Cocker's contract. Wragg, who went to consult FA Secretary Ted Croker, rejected Revie's offer out of hand.

Writing in his autobiography, *The First Voice You Will Hear Is*, Ted Croker said, 'The whole operation would cost the FA nearly £100,000! It was an amazing demand and one the FA could not possibly countenance. Wragg told him there was no suggestion that he was going to be sacked and that he spoke for the whole international committee when they said they had every confidence in him.'

After a 0–0 draw with Brazil on 8 June under Les Cocker, Revie took charge of the match against Argentina on 11 June. In a brutal game, Trevor Cherry, who had two teeth knocked out by a punch, was sent off with Bertoni in the 82nd minute.

It was Bertoni who had equalised after a third-minute goal by Stuart Pearson, who had scored with a curling free-kick in the 15th minute. The game then became bogged down in midfield, with England unable to penetrate Argentina's in-depth defence. Emlyn Hughes cleared off the goal-line in the closing moments.

The England manager appeared in a sombre mood ahead of the match against Uruguay. Talking about the rumours that he was going to be sacked after the upcoming World Cup qualifying match against Italy in November, Revie said, 'Everyone seems to be forecasting that I will go if we don't qualify, but I'll make up my mind about that when it happens. If we can't beat Italy at Wembley we don't deserve to go to Argentina and I'm sure we will beat Italy.

On 15 June, the match against Uruguay was notable for three things: first, it was to be Revie's 29th and final match as England manager; second, it was the first match where he fielded the same team; and third, it was the first time England completed a tour of South America undefeated.

The game itself was instantly forgotten. Uruguay showed interest only in defending their goal and England's tired players could not work up the energy to find a way through. They finished the tour with only one goal to show for all their effort in three matches. In Revie's mind, the sack was inevitable.

Both Revie and Elsie knew this could not go on, something had to give sooner or later. There had been moments like this in the past, but he had always overcome them. When he arrived home from South America, Revie's mind was made up: he was going to ring up the Arabs and tell him he was interested in managing their national side.

After telling the Arabs he was on his way, the next thing Revie had to do was to inform his family. The extended family of aunts and uncles was joined by son Duncan and daughter Kim to hear of Revie's plans.

For the past few months, it was obvious Revie had been unhappy but now it seemed as though a weight had been lifted off his shoulders. To start with, he said only one thing: 'I am going.' They all knew what he meant – Revie was going to leave the England job. Speaking to a BBC documentary about the England job in 1999, Elsie said, 'I think Don always knew deep down he was the wrong man for the job.'

Kim recalled: 'We all sat down and dad was quite matter of fact about it. He wanted to leave the England job. He had an offer from the Middle East and wanted to take it. We all knew he had been unhappy for a long time.'

Duncan Revie later added: 'We talked about it a great deal; I don't think dad would have accepted the job without our support. But the more we thought about it, the happier we were to give our blessing.'

In later years, Revie would say, 'All I really care about is family and good friends. As long as they are supportive, I am happy.' As Revie prepared to resign from the job every manager in English football seemed to desire, he would need their support more than ever.

'I said motor neurone disease what's that? Then he told me it can affect your speech and throat. There is no known cure. Now you can have pity parties, or you can go out and fight it. Now I have always been a fella who faces the music, like I did with the England job and now I am going to face it.'

Don Revie, upon announcing he was suffering from
motor neurone disease in August 1987

'Mr Revie was the English team manager. He held the highest post of its kind in English professional football and he published and presented to the public a sensational and notorious example of disloyalty, breach of duty, discourtesy and selfishness. His conduct brought English professional football, at a high level, into disrepute.'

Mr Justice Cantley sitting in judgment in December 1979 whilst
overturning a 10-year ban imposed on Revie by the FA after
his resignation as England manager

'He had so much to offer. People who wrote some terrible things about him should think again. He was like a father to me; he saved my England career. They should build a shrine to him in Leeds, they really should.'

Kevin Keegan, speaking after a charity match in aid of
motor neurone disease in May 1988

PART FOUR

22

IN THE DESERT (1977–83)

'I hope for his sake he learns to call out bingo numbers in Arabic!'

Alan Hardaker, Football League Secretary, upon
hearing Revie had taken up the post as national coach
of the United Arab Emirates, July 1977

On Thursday 6 July, 1977, Jeff Powell of the *Daily Mail* was preparing to travel to Turnberry in Scotland to cover the 1977 British Golf Open, when he received an unexpected call from Revie, 'How are you travelling to Turnberry?' Revie asked. When Powell told him he was flying Revie said, 'How about you drive up and drop in and see me in Leeds on the way?'

As Powell set out from his London home, he fully expected Revie to tell him he was resigning from his post as England manager. However, he never thought Revie was about to take up the offer from the UAE. Just 48 hours earlier, FA Cup holders Manchester United had sensationally sacked their manager, Tommy Docherty, for breach of contract.

Docherty had announced two weeks earlier he was leaving his wife after 27 years of marriage for a woman 18 years his junior. Things were complicated by the fact his girlfriend, Mary Brown, was the wife of club physiotherapist, Laurie Brown and they had two young children.

The story had caused a sensation in the press dominating both the front and back pages for days. It was labelled the soccer scandal of the decade.

'Everyone thought Don would return to club management and the Man United job would have been too good to turn down.' These were the thoughts in Jeff Powell's mind as he made his way up the M1 to the affluent, leafy suburb of

Alwoodley in Leeds, where Revie and Elsie made their home. When Powell pulled up to the four-bedroomed house, he was not prepared for what he was about to hear.

Once inside, Revie told the *Daily Mail* journalist he was indeed leaving the England job for the riches and uncertainty of Dubai. Jeff Powell recounts the conversation: 'Don said look, I have to talk to someone about this. Am I doing the right thing? I must secure the financial future of my family. I know I have no future with the FA. I said, the backlash is going to be significant but if the financial wellbeing of your family – and Don was a great family man – comes first that's the decision you have to make.'

Revie went on to explain he needed to travel to Switzerland to ensure the money was in the bank as promised. Powell agreed to make the necessary arrangements. Once he returned to London to file a story about the Open, he went to work.

The journey could easily have come from the imaginations of Ian Fleming or John le Carre. Powell had booked two flights under assumed names from Manchester Ringway to Dubai for 11 July, 1977. One ticket was for him, the other for Don Revie. Wearing sunglasses, no one noticed the England manager as he mingled among those bound for a holiday in the sun.

Powell recalled, 'Eventually we set off for Dubai, via Zurich, and we travelled down to Geneva to check the money had been transferred to the bank. That was the night the *Daily Mail* broke the story. We were in a restaurant overlooking Lake Geneva, a beautiful setting, at about 11 p.m. Don turned to me to ask me, what do you think is happening back home? Well, I said they have just had their first editions, so I imagine Fleet Street is in a state of turmoil.'

Back home, Powell had left three envelopes: one with the resignation, the second with the story about the UAE and the third the big interview. Knowing Revie would be the most wanted man in the country, and to throw journalists off the scent, the duo changed plans and flew to Athens before heading on to their destination of Dubai. It was there that the familiar figure of the now former England manager was spotted and greeted by a British tourist.

Thinking he had landed a scoop, the man telephoned one of the news desks back home. Luckily for both Revie and Powell, the newspaper the tourist called was the *Daily Mail*. Powell said: 'We had a chuckle about it later but at the time we breathed a sigh of relief!'

To say Fleet Street was buzzing was an understatement, and the FA were bombarded with calls from the press asking if there was any truth in the story Revie had resigned as England manager. But the FA, his employers, at this point knew nothing about it.

In a TV interview, FA Secretary Ted Croker said: 'I was surprised last night when I had several calls from newspapers and other news agencies asking if I knew about this because apparently they had already seen an early copy of the newspapers where it went into some detail and that was prior to us knowing about it.'

The FA was not the only place where there was total disbelief. Alex Montgomery of *The Sun* summed up the feeling: 'Frank Clough, who was the chief football writer, was entitled to be angry as were a few others. He knew Don from his early Leeds days and had introduced him to Jeff [Powell]. It was upsetting Don had not approached him. You can't counter a story like that or waste time trying to understand it.'

Powell said later: 'I felt bad for Frank, he was great friend and I did call him a couple of hours before the first edition came out to tip him [off] so at least he would have something for the later editions.'

The *Daily Mail* headline screamed: 'Revie Quits!' The accompanying quote told the world his reasons. 'I sat down with my wife Elsie one night and we agreed that the job was no longer worth the aggravation. It was bringing too much heartache to those nearest to us. Nearly everyone in the country seems to want me out. So, I am giving them what they want. I know people will accuse me of running away and it does sicken me that I cannot finish the job by taking England to the World Cup finals in Argentina next year. But the situation has become impossible.'

A few hours after the story broke in the *Daily Mail*, Revie's resignation letter finally arrived at Lancaster Gate, on 12 July. The letter cited a lack of support from certain sections of the FA, making 'the job of England manager... an impossible task under the present set-up.' The letter went on to tell the chairman, 'It has been brought to my attention that enquiries have been made of another manager and his club concerning the England job.'

There were more revelations the following day on 13 July when the second of Jeff Powell's envelopes were opened. Not only was Revie resigning his post, but he had been appointed manager of the UAE national team on an astounding four-year contract which would pay him an astonishing salary of £340,000 over four years, tax-free.

In the article, Revie said, 'This is an offer I cannot refuse, if everything goes through OK. It is an unbelievable opportunity to secure my family's future. I had many offers to stay in England, but the tax structure, let alone the salaries available, make it impossible to earn this type of money at home.'

Reacting to the news that Revie was bound for the Middle East, Football League Secretary Alan Hardaker quipped, 'I hope for his sake he learns to call out bingo numbers in Arabic!' in reference to Revie's way of using bingo as a team-building exercise.

Even his fellow managers were quick to stick the boot in. John Bond, manager of Norwich City, was quoted as saying, 'I didn't support him as England manager, and I didn't think he did the job well at all. The job has now lost all its dignity.'

'Don't cry for Don' said the *Daily Mirror* as they reported Revie had hit a '£340,000 oil strike!' Already there was talk from the FA that Revie was in breach of his contract and there was to be some sort of ban. Ultimately, Revie resigned from his post to avoid the heartache the job was giving him and his family but he could not foresee the pain ahead.

Reacting to the news of Revie's departure, through the pages of the *News of the World* Jack Charlton was one of the first of his former players to comment on his departure: 'It's a fallacy that his money will insulate him against public opinion. He'll try to give the impression that he doesn't care what's said about him. But I know different. He does care and so he should.

'He has cut and run, and he shouldn't have. He has angered people who respected him. But perhaps more importantly he's let himself down. He may not think that now, but when he has spent a few months in the sun and sand. I'll bet that he'll be pushed to put the timing of the resignation to the back of his mind.'

Later, Johnny Giles commented, 'It's obvious he shouldn't have done it the way he did. He didn't do himself justice. He left himself open to savage criticism by telling the *Daily Mail* first. There was no defence for it. He ruined a lot of good work and then became a baddy... which he wasn't. But who isn't greedy? The people who write the stories in the tabloid newspapers might be the greediest in the world.'

On 15 July, an extraordinary meeting of the FA council was convened to discuss the actions of the now former England manager. At its conclusion, Sir Harold Thompson released a statement that said, 'Every man present was unanimous in thinking it is long past time when we brought loyalty, dignity, integrity and above all fun to our international football.'

Thompson also made it clear that the FA were taking legal advice over Revie's resignation. Later, in response to Revie's accusation that the FA had not properly supported him, he said, 'Complaints about lack of co-operation... are serious and should not be made without better evidence.'

On 19 July, Sir Harold Thompson replied to Revie's resignation letter, and was accusing in tone. The letter informed Revie that his resignation 'is being further considered with the FA's legal advisors.' Later, he warned Revie about 'complaints about lack of co-operation which are serious and should not be made without better evidence.'

Referring to the accusation that enquiries had been made about a potential successor, Thompson asked who had told him this.

In the style to which Revie had become accustomed from his now former boss, Thompson ended his letter by chastising his former employee by stating 'this was not the kind of behaviour which I would have expected of you, nor of anyone who regarded duty, loyalty and integrity as important personal qualities.'

On 20 July, Labour MP Arthur Lewis received an answer to a written question he had submitted to the Chancellor of the Exchequer asking how much a married man would have to earn to enjoy a tax-free income of £340,000 spread over four years.

In reply, Treasury Minister, Robert Sheldon, said someone living in the UK would have to earn £458,000 to take home Revie's annual wage of £85,000. Over the course of Revie's four-year contract this would be the equivalent of £1,832,000, to arrive at £340,000.

There were even doubts about the state of football in the country Revie was about to work in. On 24 July, the *Daily Mirror* carried an interview with Abdullah Ansarki, someone who had coached in the UAE, who expressed his concerns to journalist Ken Jones about whether Revie had got it right. 'He can only be coming for money. There is nothing else for him. What can he hope to achieve? He has four years to get it right, but we are many more years behind our rivals.

'Revie is famous, he managed a famous club, he managed the English team but the more famous you are the greater the miracle that is expected... we did not need a man of Revie's stature. We need coaches who will come knowing they are not expected to wave their arms and change things overnight.'

Once back from Dubai, Revie and Elsie went on their annual holiday in Portugal. While there, on 18 August, Revie learnt he had been charged with bringing the game into disrepute.

The day before, on 17 August, Ron Greenwood had been appointed caretaker England manager. His reign got off to a dour goalless draw in a friendly with Switzerland at Wembley. There then followed a disappointing 2–0 win against Luxembourg before Greenwood secured the job on a permanent basis with a stunning 2–0 win over Italy in November. As predicted, it was not enough to qualify for the World Cup – Italy topped the group on goal difference.

It was not just the FA who were out to get Revie. From the moment it was announced Revie was to become manager of the UAE, the press were out for blood. *The Sun*'s Alex Montgomery said: 'We knew the *Mirror* was about to come out with a major anti-Revie story, we knew Don was in Portugal so they sent me to find him, sit tight and wait for his reaction to what we knew would be dirt slinging revelations. He was on a golfing holiday near Faro, I found his hotel and waited for him to come off the course with Elsie and another couple. I approached when he was alone in the foyer. He knew me, he was pleasant and adamant he would not respond to whatever the *Mirror* produced, not a word. It would be legal.'

Others went after him more aggressively. Miffed they had missed out on the sporting scoop of the decade, the *Daily Mirror* was determined to uncover any piece of dirt that may have contributed to Revie's resignation. Among other things, he was accused of asking for appearance money for the launch of the 1978 World Cup mascot and hawking himself out as a motivational speaker for £200 a time. Quite quickly the press started calling him 'Don Readies', and the name was to stick for the rest of his life.

It would not be long before investigative journalist Richard Stott of the *Daily Mirror* and his team wanted to interview the man himself.

Early in the morning on 2 September there was a loud knock on the door at Revie's Leeds home. Peering through the curtains, Elsie could make out the figures of two strangers. Opening the door, she was confronted by two men who claimed they were journalists from the *Daily Mirror*.

Startled, Elsie told them Revie was out of the country and would not say where he was. It was the second time they had visited the family home; the previous time they had received no answer.

Hearing the commotion, Revie appeared at the door dressed in blue pyjamas, telling the two men, 'She's right, I will not speak to you,' and slammed the door.

Those who had dealings with Revie at the time remember him acting like he was suffering from post-traumatic stress disorder. Nigel Clarke of the *Daily Mirror* said, 'I was in Spain and Don was there after he left for Dubai. I went up to talk to him and he looked like a rabbit caught in the headlights. You would swear I was going to shoot him.'

In his autobiography, *Dogs and Lampposts*, Richard Stott, the journalist who was leading the investigation into the now former England manager, wrote that Revie ran for the UAE job because he was terrified about what Gary Sprake, his former Leeds goalkeeper, had to say about him. The accusations of match-fixing and bribery started to fly.

The *Daily Mirror* called the Football League. They wanted to know if the paper could use footage of the controversial Wolves versus Leeds game from 1972. To Alan Hardaker, Secretary of the Football League, Revie's resignation had justified the doubts he had expressed about the Leeds manager's appointment in the first place. Without asking for an explanation, Hardaker said, 'I know what you are doing, and, in these circumstances, I do not feel justified in charging a fee.'

On 6 September, the *Daily Mirror* ran an exclusive with the headline: 'Revie: *The Mirror*'s disturbing dossier about his rise to fame.' Claiming they had been compiling a dossier since May 1977, they alleged that while Leeds United manager, Revie used a middleman to try and persuade Wolves to throw a game in 1972, acted to influence an end of season match against Nottingham Forest, and tried to offer Sunderland boss Bob Stokoe £500 to 'take it easy'.

For many years, events surrounding the game against Wolves on 8 May, 1972, had hung over Revie. Despite a police investigation, no action was ever taken. However, in September 1977, Richard Stott claimed that former Leeds United player Mike O'Grady, who was on the books of Wolves at the time, was used by Revie to approach Wolves defender, Bernard Shaw, to throw the match and Shaw then told manager Bill McGarry. Even though O'Grady initially co-operated with *Daily Mirror* journalists, he then got cold feet, telling the reporters, 'If you print any of this I will have to deny it.'

According to Gary Sprake, through the pages of the *Daily Mirror*, over a five-week period Elsie made several telephone calls to the goalkeeper and his wife. Both were invited to stay with the Revies and it was claimed Billy Bremner, now playing at Hull City, was trying to arrange a testimonial for him. Sprake thought the approach strange as he had hardly ever spoken to any of them after leaving Leeds for Birmingham.

After several attempts to arrange a meeting, Revie and Elsie waited for Sprake in the foyer of the Post House Hotel, Leicester, for lunch. Visiting Leicester was not unusual for either Don or Elsie as they still had family in the area. Bert Patrick said, 'When Don was still England manager, he would regularly visit Leicester. He would be invited into the boardroom after dropping Elsie off with her sister and while Don would watch the match, she would go shopping.'

While waiting at the hotel, a waiter told Revie he had received a phone call. It was from Robert Evans, a solicitor representing Sprake. Over the course of the short call, Evans told him that Sprake would not be appearing at the hotel as he had signed an exclusive contract with the *Daily Mirror*.

Sitting down with the paper's Richard Stott for a fee of £7,500, Sprake claimed Revie had sent Billy Bremner into the Nottingham Forest changing room before a match in 1971. A few words with the players, it was hoped, would secure the right result for Leeds.

As Stott pressed play on his tape recorder, Sprake began his tale: 'In the Leeds dressing room Revie mentioned to Bremner about going into the Forest dressing room. Billy was not changed and still in his suit. I then saw Billy leave our dressing room.

'About five minutes later, Billy came back and although I cannot remember the exact words he used it was clear to me he had been in the Forest dressing room. I think he said he'd been to see a few of the lads, or words to that effect.' In the end, Leeds ran out 2–0 winners, but the result became irrelevant as Arsenal secured the league title and eventually the double.

Later, Sprake also told Stott he was asked to tap up Welsh international colleagues when Leeds played Birmingham in Leeds' first season back in the First Division in 1964–65. He said, 'I was asked to tap up Colin Green and Terry Hennessey when we played against Birmingham in the last game of our first season back in the top flight.

'I wasn't interested and told Revie it was something I would never contemplate. I may have lost out on a championship medal, but my conscience was clear, and Revie never asked me again.'

On 6 September, 1977, the *Daily Mirror* printed their allegations. Revie was quick to deny them. In a statement issued through his solicitors, Harrisons of Albion Street, Leeds, said, 'All the allegations in today's *Daily Mirror* concerning Mr Donald Revie are completely denied and action by Mr Revie is being considered. Before leaving for Dubai, Revie had left instructions to issue a High Court writ for libel against the *Daily Mirror*.'

Already there was talk the Football League and FA were to set up a joint commission to investigate the allegations made in the *Daily Mirror* and the game between Wolves and Leeds. Both governing bodies said they would be contacting one another to discuss the matter.

West Yorkshire police said they would not investigate the allegations. Detective Chief Superintendent Dennis Hoban, deputy head of West Yorkshire CID, said: 'We have no investigation running currently. We have had no complaint and have not made any investigation. If we receive any firm evidence or complaint, we will then make an investigation.'

The chairman of Leeds United, Manny Cussins, was not available for comment, but his secretary said that he would not be calling a special meeting of the directors unless 'there is need to.' And by the time the *Daily Mirror* had made its allegations, Revie was on his way to Dubai.

Regardless of the allegations in the press, Revie's decision to leave for the UAE had caused upheaval in the family. Elsie's mother, three aunts and an uncle all lived with them in Leeds. Alternative arrangements had to be made.

Speaking to the *Sunday Times* in April 1978 Revie said, 'It was very, very hard to leave the old folk. When Elsie and I got married, I was earning £12 a week in summer and £17 in winter with Manchester City and they helped in so many ways that I felt I owed them something.

'They're now in a nice ground storey flat in Leeds, but Auntie Jennie has a bad hip, Gran's got a bad heart, Auntie Jennie has just had two bones out of her leg… Elsie's sister Agnes has now taken over where we left off and it's put a big burden on her really, not to mention the friends who have rallied around to do shopping and all kind of things.'

There had been tears on the tarmac when they departed for the UAE. Both Kim and Duncan were there to see their parents off. Revie later remarked: 'It was a leap into the unknown. I had never been abroad for work before. You do not know what is in store for you.'

Once in Dubai, Revie and Elsie were met at the airport by a chauffeur-driven Rolls-Royce and driven to the Dubai Intercontinental Hotel, to stay in a £50-a-night suite. Both were given membership of a golf club that had a joining on fee of £750. The bungalow where they would make their home would have cost £22,000 in rent.

Back at home, on 19 September, the FA finally made its move, suspending Revie from any involvement with football played under its jurisdiction. It was announced the ban would stay in force until Revie personally attended a hearing to answer the charge of bringing the game into disrepute. After receiving the news, Revie's solicitors were quick to inform the FA that their client had no intention of appearing before them to answer the charge.

The decision was made by a five-man committee chaired by Sir Harold Thompson and included league president, Lord Westwood. In a statement, Ted Croker said the ban would be purely domestic and there would be no attempt to get FIFA to impose it worldwide. Croker added, 'Mr Revie was entitled to a personal hearing but, through his solicitors, has declined to attend the commission and did not provide any written statements in reply to questions asked by letter… the ban could be indefinite if he does not appear, and the indications are that he will not answer the charge.'

When Revie arrived in Dubai, the UAE had only ever entered the Gulf Cup of Nations tournament in 1972, 1974 and 1976, together with a few minor regional competitions and some friendlies. Compared to Iraq and Kuwait, who were the giants of the region, the only role the UAE played was as the whipping boys. Their first competitive game would not be until the Gulf Cup in March 1979.

In the meantime, Revie would focus on developing football from schoolboy level right up to the national team. His first move was to extend the UAE's Under-17 league from four weeks to two and a half months. He also persuaded the authorities to scrap the Under-20 league and replace it with a reserve team league.

Speaking about his plans, Revie said, 'My main concern is the senior national team. I'm starting with them, then the Under-20s team then the Under-17s. I am giving talks to coaches, setting up medical courses and laying down training programmes for fitness.

'I want to get the same system right throughout the UAE. I want to bring some new training and coaching ideas and get coaches to pass certain coaching certificates in the schools so they will be qualified.'

Everywhere Revie looked he saw potential, from teenagers enjoying kickabouts in the sand to the building work he saw everywhere – Dubai was a place on the up. Gary James, now editor of the *Daily Express*, who at the time was working on *Gulf News*, said: 'Dubai was nowhere as well-developed as it became but every week there seemed to be a new hotel or skyscraper going up. In many ways Revie was a pioneer; he was the first person to put the Middle East on the map; they were very excited to have him there.'

On 18 March, 1978, Revie was spotted in the crowd at Elland Road for the first time since his resignation as England manager. Upon hearing the news Revie was back in the country for eight days to visit family in Leeds, the FA decided to write to all 92 clubs.

The content of the letter was simple: any club thinking of employing the services of Revie in any capacity were reminded the former England boss was currently suspended from the game until he answered a charge of bringing the game into disrepute.

When the press caught up with Revie for comment, as he left Heathrow to return to the UAE on 26 March, he simply said, 'I have no comment to make and I won't be making one in future. I have been out in the Middle East for seven months and I'm enjoying it. There is no doubt I will stay there at least until the end of my contract.'

On 11 May, Kim Revie, who had been advised by Elton John's manager, John Reid, made her singing debut at the Batley Variety Club supporting Freddie Starr. For the past six months she had been playing nightclubs in Dubai.

Later that month Liverpool manager, Bob Paisley, and his assistant, Joe Fagan, arrived in Dubai so the European Champions could play the Gulf Champions, Al Nasr. Even though Revie had nothing to do with organising the match, it did not stop the FA from trying to stop Liverpool from travelling there because of Revie's presence in the country.

On 20 July, 1978, Revie was back in the UK, being pictured looking fit and tanned at an exclusive Berkshire health hydro. His plan was to spend the rest of the summer break catching up with friends and family while playing golf. He would return to Dubai on 14 September when the UAE season kicked off.

By September, 1978, Revie's old club Leeds United were in disarray. The team that Revie built had broken up. They had finally reached their peak when Revie's feet were firmly behind the desk at Lancaster Gate. Despite dominating the 1975 European Cup Final in Paris, poor refereeing went against Leeds who were on the wrong end of a 2–0 scoreline against a Bayern Munich side captained by World Cup winner, Franz Beckenbauer.

Soon after, the stalwarts of the Leeds team of the '60s and '70s quietly left the club. The first to go was Johnny Giles. Seen as Revie's pick to replace him at Leeds, the Irishman left to manage West Bromwich Albion, while Billy Bremner was about to be appointed manager of Doncaster Rovers. Norman Hunter began turning out for Bristol City.

After the unhappy 44-day reign of Brian Clough, Jimmy Armfield came in to steady the ship. Even though there was the European Cup Final and Leeds were constantly in the top 10, they would never again challenge for the league title. In July 1978, they appointed the legendary European Cup-winning Celtic manager Jock Stein as a replacement. By coincidence, Stein only lasted 44 days before resigning to take the the Scotland job.

When he left the Leeds job in 1974, Revie had made sure that there was a consultancy role available to him at Leeds once his contact had ended at Lancaster

Gate. The Leeds board were still keen to come to an arrangement that would see Revie return to Elland Road in an advisory capacity.

But now there was a problem – the FA had banned him from working in English football, even as a consultant. This was a situation that could not continue, so on 4 September his solicitor wrote to the FA informing them that he would meet with them to hear their charge that he had brought the game into disrepute.

In a statement, the FA said: 'We have received a formal written request from Mr Revie for a meeting with the commission which heard his case, and this had been agreed to. No date has yet been fixed for the meeting, but it should not be too long.'

Responding to rumours he wanted to manage again in England, Revie said, 'A lot of people have said that it's because I want to come back and work here but that is not so. My contract in Dubai has three years to run. I am happy there and they are very good to me. It is very unlikely that I will ever come back to football in this country.'

If Revie could have seen the *Daily Mirror* on 12 October, 1978, he would have afforded himself a wry smile as it detailed journalist Frank Taylor's report about Sir Harold Thompson. In the article, Taylor reported that Douglas Goodchild, former referee and chairman of Berkshire and Bucks FA Council, wrote to the FA asking when they were going to act against Thompson.

According to Goodchild, Thompson had used foul and abusive language towards fellow members at the AGM in Bournemouth in June, describing one as a liar and accusing another of leaking stories to the press.

It was reported by Taylor that many FA councillors accused Thompson of having a dictatorial attitude. As one apparently said, 'No one can have an opinion on soccer except him,' while another allegedly claimed, 'The chairman seems to regard the Don Revie case as his personal affair when the FA would be shown as fair by setting up a panel composed of people outside the FA, preferably members of FIFA and UEFA.'

On 21 November, it was announced that Revie would be charged with negotiating with the UAE while still under contract to the FA. In doing so, he brought the game into disrepute. The date of the hearing was set for 18 December.

Even though it was argued that Thompson should not chair the disciplinary panel, the hearing went ahead. Joining Thompson was Arthur McMullen, vice-chair of the Football Association; Lord Westwood of Newcastle; Richard Strachan, a director of York City; and Bob Lord, chairman of Burnley. This was the same commission which met on 17 September, 1977, to suspend Revie from the game in the first place.

On a cold December morning, flanked by his lawyer, Gilbert Gray QC, Revie emerged from a black London cab wearing a beige raincoat and clutching a thick file of papers. Heading into the scrum of photographers and reporters he said nothing as he quickly headed up the steps of the FA headquarters.

Just a year before, the *Daily Mirror* completed its long-standing investigation into Revie. By the time he was back at Lancaster Gate to hear his fate, the paper was openly reporting that Revie had run to Dubai because he lived in fear of being exposed by its investigatory team, which had apparently sent a 330-page dossier to the FA, detailing what they termed Revie's 'dirty dealings'. The dossier has never seen the light of day.

Even though Richard Stott was adamant he sent it, in his papers donated to the Cardiff Journalism School by his widow there is scant evidence of any file, save for some notes that formed the basis of the articles that originally appeared in the *Daily Mirror*.

Taken to the second floor, Revie then came face to face with the man he had unceremoniously dropped as England captain three years earlier. Alan Ball, now with Southampton and accompanied by his lawyer, Tony Wilson, and manager, Lawrie McMenemy, was also facing a charge of bringing the game into disrepute.

In his recently published autobiography Ball had admitted accepting illegal payments from Revie to sign for Leeds United in 1966. Now both would face the five-man commission. The mood of the meeting was set by Bob Lord, who told Revie, 'Know this Don Revie, you will pay for your crimes.'

After an hour, Ball and Wilson left the meeting and announced, 'Alan Ball has pleaded guilty to a charge of meeting Mr Revie and taking payments. Mr Revie has pleaded not guilty to this charge.'

Represented by Gray, Revie called no witnesses. Over five hours, the commission heard from International Committee member, Peter Swales, and chairman, Dick Wragg, who both gave blow-by-blow accounts of the events leading up to Revie's resignation and his acceptance of the job in UAE.

It was mid-afternoon when Ted Croker appeared in the foyer to summarise the day's proceedings. Intimating that Revie had left the building through a back door, he was embarrassed when a relaxed-looking Revie burst through the doors behind him, brushing past a tinselled Christmas tree and headed straight out into the street without saying anything. The commission then retired for another hour before reaching their verdict.

At the end of their deliberations, Thompson gathered the staff together to wish them a merry Christmas before telling them, 'We have reached a decision in both cases and our verdict will be transmitted to the people concerned and that is the end of the matter. I hope so.'

On 19 December, the verdict was delivered: Don Revie was guilty of bringing football into disrepute for breach of contract. He was banned from English football for 10 years and there would be no right of appeal. The sentence was unprecedented in the history of football.

The sentence was backdated to the end of Revie's reign as England manager, which meant he was unable to work in English football until 12 July, 1987. Until then he was forbidden to be employed in any capacity under the FA's jurisdiction. The ban did not include football in Europe or elsewhere in the world. No recommendation of the ban was to be made to UEFA or FIFA.

Reacting to the news, Revie said, 'The FA gave their decision to me at 10 a.m. this morning. Since then, I have been talking over my next move with my solicitors. I am leaving everything in their hands, I am terribly disappointed in their decision and I am now going home.'

At the same time, Alan Ball was fined £3,000 with his solicitor, Tony Wilson saying, 'The FA have failed to listen to mitigation we put forward on Alan's behalf. We consider the fine unjust.'

As expected across the media there was huge support for the FA's stance with only the *Daily Mail* questioning why the FA were sitting in judgment of the man they used to employ. Where it counted, in the UAE, a leading official, Mustapha Kamil, was reported as saying, 'Don Revie is working very hard and doing well. All the players like him. There has been a big improvement in our youngsters.'

While Revie's solicitors mulled over the legal arguments, the man himself returned to Dubai. By now Revie and Elsie were living in a six-bedroomed bungalow with a swimming pool. They also employed a butler, cook and houseboy. To get around the city, Revie would get behind the wheel of a gold-coloured Mercedes. His top priority was preparing the national team for their opening game of the Arabian Gulf Cup on 24 March, 1979, against Saudi Arabia, to be held in Baghdad, Iraq.

On 1 February, 1979, it was announced Revie had decided to challenge the FA's decision in the High Court by applying for a judicial review. In a statement, Revie's lawyers said the sentence was savage, out of proportion, a restraint of trade and an infringement on his right to work.

Back on the pitch, even though he had encountered political tension in games against Cyprus and Northern Ireland as England manager, it was nothing in comparison with what he faced in the UAE. In the cauldron of the Middle East, trouble could erupt at any moment.

As a result of the Camp David Accords, on 27 March, 1979, in the middle of the Gulf Cup, the Egypt-Israeli Peace Treaty was to be signed. This made Egypt the first Arab state to formally recognise Israel. Faced with opposition from other Arab nations, tensions were particularly heightened.

Things had got off to an inauspicious start. Prior to the tournament, Revie arranged a training camp in Egypt but the hotel the team were staying in was falling apart due to an earlier earthquake. Structural experts were testing the building so Revie and the team ended up on the street, eating and resting on the team bus because they were too scared to go back into the hotel.

Even when they got to Iraq there was a bizarre situation. There was a decree that the tournament be suspended for a day as a sign of opposition to the Camp David Accords. Those present were called to convene in the hotel's lobby immediately as Iraqi Vice-President, Saddam Hussein, wanted to address the players and media. The players hurried from their rooms to listen to a fiery speech by Saddam.

When the tournament did kick-off there were high hopes. After going a goal down after 22 minutes against Saudi Arabia, Revie was pleased to see some fighting spirit in his players when they pulled one back on 51 minutes. But a goal

13 minutes before time ended any hope of a victory, so Revie would begin his tenure with a loss as Saudi Arabia recorded a 2–1 victory.

On 27 March, Revie was dismayed to see the UAE go 3–0 down in the first 20 minutes. They did well to not concede any more. By the end, Revie felt the team had some way to go before they could compete with their near neighbours. They were unlucky to lose 1–0 to Qatar two days later but it was worrying that they had scored only once in three games.

On 1 April, a 7–0 thrashing by Kuwait resulted in one of the commentators saying, 'Don't blame the players, blame Revie and the management.' This was followed up on 4 April by another hammering, this time 5–0 at the hands of tournament hosts, Iraq. A 4–0 win on 9 April over bottom-placed Oman was a confidence booster but by then the damage had been done.

In a group consisting of seven teams, the UAE finished last but one, having played six games – won one, lost five – scored five goals and conceded 18. It was a dismal performance.

On his return to Dubai from the tournament, Revie discovered his High Court action against the FA was scheduled for Monday 26 November. On 10 November, in a lunch-time interview for the *Pebble Mill at One* TV show, Revie confirmed he had been offered a consultancy post by his old club, Leeds United scheduled to start on 1 January, 1980. However, Revie said he intended to honour the remaining 18 months of his contract in the Middle East.

Revie said, 'The people out there have been very good to me and my wife and I think I will see out my contract.' He also added the job with the UAE would take about 10 years to complete and did not rule out the chance of another six-year contract.

The media, so used to seeing a downbeat man, unhappy in his final days as England manager, were surprised by his appearance at the first day of the trial. Having lost weight, Revie, accompanied by Elsie, looked tanned and relaxed and his new lifestyle certainly seemed to agree with him.

Opening for Revie, Gilbert Gray QC contended that the hostility shown by Sir Harold Thompson to Revie was such that it was not proper for him to sit on the commission that had imposed the ban. Any reasonable person, he said, might well consider there might be bias, or the risk of it.

The lawyer then detailed several occasions when Thompson had criticised team selection and Revie's position. Gray said that the FA held Revie had been guilty of bringing the game into disrepute and a 10-year ban, backdated from July, was imposed at a further hearing on 18 December, 1978. Gray submitted that the FA's decisions at the 1977 and 1978 hearings were invalid as Revie was bound only by his contract of employment, and not the FA's rules.

Gray said Revie was considered not very successful as England team manager and added, 'They only performed moderately.' He accepted there was criticism in the press and, 'It was obvious some sort of scapegoat was being sought.'

There were two and a half years of Revie's contract still to go and Revie asked for two years of that contract to be paid up, together with an additional tax-free golden handshake of £5,000.

On the second day of the trial, Revie took the stand. He told the court that he bristled whenever he was in the company of Thompson, even telling the often-repeated tale of how Thompson would never call him by his first name, sticking with the public-school tradition of calling everybody by their surname.

Revie also said that had he known Thompson was going to be his boss he would have had second thoughts about taking the job. Further to this, Revie alleged, Thompson privately criticised his predecessor as chairman, Sir Andrew Stephen, and cited Ted Croker's appointment as FA Secretary as 'the worst mistake the Football Association had ever made.'

When asked when he first offered to resign, Revie admitted he had spoken about it to Dick Wragg, the chairman of the International Committee at a football conference in Bournemouth in June 1977 after hearing rumours Bobby Robson of Ipswich Town had been sounded out about the job.

Telling the court he had no other job in mind, Revie said he had simply asked for £25,000, the value of the remaining two years of his contract as security while he found another job.

Revie then revealed he had received a £100,000 signing-on fee from the UAE and had been offered a £90,000 nine-year consultancy deal with Leeds United which meant he had to attend four board meetings a year.

On the fourth day of the trial, Bob Lord, chairman of Burnley, who was a member of the commission, took the witness stand. Responding to charges that Thompson was biased against Revie he said: 'In my estimation, Sir Harold Thompson bent over backwards to be more than fair to Mr Revie.'

Robert Johnson QC, acting for the FA, asked him, 'Did you regard yourself on the commission as some kind of a yes-man for Sir Harold?' 'I am a yes-man to nobody, and I think I am noted for that, too,' Lord replied.

At the beginning of the second week of the trial, Thompson gave evidence. 'I was totally unaware until this trial of any hostility of the kind that Mr Revie has attributed to me.'

Thompson said he had tried to recall friction between himself and Revie and could think of only two instances. The first was when Revie wanted to pull out of a fixture in Belfast against Northern Ireland because of The Troubles. Thompson said he 'took the opposite point of view' and won. The second was when he voiced fears to the FA's International Committee that too much money was being spent on the England team. 'In the end I think Mr Revie continued on the way he was going. We didn't impose cuts or anything like that,' said Thompson.

Shortly before Revie resigned, he told the court, he had agreed that the manager should have a new expensive car. 'If I had been hostile, why did I do that?' he asked. Not long before Revie quit to join the UAE, he met Revie at FA headquarters. The meeting was 'friendly and amicable in every way,' Thompson said. As they parted Revie had laughed and said, 'My God, I wish I had your brains.'

Asked about comments he was alleged to have made about certain England players picked by Revie, Thompson said, 'I can't see why the chairman of the FA can't express his opinion on the performance of players.' But he said he had never attempted to interfere with team selection. Thompson said he could not remember saying Kevin Keegan had played badly, although it was possible that he may have said it.

'Since he was quite a young player at Liverpool, I have taken a very direct interest in Mr Keegan. He has now become a world figure and at no time would I have said anything damaging or potentially damaging to his career,' he added.

Johnston QC then asked if there had been an occasion when Revie threatened to resign unless Thompson stopped interfering with the England team. He replied, 'Not in my memory.'

Questioned about a remark he is alleged to have made after England played an American team in the US in 1976, Thompson said, 'I don't think I would ever be so foolish under any circumstances to say to a stranger that Mr Revie was not fit to run the England team.' Further witnesses for the FA were Dick Wragg and Peter Swales, who repeated the evidence they had given at the commission the previous year.

On 12 December, the judge delivered his verdict. It had been an exhausting, sensational fortnight. Now there was silence in court as the Justice Joseph Cantley, dressed in flowing red robes and a wig, looked over his half-moon glasses to deliver his verdict on the 10-year ban the FA had imposed on Revie following his resignation from the England manager's position.

Revie himself was not in court to hear the verdict – he was back in the UAE. Neither was his nemesis, Thompson. Both, however, awaited a phone call and the verdict.

Finally, the judge gave his ruling. Whereas Thompson was portrayed as an honourable man who was disgusted with the selfish greed of the game and wanted to make change for the better, the image presented of Revie was the opposite, a prima donna who could not take criticism of any form. According to Cantley, Revie was 'a prickly man who brooded over imaginary wrongs.'

Despite his personal thoughts on the virtues of Revie's character, Cantley had to pass judgment based on the law. Accepting the FA were right to charge Revie with bringing the game into disrepute, he was left to remark that with Thompson in charge of the commission, it was likely the FA were biased.

His view of Revie's resignation was damning. 'Mr Revie was the English team manager. He had the highest post of its kind in English professional football and he published and presented the public a sensational, notorious example of disloyalty, breach of duty, discourtesy, and selfishness. His conduct brought English football into a high level of disrepute.'

He then refused to grant Revie any damages, ordering the FA to pay only a third of his costs. However with regret Cantley overturned the 10-year ban, allowing Revie to pursue a managerial career if he wished. While he was not in the courtroom to hear the verdict, the case had failed to do what Revie had intended – clear his name.

Thompson had not managed to come out of the episode unscathed either, with Mike Creed of the *Liverpool Echo* reporting on 15 December, 'I would think Sir Harold Thompson's days are numbered. There was an attempt to unseat him at this year's AGM, but he received 51–28 votes.

'His handling of the Revie business though will persuade a few more people that he is no longer the man for the job. It was Sir Harold's fault Revie took the action but for his insistence on being a member of the FA commission the ban may have stood.'

For Revie, with the present Leeds United manager Jimmy Adamson facing huge pressure from the Elland Road crowd there was speculation Revie would use his new position as consultant with the club as leverage to quickly take back control of his old empire.

When asked about Revie's new role as a consultant, Jimmy Adamson said: 'There can only be one manager of Leeds United. I have a highly respected staff to help me, but that does not mean I would shut the door in Don's face. He was a very successful manager and I would be ready to listen to any advice he might offer, but whether I would act upon that advice is for me to decide.'

There were concerns in Dubai that Revie's mind was on his problems back home. By May the UAE FA were discussing whether the national team might be better served with an Arabic-speaking coach. There were also frustrations for Revie who thought that the players were just not fit enough.

Not many of the plans he put forward had been carried out. The big problem for Revie was that he was unable to establish a sound training and coaching set-up at schoolboy level. For Revie, football and PE were not really part of school life in the UAE.

So, when the UAE FA decided to offer £90,000 compensation to bring his contract to an end, Revie was happy to agree. The announcement was made on 10 May and former Iran manager, Heshmatollah Mohajerani, replaced him the following month.

At the time, Revie was reported as saying, 'We lost only one of our last nine games. I am leaving a squad of good young players and am very happy about the whole business.'

Even though the results were disappointing, Revie would have been proud of his achievements there. Duncan Revie later said: 'Dad was definitely a pioneer. He introduced tactical ideas and coaching techniques that had not been seen in the Middle East before. He was proud of what he did and what he achieved. He started introducing the professionalism that eventually helped the UAE qualify for the 1990 World Cup finals in Italy.

'They had a vision, not just about sport, but events generally. The UAE is now a must-see tourist destination. These things don't happen by accident. For a lot of people of my generation, my dad's decision to take the job in Dubai was the first time they had heard of the UAE. Now, everyone knows someone who has been on holiday there.

'From a sporting point of view, you've now also got the likes of Abu Dhabi Grand Prix, the European golf tour's Race to Dubai, and the top world stars in tennis play there too. It's come a long, long way and I am proud my father played a part in that process.'

But it was not the end of the Dubai adventure. On 18 August, Revie met with the president of Al-Nasr, the premier club in Dubai, Sheik Mara Bin Khalifa Al-Maktou, and was offered a three-year contract to become the manager. For the first time in six years, Revie was a club manager again.

Even though Al-Nasr had a new stadium and had already played some of the biggest names in the game, such as Liverpool, Arsenal and Santos, there were rumours Revie had quickly become unhappy, with Nigel Clarke of the *Daily Mirror* reporting on 25 November: 'Revie rarely sees his daughter and son, he now has a grandchild and badly misses the family. The suggestion is Revie will spend six months in Spain and another six months in England. Revie, now 53, is currently with Al-Nasr although Pat Wright, the 37-year-old former Derby and Birmingham player, supervises training.'

To Revie nothing could be further from the truth. He said: 'I love life in the Gulf. We have everything we want here. My wife, Elsie, is happy, and I enjoy what I am doing. Nothing could ever tempt us back to work in England again.'

On 3 February, 1982, there was a validation for Revie, when his old Leeds United captain, Billy Bremner, won £100,000 in damages from the *Sunday People* for claiming he offered bribes to fix games. At the time it was one of the highest amounts ever awarded in a libel case.

A year later, on 11 May, 1983, Revie's contract with Al-Nasr came to an end. Despite claiming he would retire if they offered a new two-year deal, the decision was taken not to renew the contract. Within a month, Revie was back in England and claimed he would never return to club management: 'The pressure on managers today is ridiculous. I would not be prepared to put myself under that type of pressure again.'

But that did not stop Revie's name being linked with the vacant manager's job at Manchester City. On 12 June, the *Sunday Mirror* stated that, 'Don Revie is the hot tip to take over at Manchester City, who have parted company with John Benson last week and John Bond mid-season and need a top man to take them up. If Revie joined it would be as supremo with a younger track-suited manager.'

In the meantime, Revie, took on a different kind of managerial job, overseeing his daughter Kim's burgeoning pop career. On the eve of the release of her single, *Dreams in the Night*, Revie appeared with Kim in the *Sunday Mirror*, who told readers how her dad had put her on a strict training regime. Revie was quoted as saying, 'I've tried to instil in Kim the same belief as my Leeds' team had.'

By August 1984, Revie was back in sunny climes, this time as manager of Al Ahly, Egypt's biggest club. However, Elsie could not settle and had become ill. By September, just one month into the job, Revie resigned, leaving the Egyptians in shock.

The Revies returned to England, where they settled in Surrey, near Wentworth golf course. In the summer, they travelled to Marbella where Revie became a regular golfing partner for the recently retired Kevin Keegan. For all the world it looked as though Revie had settled into a happy and healthy retirement.

23

BACK HOME (1984–89)

'There is no hope for me, but I think we can help someone in the future.'

Don Revie

'The return of the man who deserted England,' read the headline in the *Daily Mirror* on 7 December, 1984. This certainly came as a surprise to those closest to Revie, who claimed he would never return to football management.

However, there it was in black and white, after seven years in the Middle East, Revie was apparently ironing out the fine details of a £50,000 six-month contract to become the new manager of Queens Park Rangers. It was reported the deal would be done by the time league leaders Everton visited Loftus Road the next day.

Three days before, on 4 December, just after QPR had beaten Stoke City 2–0, chairman Jim Gregory called manager Alan Mullery into the boardroom and sacked him on the spot. The press immediately identified West Ham's John Lyall as the favourite for the job but Gregory had other ideas.

From the moment lifelong Fulham fan Gregory bought QPR he had a vision. Having pulled up the West London side from the Third Division, he had one ambition – to win the league championship. QPR had come close in 1976 and now, in 1984, they looked as though they were on the verge of big things.

Just two years earlier they had also finished runners-up in the FA Cup. A fifth-place finish in the league promised European football. Loftus Road boasted a plastic pitch and brand-new stands. This looked like a modern, forward-thinking club.

The local Thames Television reporter, Michael Whale, recalled the night Mullery was dismissed: 'After sacking Mullery, Gregory bumped into a journalist who told him Don Revie was looking for a job.'

For a man like Gregory, who always had his eye for a headline, the appointment of Revie would see him at the heart of the most sensational story of the season. Could it be possible that Revie, having been out of the English game for seven years, could mount a spectacular comeback? According to those close to the QPR chairman, the answer appeared to be a resounding 'yes'.

By the time Gregory picked up the phone and asked Revie to make the trip from his home in Wentworth to Loftus Road to discuss the managerial vacancy, no one had heard from the former England manager in a long time. Speaking at the time to ITN, the QPR goalkeeper Peter Hucker said, 'No one has worked with him, he has been out of the game a long time.'

Revie said, 'I never thought I'd have the chance to get back into the English game, but I have discovered I have missed the involvement. I've been away seven years and don't know everything about First Division players. But I'm still able to get on to the training pitch and, after 40 years, I feel I have something to offer the game.'

Even though Gregory faced some opposition from members of his board, when the two men met at a West London hotel it seemed as though Revie would be in the dugout once again. But those who had dealt with Gregory knew he could be unpredictable – just before sacking Alan Mullery, Gregory had offered him a two-year contract extension.

And unfortunately for Revie, Gregory did change his mind about appointing the former Leeds and England boss. Following their meeting on 7 December, Gregory told the press, 'I met Mr Revie tonight, following a telephone conversation with him on Wednesday. Unfortunately, the terms Mr Revie asked for in our first conversation were not those he was seeking when I met him tonight. In view of the increased demands, I have informed him I no longer wish him to be the new manager of QPR.'

Clearly annoyed with the actions of the QPR chairman, Revie was reported in the *Daily Mirror* as saying, 'I can't help doubting whether he was serious about wanting me to join the club. I did ask for a certain salary for a six-month contract and he told me he didn't think there would be any problems.

'On reflection, and bearing in mind how the matter has been conducted, it is probably for the best that I won't be joining them. People will say it is a case of

Revie wanting more money again, but that is not true. I just wanted a slight change in the way the money would be paid.

'Gregory then told me he would get back to me the following day but later in the evening he phoned to say the deal was off. He just said, "Hello Don… no deal," and then put the phone down on me.'

The brief flirtation with QPR was the last time Revie actively pursued an opportunity to return to football management. For the next year, he whiled away his days on the golf course, coached a few days for Yorkshire Television Soccer Schools, and acted as part-time consultant to his son's Total Sport business, which offered high-end packages to events such as the British Open or Grand National.

Leeds United had had a tumultuous few years. After sacking Jimmy Adamson on 1 October, 1980, Revie old boy Allan Clarke had been appointed to replace him. Despite claiming Leeds would win the European Cup, Clarke was sacked on 25 June, 1982, after Leeds were relegated to the Second Division.

Eddie Gray then became the next member of Revie's formidable old team to be appointed manager. After failing to win promotion, he too was dismissed, on 11 October, 1985. For a brief time, Leeds United fans were led to believe Revie was to make a dramatic return to the club he built almost from scratch.

The next day, under the headline, 'Revie's way back, Don may step in as Leeds boot out Gray,' it was claimed by journalist Peter Cooper of the *Daily Mirror* that, 'Don Revie, Godfather of Leeds, may emerge from retirement to rally the club he made great.' He went on to say that as a way of reviving and building on the Revie dynasty, there was a plan to install Johnny Giles as team manager with Revie acting as the general manager.

Comments attributed to Revie, who was on holiday at the time, seemed to give fans hope that Revie was ready for an emotional return to the club. Revie said, 'I wouldn't fancy returning to league football management as I knew it but I wouldn't mind coming back as a consultant, making my experience available to the manager.'

However, on his return home to Wentworth on 15 October, Revie made it clear he had no interest in the job, telling the press, 'What we did at Leeds was a bit special and you cannot turn the clock back. I do not want the Leeds job. To return to the club would be wrong at my time of life.'

Besides, Revie and Elsie had other plans. In July 1986, Revie's promise to his wife to one day return to her beloved Scotland was fulfilled and they settled in Kinross, a stone's throw from Elsie's hometown, Lochgelly. A short article in the *Perthshire Advertiser* announced their arrival:

'Don Revie, the internationally known football personality, has decided to settle in Kinross. Mr Revie, whose wife is a Fife lass, has opted for Kinross because of the relaxed atmosphere in the town, its proximity to many famous golf courses, and the closeness to his wife's roots. Mr Revie has been staying at a Kinross hotel while finalising details of his new home.'

Revie and Elsie moved to a bungalow on Broom Road, a perfect place to enjoy their advancing years. Days would be spent playing golf or watching footage of his old Leeds side in his snug. As Revie said, 'They can take everything away from me but my memories. When I watch those tapes of the old days, that was the best football it's been my privilege to have ever seen.'

In Kinross, Don and Elsie threw themselves into local life. On 17 April, 1987, the *Perthshire Advertiser* told of Kinross RFC's 'traditional dinner on 24 April in the Green Hotel, where the guest speakers will be David Leslie, ex-Scotland; Don Revie, ex-England football manager; and Sandy Sutherland, sportswriter.'

But even before they had made the move north of the border, something had been troubling Revie. For months he had been getting pains down the backs of his legs on the last few holes of the golf course. Having had disc trouble in his back on and off since 1966, Revie thought the pains could be connected to that.

But there were more puzzling developments. As they played golf together, Elsie had observed the strange way Revie was moving, as if he was dragging his left leg. He also mentioned a sensation that made him feel as if he were floating. Tests followed, but proved inconclusive.

In May 1987, Revie went for an examination at St Mary's Hospital where motor neurone disease (MND) was diagnosed. Revie said, 'What's that? And they told me it was when the nerves don't work the muscles.' Further tests followed in Leeds and the diagnosis was the same.

From the moment Revie was diagnosed the family refused to give up hope. Kim Revie made it her business to find out everything she could about the condition. Through her research, she discovered that doctors in Houston, Texas, had had some success combatting the disease.

Revie remembered: 'So we went off to Houston for five days and I can tell you that I have never been through tests like it in my life. They took 28 separate samples of blood from me in a single day, and on another day I started having tests at 6.30 a.m. and was not finished until after midnight.'

The testing was exhaustive but the diagnosis was the same. In typical no-nonsense style Revie asked the American doctors what it meant. He was told that 10 per cent of sufferers of motor neurone disease live for 18 months; 60–70 per cent live for three to five years; and some can live 10 to 15 years – for example, the actor David Niven lived with MND for 15 years before dying in 1983.

Revie tried to remain positive: 'When it comes down to it, it is a body blow, the family just sat down and cried, but you can't do that forever and there are a lot of people in the world worse off than me. My thoughts were to get my head up and get on with it. You either curl up in a corner, cry your eyes out and die, or you can battle it out.'

By the time Revie made his diagnosis public on 10 August, 1987, this cruellest of diseases had already taken hold of the man who had prided himself on building teams based around fitness and power. It was now difficult for him to get out of the bath, get dressed or cut up his own food.

Speaking to the press, Revie said: 'What has hit me hard is that all the golf, tennis and running every day has suddenly stopped. Of course, I must be helped upstairs and that sort of thing, which is embarrassing, but you must get used to it. At least I can keep my mind occupied and I can tell you I am going to fight this thing all the way.'

Reacting to the news, Billy Bremner, now manager of Leeds United, said, 'He must fight now just like he told us to do in our great games together.' Former Leeds chairman, Manny Cussins, offered to pay for any treatment, saying, 'I am sad to hear of his illness. He was a first-class manager and we worked well together. It's a great shock that he has the disease because I always remember him as a strong, fit man.'

That fight involved fundraising for the MND Association. At one point, a newspaper appeal carrying a picture of Revie ran with the headline: 'Compared to fighting motor neurone disease, winning the FA Cup was no problem.'

On 24 August, Revie travelled to London for more tests and to talk to those who were experienced in raising money for MND research. According to an article in the *Dundee Courier* there were plans for a pop concert, a series of pro-am golf tournaments, fundraising dinners and a football match at the end of the season.

As Revie threw himself into fundraising efforts, he was resigned to the fact there was no cure for him. As he told John Helm in a Yorkshire Television interview, 'There is no hope for me, but I think we can help someone in the future.'

There was experimental treatment in America, but it was only available to American citizens. Each day, Revie underwent exercises to keep his muscles moving, which became more difficult to perform by the day. This was followed by a dip in a heated swimming pool and massages three times a week.

On 26 September, Revie returned to Elland Road to open an exclusive new members' club. It was particularly poignant as Leeds United entertained Manchester City, the club with which he made his name as a player.

After performing the opening ceremony, a physically diminished Revie was introduced to the crowd by new manager, Billy Bremner. Dressed in a smart navy suit, Revie gingerly walked onto the pitch aided by a walking stick. Looking emotional he lifted his hand slowly to acknowledge the chants of 'There's only one Don Revie! There's only one Don Revie!' which rang out throughout the stadium.

On 13 November, Revie took part in the 'Champions' series, shown as part of the BBC sports programme *Grandstand*, where he detailed the exploits of his Leeds team of the 1960s and '70s. He said, 'It was the best time of my life, they were one the greatest teams this country has ever seen.'

On 21 February, 1988, the *News of the World* printed a deeply hurtful story, claiming Revie was walking again after an Arab Sheik sent him to Moscow for revolutionary treatment. The story was only half-true. Gary James, working for *Gulf News,* said: 'It was true that Don's former boss, the president of Al-Nasr, Sheik Mara Bin Khalifa Al-Maktou, had ensured Revie received treatment in the Soviet Union but it was wrong to say he had been cured. To me it was a mark of the esteem Don was still held in in the United Arab Emirates that Al-Maktou would do that for him.'

The claims that Revie had received a 'miracle cure' for MND were greeted with disbelief by experts. And while Revie and his family made no comment, the Motor Neurone Disease Association reacted with fury on his behalf: 'It not only wounds Don and his family, but those people with the disease. It also raises false hopes for those who are struggling to look after every one of the 5,000 people who suffer from MND.

'The daily ordeal after this kind of rubbish is published is even harder to bear. We are spending £250,000 on research this year alone, and we keep in constant touch with researchers right round the world. If there was even a hint of a cure, we would have known of it long ago.

'It is sad but true that scientists and doctors internationally are baffled as to the cause of MND. It is a genuine medical enigma.'

Far from being cured, Revie's quality of life was becoming compromised by the day. His home was adapted to accommodate a wheelchair and an electric frame helped him stand up. Shaving took an hour and after his hands began to curl inwards, he used large lightweight cutlery. Kim said about her father, who was ever the competitor: 'He would challenge himself to walk a few steps, but we all knew deep down it was all in vain.'

On 11 May, there was a final reunion with the players he had loved so much from his time at Elland Road. In a gala night tribute to Revie, an All-Star XI would face Leeds United. For Revie, now confined to an electronically modified wheelchair, the trip would be difficult both physically and emotionally. However, Revie felt he had to be there. As Elsie said, 'He always cares for people. He loves people, he has always been a great humanitarian, he wants to be there because Leeds is his home.'

The proceeds of the event were divided between the Leeds City Council's Give for Life campaign and the Motor Neurone Research Appeal. Leeds were captained for the occasion by Kevin Keegan and Peter Shilton was to be in goal.

The All-Star squad, valued at more than £14 million, included four Rangers players, Graeme Souness, Chris Woods, Ray Wilkins and Mark Walters, and former Hearts striker John Robertson, playing alongside his Newcastle United teammate, Paul Gascoigne.

It was a time of tears. Revie, his face bloated with steroids and dressed in a grey leather jacket, shirt and tie, met with former players such as Norman

Hunter, Allan Clarke and Jack Charlton. Also in attendance were his two most famous captains, Bobby Collins and Billy Bremner.

Paying tribute before the match, Billy Bremner said: 'He is Leeds United; his presence is always here. It's very difficult for him, he has always been a private man, it is hard to show the state he is in.' Jack Charlton reminisced about the special relationship he and Revie enjoyed. Kevin Keegan claimed Revie 'is a battler and a fighter, he's a great person. Elland Road is Revie's stadium, he built it.'

For many, the return visit to Elland Road was the first occasion in years that they had encountered their former boss. 'It was cruel for someone associated with the physical side of life,' said Joe Jordan. Johnny Giles recalled, 'He was bad... he couldn't move his arms... but he didn't want to talk about it.'

For Revie, the emotion was too much. Leaving after 20 minutes, he did not see Paul Gascoigne get on the scoresheet in a 2–2 draw. In the end, some 7,000 people turned out to pay homage to the man known simply as 'The Don'. In doing so they raised £24,500 for the two charities.

As Revie left, he managed to speak to the press for a final time. 'It was a job to keep the tears back, but I did. I would like to thank the fans and players who travelled thousands of miles to be here. I would also like to thank Billy and his players who did such a great job for me.'

For many people, the Revie era finally ended on 28 September, 1988, when, after a poor start to the season, Billy Bremner was sacked as manager. In his place came former Sheffield Wednesday manager, Howard Wilkinson. His first act was to remove all pictures depicting the Revie glory years. For Leeds United, it was time to look to the future – something many felt Revie would have secretly approved of.

By 19 January, 1989, Elsie was in the *Perthshire Advertiser* calling on Tayside Council to provide extra funding for the Crossroads Care Attendant Scheme. The Crossroads volunteers provided vital help and relief for the families of the seriously ill and disabled. For Elsie they had come to provide a lifeline.

As Elsie explained: 'My husband cannot move himself and has to be lifted and as I have a heart condition Crossroads Volunteers assist me. They also enable me to get out to the shops knowing Don will be sufficiently looked after.'

By 20 May, the end was near. Now unable to be cared for at home, Revie was moved to the Murrayfield BUPA Hospital in Edinburgh. It was there on Friday 26 May, 1989, Don Revie, surrounded by Elsie, Duncan and Kim, died peacefully in his sleep. He was 61 years old.

The tributes came quickly. Within hours the gates of Elland Road were bedecked with scarves and posters in tribute to the man who had built Leeds United from nothing. Now languishing in the Second Division, the fans could be forgiven for the sudden rush of nostalgia that marked Revie's death. Some 15 years after leaving the club, he was still the only Leeds manager who had won anything of note.

For those who played under him, Revie's death was devastating. Billy Bremner said, 'Everyone knows the magnificent achievements he brought to Leeds United. When people talk about the club's history, they mean the period when Revie was in charge.'

Eddie Gray explained, 'He was a great man. He looked after the players as friends and got to know everyone. It was a big family and he made the club what it was. A part of Leeds United has died with him.'

Now manager of the Republic of Ireland, Jack Charlton came on Irish TV and was visibly shaken. Charlton, who had made a point of visiting Revie whenever he was in Scotland, said, 'I was very fond of Don, he was a great influence on my career. Don will be a great loss to football.'

On 30 May, Revie's funeral took place at the Warriston Crematorium in Edinburgh. A bottle of cognac was placed on top of his coffin. 'Have a few drinks on me and there must be no sad faces,' Revie had said towards the end.

Mourners at his funeral included virtually the entire Leeds United team he had led, including Billy Bremner, Allan Clarke, Frank and Eddie Gray, Mick Jones, Joe Jordan, Jack Charlton, Johnny Giles, Mick Bates and Gordon McQueen. 'It is a tragic loss,' said McQueen. 'He is still loved by all his old players as one can see from the turnout here today. He was a great manager and will be sadly missed.' Joe Jordan said Revie was an inspirational leader much loved by anyone who played for him.

Former England captain Kevin Keegan was also there, and said Revie was 'like a father to me,' adding, 'He saved my England career.' Also present was

FA International Secretary Alan O'Dell, who said both sides were upset when Revie quit as England manager, 'but I think that no one regretted it more than he did.'

O'Dell went on to say that he and current England manager Bobby Robson had visited Revie at his Scottish home a few months earlier. 'We were absolutely shocked to see the state he was in. We always remained good friends.'

Former Southampton and Sunderland manager Lawrie McMenemy, who was there as a close friend of the Revies, said, 'He had taught people that football was about much more than simply kicking a ball around. I would like him to be remembered for a lot of his successes, which were numerous, rather than the mistakes which everyone makes, which have been too well-documented at times. People have come from a tremendous distance to be here today. That shows how well he was thought of. He produced tremendous football.'

In the city of Leeds, on 14 June, 1989, hundreds of mourners paid tribute to Revie at a remembrance service at Leeds Parish Church. Many were in tears as the Bishop of Reading, the Right Reverend Graham Foley, formerly a vicar at Leeds, told the congregation that Revie's battle against MND was 'a game he couldn't win.'

The 45-minute service was attended by 500 family, friends, former players and football fans. Earlier, Revie's ashes had been scattered at Elland Road in a private ceremony watched by his family.

The bishop said, 'The man was a legend.' He compared the news of his death to the sadness felt following the Hillsborough tragedy which had occurred in April that year. 'I do not think it is an exaggeration to say that it was something like this when the football world heard of the untimely death of Don Revie. He was one of the greats in football. Don Revie was not a saint. He was a no-nonsense Yorkshireman who loved football.'

The feelings of so many people in attendance were summed up by Kevin Keegan who said, 'It saddens me that the public at large had, and still have, the wrong impression of him. He was kind, generous and caring. When he left the England job, he did the right thing for his family but did it wrongly. He knew it and was big enough to admit it. He'd have been as successful as Alf Ramsey with England if the players had been good enough. We weren't.'

Even today, 30 years after his death, Elland Road is a shrine to the man they simply refer to as The Don. The players still run out in all-white strips to the sounds of 'Marching on Together' under the Don Revie Stand, while his statue casts a shadow over all those who visit on match day.

Everywhere there are reminders of the glory years. Howard Wilkinson may have won the title in 1992 and David O'Leary took them to the Champions League semi-final in 2001, but for the faithful who come to Elland Road, there is only one Don Revie.

EPILOGUE – NO TIME
FOR REDEMPTION

On Thursday 5 May, 1955, three days before the FA Cup Final between Manchester City and Newcastle United, Clifford Webb, columnist for the *Daily Herald* and chairman of the Football Writers' Association (FWA) presented an award to the professional player who, in the words of FWA founder Charles Buchan 'by percept [perception] and example is considered by a ballot of members to be the footballer of the year.'

Accepting the award, Don Revie joined previous winners Sir Stanley Matthews and Sir Tom Finney. Future recipients would include Bobby Moore and Sir Bobby Charlton, as well as modern greats like Thierry Henry and Cristiano Ronaldo. It remains the most prestigious player award in English football.

Of all those players, only two have gone on to win the league championship as managers – Sir Kenny Dalglish, who did it with Liverpool and Blackburn Rovers, and Revie.

By that very measure alone, Revie should be recognised as a legend in the game and perhaps there is an argument to say that he, too, should have been knighted. Instead, even today, the name Don Revie stirs up strong emotions.

Whenever Leeds United play Chelsea, Liverpool or Manchester United, tales of their past battles in the 1960s and '70s are revived, and with it the tag of 'Dirty Leeds'.

When a newspaper sting claimed the scalp of newly-appointed England manager Sam Allardyce, after alluding to financial impropriety, or Sven Goran Erikson was caught touting for a non-existent job at Aston Villa by a fake sheikh from the *News of the World*, both stories were accompanied by pieces about Revie's 'crimes', real or imagined, while manager of Leeds and England.

Revie had been described as 'evil' by his peer, Bob Stokoe. David Miller of the *Sunday Express* said, 'There was always something of the hustler about Revie.' Flamboyant former Manchester City coach Malcolm Allison said, 'A lot of what Leeds did was premeditated and I would think that would make Don Revie unsuitable for the England job.'

To Emlyn Hughes and Alan Ball, both discarded by Revie when he was England manager, the man was obsessed by money. Hughes was incensed when Revie increased players' appearance fees for England matches, claiming it was the mark of the man and playing for England should be a privilege.

Newcastle's Malcolm Macdonald likes to relate the story about how Revie, then England manager, asked a BBC crew for money to interview the striker after he scored five goals against Luxembourg.

Often described as 'The Don of Elland Road', Revie's former players very rarely criticised him. 'I can't praise Don enough. Although a great player he was probably a better manager. Don's man-management was first class and, in the years I played at Leeds, very few players at the club left as they all wanted to be part of the success he generated,' said Mick Jones.

Eddie Gray said, 'Everything he did was so enthusiastic. If you had a happy football club, you had a fair chance of becoming a successful football club and that is what the club was like in the 1960s.'

'The Gaffer wanted Elland Road to be a fortress. When opponents saw the sign Leeds on the motorway, he wanted opponents to tremble. We didn't win every game at home, but opponents always knew they were in for a hard match,' was Paul Reaney's view.

Speaking before a charity game at Elland Road Kevin Keegan said, 'I put him up there with Bill Shankly and in my book that is the highest compliment I can pay anyone. I have no doubt he would have won the World Cup, but we just didn't have the players.'

It can be seen in the Leeds players' attitude to Gary Sprake, the Welsh goalkeeper who told journalist Richard Stott that Revie was a match-fixer. Shunned and scorned for the rest of his days, Sprake was never invited to get-togethers and was labelled 'useless' and 'rubbish' by players such as Bremner and Giles. No wonder Brian Clough claimed, 'Don Revie's so-called family had more in keeping with the Mafia than Mothercare.'

...

The Yorkshire Television documentary, *The Don of Elland Road*, filmed as Leeds chased the 1974 league championship, offers a glimpse into the duality of Revie's personality. It opens with Revie dressed in an overcoat walking up a street outside Elland Road.

Narrating, Revie says, 'I'm a superstitious man. I had the same lucky blue suit on since the beginning of the season, same lucky tie and a couple of lucky charms in my pocket. I walk up to the traffic lights every time and I walk back down to the hotel.'

The documentary then moves to Revie reading from one of his dossiers: 'I have had Liverpool watched three times; each player is broken down and what we are going to do.

'One or two players have been really making them tick. Callaghan is a tremendous little professional, doesn't know when he's beaten. Keegan is very, very dangerous at coming off people and getting the ball when he has his back into someone and he is very tightly marked, one finger behind each other (holds up two fingers) like that. He can turn players like that and turn them out of the game.'

These two scenes demonstrate a need to leave nothing to chance, something which marked his entire life. Perhaps the basis of this can be found in his childhood. By his own admission, the death of his mother when he was just 11 left him with a sense of loneliness and a feeling anything could go wrong without warning at any given moment. The passing of his mother meant he dropped to his knees each night and prayed to god before he went to sleep.

When he left his native Middlesbrough for Leicester at 17, Revie said he had never been 'anywhere further than Redcar'. On his own in a strange city, with no friends and having to train at night while completing a bricklaying apprenticeship by day, by his own admission, Revie felt extremely lonely. The loneliness was not really resolved until he met and married his wife Elsie, and in doing so embraced her extended family.

Two themes run through Revie's life: fear and control. The fear of losing overrode everything. Johnny Giles said, 'He just could not fathom you cannot win them all. I think it drove him mad in the end.'

That fear ran through the detailed dossiers he produced, to the point some of the players felt overloaded by the amount of information. Peter Lorimer said, 'I remember playing Colchester United and the way Don prepared us and wound you up, you would think you were playing Real Madrid.'

The dossiers, alongside an interest in players' private lives, was all part of controlling everything from top to bottom. However, there was more to it than just caring for his players. Revie was to say in 1973, 'I like to be out there every day with them and do a little bit with them then I massage them. I've been here 12 years and I like to be with them; I like to be part of them. I look on all of them as my sons.'

Paul Reaney said, 'Don was like my second father and that was the case for a lot of the players at the club at that time. Don was a real people's man. He knew all his players, individually and collectively, knew our families and our lives away from football.'

Allan Clarke recalled, 'The gaffer was dedicated to his players; trusted us and knew we would not let him down. He was very much a father figure to us all and genuinely cared about us as people not just players.'

Arthur Hopcraft, writing in *The Football Man* in 1968 said this about Revie's attitude to his players: 'There are regular homilies about keeping their hair short and their clothes smart and not getting caught up with loose girls.'

At times Revie would seek to influence events beyond his control. Always a superstitious man, as Revie changed for the 1956 FA Cup Final one of his teammates noticed he was carrying two blocks of wood that had been blessed by a gypsy for luck.

As the years went on the superstitions became more outlandish and another gypsy was employed to remove a supposed curse from Elland Road. From that point on, Revie was convinced the team's luck changed for the better.

In many respects Revie was a man of contradictions. Certainly, he was insecure, hence his superstitious nature, and the footballing world in which Revie worked did not help any anxiety he may have suffered from. Former Wolves manager Stan Cullis, speaking to Hopcraft, said, 'The atmosphere in the game was tense and the manner never delicate. It was the survival of the fittest... there was a feeling of great uncertainty. If you didn't make the grade you were on the dole.'

On the footballing side, Revie was a visionary who was always unshakeable in his belief that he wanted Leeds United to be the best club in the world. He was a family man who took those values into the club.

In one of his last interviews Revie said, 'I lived for the day we were champions, then I lived for the days we were champions of Europe. I really wanted to win the European Cup then go on and play for the World Club Championship. I never achieved that.'

Leeds United president Lord Harewood said, 'I think Don's weakness was the fear of not knowing everything there was to be known about the opposing side; that might have been carried to excess.' Did this lead him to the darker side of the game?

...

To many, walking away from the England job, seen as the pinnacle of the profession, then leaving for a lucrative contract in the United Arab Emirates, confirmed what many people already thought of Revie – that his sole motivation in life was money.

Things were made worse when he sold the exclusive rights of his England exit to the *Daily Mail*. As Alex Montgomery of *The Sun* said, 'After that the knives were out for Revie in Fleet Street.' There can be little doubt the press were out to destroy him. Frank Taylor of the *Daily Mirror*, who also acted as ghost writer on Revie's biography *Soccer's Happy Wanderer,* dubbed the former Leeds manager in his obituary as 'money mad'.

The supposed obsession with money dogged Revie throughout his career. Despite winning plaudits with his performance in the FA Cup Final with Manchester City in 1956, he wanted to leave.

When pushed by Manchester City half-back Ken Barnes for the reasons for his departure it's claimed Revie said, 'There is one thing which will tell you if you have been a good player: how much money you have in the bank.' During his spell at City he had requested to be put on the transfer list on three separate occasions and was reported to be agitating for a move when he was playing for Leeds.

Long before Leeds and England, a cloud of financial impropriety hung over Revie. Some five years after Revie's departure from Manchester City, his captain Roy Paul made allegations that he and his teammates would take bribes to throw matches. At the time, Revie's name was never mentioned but when the papers came looking for dirt on Revie in the mid-1970s it did not take them long to link him to the allegations.

During the 1950s, there was always a climate of financial skulduggery within football. Revie's new club at the time, Sunderland, was fined for making illegal payments to players and, in 1964, three Everton players were banned for life for throwing matches.

The question that has hung over Revie since he resigned as England manager is, did his desire for complete control and to guarantee outcomes lead him to attempt to bribe opposing sides to throw games? The question became central to the *Daily Mirror* investigation led by journalist Richard Stott in 1977.

Even as far back as the early '70s there had been rumours. Brian Clough, who ironically only avoided being charged by the FA with misconduct for receiving illegal payments in the early '90s because of ill health, alluded to gossip

343

in an interview with David Frost by saying, 'If I revealed what he [Revie] got up to we would probably be taken off air, David.'

The first time that bribes were ever mentioned was by *The People* newspaper when Leeds, having won the 1972 FA Cup, had to face Wolves two days later to complete a historic double. Despite claims Wolves were offered money to throw the game, an injury-ravaged Leeds lost 2–0 and with it the championship to Derby County. Johnny Giles said, 'If we were bribing teams, we must have been awful at it as we lost all the games we were accused of trying to buy.'

A more serious allegation was made 10 years earlier by former Sunderland manager Bob Stokoe, who in 1962 was managing Bury. Stokoe claimed Revie tried to personally bribe him to lose as Leeds, threatened with relegation, needed the points to stay up. When Stokoe turned Revie down it was alleged he asked to speak with Bury's players in the dressing room.

The allegation did not surface until 1977, a full 15 years after the event, when Stokoe found himself out of work. Journalist Jeff Powell of the *Daily Mail* said, 'Stokoe was an awkward man. Jealous of both Clough and Revie, he was aggrieved he was never offered a big job, even though both Revie and Clough weren't either; they both built clubs up from nothing.'

But the fact remains that even though *Daily Mirror* journalist Richard Stott, who in 1977 was named Reporter of the Year for his scoop on Revie, claimed a 330-page dossier was sent to the FA detailing Revie's crimes, over 40 years later there is no record of a dossier in either the FA archive or in any the 14 boxes of papers Stott's widow donated to the Cardiff School of Journalism upon his death.

In an age when footballers were tied to the maximum wage and their careers could be cut short by one mistimed tackle, football was a precarious profession at the best of times. Even if a player survived league football, he was usually retired at 35.

In his biography, Jack Charlton relates tales of how he would sell pieces of cloth or rabbits he had shot to make extra money on the side. Moving clubs like Revie did during the 1950s was on the less serious end of the spectrum.

As a manager he knew that a run of bad results would mean being out of work. So, when an offer came from the UAE, when he thought he was on the verge of being sacked, he was going to take it. The offer represented something he had been chasing all his life – financial security.

As Leeds manager, Revie took tactical innovations inspired by the 'Revie Plan' from his time at Manchester City. He used his experience as a player and his willingness to learn from anyone and everyone to bring about changes in the club.

Revie even turned a disinterested Jack Charlton into a World Cup-winning centre-half. Brian Clough would say of Charlton, 'At 25 or 26 I would not have touched him but at 27 or 28 he was world class and that was down to Don Revie.'

The other legacy Revie is tarred with is the one of 'Dirty Leeds'. Watch any game in isolation and Leeds were certainly a hard team. Much is made of this reputation, to the point of being accused of bringing violence to the field of play.

For a flavour of the time, Hopcraft laments the level of violence seen on English pitches. However, it is not Leeds who are held up as an example but Arsenal, under former England captain Billy Wright, for their rough play. The only time Revie gets a mention is for his unique bond and loyalty to his players.

In the same book, Hopcraft interviewed two former professionals who demonstrate hard play did not begin upon the promotion of Leeds United to the top flight in 1964. Legendary Wolves manager Stan Cullis, when commenting on the game in the 1960s, said of his time as a player in the 1930s and '40s, 'It was more rugged. There was more physical contact. We always had what you call killers in the game, players who went deliberately over the ball to get the man. They were well known, and you took special precautions against them. The play was harsher and dirtier than it is now.'

Sheffield Wednesday striker Derek Dooley, whose career ended with an amputated leg in 1951 after a clash with a goalkeeper, said about the game, 'Nobody was averse to catching you on one leg and having you over or coming up behind and giving you a good dig.'

Looking through modern eyes, the game was completely different in Revie's day. Muddy pitches, substandard and dangerous stadiums, and players who played it hard. Take, for example, the 1958 FA Cup Final when Bolton's Nat Lofthouse deliberately came from behind to shoulder charge Manchester United goalkeeper Harry Gregg as he caught the ball in mid-air. Lofthouse, Gregg and the ball all ended up in the net.

These days Lofthouse would receive a straight red card, an FA charge for violent play, a fine and a suspension. Then, not only was he allowed to stay on the pitch but Bolton took the cup in a 2–0 win.

Every team also had its resident hard man. There was 'Anfield Iron' Tommy Smith of Liverpool and Ron 'Chopper' Harris of Chelsea, as well as Pat Crerand of Manchester United and Peter Storey of Arsenal. Johnny Giles said, 'You learned pretty quickly to look after yourself, every week someone had their career ended through a broken leg, it was a common occurrence.' Even Revie was moved to say about himself, 'I was never a hard player but I wish I was.' In the end Leeds United were no better or worse than anyone else playing in that era.

Revie's tenure at Leeds was marked by his man-management. Turning Jack Charlton into a world class centre-half was an achievement. Charlton was a player, Revie said during his playing days, that he would kick out of the club if he was manager.

Likewise, he convinced a young homesick Billy Bremner to stay in Leeds when he was set on returning to Scotland. Then moulding a group of young players like Norman Hunter, Paul Reaney and Gary Sprake into internationals showed a keen eye for player developement. When Leeds lifted the league championship in 1969, eight of the first-team regulars had come through the youth system.

Matches like the ill-tempered 1965 FA Cup semi-final against Manchester United or the League Cup Final win over Arsenal three years later seemed to underline this. Accusations of time wasting and stifling play were added to the mix. Much of this behaviour was explained away by Revie as simply an overwhelming desire to win.

By Revie's own admission, in his early years they played for results. Years later he was to say he did not realise the talent they had until much later when he said he 'let them off the leash'. From that point on 'Dirty Leeds' became 'Super Leeds'. By the time the second championship was secured in 1974, Bremner and Giles were the best midfield combination in the country.

Signings like strikers Allan Clarke, who came in for a record fee from Leicester in 1969, and Mick Jones were more nuanced in their play. Replacing a retiring Jack Charlton with the more cultured Gordon McQueen indicated a change in the approach Leeds were taking.

Under Revie, Leeds were the most consistent side during the late 1960s and early '70s. In doing so he built a group of players who would have, in Revie's own words, 'died for each other'.

However, the mark of greatness which set managers like Bob Paisley and Sir Alex Ferguson apart from the rest was their ability to break up a successful side and rebuild a new, and very often, better one. Leaving for England he never had to find replacements for Giles, Bremner or Hunter, players who were already in their 30s when they won the title in 1974 and had reached their peak.

Ultimately, Revie thrived on day-to-day management. At his desk at 8.30 a.m. ahead of the players' arrival at 10.00 a.m., he would attend a weekly board meeting where he could set out his plans and get answers almost straight away. By the time he arrived at Lancaster Gate he was used to, and expected, total control.

Over 13 years at Leeds, Revie proved himself best suited as a club manager, thriving in the day-to-day involvement with players. As an international manager he could go months without seeing his players and it was something Revie, who tried to foster a club atmosphere, found difficult to handle.

Commenting on the difference between club and country, former Arsenal manager Arsene Wenger said, 'If you want to be part of coaching, then I think, of course, it's club. For me, international coaching is not coaching. It's only really interesting during the big tournaments. It's a very pressured job for the England coach and every week you go to a game and think, "Has the guy got to the level? Do I put him in or not?" But you are very frustrated daily.'

One of Revie's much-maligned successors as England manager, Graham Taylor, said, 'In international football you have 10 games a season with players from different clubs. There's no time for proper coaching; they're just recovering from playing on the Saturday.'

The contrast between the jobs was massive. The pace of management at international level is slow and there are weeks where there is very little to do apart from watch games. Kevin Keegan, reflecting on his time as England manager, said, 'I had nothing to do all day. I would fill my time by coaching the deaf or blind teams at Keele. You see the players for a day or two a week, get them ready to play then that's it.'

When Revie left Leeds for England, he was not just leaving a football club but a small empire which he controlled every part of. Giles added, 'The directors could have fought to keep Revie but after years of such strong management they wanted to be in charge for once.'

In the England job, Revie did not enjoy the freedom to do as he pleased as he had at Leeds, often butting heads with the International Committee tasked with running the England side.

The transition was difficult for Revie who was not prepared to give any ground to people he felt knew nothing about football. As Revie told BBC commentator Gerald Williams on his *Word with Williams* radio programme in 1984, 'I did not like people who knew nothing about the game telling me how to do my job or questioning my methods. I wasn't used to that at Leeds and we used to have a weekly board meeting. With the International Committee I had to wait six months for an answer to anything. It was very frustrating.' Making an enemy out of Football League Secretary Alan Hardaker did not help him either. Hardaker steadfastly refused to postpone league fixtures the weekend before international fixtures.

From the outset, the pressure on Revie was immense. Not only had his predecessor Sir Alf Ramsey won the 1966 World Cup, but he had only lost 13 matches in 12 years. Revie was always aware it was the failure to qualify for the 1974 World Cup that spelled the end for Ramsey. As Revie said of Ramsey's dismissal, 'I thought it was diabolical when they sacked him; here was a man who won the World Cup and they sacked him after he lost one game against Poland. I thought if they sack him over one game then they can certainly sack me.'

By common agreement, Ramsey's biggest failing was his ability to deal with the press. From the moment he was appointed Revie sought to rectify this, serving drinks and sandwiches at press conferences while making himself readily available to journalists. John Wray of the *Yorkshire Evening Post* said, 'He was great, if you asked him for a story, he always had one even if he made it up.'

A question often levelled at Revie, even while he was still England manager was, did his desire to be liked by the press influence his selection decisions? In three years, some 52 players were given caps. Malcolm Macdonald said he was told by Revie, 'I only picked you because the press told me to.' Another flair player, Arsenal's Charlie George, who had a large following in the press, played a solitary game after a press campaign which it was hoped would exploit George's quality for England.

The deft touch he had with the Leeds players seemed to desert him with England, the most famous example being Alan Ball. When Revie made Ball England captain it was met with nothing but praise from the press. Ball was the last surviving member of the 1966 World Cup team and it was painted as a nice little acknowledgement for his service to the country.

Any goodwill was destroyed when Ball let it be known he was informed in an official letter from the FA that his services would no longer be required. The letter was not even signed by Revie but a secretary in his absence. There were similar complaints from Liverpool's Emlyn Hughes, who had his international career ended in much the same way only for it to be resurrected for a crunch qualifier against Italy. Both Ball and Hughes would become vocal critics of Revie in the coming years.

The tipping point for Revie as England manager came in February 1977 when the all-conquering Dutch came to Wembley with stars like Johnny Rep and, most notably, Johann Cruyff, who was universally recognised as the best player in the world. Despite priding himself on his tactical nous, England looked clueless against the Total Football of the Netherlands. Writing in the *Daily Mail* Jeff Powell said, 'England joined the rest of the second-raters in the gutter of world football last night. The last dregs of self-respect drained away to the accompaniment of "what a load of rubbish", for England were not just beaten by Holland [the Netherlands] they were torn apart.'

Further spluttering displays against Scotland and Wales and an unhappy tour of South America and Revie was gone, off to Dubai and tax-free cash. Where, depending on which source you want to believe, he was either blissfully happy or intensely miserable. By 1984, he was back in the UK, lamenting his decision with Gerald Williams: 'It was completely wrong, the way I went about it'.

Was Revie such a failure as England manager? His record of 29 games, 14 wins, 8 draws and 7 losses puts him above Euro '96 manager Terry Venables in terms of win percentages. On his appointment, he set out his goal to win the 1978 World Cup and boldly commented that England had been good enough to reach the semi-finals in West Germany in 1974.

Failing to qualify for the 1976 European Nations Cup and indifferent performances, especially in the 1978 World Cup qualifying campaign, made Revie's tenure as England manager a huge disappointment.

There were times under Revie when it looked as though England could compete with the very best. A 2–0 win at Wembley in March 1975 over a West Germany side that had Franz Beckenbauer in it, and a 3–2 win over Italy in May 1976 were highlights – but they were few and far between.

The trait of falling at the final hurdle, which dogged him at Leeds United, seemed to follow him to the England job. Going into the final two qualifying games of the 1976 European Nations Cup England looked as though they were odds-on to qualify for Revie's first major championship. But a loss to Czechoslovakia and a draw against Portugal not only stopped them progressing, but had repercussions for their World Cup campaign.

Unseeded, they were drawn in a group with Italy, Finland and Luxembourg, with only one team able to qualify. It seemed like a mountain to climb. Unspectacular wins over Finland and Luxembourg and a loss to Italy meant England were struggling on the day Revie resigned, leaving behind him more questions than answers.

Sitting down with Jeff Powell of the *Daily Mail*, Revie said his reasons for resignation were simple: 'Everyone wants me out, so I am giving them what they want.'

During the mid-1970s, the tabloids became engaged in a circulation war that got hotter as the decade gave way to the 1980s. Both Nigel Clarke of the *Daily Mirror* and Alex Montgomery of *The Sun* had given descriptions of Revie suffering from something akin to PTSD when they approached him after his resignation.

Perhaps Revie's biggest crime was simply to resign from a job he did not enjoy, even if the press was unhappy with his decision. As late as 1990, the press would not accept the resignation of an England manager. When Bobby Robson announced he was leaving England to coach PSV Eindhoven he was called a traitor and faced all sorts of false allegations about his private life even though it was common knowledge there were no plans to renew his contract after the World Cup.

There is an argument that said that Revie was the first England manager whose day-to-day activities were placed under the microscope. For someone who was used to commanding respect from his players and the press in Yorkshire, the constant criticism was something Revie had never encountered before – and he did not like it.

...

Despite being only 56 upon his return to England, Revie never worked in football again. His last public appearance was at Elland Road in May 1988 for a charity match in aid of the Motor Neurone Disease Association. On the scoresheet that night was a young Paul Gascoigne, who was to be so pivotal in English football's renaissance.

Revie died on 26 May, 1989; the same night that Arsenal pipped Liverpool to the title with the last kick of the season.

Seven years later, on 30 June, 1996, when England faced Germany in the semi-final of the European Championship, English football had gone through a remarkable renaissance.

By the time fans were chanting 'football's coming home' as England made their way through Euro '96, football was everywhere. From the Britpop bands who wore soccer shirts on *Top of the Pops*, to New Labour leader Tony Blair playing head tennis with Newcastle United manager Kevin Keegan, to Geoff Hurst being knighted, football epitomised the national pride that had enveloped the country.

As Cool Britannia looked back to the 1960s and '70s for inspiration, it was inevitable that faces from the past were going to enjoy their moment in the sun. It was not unusual to see footballers from yesteryear offering comment about football.

Sadly, Revie was never forgiven. His Leeds team remains the face of violence on the pitch and hooliganism on the terraces. His tenure as England manager coincided with industrial unrest and a general malaise in society. No one looks back on that period with fond memories.

Not being around to give his side of the argument meant his story is framed by others. Despite dominating the late 1960s and early 1970s he is unloved and held responsible for ushering in a dark chapter in English football. And by dying relatively young he was robbed of the opportunity to explain himself.

Had Revie died in 1974 his obituary would have been completely different. He would have been remembered as a visionary, a tactical master and as the man who redefined the role of a football manager. As it is, he is remembered as the man who sold out England for 30 pieces of silver in the form of £340,000 from the UAE. His crime was not only disloyalty, but greed.

Regardless, his influence in the game can be felt today. It is there in the pages of dossiers clubs rely on when they are preparing their team for an upcoming match. Whenever someone buys a replica shirt of their favourite club, they can thank Revie, who oversaw the first shirt deal when Admiral paid Leeds United to wear their shirts.

It was Revie who first came up with the idea of a club displaying a sponsor's name across the shirt or having executive boxes at grounds. It was Revie who developed a public relations strategy and encouraged players to sign endorsement deals.

On the training ground, he was one of the first to get into a tracksuit and talk tactics with his players. His ideas on diet, rest and massage were ahead of their time. In many respects Revie was the template for the modern-day manager.

Revie remains the most controversial figure in football history. Therein lies the tragedy of the story, for all his triumphs he is remembered simply for resigning from a job. The problem is that job was England and in the words of Revie, 'Any Englishman that is worth his salt would want to manage the England team.' So no one could quite understand why anyone would want to walk away from it.

Even today, no one has left the England job without their reputation in ruins. For too long Revie's entire career has been overshadowed by his three years as England's manager and that is unfair.

Upon his England resignation speculation was rife that Revie was about to be appointed manager of Manchester United in place of Tommy Docherty, who had been sacked the same week. This development could be seen to be one of the great 'what ifs'. Going to Old Trafford rather than Dubai would have seen Revie taking charge of a club which had just won the FA Cup and was in a position to challenge for the league title. Crucially, after a disappointing tenure at England, would he have been given the opportunity to redeem himself?

Between 1965 and 1974, Leeds United were the most consistent and dominant side in England. Their record ranks among the very best teams of that era. It is for that reason Revie should take his place alongside Sir Matt Busby, Bill Shankly and Sir Alex Ferguson as one of the greatest managers this country has ever seen.

ACKNOWLEDGEMENTS

By the time I began watching football in the 1980s, Leeds United were in the Second Division. The only teams that appeared regularly on television were either Liverpool or Manchester United, so it was little wonder then that everyone in school wore their shirts.

The first time I ever came across Leeds United was when they reached the 1987 FA Cup semi-final. I can well remember the build-up on ITV. Against a cool T-Rex soundtrack, there was this team in white, ripping apart Manchester United, Billy Bremner lifting the 1972 FA Cup and their manager, Don Revie, parading the 1974 League Championship.

When Leeds United pipped Manchester United to the First Division title in 1992, I was amazed former professionals like Emlyn Hughes, then known for his light-hearted nature on the BBC's *Question of Sport*, went on record to declare their hatred for Leeds United and, in particular, Revie.

Nearly every article that appeared during that period included some reference to 'Dirty Leeds' or the word 'disgraced' affixed to Revie's name. The more that was written about Revie, the more fascinating I found the man.

Even today, ask anyone to name their top managers and they will throw names at you such as Sir Alex Ferguson, Sir Matt Busby, Bill Shankly and Bob Paisley. Some will even mention Brian Clough and his exploits at Derby County and Nottingham Forest. Few will recall Don Revie and the magnificent team he built at Leeds United, and when they do it will be with disdain. I wanted to know why.

This book began as a conversation about controversial sporting figures with my agent, Nick Walters of David Luxton Associates. Thanks to Nick's enthusiasm and encouragement, a vague idea developed into a proposal and then finally this book. For that I am eternally grateful.

I can give no higher praise to my editor, Matt Lowing of Bloomsbury, than to say he is a force of nature who seems to know something about everything! I would also like to thank him for his understanding and patience as the writing of this book coincided with the 2019 General Election and then the COVID-19 pandemic.

Matt is of course part of the wonderful team at Bloomsbury, who have all been an absolute joy to work with. I would like to thank Holly Jarrald, for her good humour and attention to detail while painstakingly working on the book. Conor Kilgallon for reading the book and coming up with some great suggestions. Thanks also to Katherine MacPherson and fact checker Robert Lodge for their help in bringing this book to life.

This book has also meant a lot of long train journeys, the first being a visit to Middlesbrough in April 2019 where my friend and local MP, Andy McDonald, was kind enough to arrange a tour of the town with *Fly Me to the Moon* fanzine editor, Rob Nichols.

After visiting all of Revie's old haunts, I was introduced to former England striker, Alan Peacock, who was to become the first of Revie's players I met. Over the course of writing this book, sadly Norman Hunter passed away. I feel incredibly privileged to have been able to have spoken to him at Elland Road.

Other players who generously gave their time were Johnny Giles, Eddie Gray, Gordon McQueen, Mick Bates, Allan Clarke, Chris Galvin, Terry Cooper, Joe Jordan and Mick Jones, as well as Sonny Sweeney and Sean O'Neill. For memories of Revie's time at England I would like to thank Malcolm Macdonald, Kevin Keegan, Peter Barnes, Lawrie McMenemy, Bert Patrick, Howard Wilkinson and Mike Summerbee, as well as Peter Jackson, Alan Curtis and Derek Temple.

As one of the most controversial figures in football, Revie generated more than his fair share of headlines. Therefore, I would like to thank journalists Nigel Clarke, Alex Montgomery, John Helm and Jeff Powell for their thoughts on Revie as both a club and international manager. I would also like to thank artist Paul Trevillion for his time.

I am also grateful to the various club historians I have been in contact with. John Hutchinson oversees a remarkable archive at Leicester City, while Dave Bond at Hull City was always on hand with an email suggesting another avenue of research. Material from Manchester City's Gary James was incredibly helpful. Rob Mason of Sunderland gave an entertaining account of Revie's time there. I must thank Rob Sawyer at Everton for his insight into Revie's various flirtations with the club.

I was also able to travel to Birmingham and sit down with Jim Cadman and learn how the Don Revie statue came to be placed at Elland Road. I would like to thank both Jim and his wife for their hospitality.

In August 2019, I travelled to Elland Road, where I met player liaison officer Stix Lockwood. I thank him and all the staff there for making the day so enjoyable and informative. This visit would never have happened without the help of Hilary Benn MP and John Mann MP.

I must thank Mark Hendricks MP for taking me around what used to be Maine Road and for introducing me to one of Don Revie's oldest surviving teammates, Johnny Williamson and his wife, Lorraine. Also, my former colleague and former Sports Minister, Gerry Sutcliffe, should get a mention for opening his contact book so I could interview so many people for this book. Thanks also, to my friend, Murray Stewart, for helping to arrange interviews.

For Revie's time in the Middle East, I spoke with the United Arab Emirates Embassy in London, who were very helpful, as well as journalist Ali Khalid and player Eammon O'Keefe.

To learn more about the MND that claimed Revie's life, I would like to thank the Motor Neurone Disease Association, not only for their assistance but for the vital work they do for sufferers everywhere. After speaking to Professor Nigel Leigh, I am hopeful one day we can find a cure for this cruel disease.

Of all the people I met for this book, I would particularly like to pay tribute to Kim Revie. She generously gave me hours of her time, sent me various materials by email and was always quick to respond to any questions or queries I had.

Anyone with a passing interest in Don Revie will know family was the most important thing in his life and I would like to thank mine. Whenever I visited my mother, the picture of Don Revie and Billy Bremner that hangs in her living room was a constant spur to get the book completed. My stepfather, Bob, is a huge Leeds United fan and has been great company on many of my fact-finding train journeys.

The one person I really need to thank is my wife, Julia. From the very start she has been nothing but encouraging and supportive. During the writing of this book she was expecting our beautiful daughter, Jasmine, while looking after our fantastic young son, Zachariah, all the while holding down a full-time job. She is an absolute star and I am so lucky to have her and our children in my life.

It is now over 30 years since Don Revie died and 60 years since he was appointed Leeds United manager. It is time he took his rightful place among the greats of the game. In writing this book I hope I can contribute in some small way to that finally happening.

BIBLIOGRAPHY

BOOKS

Bremner! The Legend of Billy Bremner, Bernard Bale

Biting Talk: My Autobiography, Norman Hunter

Keep Fighting! The Billy Bremner Story, Paul Harrison

Billy Bremner's Book of Soccer, Billy Bremner and Don Revie

Bremner: The Real King Billy – The Complete Biography, Richard Sutcliffe

The Biography of Leeds United: The Story of the Whites, Paul Bagchi

Dirty Leeds: The First Title: Don Revie, Harry Reynolds and the Team of the Sixties, Dave Tomlinson

Revie's Boys, David Saffer

Revie: Revered and Reviled, Richard Sutcliffe

The Unforgiven, The Story of Don Revie's Leeds United, Paul Bagchi and Paul Rogerson

Jack Charlton, The Autobiography, Jack Charlton

Kevin Keegan: My Life in Football, Kevin Keegan

100 Years of Leeds United: 1919–2019, Daniel Chapman

No Glossing Over It: How Football Cheated Leeds United, Gary Edwards

The Biography of Leeds United: The Story of the Whites, Paul Bagchi

Ups and Downs: The Inside Story of Leeds United's Biggest Matches, James Willoughby

Fifty Shades of White: Half a Century of Pain and Glory With Leeds United, Gary Edwards

The Life and Times of Mick Jones, David Saffer

Leeds United, A History, Dave Tomlinson

The Damned United, David Peace

We Are The Damned United, The Real Story of Brian Clough at Leeds United, Phil Rostron

John Giles: A Football Man, My Autobiography, John Giles

Shankly: My Story, John Roberts

The Singing Winger, Colin Grainger with Hyder Jawad

The Black Flash: The Albert Johanneson Story, Paul Harrison

How Leeds United Won The Centenary FA Cup, Clarke... 1–0, Martin Jarred

Best, Pele and a Half-Time Bovril: A Nostalgic Look at the 1970s – Football's Last Great Decade, Andrew Smart

The Mavericks: English Football When Flair Wore Flares, Rob Steen

When Footballers Were Skint: A Journey in Search of the Soul of Football, Jon Henderson

Quiet Genius: Bob Paisley, British Football's Greatest Manager, Ian Herbert

Sir Matt Busby: The Man Who Made a Football Club, Patrick Barclay

Sir Alf: A Major Reappraisal of the Life and Times of England's Greatest Football Manager, Leo McKinstry

Alan Ball: The Man in White Boots: The Biography of the Youngest 1966 World Cup Hero, David Tossell

Lawrie McMenemy: A Lifetime's Obsession, Lawrie McMenemy

Don Revie: Portrait of a Footballing Enigma, Andrew Morant

Clough and Revie: The Rivals Who Changed the Face of English Football, Roger Hermiston

Brian Clough: Nobody Ever Says Thank You: The Biography, Jonathan Wilson

Football in the Dock, Simon Inglis

Leeds United and Don Revie, Eric Thornton

Leeds United Book of Football, Don Revie

Leeds United Book of Football Number Two, Don Revie

Nowt For Being Second, Billy Bremner

Gentleman George: The Autobiography of George Hardwick, George Hardwick

Stokoe, Sunderland and '73, The Story of the Greatest FA Cup Shock of all Time, Lance Hardy

Soccer's Happy Wanderer, Don Revie

Farewell But Not Goodbye: My Autobiography, Bobby Robson

Dogs and Lampposts, Richard Stott

Golden Boy: A Biography of Wilf Mannion, Nick Varley

The Park Drive Book of Football 1970, ed Gordon Banks
Fifty Years of Hurt: The Story of England Football and Why We Never Stop Believing, Henry Winter
Inverting the Pyramid: The History of Football Tactics, Jonathan Wilson
Careless Hands: The Forgotten Truth of Gary Sprake, Stuart Sprake and Tim Johnson
Dirty Leeds, Robert Endeacott
Disrepute, Robert Endeacott

NEWSPAPERS

Daily Express
Daily Mirror
Daily Herald
Daily Mail
News Chronicle
The Daily Telegraph
Daily Sketch
The Times
Manchester Guardian
The Sun
Daily Star
Daily Record
The Guardian
The Independent
News of the World
Sunday Mirror
The Mail on Sunday
The People
The Sunday Times
Sunday Express
The Sunday Telegraph
Sunday Mail

Sunday Post
The Observer
The Mirror
Independent on Sunday
Sunday Graphic
Empire News
Sunday Chronicle
Western Mail
Dundee Courier
Perth and Kinross Advertiser
The Sports Argus
The Northern Telegraph
Newcastle Chronicle
Yorkshire Evening Post

WEBSITES

www.mightyleeds.co.uk
www.leedsunited.com
www.ozwhitelufc.net.au
www.motforum.com
www.fmttmboro.com
www.bluemoon-mcfc.co.uk
www.britishnewspaperarchive.co.uk

OTHER

Richard Stott collection, Cardiff School of Journalism
Sir Harold Thompson papers, Royal Society, London

INDEX

AC Milan FC   225, 230
Adamson, Jimmy   325, 330
Admiral   233–4, 240, 264–5, 285, 351
Al Ahly FC   327
Al Nasr FC   316, 326–7, 333
Allardyce, Sam   339
Allison, Malcolm   219, 340
Amsterdam FC   143
Ankaragücü FC   214, 215
Ansarki, Abdullah   309–10
Arabian Gulf Cup (1979)   320–1
Argentina national football team   299
Armfield, Jimmy   316
Arsenal FC   19–20, 26, 33–4, 36, 45, 50, 55, 58,
    112, 116, 143, 155–6, 163, 167, 168, 174,
    187, 190, 193, 194, 197, 198, 202, 205, 206,
    210, 217, 226, 228, 235, 237, 240, 241, 345,
    346, 350
Astle, Jeff   195, 197
Aston Villa FC   50, 113, 115–16, 125, 143, 215

Ball, Alan   130–1, 133, 141, 228, 260, 263,
    267, 268, 270, 272, 273, 281, 318, 319,
    340, 348, 350
Barcelona FC   203
Barnes, Ken   36, 41, 43, 44–5, 47, 50, 55, 126, 343
Barnes, Peter   39
Barnstaple FC   50–1
Bates, Mick   89, 95, 179, 180, 199, 209, 226–7,
    236, 246
BBC (British Broadcasting Corporation)   108,
    110, 195, 196, 260, 270–1, 289–90, 340
Beattie, Kevin   257, 260, 263, 271, 294
Beckenbauer, Franz   x, xiii, xiv, 284, 316,
    349, 351
Belfitt, Rod   136, 149, 151, 162, 165
Bell, Colin   265, 267, 268, 272
Bell, Willie   121, 152
Bertoni, Daniel   299
Best, George   113, 187, 284, 289
Bingham, Billy   56, 61, 235, 292
Birmingham City FC   19, 45, 51, 52, 57, 61, 74,
    125, 206, 217, 220, 235, 236

Birmingham Daily Post   78
Birmingham Gazette   45, 54
Blackburn Rovers FC   22, 122
Blackpool FC   46, 119, 130, 131, 138, 141, 144,
    193, 222
Blanchflower, Danny   108
Bologna FC   146
Bolton, Sam   64, 70, 72, 74, 76, 77, 78
Bolton Wanderers FC   76, 178, 179, 345
Bond, John   308
Bonetti, Peter   183–4
Bournemouth FC   75
Bowles, Stan   260, 281, 290
Brazil national football team   284, 297, 299
Bremner, Billy   73–4, 77, 79–80, 83, 86, 88, 90,
    101, 102, 103, 109, 111, 112, 113, 115,
    116, 123, 124, 127, 128, 133, 142, 143, 144,
    145, 146, 148, 152–3, 155, 157, 161, 163,
    164, 165, 167, 168, 172, 174, 175, 178, 179,
    181, 183, 184, 187, 188, 192, 195, 197–8,
    206, 209, 216, 219, 222, 223, 230, 236,
    241–2, 255, 256, 312–13, 316, 327, 332,
    335, 346
Bristol City FC   157, 163, 237
Bristol Rovers FC   204
Broadis, Ivor   37–8, 39–40
Bromilow, Tom   11
Brook, Eric   48
Brooking, Trevor   265, 267, 288, 290, 291
Brown, Alan   60–2, 63–4, 101, 117–18
Brown, Sandy   121
Brown, Tony   194–5, 196
Burden, Tommy   73
Burgess, Ronnie   17
Burnley FC   60, 164, 174, 180, 187, 194, 214,
    238–9
Burns, Ken   147, 148
Bury FC   82–3, 98, 100, 135, 145, 152, 221, 345
Busby, Sir Matt   80, 93–4, 99, 115, 170, 173, 187,
    190, 224, 240
Butler, Ernest   20–1
Byrne, Gerry   110, 127
Byrne, Roger   93